The Psychology of Gratitude

SERIES IN AFFECTIVE SCIENCE

Series Editors
Richard J. Davidson
Paul Ekman
Klaus Scherer

The Psychology of Gratitude

Edited by

ROBERT A. EMMONS &
MICHAEL E. McCULLOUGH

OXFORD
UNIVERSITY PRESS

2004

OXFORD

UNIVERSITY PRESS

Oxford   New York
Auckland   Bangkok   Buenos Aires   Cape Town   Chennai
Dar es Salaam   Delhi   Hong Kong   Istanbul   Karachi   Kolkata
Kuala Lumpur   Madrid   Melbourne   Mexico City   Mumbai   Nairobi
São Paulo   Shanghai   Taipei   Tokyo   Toronto

Copyright © 2004 by Oxford University Press, Inc.

Published by Oxford University Press, Inc.
198 Madison Avenue, New York, New York 10016

www.oup.com

Oxford is a registered trademark of Oxford University Press

Library of Congress Cataloging-in-Publication Data
The psychology of gratitude / edited by Robert A. Emmons and Michael E. McCullough
  p. cm.
Includes bibliographical references and index.
ISBN 0-19-515010-4
1. Gratitude. I. Emmons, Robert A. II. McCullough, Michael E.
BF575.G68 P79 2003
155.2'32—dc21   2003005497

9 8 7 6 5 4 3 2 1

Printed in the United States of America
on acid-free paper

Foreword

Robert C. Solomon

> So after every case, you have to go up to somebody and say "thank you"? What a . . . nightmare.
> —*My Cousin Vinny* (Launer, Schiff, & Lynn, 1992)

Gratitude is one of the most neglected emotions and one of the most underestimated of the virtues. In most accounts of the emotions, it receives nary a mention. Even in broader surveys of the attitudes, it is often ignored. And in the most prominent lists of the virtues, notably Aristotle's, it is not included. Gratitude is often included, of course, in Christian treatises on the virtues, but then it is usually directed only toward a single if exceptional object, namely God the Almighty. And yet gratitude is one of those responses that seems essential to and among civilized human beings, and perhaps it is even significant among some social animals, as de Waal and others have persuasively shown.

The neglect of gratitude is, in itself, interesting. Why does it not come to mind immediately when the social emotions and virtues are in question? Why should we be loathe to admit that we feel and should feel indebted to someone who is our benefactor and has helped us in some way? This way of describing the emotion is already a clue. We (especially in this society) do not like to think of ourselves as indebted. We would rather see our good fortunes as our own doing (whereas the losses and sufferings are not our fault), thus the neglect of gratitude. Like the emotion of trust (to which it is closely akin), it involves an admission of our vulnerability and our dependence on other people. Thus gratitude lies at the very heart of ethics. It is more basic, perhaps, than even duty and obligation.

The neglect of gratitude as an emotion might be partially explained by the fact that it is obviously what Hume called a "calm passion," with none of the vehemence and drama of the "violent" passions. There is gushing gratitude, to be sure, but such behavior is hardly the norm, even in cases where the boon is enormous and one's gratitude is appropriately expansive. Usually, even when one is grateful to someone for saving one's life, gratitude is better expressed through a quiet thanks and an appreciative silence, followed (usually after a decent interval) by an appropriate gift or return favor.

Gratitude is thus a poor candidate for a basic emotion or affect program of the sort that have been prominently defended by many recent psychologists (e.g., Paul Ekman) and philosophers (e.g., Paul Griffiths). As far as we know, it displays no regular or recognizable facial expression; leads to no single sort of hardwired behavioral response; and cannot plausibly be traced, much less reduced, to any particular neurological processes. Also, gratitude endures. It is not, as Carroll Izard defined *emotion*, a "brief . . . response" (Izard, 2002, p. 248) If it is just a fleeting feeling, it hardly counts as gratitude. And gratitude, unlike hardwired behavioral responses, can be appropriate or inappropriate. Gratitude should be sincere.

Perhaps, on occasion, gratitude may feel good, and we do speak of heartfelt gratitude, but I think the more usual feeling is one of slight discomfort (for reasons suggested previously) or, often, nothing at all. We may say that we feel grateful in describing or expressing our gratitude, but this is not usually a phenomenological report of a unique kind of experience. (Most emotions, I argue, lack any specific feeling in this sense. Our phenomenological reports more likely consist of various perspectival and value-laden descriptions of the situation and objects of our emotion.) Some theorists (e.g., Paul Griffiths) might include gratitude among our higher cognitive emotions, if, that is, it were to count as an emotion at all. But emotions comprise a varied and expansive category in which all sorts of feelings are included, and it seems to me that excluding gratitude too readily suggests that gratitude isn't "felt" at all. But to say this is to suggest that gratitude is *just* a social performance, like unthinkingly saying "thank you" when the waiter brings some extra pads of butter to the table.

As for the virtues, gratitude is not as active as most (courage and generosity, for instance), nor is it an ongoing disposition to behave in a socially responsible or congenial manner (temperance and truthfulness, for example). We do not usually think of it as being cultivated as a habit (although some of its superficial trappings, such as saying "thank you," obviously may be), and (like many virtues) its status as a virtue as opposed to an emotion is in much dispute. (Aristotle, in his *Nicomachean Ethics*, opposed the virtues, which he insisted were "states of character," to the passions, which he considered merely episodic. Many philosophers have followed him in this; for example, Bernard Williams in his 1985 *Ethics and the Limits of Philosophy*.)

But it is not always easy to distinguish between a dispositional state of character and a recurring passion, and (as Aristotle clearly argued) it is as necessary to cultivate the right passions as it is to cultivate the right habits and states of character. Both are essential to virtue. Indeed, they are often identical. Cultivating courage, for example, is cultivating the right amount of and the right attitude to fear, and cultivating generosity is cultivating the right amount of and the right attitude to sympathy or compassion. It may be that when we speak of a grateful person (or a grateful nation) we are more often referring to a particular episode rather than a consistent state of character. But it does not follow that gratitude cannot be cultivated, or that it has nothing to do with character. Indeed, a single feeling of gratitude—for example, to one's parents, to an influential teacher or guru, or to someone who has serious changed or even saved one's life—may come to define a good deal of one's character and one's sense of one's own life.

By contrast, being ungrateful is clearly the mark of a vice, whether in a single instance or as a long-term defect of character. Where gratitude is appropriate, even mandatory, being ungrateful is a sign or symptom of lack of socialization, whether evident in the inability to appreciate what others have done for one or, worse, the grudging resentment of one's own vulnerability and the refusal to admit one's debt to others. Gratitude directed to God may not be demeaning. After all, it is God we are acknowledging as our benefactor. But gratitude toward other people may be more of a problem. A decade or so ago, the late social psychologist Shula Sommers studied attitudes toward gratitude (and other emotions) in U.S. and Israeli society. She found that Americans in general ranked gratitude comparatively low on a scale of comfortable and uncomfortable emotions and that U.S. men, in general, found gratitude to be a humiliating emotion (Sommers, 1984). But uncomfortable though it may be, we recognize that none of us is wholly self-sufficient and without the need of help from others. To deny that obvious truth is not just to be philosophically mistaken: It is to be a person of poor character, whatever one's other virtues.

Which is not to say that gratitude is good in itself, as philosophers say, and as many of the authors in this book are well aware. As Aristotle said of all of the passions, it is appropriateness that counts—the right passion, in the right circumstance, with the right target, to the right degree. Thus Aristotle talked about perception as the key to ethics, the practiced ability to see in a situation the appropriateness (or the inappropriateness) not only of gratitude but of its specific expression. There are occasions in which gratitude is inappropriate despite the benefit. (I have heard people say that gratitude is inappropriate if someone is just doing his or her job, although I suspect that this is just an excuse not to thank them.) There are occasions on which gratitude is appropriate even though the benefit in question is slight indeed. (I would argue that the waiter bringing the butter is one modest example.) Sometimes the best expression of gratitude is a slight nod of the head. Sometimes nothing less than pledging one's life will do. Both Seneca and Adam Smith spent considerable time discussing the question of appropriateness, but the point to be made is that the matter of appropriateness is one that escapes the confines of psychology and moves to manners and ethics.

I argue, as do many of the authors in this book, that being capable of and expressing gratitude is not only a virtue but part and parcel of the good life. It is not just an acknowledgment of debt and an expression of humility but is also a way to improve one's life. One can take one's life and its advantages for granted, but how much better it is to acknowledge not only these advantages but one's gratitude for them. Thus Barbara Fredrickson rightly argues that gratitude broadens and builds. It is not just a positive view of life. It is a way of putting one's life in perspective. Ultimately, as Nietzsche (1967) exclaimed in one of his most heartfelt aphorisms, one should be grateful for one's life as such ("How could I fail to be grateful to my whole life?"—*Ecce Homo*, "Why I Am So Clever," section 10, p. 221). A person who feels such cosmic gratitude, even if just on occasion, is a better person and a happier one.

But one of the questions that has always intrigued me about such cosmic gratitude, and it certainly bothered Nietzsche as well, is *to whom* should one feel this gratitude?

As an emotion (as opposed to a mood or a mere state of character), gratitude is defined, at least in part, by its object. But the object (in this case one's whole life) seems to be incomplete. If a good friend gives me a book, I am not just grateful for the book; I am grateful to him for giving me the book. This acknowledgment of the other's agency seems essential to the emotion. But if one does not believe in God, then how can one be grateful for one's life and all of its blessings? Nietzsche talks rather obscurely about affirming one's life, but this seems to rather beg the question. *To whom* should one be grateful for one's life? Robert C. Roberts has no problem with this question, nor do most Christians, Jews, Hindus, and Muslims. But I do, as do some Buddhists, who may well share the problem with atheists.

Being grateful "to the universe" is a limp way out of this quandary. But personifying the universe solves the God problem only by displacing it. Thus Camus (1946), another atheist, populates his hero Sisyphus's world with gods and goddesses who are maliciously enjoying his fate (and at whom he can rail in scorn and defiance). But this literary ploy is part and parcel of Camus's own recognition that the universe cannot be, as he so often claims, merely indifferent. (Indeed, he gives the game away when he has his antihero

Meursault "open his heart to the *benign* indifference of the universe" at the end of *The Stranger*) (emphasis added). But does it make sense to be grateful *to the universe*? I can imagine Dr. Roberts saying, "Isn't this really being grateful to God without admitting it?"

Perhaps one can avoid God by claiming to be thankful to chance, or perhaps to luck, as one might be thankful in roulette or the state lottery (one is surely not thankful to the casino or to the state). But, again, the effort seems limp. The "to whom?" question gets begged again. Manufacturing an evasive impersonal agent to whom to be grateful does not seem convincing. But, then, are atheists stuck with being ungrateful about the single gift that matters most?

Rather, I think the "to whom?" question is misplaced here. The easy move from gratitude as an interpersonal social emotion to cosmic gratitude for one's whole life is unwarranted. It may make good sense for a theist, for whom there is something akin to an interpersonal relationship with God (but even the most powerful author on this topic, the Danish existentialist Søren Kierkegaard, expressed deep anxiety about the peculiar one-sidedness of this particular interpersonal relationship). And one can, of course, personify the universe as Camus did, but it is instructive that Camus felt compelled to belittle science (and the scientific worldview) at the same time. But I think that there is another solution, more radical in that it severs gratitude for one's life from the interpersonal emotions. It is, I think, still gratitude, but it shines a light on what even interpersonal gratitude is all about, which is not merely being thankful to X for boon or gift Y.

Gratitude should not be conceived just in terms of a particular relationship. Gratitude is a philosophical emotion. It is, in a phrase, seeing the bigger picture. In relationships, it is seeing a particular act or transaction as part of a larger and ongoing relationship. The limiting case, in which one is briefly grateful to a stranger whom one will (probably) never see again, underscores the nature of the more usual case in which one probably will see the other person again. The bigger picture in such a case is not the one-off nature of the episode but the frequency of such episodes and one's need to be grateful to any number of strangers, of which this is just one instance. Thus Blanche Dubois's classic statement that she had always depended on "the kindness of strangers" (Tennessee Williams, 1947) expressed an astute philosophy, not just a personal observation. So viewed, opening one's heart to the universe is not so much personifying the universe as opening one's heart, that is, expanding one's perspective.

And so viewed, being grateful for one's whole life is not a "grateful to whom?" question so much as it is a matter of *being aware* of one's whole life, being reflective in a way that most of us are not, most of the time. And when one is reflective and aware of one's whole life, one recognizes how much of life is out of one's hands, how many of advantages one owes to other people, and how indebted one is or should be to parents, friends, and teachers. Such general recognition takes the sting out of acknowledging vulnerability in more particular instances. If we are always vulnerable and dependent beings, then acknowledging our vulnerability and dependency and being grateful in any particular instance should not be so much of a problem. It is gratitude and humility, not gratitude and humiliation, that form the natural pair. To be sure, such gratitude typically involves a "to whom?" as part of its structure, but this is not essential. Like many moods, gratitude expands beyond the focus on a particular object to take in the world as a whole. Thus Fredrickson rightly recognizes gratitude in terms of broadening and building, not only in its effect and expression, but by virtue of its internal structure as well.

One thus could look at gratitude as one of the essential but usually neglected emotions of justice. To be a bit shocking, it is a positive counterpart to vengeance. Whereas vengeance is characterized (by Socrates, for instance) as the return of evil for evil, gratitude is the return of good for good. Socrates both shared Plato's view of justice as giving a person his or her due. But whereas vengeance leads to a deadly downward spiral of escalation and destruction, gratitude often results in a mutually supportive dialectic in which our world opens up with new possibilities. The same is true, I have elsewhere argued, with trust. Moreover, it is pretty clear why, though agreeing in their basic theory of justice, gratitude and vengeance are likely to prove mutually incompatible. Those who feel gratitude are less likely to be vengeful and vice versa. Thus gratitude and forgiveness are also related, and given the existential choice between living a life based on gratitude and forgiveness and living a life based on resentment and vengeance, the choice to be made is obvious. Nietzsche, for all of his personal venom, saw this quite clearly. So, too, do others of us who do not share the sensibilities of those who enjoy a personal relationship with the Almighty. Gratitude (and, I argue, trust and forgiveness) is an essential emotion of the good as well as the virtuous life.

Dedicated, with much gratitude, to my old teacher, Frithjof Bergmann, on the occasion of his retirement.

References

Camus, A. (1946). *The stranger.* S. Gilbert, trans. New York: Knopf.

Izard, C. E. (2002). Emotion, human. *Encyclopaedia Britannica*, 15th ed. (pp. 248–256). Chicago, IL: Encyclopaedia Britannica.

Launer, D. (Writer/Producer), Schiff, P. (Producer), & Lynn, J. (Director). (1992). *My cousin Vinny* [Motion picture]. United States: Twentieth Century Fox in association with Peter V. Miller Investment Corp.

Nietzsche, F. (1967). *Ecce homo.* W. Kaufmann, trans. New York: Random House.

Sommers, S. (1984). Adults evaluating their emotions. In C. Izard & C. Malatesta (Eds.), *Emotions in adult development* (pp. 319–338). Beverly Hills, CA: Sage.

Williams, B. A. O. (1985). *Ethics and the limits of philosophy.* Cambridge, MA: Harvard University Press.

Williams, T. (1947). *A streetcar named Desire* [Play]. New York: New Directions.

Contents

   Developmental-Interactionist Perspective of Moral Emotion   100
   Ross Buck

7 Parent of the Virtues? The Prosocial Contours of Gratitude   123
   Michael E. McCullough and Jo-Ann Tsang

PART III: PERSPECTIVES FROM EMOTION THEORY

8 Gratitude, Like Other Positive Emotions,
   Broadens and Builds   145
   Barbara L. Fredrickson

9 Gratitude and Subjective Well-Being   167
   Philip C. Watkins

PART IV: PERSPECTIVES FROM ANTHROPOLOGY
          AND BIOLOGY

10 Gratitude and Gift Exchange   195
    Aafke Elisabeth Komter

11 Primate Social Reciprocity and the Origin of Gratitude   213
    Kristin E. Bonnie and Frans B. M. de Waal

12 The Grateful Heart: The Psychophysiology of Appreciation   230
    Rollin McCraty and Doc Childre

PART V: DISCUSSION AND CONCLUSIONS

13 Gratitude: Considerations from a Moral Perspective   257
    Charles M. Shelton

14 Gratitude as Thankfulness and as Gratefulness   282
    David Steindl-Rast

    Appendix: Annotated Bibliography of Psychological Research
    on Gratitude   291
    Jo-Ann Tsang and Michael E. McCullough

    Index   343

Contributors

Jack J. Bauer
Department of Psychology
Northern Arizona University
Flagstaff, Arizona 86011-5106
E-mail: jack.bauer@nau.edu

Kristin E. Bonnie
Department of Psychology
Emory University
532 North Kilgo Circle
Atlanta, Georgia 30322
E-mail: kebonnie@emory.edu

Ross Buck
Department of Communication
    Sciences
University of Connecticut
Storrs, Connecticut 06269-1085
E-mail: ross.buck@uconn.edu

Doc Childre
Quantum Intech, Inc.
14700 West Park Avenue
Boulder Creek, California 95006

Frans B. M. de Waal
Department of Psychology
Emory University
532 North Kilgo Circle
Atlanta, Georgia 30322
E-mail: dewaal@emory.edu

Robert A. Emmons
Department of Psychology
University of California
One Shields Avenue
Davis, California 95616
E-mail: raemmons@ucdavis.edu

Barbara L. Fredrickson
Department of Psychology
University of Michigan
525 East University Avenue
Ann Arbor, Michigan 48109-1109
E-mail: blf@umich.edu

Edward J. Harpham
Department of Social Sciences
University of Texas at Dallas
Richardson, Texas 75083-0688
E-mail: harpham@utdallas.edu

Aafke Elisabeth Komter
Department of General Social
    Science
Utrecht University
Heidelberglaan 2
3508 TC Utrecht
The Netherlands
E-mail: A.Komter@fss.uu.nl

Dan P. McAdams
School of Education and Social
    Policy and Department of
    Psychology
Northwestern University
2115 North Campus Drive
Evanston, Illinois 60208
E-mail: dmca@northwestern.edu

Rollin McCraty
HeartMath Research Center
Institute of HeartMath
14700 West Park Avenue
Boulder Creek, California 95006
E-mail: rollin@heartmath.org

Michael E. McCullough
Department of Psychology
University of Miami
P. O. Box 248185
Coral Gables, Florida 33124-2070
E-mail: mikem@miami.edu

Robert C. Roberts
Department of Philosophy
Baylor University
Waco, Texas 76798-7273
E-mail: Robert_Roberts@baylor.edu

Solomon Schimmel
Department of Education and
    Psychology
Hebrew College
43 Hawes Street
Brookline, Massachusetts 02446
E-mail:
    sschimmel@hebrewcollege.edu

Charles M. Shelton
Department of Psychology
Regis University
3333 Regis Boulevard
Denver, Colorado 80221-1099
E-mail: cshelton@regis.edu

Robert C. Solomon
Department of Philosophy
University of Texas at Austin
Austin, Texas 78712
E-mail: rsolomon@mail.utexas.edu

David Steindl-Rast
Benedictine Hermitage
442 Savage Farm Road
Ithaca, New York 14850-6507
E-mail: David_osb@hotmail.com

Jo-Ann Tsang
Department of Psychology and
    Neuroscience
Baylor University
P. O. Box 97334
Waco, Texas 76798-7334
E-mail: JoAnn_Tsang@baylor.edu

Philip C. Watkins
Department of Psychology, MS-94
Eastern Washington University
526 5th Street
Cheney, Washington 99004-2431
E-mail: pwatkins@mail.ewu.edu

The Psychology of Gratitude

1   The Psychology of Gratitude

An Introduction

Robert A. Emmons

Over the past quarter century, unprecedented progress has been made in understanding the biological, psychological, and social bases of human emotions. As psychologists further unravel the complexities of emotions, gaps in understanding are revealed. One of those gaps concerns the psychology of gratitude. A distinguished emotions researcher recently commented that if a prize were given for the emotion most neglected by psychologists, gratitude would surely be among the contenders. In the history of ideas, the concept of gratitude has had a long life span, but in the history of psychology, a relatively short past. For centuries, gratitude has been portrayed by theologians, moral philosophers, and writers as an indispensable manifestation of virtue—an excellence of character. For example, gratitude is not only a highly prized human disposition in Jewish, Christian, Muslim, Buddhist, and Hindu thought (Carman & Streng, 1989), it is deemed an unrivaled quality in these traditions, essential for living life well. The consensus among the world's religious and ethical writers is that people are morally obligated to feel and express gratitude in response to received benefits. For example, Adam Smith, the legendary economist and philosopher, proposed that gratitude is a vital civic virtue, absolutely essential for the healthy functioning of societies (Smith, 1976).

Much of contemporary culture is similarly enamored with gratitude. The construct of gratitude has inspired considerable interest in the general public. An increasing prevalence of books targeted to general audiences on the topic testifies to this concept's widespread appeal. Following a similar format, these popular books generally consist of reflections on the value of gratefulness, along with strategies for cultivating an attitude of gratitude. The essential message of these volumes is that a life oriented around gratefulness is *the* panacea for insatiable yearnings and life's ills. One writer, skeptical of this trend, wrote that an "epidemic of gratitude is sweeping the nation" (Duplantier, 1998). Some of the claims for gratitude are sweeping. Gratitude has been called not only the greatest of the virtues, but the parent of all others, the moral memory of mankind, the most passionate transformative force in the cosmos, the key that opens all doors, the quality that makes us and keeps us young. One popular book on gratitude asserted that "whatever we are waiting for—peace of mind, contentment, grace . . . it will surely come to us, but only when we are ready to receive it with an open and grateful heart" (Breathnach, 1996).

In contrast to philosophers, theologians, and popular writers, psychologists are relative latecomers to the study of gratitude. Until recently, psychologists have had very little to offer in the way of insights into the nature of gratitude. Even those psychologists who specialize in the study of emotion have, for the most part, failed to explore its contours. The term *gratitude* rarely appears in the emotion lexicon (Shaver, Schwarz, Kirson, & O'Connor, 1987). *Gratitude* appears nowhere in the index of the *Handbook of Emotion* (Lewis & Haviland-Jones, 2000), only once in the wide-ranging *Handbook of Cognition and Emotion* (Dalgleish & Power, 1999), and not at all in the presumably comprehensive *Encyclopedia of Human Emotions* (Levinson, Ponzetti, Jr., & Jorgensen, 1999). Widespread ambiguity and uncertainty concerning its status as an emotion account for its scant attention. Unlike anger, fear, or disgust, gratitude does not seem to qualify as a basic emotion. There is unlikely to be a biologically based universal facial expression for it or a unique physiology underlying it.

ON THE MEANING OF GRATITUDE

What exactly is gratitude? The *Oxford English Dictionary* (1989) defined gratitude as "the quality or condition of being thankful; the appreciation of an inclination to return kindness" (p. 1135). The word *gratitude* is derived from the Latin *gratia*, meaning favor, and *gratus*, meaning pleasing. All derivatives from this Latin root "have to do with kindness, generousness, gifts, the beauty of giving and receiving, or getting something for nothing" (Pruyser, 1976, p. 69). We are all familiar with the feeling of gratitude—we receive a gift, and we are thankful to the person who has provided this kindness to us.

We recognize that the other need not have made this gesture but did so out of goodwill toward us.

Psychologists and philosophers are rarely content with dictionary definitions. Gratitude has been defined in a number of ways throughout history. Kant (1797/1964) defined gratitude as "honoring a person because of a kindness he has done us" (p. 123). Scottish philosopher Thomas Brown (1820) defined gratitude as "that delightful emotion of love to him who has conferred a kindness on us, the very feeling of which is itself no small part of the benefit conferred" (p. 291). In psychological parlance, gratitude is the positive recognition of benefits received. Gratitude has been defined as "an estimate of gain coupled with the judgment that someone else is responsible for that gain" (Solomon, 1977, p. 316). Gratitude has been said to represent "an attitude toward the giver, and an attitude toward the gift, a determination to use it well, to employ it imaginatively and inventively in accordance with the giver's intention" (Harned, 1997, p. 175). Gratitude is an emotion, the core of which is pleasant feelings about the benefit received. At the cornerstone of gratitude is the notion of *undeserved merit*. The grateful person recognizes that he or she did nothing to deserve the gift or benefit; it was freely bestowed. This core feature is reflected in one definition of gratitude as "the willingness to recognize the unearned increments of value in one's experience" (Bertocci & Millard, 1963, p. 389). The benefit, gift, or personal gain might be material or nonmaterial (e.g., emotional or spiritual). Gratitude is other-directed—its objects include persons, as well as nonhuman intentional agents (God, animals, the cosmos; Solomon, 1977). It is important that gratitude has a positive valence: It feels good. Solomon (1977) described it as "intrinsically self-esteeming" (p. 317).

Although a variety of life experiences can elicit feelings of gratitude, gratitude prototypically stems from the perception of a positive personal outcome, not necessarily deserved or earned, that is due to the actions of another person. Fitzgerald (1998) identified three components of gratitude: (1) a warm sense of appreciation for somebody or something, (2) a sense of goodwill toward that person or thing, and (3) a disposition to act that flows from appreciation and goodwill. Bertocci and Millard (1963) noted that the virtue of gratitude is the willingness to recognize that one has been the beneficiary of someone's kindness, whether the emotional response is present or not. They thus conceived of it as a "moral virtue-trait" (p. 388) that leads a person to seek situations in which to express this appreciation and thankfulness. Social psychologist Fritz Heider (1958) argued that people feel grateful when they have received a benefit from someone who (the beneficiary believes) *intended* to benefit them. Heider posited that the perceived intentionality of the benefit was the most important factor in determining whether someone felt grateful after receiving a benefit. He also predicted that situations in which a benefactor calls on the beneficiary's *duty* to be grateful would produce the opposite effect. Moreover, Heider noted that beneficiaries prefer to have their gratitude attributed to internal motivations rather than extrinsic ones (e.g., duty or social norm).

FACTORS CONTRIBUTING TO AN INCREASED FOCUS ON GRATITUDE

A number of contemporary trends have emerged that have helped to make this a propitious time for a volume on gratitude. First, the positive psychology movement (Seligman & Csikszentmihalyi, 2000) has directed attention toward human strengths and virtues—those inner traits and psychological processes that most cultures, philosophies, and religions have commended as qualities that fit people well for living in the world. Gratitude is a virtue, the possession of which enables a person to live well, and therefore must receive a hearing in any comprehensive treatment of the topic. The positive psychology movement has also called increasing attention to pleasant emotional states or to what Ben Ze'ev (2000) has referred to as the "sweetest emotions": happiness, joy, love, curiosity, hope, and gratitude. German theologian Dietrich Bonhoeffer (1967) wrote, "In ordinary life we hardly realize that we receive a great deal more than we give, and that it is only with gratitude that life becomes rich" (p. 370). Psychologists who have aligned themselves with positive psychology are quite interested in those psychological propensities that lead to a rich life, and several contributors to this volume maintain that gratitude is one of those propensities.

Second, there is a renewed interest among social scientists in people's religious and spiritual lives. The roots of gratitude can be seen in many of the world's religious traditions. Thus, interest in personal manifestations of religion and spirituality may transport the scientist into the realm of gratitude. In the great monotheistic religions of the world, the concept of gratitude permeates texts, prayers, and teachings. The traditional doctrine of God portrays God as the ultimate giver. Upon recognition of God's outpourings of favor, humans respond appropriately with grateful affect, and gratitude is one of the most common emotions that Judaism, Christianity, and Islam seek to evoke and sustain in believers. The Hebrew Bible is replete with the motif that man owes God gratitude for life, health, and sustenance. There are numerous thanksgiving psalms and other prayers in which the person or the community that is praying pours forth expressions of gratitude. In one of the earliest psychological studies of religion, Leuba (1912) characterized gratitude as a religious emotion and a distinguishing mark of religious experience.

Even though gratitude has a clear religious connotation, a distinction can be made between transpersonal gratitude and theistic gratitude. Transpersonal gratitude may be gratefulness to God, or to a higher power, but may also be directed toward the cosmos more generally (Nakhnikian, 1961). It is the gratitude that one feels when contemplating a starry sky or a majestic mountain peak. Such a vast thankfulness, Nakhnikian contends, cannot be directed toward a person or even a supernatural agent and occurs in the absence of a belief that a favor has been intentionally conferred upon a person by a benefactor. The spiritual quality of gratitude was aptly conveyed by Streng (1989): "In this attitude people recognize that they are connected to each other in a mysterious and miraculous way that is not fully determined by physical forces, but is part of a wider, or transcendent context" (p. 5).

A third factor that makes this a propitious time for gratitude is the resurgent interest in virtue ethics, a subfield of moral philosophy (Hursthouse, 1999; Taylor, 2002). Philosophers have counted gratitude among the most important of the virtues, and as a necessary ingredient for the moral personality. Viewed through the lens of virtue ethics, gratitude is a purely person-to-person phenomena, apart from any reference to the divine. Ingratitude, on the other hand, is seen as a profound moral failure. For example, Hume (1888) called ingratitude "the most horrid and unnatural of all crimes that humans are capable of committing" (p. 466), and Kant (1797/1964) listed ingratitude as one of three vices that are the "essence of vileness and wickedness." In the present volume, Harpham (chap. 2) provides an overview of gratitude in the history of moral and political philosophy. As Elster (1999) pointed out, the writings of the moralists can teach us much, both about an emotion and the place of that emotion in the society in which they live. Grateful people are those who respond with thankfulness in situations that call for it. Moralists generally see gratitude as an obligation, and stressed its dutiful aspects rather than its emotional quality. In the thirteenth century, Thomas Aquinas (1981 version) understood gratitude as a secondary virtue associated with the primary virtue of justice (rendering to others their right or due, and in accord with some measure of basic equality). Gratitude is a motivator of altruistic action, according to Aquinas, because it entails thanking one's benefactors and generating a fitting and appropriate response. A century ago, the sociologist Georg Simmel (1908/1950) argued that gratitude is a cognitive-emotional supplement to sustain one's reciprocal obligations. Because formal social structures such as the law and social contracts are insufficient to regulate and insure reciprocity in human interaction, people are socialized to have gratitude, which serves to remind them of their need to reciprocate. From these perspectives, the crucial role that exchanging services plays in a moral human society underscores the importance of gratitude as a force to encourage acts of beneficence, leading philosophers such as Cicero to state that gratitude is the greatest of the virtues. The moral nature of gratitude is discussed most explicitly in the chapters in this volume by Buck, McCullough and Tsang, and Shelton.

GRATITUDE AS AN EMOTION

Psychologists have preferred the language of emotion in speaking about gratitude. One of the earliest psychological treatments of gratitude as an emotion appeared in the writings of William McDougall. In the chapter on emotion in his *Outline of Psychology*, McDougall (1929) viewed gratitude as a secondary, or blended, emotion that includes awe, admiration, reverence, envy, resentment, embarrassment, and jealousy. Gratitude, as seen by McDougall, is a compound of "tender emotion and negative self-feeling" (p. 334). By *negative self-feeling*, McDougall was referring to the perceived inferiority of the receiver relative to the giver. He went on to state that "the act that is to inspire gratitude must make us aware not only of the kindly feeling, the tender emotion, of the other toward us; it must also make us aware of his power, we must see that he is able to do for us something that we cannot do for ourselves. . . . This element of negative self-feeling renders gratitude an emotion that is not purely pleasurable to many natures, makes it one that a proud man does not easily experience" (pp. 334–335). McDougall identified an important characteristic of gratitude, namely that although normally considered desirable, gratitude does contain some features that may lead one to be ambivalent about its status. A contemporary of McDougall, Edwin Westermarck (1932), viewed gratitude as a moral emotion, or more accurately, a "retributive kindly emotion" that consists of a desire to give pleasure in return for pleasure received. Unlike McDougall, Westermarck did not believe that gratitude required a negative self-feeling evoked through sensing one's inferiority with respect to the more powerful benefactor.

Following McDougall, we do not wish to convey the impression that gratitude has always been seen as unequivocally positive and desirable. The notion of whether gratitude places a person in an inferior position vis-à-vis his or her benefactor and is therefore at least somewhat undesirable has been debated throughout history. Aristotle, for example, viewed gratitude as incompatible with magnanimity and therefore did not include it on his list of virtues. Magnanimous people, according to Aristotle, insist on their self-sufficiency and therefore find it demeaning to be indebted and thus grateful to others. Solomon (1995) noted that "Gratitude presupposes so many judgments about debt and dependency that it is easy to see why supposedly self-reliant American males would feel queasy about even discussing it" (p.

282). It has been argued that conventional males may be averse to experiences and expressions of gratefulness, insomuch as they imply dependency and indebtedness. Sommers and Kosmitzki (1988) found that American men were less likely to evaluate gratitude positively than were German men, and that they viewed it as less constructive and useful than did their German counterparts. There is also some empirical evidence that gratitude is associated with feminine gender-role stereotypic traits (Brody, 1993). Finally, experiences of gratitude can be commingled with conflicting emotions, as when the same person confers both benefits and harms (Nussbaum, 2001). For these reasons, we should not expect any simple relationships between gratitude and happiness.

Still another important issue is the degree to which the emotion of gratitude is distinct from the virtue of gratefulness. One can be prone to experiencing and certainly expressing gratitude on appropriate occasions without necessarily being a grateful person. Researchers have found it helpful to distinguish among different levels of gratitude (McCullough, Emmons, & Tsang, 2002; Shelton, chap. 13, this volume). As Webb (1996) pointed out, gratitude can be a vague attitude or an intense emotion; it can also be organized into value systems, elaborate rituals, and daily habits. As an emotion, gratitude is an attribution-dependent state (Weiner, 1985) that results from a two-step cognitive process: (a) recognizing that one has obtained a positive outcome and (b) recognizing that there is an external source for this positive outcome. Lazarus and Lazarus (1994) argued that gratitude is one of the "empathic emotions" whose roots lie in the capacity to empathize with others. The core relational theme associated with gratitude is recognition or appreciation of an altruistic gift. Ben-Ze'ev (2000) referred to gratitude as a "short-term state," reflecting a praiseworthiness of another's actions. It is clear from these conceptualizations that gratitude is a complex state that belongs to the category of affective-cognitive conditions (Ortony, Clore, & Collins, 1987) in which both affect and cognition are predominant meaning components of the term. McCullough, Kilpatrick, Emmons, and Larson (2001) reviewed data from several studies to conclude that people experience the emotion of gratitude most consistently and strongly when they perceive themselves to be recipients of an intentionally rendered benefit that is both valuable to the beneficiary and costly to the benefactor. In addition, McCullough et al. (2001) posited that the emotion of gratitude has a specific action tendency, which is "to contribute to the welfare of the benefactor (or a third party) in the future" (p. 252). Indeed, grateful emotions appear to motivate people to reciprocate the benefits they have received by rendering further benefits. It is important to note that this action tendency is adequately distinct from the action tendencies associated with indebtedness (Gray & Emmons, 2001; Greenberg, 1980).

This brief overview of gratitude in contemporary conceptions of emotion suggests that there may be a number of ways in which gratitude might be profitably conceptualized and measured. Gratitude is a multilayered concept that defies easy description or analysis. It will be important for researchers to be explicit in choosing at which level to identify gratitude so that shared meanings can be achieved and empirical results may be compared across studies. The many meanings of gratitude and the implications for measurement will be made apparent throughout the chapters in this volume.

OVERVIEW OF THE PRESENT VOLUME

In the present volume, we have drawn together diverse perspectives on gratitude from a variety of disciplines. In our initial identification of persons who could advance scholarship on the topic, we were struck by the range of disciplines that could be brought to the gratitude table. Although many scholars have spoken about gratitude, either directly or in passing, contemporary research on gratitude is still in a fledgling state. Our goal in this volume is to jumpstart the scientific study of gratitude by bringing together perspectives from anthropology, moral and political philosophy, psychology, sociology, theology, and primatology. Representatives from these fields have distinctive insights to offer concerning the nature of gratitude and how its academic study can be furthered.

The first section of the book explores philosophical and theological foundations of gratitude. Edward Harpham traces the idea of gratitude throughout the history of ideas, focusing primarily on the influential writings of the eighteenth-century economist and philosopher Adam Smith. Smith's writings on the moral sentiments have influenced scores of scholars in a variety of disciplines, and a number of years ago Truzzi (1966) suggested that Smith can be read with profit by psychologists. Harpham also provides a scholarly overview of several other philosophers for whom gratitude was central in their thinking, including Seneca, Aquinas, Hobbes, and Samuel Pufendorf. From these historical analyses, he derives insights into the functions that gratitude has served and continues to serve in civic society.

In chapter 3, Solomon Schimmel examines the concept of gratitude in the religious traditions of Judaism. He identifies two themes in Jewish teaching on gratitude: cultivating gratitude to God and nurturing gratitude in human relationships. His chapter is a rich tapestry of prayers and teachings on gratitude and related concepts (such as thanksgiving) throughout Hebrew scriptures, and he suggests ways in which religion-based conceptions of gratitude might be translated into empirical research questions.

Robert Roberts (chap. 4) emphasizes the relationship between gratitude and well-being, though he also devotes considerable effort to a conceptual analysis of gratitude. As a philosopher, Roberts has specialized throughout his career in articulating the meaning of constructs. Elsewhere, he has written that philosophy is a process of clarification, of shedding light into corners of life that might otherwise remain unilluminated. Not surprisingly, then, he clarifies the concept of gratitude by presenting a conceptual grammar that states precisely what the emotion of gratitude is and under what conditions it is activated. He is concerned with what gratitude is, what it is not, and how to think clearly about it. He brings to bear on this task an explicitly Christian perspective on the nature and vicissitudes of gratitude.

The next section of the book deals with personality, social, and developmental perspectives. McAdams and Bauer (chap. 5) are personality psychologists who study adult personality development. They take a developmental perspective on gratitude in their chapter, providing a framework for thinking developmentally about gratitude and reviewing the scant research on the development of gratitude in childhood and adolescence. They then present some original research on gratitude and identity development, and gratitude and generativity.

Ross Buck (chap. 6) returns to the developmental perspective in his developmental-interactionist approach to gratitude. Buck distinguishes between a gratitude of exchange and a gratitude of caring. This is an important distinction and is one that has a long history in ethical treatments of gratitude. For example, Aquinas saw gratitude as a component of justice, whereas Spinoza (1677/1981) viewed gratitude as the reciprocation of love with love. Complete treatments of gratitude must recognize this dual nature. Important implications of failing to do so follow. Conceptions of gratitude rooted in reciprocity theory, the approach favored by social scientists, risk reducing gratitude to mere economies of exchange. Buck relates each form of gratitude to its biological origins in curiosity and attachment, and he fleshes out the implications of this distinction for understanding important social issues such as the nature of evil.

McCullough and Tsang (chap. 7) describe the prosocial basis of gratitude by identifying three distinct functions of grateful emotions. They argue that gratitude serves as a moral barometer, a moral motive, and a moral reinforcer and review existing research that illustrates these three hypothesized functions. Measurement is also a concern of McCullough and Tsang; they delineate various levels of analysis at which gratitude and gratitude-related phenomena can be studied.

The next section includes two chapters that consider gratitude primarily as an emotion. Fredrickson (chap. 8) asks the question, what good is feeling grateful? She likens gratitude to other positive emotions that broaden an individual's thinking and build the person's enduring personal resources. She discusses a variety of ways in which gratitude might transform individuals, organizations, and communities in positive and sustaining ways.

Watkins (chap. 9) is interested in the ways in which the conscious practice of gratitude might transform individuals' emotional lives. He reviews research that demonstrates that gratitude has a causal influence on mood, especially positive mood, and also argues that the cultivation of grateful emotions might be efficacious in the treatment and prevention of depressed affect. Given the somewhat grand pronouncements of the power of gratitude referred to earlier, a critical examination of research on gratitude and well-being becomes paramount.

Part IV consists of three chapters that examine gratitude from anthropological and biological perspectives. The giving and receiving of gifts and the feelings generated in these exchanges appear to be one of the "*universalia* of human civilizations" (Burkert, 1996, p. 130). Reciprocal gift exchange is ubiquitous. Furthermore, gratitude has long been posited as the emotional core of reciprocity (Becker, 1986). In chapter 10, anthropologist Aafke Komter emphasizes the imperative nature of gratitude. She highlights the ways in which gratitude compels us to return the benefit that we have received, and she marshals evidence for this "gratitude imperative" in cross-cultural studies of gift giving and receiving. The link between gratitude and generosity is one that intrigues moralists, and Komter brings both an anthropological and an object relations perspective to bear on this aspect of gratitude. She also discusses how gratitude can be complicated by issues of power, status, and dependence in instances of asymmetrical reciprocity.

Giving, receiving, and gratitude are also the focus of chapter 11, but here Bonnie and de Waal are concerned not with human exchange, but with exchange in nonhuman primates. These authors remind us that "Reciprocal exchanges govern the lives of many social beings, including fish, birds, and mammals" (p. 213). The lives on which they have chosen to focus are those of chimpanzees and capuchin monkeys. Do these animals show gratitude? How would gratitude be inferred in these species? You'll have to read their chapter to find out. Their conclusions are an argument for the universality of gratitude grounded in biological systems, echoing a sentiment expressed nearly a century ago by moralist Henry Sidgwick (1907), who contended that "gratitude is a truly universal intuition" (p. 230).

McCraty and Childre (chap. 12) present a framework for the study of the emotional physiology of gratitude. More precisely, they examine the cardiovascular contours of appreciation, an emotion that is seen as overlapping with gratitude. They use state-of-the-art monitoring techniques to draw innovative conclusions about the heart's role in appreciation and other positive emotions, and they review intervention studies demonstrating benefits of various techniques that enable people to develop a greater awareness of their emotional responses, including appreciation.

In one of the two concluding chapters, Charles Shelton (chap. 13) further probes gratitude's meaning by situating it within a moral framework. In an important illustration of the interdisciplinary thought needed to understand gratitude, he blends perspectives of the humanities with those of the social sciences. Shelton provides an important counterpoint to the prevailing sentiment, expressed throughout the book, that gratitude is inevitably positive and desirable. He argues for the necessity of a moral underpinning for gratitude, lest the meaning of the concept lose its distinctive character.

David Steindl-Rast is a Benedictine monk who holds a Ph.D. in psychology from the University of Vienna and is one of the world's foremost Christian devotional writers. His is a conceptual piece, and in this brief final chapter, he advocates distinguishing between gratefulness and thankfulness. He maintains that there are phenomenologically different modes of experience that require this terminological difference, and he highlights the respective uses of each in the other chapters in the volume.

Finally, because we hope to kindle a science of gratitude with this volume, it is appropriate to present a systematic review of existing studies on gratitude. Thus the book concludes with an annotated bibliography of research on gratitude compiled by Jo-Ann Tsang and Michael McCullough.

SUMMARY

The philosopher Søren Kierkegaard suggested that, in thankfulness, a person's relationship to God and others gives birth to a self-awareness that constitute his being (Minear, 1962). Experiences and expressions of gratitude thus shape identity. Given that gratitude is a fundamental attribute of human beings and a potential key to human flourishing, we should endeavor to learn as much as we can about its origins, its forms of expressions, and its consequences for individual and collective functioning. Our conviction is that its study can provide significant insights into human nature. Our hope is that both the science and applications of gratitude will advance with the publication of this volume, and that this volume will serve as a benchmark text defining the field of gratitude research. We hope that readers will develop an appreciation for the interdisciplinary nature of gratitude and how further progress in the psychology of gratitude must remain true to its multidisciplinary roots. If this volume contributes to those aims, then its editors will be very grateful. With gratitude to the John Templeton Foundation for their support of this project.

References

Aquinas, T. (1981). *Summa theologica* (Fathers of the English Dominican Province, Trans.). Westminster, MD: Christian Classics.

Becker, L. C. (1986). *Reciprocity.* London: Routledge, Kegan Paul.

Ben-Ze'ev, A. (2000). *The subtlety of emotions.* Cambridge: MIT Press.

Bertocci, P. A., & Millard, R. M. (1963). *Personality and the good: Psychological and ethical perspectives.* New York: David McKay.

Bonhoeffer, D. (1967). *Letters and papers from prison* (E. Bethge, Ed.). New York: Macmillan.

Breathnach, S. B. (1996). *The simple abundance journal of gratitude.* New York: Warner.

Brody, L. R. (1993). On understanding gender differences in the expression of emotion. In S. L. Ablon (Ed.), *Human feelings: Explorations in affect development and meaning* (pp. 87–121). Hillsdale, NJ: Analytic Press.

Brown, T. (1820). *Lectures on the philosophy of the human mind.* Edinburgh, UK: Black.

Burkert, W. (1996). *Creation of the sacred: Tracks of biology in early religions.* Cambridge, MA: Harvard University Press.

Carman, J. B., & Streng, F. J. (Eds.). (1989). *Spoken and unspoken thanks: Some comparative soundings.* Cambridge, MA: Harvard University Center for the Study of World Religions.

Dalgleish, T., & Power, M. J. (Eds.). (1999). *Handbook of cognition and emotion.* Chichester, UK: Wiley.

Duplantier, F. R. (1998, November). An epidemic of gratitude is sweeping the nation. *New Oxford Review, 65,* 23–27.

Elster, J. (1999). *Alchemies of the mind.* New York: Cambridge University Press.

Fitzgerald, P. (1998). Gratitude and justice. *Ethics, 109,* 119–153.

Gray, S. A., & Emmons, R. A. (2001, August). *Distinguishing gratitude from indebtedness in affect and action tendencies.* Poster presented at the annual meeting of the American Psychological Association, San Francisco.

Greenberg, M. S. (1980). A theory of indebtedness. In K. J. Gergen, M. S. Greenberg, & R. H. Willis (Eds.), *Social exchange: Advances in theory and research* (pp. 3–26). New York: Plenum.

Harned, D. B. (1997). *Patience: How we wait upon the world.* Cambridge, MA: Cowley.

Heider, F. (1958). *The psychology of interpersonal relations.* New York: Wiley.

Hume, D. (1888). *A treatise of human nature.* Oxford, UK: Clarendon Press.

Hursthouse, R. (1999). *On virtue ethics.* New York: Oxford University Press.

Kant, I. (1964). *The metaphysical principles of virtue: Part II of The metaphysics of morals* (J. Ellington, Trans.). Indianapolis, IN: Bobbs-Merrill. (Original work published 1797)

Lazarus, R. S., & Lazarus, B. N. (1994). *Passion and reason: Making sense of our emotions.* New York: Oxford University Press.

Leuba, J. H. (1912). *A psychological study of religion: Its origin, function, and future.* New York: AMS Press.

Levinson, D., Ponzetti, J. J., Jr., & Jorgensen, P. F. (Eds.). (1999). *Encyclopedia of human emotions*. New York: Macmillan.

Lewis, M., & Haviland-Jones, J. M. (Eds.). (2000). *Handbook of emotions* (2nd ed.). New York: Guilford Press.

McCullough, M. E., Emmons, R. A., & Tsang, J. (2002). The grateful disposition: A conceptual and empirical topography. *Journal of Personality and Social Psychology, 82,* 112–127.

McCullough, M. E., Kilpatrick, S. D., Emmons, R. A., & Larson, D. B. (2001). Is gratitude a moral affect? *Psychological Bulletin, 127*(2), 249–266.

McDougall, W. (1929). *Outline of psychology.* New York: Charles Scribner's Sons.

Minear, P. S. (1962). Thanksgiving as a synthesis of the temporal and eternal. In H. A. Johnson & N. Thulstrup (Eds.), *A Kierkegaard critique* (pp. 297–308). New York: Harper & Brothers.

Nakhnikian, G. (1961). On the cognitive import of certain conscious states. In S. Hook (Ed.), *Religious experience and truth* (pp. 156–164). New York: New York University Press.

Nussbaum, M. C. (2001). *Upheavals of thought: The intelligence of emotions.* New York: Cambridge University Press.

Ortony, A., Clore, G. L., & Collins, A. (1987). *The cognitive structure of emotions.* New York: Cambridge University Press.

Oxford English dictionary (2nd ed.). (1989). Oxford: Oxford University Press.

Pruyser, P. W. (1976). *The minister as diagnostician: Personal problems in pastoral perspective.* Philadelphia: Westminster Press.

Seligman, M. E. P., & Csikszentmihalyi, M. (2000). Positive psychology: An introduction. *American Psychologist, 55,* 5–14.

Shaver, P. R., Schwarz, J., Kirson, D., & O'Connor, C. (1987). Emotion knowledge: Further exploration of a prototype approach. *Journal of Personality and Social Psychology, 52,* 1061–1086.

Sidgwick, H. (1907). *The methods of ethics* (7th ed.). New York: Macmillan.

Simmel, G. (1950). *The sociology of Georg Simmel* (K. H. Wolff, Ed. & Trans.). Glencoe, IL: Free Press. (Original work published 1908)

Smith, A. (1976). *The theory of moral sentiments* (6th ed.). Oxford, UK: Clarendon Press. (Original work published 1790)

Solomon, R. C. (1977). *The passions.* Garden City, NY: Anchor Books.

Solomon, R. C. (1995). The cross-cultural comparison of emotion. In J. Marks & R. T. Ames (Eds.), *Emotions in Asian thought* (pp. 253–294). Albany: SUNY Press.

Sommers, S., & Kosmitzki, C. (1988). Emotion and social context: An American-German comparison. *British Journal of Social Psychology, 27,* 35–49.

Spinoza, B. (1981). *Ethics* (G. Eliot, Trans., & T. Deegan, Ed.). Salzburg, Austria: University of Salzburg. (Original work published 1677)

Streng, F. J. (1989). Introduction: Thanksgiving as a worldwide response to life. In J. B. Carman & F. J. Streng (Eds.), *Spoken and unspoken thanks: Some comparative soundings* (pp. 1–9). Cambridge, MA: Harvard University Center for the Study of World Religions.

Taylor, R. (2002). *Virtue ethics: An introduction.* Amherst, NY: Prometheus Books.

Truzzi, M. (1966). Adam Smith and contemporary issues in social psychology. *Journal of the History of the Behavioral Sciences, 2,* 221–224.

Webb, S. H. (1996). *The gifting God: A trinitarian ethics of excess.* New York: Oxford University Press.

Weiner, B. (1985). An attributional theory of achievement motivation and emotion. *Psychological Review, 92,* 548–573.

Westermarck, E. (1932). *Ethical relativity.* London: Kegan Paul.

PART I

Philosophical and Theological Foundations

2 Gratitude in the History of Ideas

Edward J. Harpham

He who receives a benefit with gratitude repays the first installment on his debt.

—Seneca (*On Benefits*, 2.22.1)

I hate ingratitude more in a man
than lying, vainness, babbling, drunkenness,
Or any taint of vice whose strong corruption
Inhabits our frail blood.

—Shakespeare
(*Twelfth Night*, Act 3, Scene 4)

Blow, blow, thou winter wind!
Thou art not so unkind
As man's ingratitude.

—Shakespeare
(*As You Like It*, Act 2, Scene 7)

As justice dependeth on Antecedent Covenant; so does Gratitude
depend on Antecedent Grace; that is to say, Antecedent Free-gift;
and is the fourth Law of Nature; which may be conceived in this
Forme, *That a man which receiveth Benefit from another of meer
Grace, Endeavour that he which giveth it, have no reasonable cause to
repent him of his good will.*

—Thomas Hobbes (*Leviathan*, p. 105)

Gratitude in the generality of men is only a strong and secret desire
of receiving greater favours.

—La Rochefoucauld (*Maxims*, 298)

Although an ungrateful heart is not an offence in itself, still a
name for ingratitude is regarded as baser, more odious and more
detestable than a name for injustice.

—Samuel Pufendorf (*On the Duty of Man and
Citizen According to Natural Law*, p. 66)

Of all the crimes that human creatures are capable of committing,
the most horrid and unnatural is ingratitude, especially when it is
committed against parents, and appears in the most flagrant instances of wounds and death.

—David Hume (*A Treatise of Human Nature*, p. 466)

Gratitude, as it were, is the moral memory of mankind.

—Georg Simmel (1908/1996, p. 45)

No other animal plays non-zero sum games as tirelessly as we do.
Much of your emotional life is natural selection's way of getting
you to play. Gratitude for favors rendered and guilt over neglecting
a friend help you start or sustain potentially win-win games.

—Robert Wright (2000, p. 59)

Ours is a commercial age, one driven by the impulse of self-
interest. Adam Smith understood this well when he noted in *The Wealth of
Nations* (1776/1981) that it is not benevolence or love of our fellow human
beings that brings food to our table. We receive our daily bread by appealing
to the self-interest of the baker and offering something in return that is
needed. Two factors lay behind Smith's defense of self-interest over benevolence. First, he believed that self-interest was a more steady passion than
benevolence because the unintended consequences of self-interest could be
calculated and projected into the future. We can rely on the self-interest of
others more readily than we can their benevolence or love. Second, Smith
believed that an appeal to self-interest was also an appeal to the dignity of
the individual. Only a beggar depends on the benevolence of others for
everyday subsistence, and even then only on a limited basis. In contrast to
benevolence, self-interested exchange was predicated on the idea that individuals could enter into market exchanges and affirm their existence as free
and autonomous human beings.

Given the central role of self-interest in Smith's economic theory of
commercial society, it is tempting to conclude that Smith believed—as all
too many of his twentieth- and twenty-first-century counterparts now seem
to believe—that humans are at heart self-interested creatures who care little
for the concerns or interests of others. As any reader of his *Theory of Moral*

Sentiments soon discovers, however, this would be a serious mistake. To be sure, individuals are driven by self-interest. But, according to Smith, they are also capable of love, compassion, pity, self-sacrifice, resentment, and gratitude. Smith the moral philosopher was less concerned with trumpeting the triumph of self-interest in commercial society than coming to terms with the proper balance that should exist between self-interest and other passions and virtues.

Far from believing that a commercial society could flourish solely on the basis of the drive of self-interest, Smith argued that a certain moral capital was needed if a society was to flourish. For contracts to work, people had to keep their word. Property had to be respected for exchange transactions to take place. People also had to be willing to respect and tolerate one another, particularly on divisive matters like theology. The values of friendship, family, and love had to be preserved and promoted. Individuals had to be willing to sacrifice their own good for the good of the whole, particularly in times of war where the nation's very existence was in question. The individual championed in Smith's moral theory as well as his political economy was not simply an isolated utility maximizer. He or she was a social creature linked closely to others in the community through passions and affections.

What Smith recognized as obvious, many social, political and economic theorists consider today to be a heresy. The rational actor that underlies much contemporary theory in the social sciences is a far cry from the individual analyzed by the father of modern economics. In a quest for an internally consistent predictive empirical theory, many theorists have lost touch with a dimension of human existence that is obvious to everyone in everyday life. This is particularly apparent when we consider what has happened to our understanding of gratitude. For Smith, gratitude was one of the major topics that must be considered in a theory of the moral sentiments. For most modern theorists, gratitude is but an afterthought, an idea better left alone than seriously investigated.

Gratitude is defined by the *Random House Dictionary of the English Language* as "the quality or feeling of being grateful or thankful" (1967, p. 617). Be grateful to those who do good to you; be grateful for your blessings. This is something that we teach to our children at the youngest of ages. Gratitude is an important dimension of life as we interact with one another in our everyday affairs. It is impossible to imagine a world where individuals don't receive and give gratitude regularly. Gratitude is one of the building blocks of a civil and humane society.

Although an appreciation of gratitude lies at the heart of common life—even in our commercial age—it has all but been forgotten by the modern academy. As we will see, this was not always the case. The Roman philosopher Seneca wrote an entire book on the subject, entitled *On Benefits*, around A.D. 54. The idea of gratitude was an important topic taken up by philosophers as diverse as Thomas Aquinas, Thomas Hobbes, Samuel Pufendorf, and Adam Smith and remained an important idea throughout the Middle Ages (see Dunn, 1946; Galloway, 1994; Tronto, 1999). Over the past hundred years, the philosophical essays published on the topic have been few and far between. Although a number of articles have been written on the subject of gratitude as a foundation for political obligation (see Klosko, 1989; Walker, 1998, 1999), Terrance McConnell's (1993) book, *Gratitude*, is notable because it almost stands almost alone in its attempt to provide a general philosophical account of gratitude (see also Fitzpatrick, 1998; Roberts, 1991; Simmel, 1908/1996). The disjuncture between our common life and our academic endeavors at the very least should raise troubling questions.

This chapter is an attempt at recovery. It begins by exploring the idea of gratitude in the history of ideas, focusing particular attention on the thought of Seneca, Thomas Aquinas, Thomas Hobbes, and Samuel Pufendorf. I then turn to consider Adam Smith's discussion of gratitude. Smith placed an analysis of the phenomena of gratitude at the heart of his moral thought. He was particularly concerned with understanding the role that gratitude plays in modern society and the forces that threaten to undermine it. Understanding his analysis sheds light on how we moderns have come to think about gratitude and its place in the life of a commercial society grounded on the workings of self-interested behavior. At the end of this chapter, I suggest that the time may have come to resurrect the idea of gratitude by reconsidering the proper role that it should play in human affairs in a commercial society. By taking up the subject of gratitude in a historical context, I hope to nudge our theories of the human condition into a little closer contact with the everyday life that we live.

THE IDEA OF GRATITUDE PRIOR TO SMITH

The first (and, for many centuries, the only) great treatise on gratitude in Western thought was *On Benefits*, written by the Roman Stoic philosopher Seneca. Addressed to a friend, Aebutius Liberalis of Lyons, the work is long-winded and repetitious. But it raises many of the concerns that would define how later thinkers conceptualized the problem of gratitude. The importance of understanding the place of gratitude in human society was stated clearly in the first paragraph: "Among the many and diverse errors of those who live reckless and thoughtless lives, almost nothing that I can mention, excellent Liberalis, is more disgraceful than the fact that we do not know how either to give or to receive benefits. For it follows that, if they are ill placed, they are ill acknowledged, and when we complain of their not being returned, it is too late; for they were lost at the time they were given. Nor is it surprising that among all our many and great vices, none is so common as ingratitude" (trans. 1935, p. 3).

Identifying ingratitude as our most common vice is intriguing. It may be because it is such a common vice that we do not properly understand its complexity. Throughout the treatise, Seneca tried to provide a perspective for sorting out the complexity underlying the problem of gratitude.

He began his inquiry into gratitude by noting that gratitude must be understood as part of a dyadic relationship between a giver of benefits and a receiver of benefits (Tronto, 1999, pp. 12–14). To understand gratitude, one must grasp both sides of the relationship fully. In regard to giving, Seneca posed a series of questions that must be addressed: What exactly is a benefit? To whom should benefits be given? What is the proper way to give a benefit? One of Seneca's major arguments was that for gratitude to be properly expressed in the world, a gift must be properly given. Similar questions were raised in regard to the actions of a person who receives a benefit from another: How does one properly show gratitude for a benefit given? Are there different forms of gratitude? Is gratitude more than just being grateful for a benefit provided? Does gratitude involve something more substantial than just thanks under certain conditions, such as an equal or greater return of benefits given for those received? Is gratitude only a relationship that can exist between equals, or can a master be grateful to a slave for benefits provided?

A number of general ideas that emerged from Seneca's inquiry are worth highlighting. First, he argued that the intentions of both the givers and the receivers of benefits are of the utmost importance in understanding gratitude (trans. 1935, p. 23). Good consequences devoid of good intentions do not create a debt of gratitude (p. 91). If the intention of a giver is not to help another individual, but to bind the receiver or to make that person feel bad, then a benefit has not been given, and gratitude is not required. Similarly, a debt of gratitude has not been fulfilled if the receiver of the benefit does not truly feel thanks to the giver but responds to the benefit merely out of a sense of duty or guilt or anger. Rules join together providers and receivers of benefits, and these are the foundation on which gratitude rests (see p. 67).

Second, an egalitarianism ran through Seneca's arguments, as it did through the work of many other Stoic writers. Providing benefits and creating bonds of gratitude tie people together in society, whatever their place in the social hierarchy. According to Seneca, it is a mistake to believe that "slavery penetrates into the whole being of a man" (trans. 1935, p. 165). Only the body is at the mercy of the master; the mind remains free. As Seneca explained, "He who denies that a slave can sometimes give a benefit to his master is ignorant of the rights of man; for, not the status, but the intention, of the one who bestows is what counts" (p. 161). Social inferiors thus can provide a benefit to their superiors. Masters can come under a debt of gratitude to their slaves under the proper circumstances.

Third, Seneca sharply distinguished debts in the marketplace and debts of gratitude. Gratitude does not arise as a result of an exchange in which one individual gives another a gift with the expectation that something of equal value will be given in return. On the contrary, gratitude arises in response to a gift freely given by another. A person does not provide another with a benefit because he or she expects something in return. That would be an exchange in the marketplace, subject to different sorts of sanctions. A gift is given freely because of a desire, in and of itself, to assist another person. Similarly, a person does not simply respond to a benefit with an equal benefit, not more, not less, in return. That would be to treat gratitude as a commodity exchanged between individuals for an equal benefit. As Seneca explained, "Although to repay gratitude is a most praiseworthy act, it ceases to be praiseworthy if it is made obligatory; for in that case no one will any more praise a man for being grateful than he will praise one who has returned a deposit of money, or paid a debt without being summoned before a judge. So we spoil the two most beautiful things in human life—a man's gratitude and a man's benefit. For what nobility does either one show—the one if, instead of giving, he lends a benefit, the other if he makes return, not because he wishes, but because he is forced?" (trans. 1935, pp. 137–139).

Lurking in the background of this line of argument is the idea that a free gift should touch off a feeling of gratitude in the recipient that, in turn, sparks additional actions of benevolence and feelings of gratitude. Giving benefits and feeling grateful is, in the language of modern game theory, a positive-sum game.

Finally, Seneca argued that providing benefits freely and expressing gratitude are to be desired in and of themselves and for their consequences. In many ways, the ideal model of a giver is God (or Nature), who bestows his many gifts upon mankind with no thought of any return. Because God needs nothing, when he bestows a benefit he is only concerned with the advantage of the recipient. A benefit, in this respect, is good in and of itself. Gratitude also makes one a better person, a more virtuous person. It builds bonds of harmony and community in the world. Ingratitude, on the other hand, is a vice to be avoided, one that destroys the individual and society by disrupting the harmony that ties us to one another. As Seneca explained:

> For how else do we live in security if it is not that we help each other through an exchange of good offices? It is only through the interchange of benefits that life becomes in some measure equipped and fortified against sudden disasters. Take us singly, and what are we?

The prey of all creatures, their victims, whose blood is most delectable and most easily secured. For, while other creatures possess a strength that is adequate for their self-protection, and those that are born to be wanderers and to lead an isolated life have been given weapons, the covering of man is a frail skin; no might of claws or of teeth makes him a terror to others, naked and weak as he is, his safety lies in fellowship. (trans. 1935, p. 241)

There are many problems with Seneca's general approach to the subject of gratitude. His analysis was far from systematic and never linked to a larger theory of moral judgment. Indeed, the argument proceeded from one question to another in an almost haphazard manner. Interesting ideas were introduced, then dropped, only to taken up in later works. Most disturbing of all, it is often unclear to the reader what the standards are by which we are to judge appropriate behavior on the part of both the giver and the receiver of the benefits. Understanding gratitude, for Seneca, seems to have meant simply mastering the complexity of the situation under which a particular example of gift giving has taken place. Other than reading Seneca's own explanation for understanding a particular situation, the student is left on his or her own to master a new situation, with insight (it is hoped) provided by earlier discussions. Finally, there is the problem of gratitude to God for the blessings bestowed on us. We clearly must be grateful to God for the many benefits given to us, but how are we to express this gratitude? Through prayers of praise and thanksgiving to God? Through beneficent actions aimed at others?

In the Middle Ages, there was an important shift away from Seneca in how gratitude came to be understood. According to Andrew Galloway (1994), the Latin term *gratitude* is of scholastic origin and never appeared in the work of Augustine. Moreover, Augustine's use of the term *gratia* was almost always in terms of divine grace rather than human obligation. In Aquinas, many of the issues surrounding gratitude taken up by Seneca were given a particularly Christian reading. Gratitude was a sentiment or emotion that people feel in response to a particular situation or action. For Aquinas as for Seneca, intentions continued to play an important part in defining the relationship between benefactor and recipient. But the egalitarian underpinnings were largely missing. People were linked to others up and down the social hierarchy in a great chain of being through various types of debts of gratitude: humankind to God, child to father, servant to master, and recipient to benefactor. Gratitude, for Aquinas, was a complex phenomenon that must be understood as a continuous scale of obligations; he wrote, "The nature of a debt to be paid must needs vary according to various causes giving rise to the debt, yet so that the greater always includes the lesser. Now the cause of debt is found primarily and chiefly in God, in that He is the first principle of all our goods: secondarily it is found in our father, because he is the proximate principle of our begetting and upbringing: thirdly it is found in the person that excels in dignity, from which general favors proceed; fourthly it is found in a benefactor, from whom we have received particular and private favors, on account of which we are under particular obligation to him" (trans. 1920/2003, Q.106, A.1).

Another shift away from Stoic egalitarianism took place when discussions of gratitude were joined to a notion of one's larger social duties given one's place in the social hierarchy. As Catherine Dunn (1946) showed, during the late Middle Ages and early Renaissance notions of gratitude and fealty became closely linked together, as did those of ingratitude and treason. To be ungrateful in the feudal world could be tantamount to engaging in treasonable actions against one's lord (see Dunn, 1946).

Along a different line of thought, theologians throughout the Middle Ages and into the Renaissance considered the problem of gratitude and ingratitude in terms of one's relationship to God. Ingratitude to God was condemned as being worse than ingratitude to one's fellow human beings. Not only was it a rejection of God's infinite love and the sacrifice of Christ on the cross, but it was an enemy of the soul's salvation (see Dunn, 1946, pp. 91–121).

In the sixteenth and seventeenth centuries, a series of economic, political, and religious revolutions helped to transform the intellectual environment of Europe. The Reformation destroyed the religious unity that had held Western Christendom together for over a thousand years. A commercial revolution introduced market forces into many parts of Europe, replacing forever the insularity of a feudal economy with the dynamics of international trade and production. Finally, a series of political revolutions put into place new political regimes based on new understandings of the origins and nature of political power.

Awareness of the role of self-interest in both the modern commercial economy and in modern political systems helped to stimulate the rise of modern social contract theory in the seventeenth century. In the work of philosophers such as Thomas Hobbes in England and Samuel Pufendorf in Germany, sophisticated social contract theories were developed to explain the origins of political power in terms of self-interest. (It is not my purpose to inquire into social contract theory per se, only to note that in the work of at least two of the leading philosophers of the day, the problem of gratitude was important.)

Hobbes is known for his rather dismal assessment of the human condition as being "nasty, brutish, and short." Humans surrender their natural right to all things to an absolute sovereign to escape the uncertainties of the state of nature and enter into civil society. It is interesting that, in Hobbes's *Leviathan*, gratitude is considered to be the fourth law of nature, following the laws of seeking peace, contracting for peace, and performing one's contracts (that is, following the rules of justice). As Hobbes explained the fourth law of nature, "That a man which receiveth Benefit from another of mere Grace, Endeavor that he which giveth it, have no reasonable cause to repent of his good will" (Hobbes, 1651/1991, p. 105). From a Hobbesian position, gratitude is a necessary condition in society to assure us that self-interested people will be willing to act in disinterested ways for the benefit of others and for society in general. To use a slightly different terminology, the fourth law of nature helps to overcome problems of collective action when people do things that do not directly benefit themselves. Gratitude is thus less a result of the relationship between two people than it is a general social condition (or social virtue, as Joan Tronto put it) that promotes general sociability in society as a whole (see Tronto, 1999).

Similarly, Samuel Pufendorf, an individual whose political philosophy was written in response to Hobbes, provided a central place in his thought for gratitude. Unlike Hobbes, however, he returned to the idea that gratitude is based on a dyadic relationship between a giver and a receiver of benefits. According to Pufendorf, our first two duties in society are not harming others and recognizing the equality of others with ourselves. The third duty is being useful to others, so far as one conveniently can. Providing charity and gifts to others was, for Pufendorf, one of the best ways individuals can promote commodious living, particularly when the response to such beneficence is gratitude. Echoing Seneca, Pufendorf noted how complex the entire problem of gratitude is. Intentions must be taken into account. Debts of gratitude must not be confused with debts of exchange. Neither the giver nor the receiver of benefits must be harmed by either the original gift or the gratitude in response (see Pufendorf, trans. 1991, chap. 8).

In echoing the concerns of Seneca, however, Pufendorf's analysis of gratitude shows how little thought had progressed since the first century. For Pufendorf as for Seneca, it was essential to master the particular situation in which gift giving was taking place, to understand gratitude. Although he did link his discussion of gratitude to a general theory of moral judgment, he offered little more than very abstract guidelines as to how one might go about mastering that situation outside the existing manners found in a particular society at a particular time. Readers are left to master a new situation on the basis of inferences drawn from earlier discussions.

In the mid-eighteenth century, the Scottish philosopher and political economist Adam Smith changed the way the gratitude was conceptualized in the West. Rather than rationally accounting for gratitude, he tried to describe the mechanism that gives rise to the feeling of gratitude and to explain how this mechanism relates to other moral issues. He then turned to developing a perspective for explaining when and why gratitude is an appropriate response to certain situations, a perspective that was far more sophisticated than the thought of most earlier moral philosophers.

To consider Smith to be one, if not the most, important modern philosopher of gratitude may strike some people as strange. He is, after all, considered to be the father of modern political economy and one of the first students of the dynamics of self-interest in a market economy. But before he wrote the *Wealth of Nations* in 1776, Smith authored in 1759 *The Theory of Moral Sentiments*, a work that would go through six editions in his lifetime and mark him as one of the leading moral philosophers of his generation. Deeply embedded in his thought from the outset was the desire to understand the role that gratitude could and should play in a modern commercial order.

SMITH ON GRATITUDE

Adam Smith is often identified with the so-called moral sense school of the eighteenth century. Responding to rationalist philosophers such as Thomas Hobbes or John Locke, moral sense philosophers such as the first Earl of Shaftesbury, Francis Hutcheson, and David Hume rejected the idea that morality was based solely on reason, arguing instead that morality was ultimately derived from emotions and feelings. Morality was something felt, and not just a conclusion of reason. If one wanted to understand moral norms, including gratitude, one had to understand the moral sentiments.

According to Smith, gratitude is the passion or sentiment that prompts us to reward others for the good that they have done us. Like the passions of love, esteem, and resentment, gratitude takes us beyond ourselves and interests us in the happiness or misery of others. Smith thus took the existence of the passion of gratitude as a given. His problem was not so much to account for this passion as to analyze the implications that it has for human society. More specifically, he wanted to provide an account of three dimensions of the phenomena of gratitude in the world: First, under what circumstances do individuals feel gratitude? Second, when is the feeling of gratitude proper and when is it not? Third, how is an individual's sense of gratitude channeled in directions that are socially beneficial?

Smith's explanation of the propriety of gratitude is an essential part of the analysis of moral judgment found in Parts I and II of *The Theory of Moral Sentiments* and works directly out of the moral sense tradition. Through an account of the emotions and the passions, Smith sought to provide an explanation of moral judgment in the world. As he explained in one of the few lengthy footnotes in the text, "The present enquiry is not concerning a matter of right, if I may say so, but concerning a matter of fact. We are not at the present examining upon what principles a perfect being would approve of the punishment of bad actions, but upon what principles so weak and imperfect a creature as man actually and in fact approves of it" (1790/1982, 77–78).

The first part of Smith's *Theory of Moral Sentiments* is an explanation of the process by which humans judge actions and motives to be right or wrong. At the heart of this theory of moral judgment lies the idea of sympathy. According to Smith, there are principles in our nature that interest us in the fortune of others, regardless of our own self-interest. Sympathy is an inborn mechanism of the imagination that enables us to place ourselves in the situation of another, allowing us to experience the passions, affections, and emotions that arise from this situation. Sympathy, for Smith, thus was not the same as empathy. When we sympathize with other people, we do not empathize with them or feel their actual emotions. Rather, we imaginatively place ourselves in the actual situation of others and experience analogous emotions that rise from such situations in attentive spectators. This capacity to sympathize with others' situations is the way in which we come to judge the propriety or impropriety of a sentiment, emotion, or action of another individual in a particular situation. As Smith explained, "To approve of the passions of another, therefore, as suitable to their objects, is the same thing as to observe that we entirely sympathize with them; and not to approve of them as such is the same thing as to observe that we do not entirely sympathize with them" (1790/1982, p. 16).

A second idea Smith used to explain moral judgment in the world was that of mutual sympathy. There is planted in the human breast, Smith argued, a desire for mutual sympathy. By this, he essentially meant that individuals want other people to feel the same passions and emotions that they feel. According to him, "Nothing pleases us more than to observe in other men a fellow-feeling with all the emotions of our own breast; nor are we ever so much shocked as by the appearance of the contrary" (1790/1982, p. 13). Mutual sympathy is a powerful socializing force that works through sympathy. To realize this mutual sympathy, individuals are willing to moderate and bring under control their passions and emotions when these are too strong for others to enter into completely. For example, an individual who is experiencing overwhelming hate will attempt to temper or cool his passion so that others are able to enter into it through sympathy and judge it to be a proper response to a particular situation. The net effect of sympathy is to help bring about a certain harmony between the sentiments expressed by people in society: "As their sympathy makes them look at it, in some measure, with his eyes, so his sympathy makes him look at it, in some measure, with theirs, especially when in their presence and acting under their observation: and as the reflected passion, which he thus conceives, is much weaker than the original one, it necessarily abates the violence of what he felt before he came into their presence, before he began to recollect in what manner they would be affected by it, and to view his situation in this candid and impartial light" (Smith, 1790/1982, p. 22).

A third idea that lies at the heart of Smith's theory of moral judgment is that of the impartial spectator, an idea that follows directly from his analysis of the mechanism of sympathy and our desire for mutual sympathy. We judge the propriety of other people's passions and emotions as spectators who imagine ourselves in their situation. Over time and with experience, we learn to view others impartially, that is, in the manner that indifferent third-party spectators might observe them. Finally, we come to extend this capacity of being impartial observers of others to being impartial observers of ourselves. Through experience, we learn to view and to judge our own affections and sentiments as imaginary impartial spectators might observe them. The idea of the impartial spectator thus embodies Smith's notion that within each individual is the imaginative capacity to judge himself or herself as that person would judge others or as others might judge him or her.

Smith's discussion of gratitude is part of the larger discussion found in Part II of *The Theory of Moral Sentiments* regarding merit and demerit. Part I investigates how we come to judge actions as being proper or not proper. Part II takes up the question of what action or conduct is deserving of our reward or punishment. Smith began his inquiry by arguing that actions deserve to be rewarded if they are the proper object of gratitude; they deserve to be punished if they are the proper objects of our resentment.

Like Seneca, Smith thus began his analysis of gratitude on the dyadic relationship between an actor and a receiver of benefits. But he immediately took up the question of the propriety of gratitude in terms of a third-party spectator who is removed by the relationship itself. How are we to know if a recipient's response of gratitude is appropriate or not? Smith's answer was clear: "But these, as well as all the other passions of human nature, seem proper and are approved of, when the heart of every impartial spectator entirely sympathizes with them, when every indifferent by-stander entirely enters into, and goes along with them" (1790/1982, p. 69).

Gratitude is a natural response to a particular situation when good things happen to an individual, but it also may be an incorrect response. We may be so biased by good things that happen to us that we respond incorrectly to a particular situation. For example, we may feel gratitude toward an individual whose intentions do not deserve such a response. We may credit inanimate objects for saving our lives or bringing us luck, to the point that we feel gratitude to the objects. We deceive ourselves into thinking that we should be grateful to things. Only by adopting the position of an impartial spectator can we successfully judge whether our response has been appropriate.

How does the impartial spectator come to judge the propriety of gratitude? First, the impartial spectator comes to sympathize with the gratitude felt by the recipient of free gifts. Much like we sympathize with the joy of our companions, we sympathize with the love and affection that they feel for an object or individual that has brought them joy. But before we can sympathize entirely with the gratitude of a recipient, we as impartial observers must also sympathize with the motives and affections of the original provider of the benefits. If the motives themselves are not deserving of reward—for example, if they are based on the self-interest of the actor rather than the best interest of the recipient—impartial spectators will not approve of the gratitude being felt by the recipient for the good things that befall him or her in this life. Similarly, impartial spectators will not sympathize with the gratitude felt by an individual for inanimate objects incapable of intending anything at all.

Smith's understanding of the social dynamics did not end here. Through his notion of mutual sympathy, he explained how an individual's feeling of gratitude can be modified and corrected by the judgments of others in society. An individual wants others to feel the sentiments in their breasts. When others cannot, the individual moderates his or her passions to the point that they can be adopted and approved by others. By looking through the eyes of others and by adopting the position of the impartial spectator and viewing my own passions and responses to a particular situation, I learn to be grateful in socially appropriate and socially approved ways. The impartial spectator thus functions as a mechanism for ensuring the proper functioning of gratitude. Much as the state enforces contracts and maintains justice in civil society, the impartial spectator stands behind benevolence and gratitude, making sure that the benefits of each can spread from one individual to another.

Smith's analysis of merit and demerit moves our understanding of gratitude forward along a number of different dimensions. First, it explains clearly where gratitude fits into our social world and why self-interest is not enough to tie people together or bring about the many benefits of social interaction. *The Wealth of Nations* (1776/1981) was predicated on the assumption that self-interest is a more reliable foundation than beneficence and gratitude for securing the basic economic needs of a society. But it did not eliminate the need for either benevolent acts or responses of gratitude. As Smith showed in *The Theory of Moral Sentiments* (1790/1982), gratitude plays a vital role in making the world we live in a better place. Second, Smith's analysis provided a secular account of gratitude that freed itself from many of the theological and hierarchical assumptions of medieval thought. Gratitude is a human phenomenon that binds people together in society. As such, it is subject to the frailties and tensions that threaten the human condition as well. Third, Smith's analysis explained how feelings of gratitude are socialized through interaction with other people and how the prevailing standards of gratitude found in a society can be improved by a deeper appreciation of the psychological forces that give rise to and sustain gratitude in the world. Fourth, Smith identified with great clarity the forces that might threaten proper feelings of gratitude in the modern world. Self-interest, in particular, was identified as a factor that can warp and even pervert proper feelings of gratitude in a human being. Failing to place oneself in the position of an impartial spectator can cause one to both overestimate and underestimate the gratitude that may be owed to another individual. Learning to adopt the proper perspective for viewing moral questions is the key for giving gratitude its proper place in a modern commercial order.

In *The Wealth of Nations*, this theme about possible threats to gratitude is extended into a wholesale analysis of the problems that accompany the division of labor in a market-oriented society. In Book I, Smith argued that the key to wealth and economic growth in a commercial order is an extensive division of labor. In Book V, however, he noted that an extensive division of labor brings with it serious and disturbing unintended consequences. Workers who are engaged in highly specialized jobs in the production process may become dehumanized to the point that they lose touch with their basic humanity. An extensive division of labor confines some men's mental capacities to a few simple functions, rendering them stupid and narrow minded. As Smith explained:

> The man whose whole life is spent in performing a few simple operations, of which the effects too are, perhaps, always the same, or very nearly the same, has no occasion to exert his understanding, or to exercise his invention in finding out expedients for removing difficulties which never occur. He naturally loses, therefore, the habit of such exertion, and generally becomes as stupid and ignorant as it is possible for a human creature to become. The torpor of his mind renders him, not only incapable of relishing or bearing a part in any rational conversation, but of conceiving any generous, noble, or tender sentiment, and consequently of forming any just judgment concerning many even of the ordinary duties of private life. (1776/ 1981, p. 782)

According to Smith, the modern economy may undercut the psychological forces that naturally give rise to gratitude in society. Efforts thus must be made to counteract these tendencies, particularly through the institution of public education among the laboring classes and the teaching of science and philosophy. Gratitude has a place in the modern world, but it is a place that must be defended against the corrupting influences of modern life.

Promoting sentiments like proper gratitude is by no means an easy task. Smith noted that the civil magistrate is entrusted with preserving the public peace and restraining injustice as well as "promoting the prosperity of the kingdom" (1790/1982, p. 81). This means that the state must establish good discipline in society by promoting virtue and discouraging vice and by commanding "mutual good offices to a certain degree" (p. 81). This is easier said than done. As Smith explained, "Of all the duties of law-giver, however, this, perhaps, is that which requires the greatest delicacy and reserve to execute with propriety and judgment. To neglect it altogether exposes the commonwealth to many gross disorders and shocking enormities, and to push it too far is destructive of all liberty, security, and justice" (p. 81).

Like Seneca, Smith recognized that there are limits to what could be done to promote sentiments of gratitude in the world. Allowing the legislator, rather than the impartial spectator, to be the judge and enforcer of debts of gratitude may undercut one of the most important psychological bonds that naturally tie one person to another.

CONCLUDING THOUGHTS

Not all eighteenth-century philosophers had the insight or ability of Adam Smith to explain the interrelations between self-interest and gratitude in modern commercial societies. His contemporary Jean-Jacques Rousseau, the great eighteenth-century critic of the modern commercial order, seemed at a loss to explain either the positive features of self-interest or the role that gratitude continued to play in modern society. In his last autobiographical work, *Reveries of the Solitary Walker* (1782/1979), Rousseau lamented the fact that ordinary human dealings were no longer based on "natural kindness and sociability" but had become sullied and polluted by venal motives such as self-interest. In the past, he argued, Europeans could receive housing free of charge by relying on the hospitality of the host and the gratitude of the lodger. He noted that, in modern times, the situation is different. Self-interest has displaced all. Rousseau wrote, "I have noticed that only in Europe is hospitality put up for sale. Throughout Asia you are lodged free of charge. I know that it is harder to find the comforts that you are used to. But then it is something to be able to say to yourself: 'I am a man and I am the guest of my fellow-men; it is pure humanity that I have to thank for my sustenance.' Little hardships are easy to endure when the heart is better treated than the body" (pp. 151–152).

In this passage, it appears that Rousseau was decrying that European commercial societies have lost something that Asian societies have not: a sentiment of hospitality and the pleasures of receiving such hospitality and being grateful for it. For Rousseau, hospitality and gratitude were exemplars of "pure humanity." Unlike Smith, who provided a place for both self-interest and gratitude, Rousseau offered nothing but a stark dichotomy between them. Significantly, it was a dichotomy in which Rousseau himself was caught.

At first blush, it seems that Rousseau (1782/1979) was rejecting the world of commercial prosperity for a simpler one based on natural human sentiments. In an earlier passage in *Reveries*, he noted that gratitude is part of a sacred bond that links a benefactor and a recipient in a close personal relationship. These bonds naturally flow from the pleasure that individuals have in interacting with one another and thus differ sharply from the bonds of duty established by self-interest (see p. 97). Nevertheless, despite his apparent championing of hospitality and gratitude over self-interest, he would not personally accept the conclusion that we are better off relating to one another through gratitude rather than self-interest. Experience had taught him that natural sentiments such as gratitude embodied a downside. As a young man, Rousseau claimed, he trusted others and allowed such relations based on beneficence and gratitude to blossom. Age and experience, however, caused him to distrust others and the natural sentiments that tie people together, because he came to believe that the bonds of dependency that were being forged were more dangerous to the individual in the modern world than connections that were being established (see pp. 98–99). Paradoxically, Rousseau, the champion of sentimentality, could not accept the human consequences that followed from expressions of gratitude. Benevolence and gratitude may be expressions of our deepest humanity, but they also threaten us with chains no free man could desire. Forced to choose between freedom and humane sentiments, Rousseau chose the former.

But even in this choice, Rousseau found it difficult to be consistent. Ironically, his final word on the subject of gratitude at the end of *Reveries* (1782/1979) was hardly consistent with this rejection. In the final sentence of the book, he stated that he would employ his remaining leisure hours "to repay the best of women for all the help she had given me" (p. 154). Earlier protestations aside, his last thoughts were to thank the one individual who helped him most along the path to enlightenment. For Rousseau, gratitude bubbled to the surface, whatever else was done to keep it under control.

Rousseau's ambivalence about the place of gratitude in the modern world is echoed by many of our contemporaries today. Abandoning Smith's attempt to understand the place of both gratitude and self-interest in our modern world, too much theory has ignored the former and misconstrued the latter. Like Rousseau, we find ourselves lost in a false choice between the world of cold rational calculation and the sweets sentiments of humanity. If we are to bring our social, political, and economic theory into closer contact with the everyday world in which we live, we must recognize, as Smith did, that gratitude is a significant force in developing relationships to others and organizing society as a whole. Self-interest may be the driving force of our modern capitalist economy, but it has not made gratitude a vestigial passion. On the contrary, the triumph of self-interest and the modern market economy may demand that we intensify our awareness of gratitude and the dynamic forces it unleashes. Failure to do so may not only cause us to miscast our theories about our social world, but may also undercut positive social consequences that follow from these theories.

I would like to thank Douglas Dow for his close reading and insightful comments.

References

Aquinas, T. (2003). *Summa theologica* (Fathers of the English Dominican Province, Trans.) [Electronic version]. (Original translation published 1920). Retrieved May 7, 2003, from http://www.newadvent.org/summa/

Dunn, E. C. (1946). *The concept of ingratitude in Renaissance English moral philosophy.* Washington, DC: Catholic University of America Press.

Fitzgerald, P. (1998, October). Gratitude and justice. *Ethics, 109,* 119–153.

Galloway, A. (1994). The making of a social ethic in late-medieval England: From gratitudo to "Kyndeness." *Journal of the History of Ideas, 55*(3), 365–383.

Hobbes, T. (1991). *Leviathan* (R. Tuck, Ed.). Cambridge, UK: Cambridge University Press. (Original work published 1651)

Klosko, G. (1989). Political obligation and gratitude. *Philosophy and Public Affairs, 18*(4), 352–358.

La Rochefoucauld, F. de. (1997). *Maxims.* Hertfordshire, UK: Wordsworth Classics.

McConnell, T. (1993). *Gratitude.* Philadelphia: Temple University Press.

Pufendorf, S. (1991). *On the duty of man and citizen according to natural law* (J. Tully, Ed., & M. Silverthorne, Trans.). Cambridge, UK: Cambridge University Press.

Roberts, R. C. (1991). Virtues and rules. *Philosophy and Phenomenological Research, 51*(2), 325–343.

Rousseau, J.-J. (1979). *Reveries of the solitary walker* (P. France, Trans.). Harmondsworth, UK: Penguin. (Original work written 1789)

Seneca, L. A. (1935). On benefits. In *Moral essays, with an English translation by John W. Basore: Vol. III* [Loeb Classical Library]. Cambridge, MA: Harvard University Press.

Simmel, G. (1996). Faithfulness and gratitude. In A. E. Komter (Ed.), *The gift: An interdisciplinary perspective* (pp. 39–48). Amsterdam: Amsterdam University Press. (Original work published 1908)

Smith, A. (1981). *An inquiry into the nature and causes of the wealth of nations* (R. H. Campbell & A. S. Skinner, Eds., & W. B. Todd, Textual Ed.). Indianapolis, IN: Liberty Classics. (Original work written 1776)

Smith, A. (1982). *The theory of moral sentiments* (A. L. Macfie & D. D. Raphael, Eds.). Indianapolis, IN: Liberty Classics. (Original work published 1790)

Stein, J. (Ed. in Chief), & Urdang, L. (Managing Ed.). (1967). *The Random House dictionary of the English language.* New York: Random House.

Tronto, J. C. (1999, September). *Politics and gratitude: Revisiting Hobbes's "social virtues."* Paper presented at the annual meeting of the American Political Science Association, Atlanta, GA.

Walker, A. D. M. (1988). Political obligation and the argument from gratitude. *Philosophy and Public Affairs, 17*(3), 191–211.

Walker, A. D. M. (1989). Obligations of gratitude and political obligation. *Philosophy and Public Affairs, 18*(4), 359–364.

Wright, R. (2000, January 24). Games species play. *Time,* vol. 155, no. 3.

3 Gratitude in Judaism

Solomon Schimmel

Jewish teachings on gratitude are attempts to cultivate a sense of gratitude to God, and to nurture gratitude in human relationships. Although these two manifestations of gratitude can be considered independently, in the religious literature of Judaism they are often connected. We begin with the human-divine relationship.

GRATITUDE IN BIBLICAL THEOLOGY

In their analysis of the sentiment of gratitude McCullough, Kilpatrick, Emmons, and Larson (2001) conceptualized gratitude as having three morally relevant functions, that of a moral barometer, a moral motivator, and a moral reinforcer. In examining the role of gratitude in Judaism, in the individual's relationship to God whom he or she believes is the benevolent provider of life and all that sustains it, the motivating and reinforcing functions of gratitude are evident. Feelings of gratitude to God *motivate* proper behavior toward him, which means obeying his commandments and loving him. In the dominant paradigm of divine theodicy in the Hebrew Bible and in later rabbinic literature, gratitude also functions as a *reinforcer* of God's munificence. God will confer further prosperity and other rewards on those who express their gratitude to him, whether in sacrifice, in prayer, in good deeds directed toward others, or in performing rituals, all of which he has prescribed in his Torah (teachings).

We need to take note, however, of a major biblical exception to the notion of a God who rewards fidelity, love, and gratitude, which is articulated in the poetic section of the book of Job (in contrast to the prose prologue and epilogue of the book). Job challenged the prevailing belief that God rewards obedience and righteousness. Job did so on the basis of his personal experience, and in the absence in general human experience, as he perceived it, of any positive correlation between righteousness and well-being and between wickedness and suffering. Gratitude to God, however manifested or expressed, does not seem to affect how God behaves to people, or at least not in any way humans can unequivocally discern. Implicit in the view of the author of Job is that one should not expect gratitude to God to function as a reinforcer of God's benevolence, because reality demonstrates that too often it is the grateful righteous who suffer and the ungrateful wicked who prosper. Although gratitude to God for life, and for whatever in life one cherishes, as a *motivator* of human response to God, is possible in Job's theological worldview,[1] gratitude as a *reinforcer* of God's benevolence is not.

Notwithstanding the poetic power and persuasiveness of Job's challenge to the existence of a divinely regulated and reliable moral order in the universe that makes gratitude relevant, his view never supplanted the dominant biblical belief and trust in God's justice and in God's love for Israel. God's justice linked righteous behavior with a divine reward and God's love with the bestowal of an abundance of blessings on those faithful to him. This dominant view, expressed in biblical narrative, law, historiography, psalms and theology, nurtured the sentiment of gratitude as both a motivator for human behavior toward God and a reinforcer of and influence on divine behavior toward man, in response to expressions of gratitude to God.

The Hebrew Bible is replete with the motif that humans owe God gratitude for life, health, and sustenance. There are numerous thanksgiving psalms[2] and other prayers in which the person or the community that is praying pours forth expressions of gratitude. Many of the sacrifices offered on altars and, later, in the Temple in Jerusalem, were infused with the sentiment of gratefulness and thanks, as was the elaborate ceremony of bringing the first fruits—*bikkurim*—to the priests, the representatives of God in the Temple. This ceremony (Deuteronomy 26:1–16) includes a long recitation, by the donor, of the Lord's redemptive actions on behalf of the nation of Israel and his gracious gift to Israel of the land flowing with milk and honey. "So now I bring the first of the fruit of the ground that you, O Lord, have given me" (Deuteronomy 26:10, New Revised Standard Version). Moreover, the gratitude of the donor is to be expressed not only in the offering of the first fruits to the priest, but also in compassion for the resident aliens, the orphans, and the widows through various tithes that were to be given to them.

Along with these powerful sentiments of gratitude and thanks, there is a plea for future blessings, so the *bikkurim* ceremony and sacrifices are not lacking in self-interest. The assumption is that gratitude and thanksgiving will be rewarded by further bounty and divine protection, and ingratitude can be dangerous because it will evoke God's wrath. Thus, there is more to expressions of gratitude and offerings of thanksgiving than pure appreciation of favors bestowed. There is, as well, an underlying anxiety about the future. It would be naive to assume that expressions of gratitude and thankfulness aren't often motivated by self-interest, and the Bible does not seem to be bothered by this fact. Indeed, it unabashedly employs self-interest as a primary reason for people to express and act on their feelings of gratitude toward God.

The sentiment of gratitude is central to the very relationship between God (YHWH) and the people of Israel. Levenson (1985), analyzing the nature of the covenant between YHWH and Israel, examines in depth its components as reflected in chapter 24 of the book of Joshua:

> The dominant theme of this recitation of history (Joshua 24:1–28) is the unceasing grace of YHWH toward Israel. He has given them more than they deserve. Time and again he has rescued them; time and again he has frustrated their enemies. Thus, at this moment at the end of the book of Joshua, as the great epic of deliverance and conquest draws to a close . . . the message is clear; God has benefited Israel beyond her deserts. . . . Awareness of divine grace sets the stage for the stipulations [of the covenant]. These are expressed in the form of three imperatives: "hold YHWH in awe," "serve him with undivided loyalty and in truthfulness," and "banish the [alien] gods" (v 14). (p. 33)

In turn, Israel's gratitude to God for his beneficence and love is expected to generate fidelity to Him, obedient fulfillment of His commandments, and reciprocal love of Him. "'And now what does YHWH your God demand of you? Only this: to hold YHWH your God in awe, to walk in all his paths, to love him, and to serve YHWH your God with all your heart and all your soul, to observe YHWH's commandments and his laws, which I enjoin upon you this day, for your own benefit' (Deuteronomy 10:12–13). Israel . . . is to realize her love in the form of observance of her master's stipulations, the mitsvot, for they are the words of the language of love, the fit medium in which to respond to the passionate advances of the divine suzerain. It is not a question of law *or* love, but law conceived in love, love expressed in law" (Levenson, 1985, p. 77).

GRATITUDE IN THE PASSOVER SEDER AND JEWISH LITURGY

In her gratitude to God, Israel feels an *obligation* to praise and thank him. In the Passover Seder ceremony, after concluding the recounting of the story of the redemption from slavery in Egypt, there is a recitation of the Hallel, psalms of praise and thanksgiving to God. The following passage acts as the transition from the recapitulation of redemptive history to the Hallel: "Therefore it is our *duty* to thank, to praise, to laud, to glorify, to exalt, to honor, to bless, to extol and give respect to Him who performed all these miracles for our fathers and for us. He has brought us from slavery to freedom, from sorrow to joy, from mourning to festivity, from darkness to bright light, and from bondage to redemption! Therefore let us recite a new song before Him. Hallelujah!" (*Passover Haggadah*, 1977, pp. 148–152) (emphasis added).

The *dayenu* prayer that is part of the Passover Haggadah lists 14 redemptive events and gifts of God for which Israel is grateful. However, it uses an unusual format in doing so. The pattern it follows is shown in the following excerpt:

> For how many favors do we owe thanks to the Omnipresent!
> If He had brought us out of Egypt, but had not executed judgments upon the Egyptians, it would have sufficed for us. . . .
> If He had given us the Sabbath but not brought us to Mount Sinai, it would have sufficed for us. . . .
> If He had given us the Torah, but not led us into the land of Israel, it would have sufficed for us.

Thus, the prayer lists the 14 acts of God in sequential order, saying after each one mentioned that it would have sufficed for us had he stopped at that juncture. It then concludes, "Thus, how much more so do we owe thanks to the Omnipresent for all His manifold favors. He brought us forth from Egypt, executed judgments . . . gave us the Sabbath, brought us to Mount Sinai, gave us the Torah, brought us into the land of Israel," (Passover haggadah, 1977, pp. 136–137) and so on, repeating the 14, all of which, in the biblical account, God actually did perform.

One may ask, if the purpose of the song is to express gratitude to God for all that God had done, as the concluding passage indeed does, what function is served by the hypothetical "If he had done X but not done Y," given that He had done Y? Why doesn't the concluding, summary passage suffice to express Israel's gratitude to God?

One interpretation of the structure of this poem is that when we reflect on a benefit that God (or, by extension, another person) has done for us, we should break it into its multiple components, meditating on each element. This will engender a greater appreciation of the effort that was expended by the benefactor and of the multiplicity of the benefits that inhere in the "global one," that a more hurried and superficial acknowledgment of gratitude might overlook. For example, to simply say that I am grateful to my mother for the sacrifices she made so that I could get an education is less grat-itude-inducing than consciously and deliberately trying to think about or overtly mention and remind myself of, thereby, the thousands of hours and days and weeks and years of hard work that she invested on my behalf.

In a similar vein, Emmons and Shelton (2002) noted that "many reli-giously oriented events such as reflection days or scheduled week-long re-treats have as a recurring theme the idea of 'gift' . . . as do many self-help groups and organizations. . . . All in all, setting aside time on a daily basis to re-call moments of gratitude associated with even mundane or ordinary events, . . . or valued people one encounters has the potential to interweave and thread together a sustainable life theme of highly cherished personal mean-ing" (p. 466).

Another idea suggested by the structure of the *dayenu* poem is that we should be grateful for benevolent efforts expended on our behalf even if they did not ultimately come to fruition. The Israelites would have owed God gratitude for each effort or action he took on their behalf even if these ac-tions would not have reached all of their ultimate goals.[3]

The idea that one should reflect on the *abundance* of God's gifts and ex-press that in thanksgiving and praise, as a means of accentuating the emotion of gratitude, is illustrated by another prayer, the *Nishmat*, recited in the Sab-bath morning service:

> Were our mouth filled with song as the sea [is with water], and our tongue ringing praise as the roaring waves; were our lips full of ado-ration as the wide expanse of heaven, and our eyes sparkling like the sun or the moon; were our hands spread out in prayer as the eagles of the sky, and our feet as swift as the deer—we should still be unable to thank thee and bless thy name, Lord our God and God of our fa-thers, for one thousandth of the *countless millions of favors which thou hast conferred on our fathers and on us*. Thou hast delivered us from Egypt, Lord our God, and redeemed us from slavery. Thou hast nourished us in famine and provided us with plenty. Thou hast res-cued us from the sword, made us escape the plague, and freed us from severe and lasting diseases. (Birnbaum, 1949, p. 332)

If one were to to list the gifts bestowed upon Israel as recorded in the Bible and in postbiblical Jewish literature, I suppose it would be difficult to come up with "countless millions." However, if every minute of life for every member of Israel, for the nearly two thousand years from Abraham to the composition of this prayer, were counted as separate gifts, I suppose "count-less millions of favors" might not be an exaggeration, and perhaps this is the sense of the prayer. Another interpretation, based on the fact that the prayer seems to have been associated with the rain (*Babylonian Talmud*, Tractates

Berakhot 59b, Ta'anit 6b), is that countless millions of favors "might refer to the drops of rain, with each drop being counted as a separate favor, in accordance with the talmudic suggestion that thanks should be given for every drop of rain" (Birnbaum, 1949, pp. 331–332).

Another manifestation of the importance of specificity in thanking a benefactor for his or her gifts is in the rabbinic formulations of blessings of thanks to God that are to be recited before partaking of food. These blessings, known as *birkhot hanehenin*—blessings for things that we enjoy in life—include separate ones for bread, pastries, fruits, vegetables, wine, water, and other drinks and foods. Instead of formulating a single generic blessing to be recited before partaking of any food, the rabbis formulated different blessings for several different categories of food. Perhaps another idea implicit here is that the pleasures or benefits derived from drinking wine or eating a fruit, a piece of bread, and so on are not identical; therefore each gift is unique, and gratitude and thanksgiving should acknowledge this uniqueness. Although these notions about how gratitude should be expressed refer to human gratitude to God, they are applicable as well to interpersonal gratitude.

The rabbinic sages also taught that "One blesses over misfortune just as one blesses over good, for it is said 'Love the Lord your God . . . with all your soul' (Deuteronomy 6:5), even if he takes your soul" (*Mishnah*, Berakhot 9:5).

The blessing one recites over misfortune may not be an expression of gratitude, but rather an acceptance of the divine judgment as being just. However, it might also be interpreted as an expression of gratitude, because what may appear tragic to the limited understanding of a human might, from am omniscient divine perspective, actually be for the ultimate benefit of the person who suffers.

An extreme example of this attitude is the story about Rabbi Akiva, who laughed joyously as he was being tortured to death by Romans who had caught him studying Torah in violation of their decree forbidding it. His disciples asked him how he could rejoice while in such excruciating pain. Rabbi Akiva said to them that all of his life he had been troubled that he might not be able to fulfill the commandment to love God with all of his soul. Now that the opportunity presented itself to him, he rejoiced in it. Rabbi Akiva did not seek opportunities to die as a martyr, but when he found himself in such a situation, he was grateful for it.

Analogously, Emmons and Shelton (2002, p. 467) ask, "Is the Biblical injunction to be 'thankful in all circumstances' (1 Thessalonians 5:18, RSV) realistic, even for religious persons?" They respond that "in this regard, the examination of gratitude in the lives of people coping with major adversities might be illuminating. An attitude of gratitude may be one means by which tragedies are transformed into opportunities for growth, being thankful not so much for the circumstances but rather for the skills that will come from dealing with it. The ability to discern blessings in the face of tragedy is a magnificent human strength" (p. 20).

INTERPERSONAL GRATITUDE IN BIBLICAL NARRATIVES AND LAW

Although the Hebrew Bible is mostly concerned with the gratitude to God owed by the people of Israel and by individual Israelites, several biblical stories reflect gratitude to humans for favors bestowed or for good deeds that are appreciated. Joshua rewarded Rahab of Jericho (for assisting the spies he sent to the city) by saving her and her family from destruction when he conquered and destroyed Jericho (Joshua 2:12, 6:25). In this case, gratitude was an expression of reciprocity, unlike many other instances in which the beneficiary cannot bestow, and cannot in the future bestow, any favor or gift upon his or her benefactor that is in any way commensurate with what has been received. Rahab asks for a quid pro quo, "Now then, since I have dealt kindly with you, swear to me by the Lord that you in turn will deal kindly with my family" (Josh. 2:12, NRSV). The concept of measure for measure is widely used in postbiblical rabbinic literature in several contexts, especially that of reward and punishment. It also can reflect gratitude, in that the recipient wants, or feels obligated, to repay the donor at a comparable level with or in a similar manner to the benefit he or she received.

Ruth the Moabite, daughter-in-law of Naomi the Israelite, returned with Naomi to Judea after both were widowed. Ruth could have returned to the safety and security of her native home and homeland, but (notwithstanding Naomi's encouraging her to do so) chose to cast her lot with Naomi and Israel. She also decided to follow the custom in Israel of giving to a kinsman of the deceased husband first marriage rights to his widow. She sought out the kinsman Boaz rather than putting herself on the free market, so to speak, where she might have made out quite well for herself. Boaz appreciatively told her, "May you be blessed by the Lord, my daughter; this last instance of your loyalty is better than the first; you have not gone after young men, whether poor or rich. . . . I will do for you all that you ask" (Ruth 3:10–11, NRSV). He took her as his wife, and she bore Obed, the grandfather of King David. Boaz was grateful to Ruth not so much because she chose him, although he might have appreciated that as well, but because she followed Naomi to Judea and was faithful to the Israelite custom of perpetuating the name of a deceased husband by marrying his kin, so that the first child born of this marriage was considered the legal heir and descendant of her first husband. The author of the book of Ruth appreciated Ruth's loyalty to Naomi, to Israel, and to Israel's customs, all the more so because she was a foreigner with other options. He explained that God rewarded her with the honor of becoming the great-grandmother of Israel's greatest king. Gratitude here is not for a personal favor rendered, but for noble deeds performed.

The biblical admonition to the Israelites "You shall not abhor any of the Egyptians, because you were an alien residing in their land" (Deut. 23:7, NRSV) reflects gratitude extending across generations. The admonition is strange, considering that the Egyptians weren't exactly kind to the Israelites in Egypt, enslaving and oppressing them for centuries. One interpretation of the admonition is that, although the Egyptians enslaved the Israelites after the death of Joseph, while he was alive they invited Jacob and his family to reside in Goshen and provided them with a haven from famine. Whatever wicked deeds the Egyptians later did, they did not entirely cancel the debt of gratitude owed to them for the benefits they had earlier conferred. The verse doesn't say, "Love the Egyptians"; it says only, "Don't abhor them." However, in the context of Deuteronomy 23:3–6, to not abhor was a much better attitude than the one the Israelites were to have toward Ammon and Moab, who were hostile toward Israel when she was in dire need, and therefore "You shall never promote their welfare or their prosperity as long as you live" (Deut. 23:6, NRSV). The gratitude and appreciation expressed toward Ruth the Moabite is especially striking in light of this hostility toward the nation of Moab.

Another interpretation (albeit somewhat forced) of the modicum of appreciation owed by the Israelites to Egypt is that, even as they were oppressed strangers in that land, they did receive some benefits from the Egyptians—a place to live and food to eat. The Egyptians didn't annihilate them (although they tried unsuccessfully to kill all the male children) as some nations of old were wont to do to those they conquered.

GRATITUDE IN TALMUD AND MIDRASH
(RABBINIC BIBLICAL EXEGESIS)

The Midrash notes that in the description of the first 3 of the 10 plagues in Exodus—the blood, frogs, and lice—it was Aaron rather than Moses who struck the Nile River and the sand, the sources of these plagues. Why so? Because the Nile, where Moses had been hidden in a basket by his mother, had protected him from Pharaoh's decree that all male Israelite infants be drowned at birth. Similarly, the sand—which had concealed the body of the Egyptian taskmaster Moses had killed in his righteous indignation at seeing him mercilessly beating a Hebrew slave—had saved Moses from Pharaoh's wrath and from prosecution and death. In gratitude to the Nile and to the sand, Moses did not want to be the one to smite them with his staff, and Aaron was delegated by God to do so. The moral the rabbis were conveying is that if one has to show gratitude even to inanimate objects, how much more must we show gratitude to humans who have benefited us (see Fendel, 1986, p. 222)?

Another Midrash, commenting on the verse "There arose a new king over Egypt, who knew not Joseph" (Exodus 1:8), teaches,

> "Why does Scripture severely chastise ungrateful individuals? Because ingratitude is similar to disavowal of God. The atheist is also an ingrate. An individual may begin by manifesting ingratitude for the kindness shown to him by his fellow man; it is not long before he disavows the kindness of his Creator.
>
> So, too, does it say concerning Pharaoh, 'he knew not Joseph.' Yet surely, even today, Egypt recalls the kindness of Joseph. This must mean, rather, that Pharaoh surely knew [Joseph], but he took no heed of him, and he disavowed his kindness. Subsequently, he disavowed the kindness of the Almighty, as he said, 'I know not God' (Exodus 5:2).
>
> From here we may derive that ingratitude may be likened to denial of God. (pp. 223–224)[4]

About this midrash, Fendel, basing himself on Maimonides and other medieval Jewish moralists who emphasized the importance of the regular practice of virtuous behaviors as a means of inculcating virtuous traits and attitudes, wrote, "The individual, therefore, who does not continually train himself to express gratitude and appreciation in his daily interaction with his fellow man, cannot possibly hope to acquire mastery of the trait of [gratitude]. Consequently, he will hardly be prepared to express sincere, heartfelt gratitude when called upon to do so in his interaction with God" (p. 225).

The Talmud criticizes several biblical characters for their lack of gratitude. For instance, Adam, instead of thanking God for fashioning Eve as a companion-helper for him, blamed God for having given Eve to him, as he shunted responsibility onto Eve and even to God for his own disobedient eating of the fruit of the forbidden tree. When God asked, "Have you eaten of the tree of which I commanded you not to eat?" Adam responded, with hutzpah and ingratitude, "The woman whom *you* gave to be with me, *she* gave me fruit from the tree, and I ate" (Genesis 3:11–12, NRSV) (emphasis added).

The Israelites, rather than thanking God for redeeming them from slavery and for the manna from Heaven which sustained them in the wilderness, complained. "The people spoke against God and against Moses, 'Why have you brought us up out of Egypt to die in the wilderness? For there is no food and no water, and we detest this miserable food' (Numbers 21:5)" (*Babylonian Talmud*, Tractate Avoda Zarah, 5a–5b and commentaries ad loc).

Not long after the great flood, the descendants of Noah attempt to scale Heaven and challenge God's sovereignty, by building the Tower of Babel. In Genesis we read, "The Lord came down to see the city and the tower, which the *sons of the Adam* [literally, the 'sons of the ground,' i.e., humans or mortals], had built." (Genesis 11:5, emphasis added). Why, asks the Midrash, as paraphrased by Rashi, the eleventh-century Jewish commentator on the Bible, do we have to be told that the people who were building the Tower were "sons of humans," as this is self-evident? They surely weren't children of asses or camels!

The reason, answers the Midrash, for the expression *bnai ha'adam* (reading it as "the sons of the Adam") is that the Torah wants to attribute their descent to Adam of the Garden of Eden, to teach us that they were like their ancestor Adam, ingrates such as he was. How so? Rather than being grateful to God for having saved them from the flood (i.e., they were descended from Noah), they instead rebelled against him.

The teaching here seems to be not only that gratitude is important, and that it prevents hubris and sin, but that parents have a crucial role in transmitting to their children attitudes of gratitude or of ingratitude (Fendel, 1986).

BAHYA IBN PAKUDA ON GRATITUDE TO HUMANS AND GRATITUDE TO GOD

The idea that gratitude to other human beings is one pathway to developing an attitude of gratitude toward God, was elaborated on at length by Bahya Ibn Pakuda, the tenth-century Spanish Jewish author of one of the most influential of Jewish devotional treatises, *Duties of the Heart*. Bahya analyzed the psychology of gratitude in interpersonal relationships, not for its own sake but to provide grounds for our obligation to be thankful and obedient to God. He wrote:

> It is a known and accepted fact that our obligation to thank our benefactor should be according to his good intention towards us. Although he may fail in his deed for some reason or because of some obstacle, we must nevertheless be grateful to him once we have ascertained his favorable conduct and beneficial intention toward us. On the other hand, when a favor is done for us unintentionally, we have no obligation of gratitude to anybody.
>
> When we consider the favors men do for each other we find them all falling under one of the five following categories: first, the

favors done by parent for child; second, those done by a master for a slave; third, favors by the wealthy for the poor, for the sake of heavenly rewards; fourth, favors done by one man for another for the sake of praise, honor, and earthly rewards, and fifth, those done by the powerful for the sake of the weak, out of pity and compassion. (trans. 1973, p. 176)

Bahya went on to analyze the motives for each of these five categories of benefactors. He asserted, "It is clear that the parent's intention is to benefit himself through the child, for the child is part of the parent, who places great hopes in him" (trans. 1973, p. 177). Moreover, he said that parents are motivated by their nature to protect and nurture their children, and as "the parent is forced to it by his nature, he is only a medium, and the grace belongs to God" (p. 177). Yet notwithstanding the fact that the parent cares for and nurtures the child out of self-interest and instinct, "both the Law [i.e., the Torah] and Reason oblige the children to obey, honor, and fear their parents" (p. 177).

The favors done by a master for a slave are also motivated by self-interest, because "his intention is to enlarge his wealth by improving his property. In addition, he need the slave's services, so his only intention is to improve himself. Nevertheless, God has obliged the slave to thank his master and obey him, as it is said 'A son honoreth his father, and a servant his master; If then I be a father, where is my honor? And if I be a master, where is my fear? Saith the Lord of hosts unto you . . . '(Malakhi 1:6)" (Bahya, trans. 1973, p. 177).

The wealthy man does favors for the poor man only because he is seeking "the adornment of his own soul in the next world" (p. 177). Even so, "it is generally accepted that he should be greatly thanked and praised for it" (p. 177).

Why do people do favors for one another? Here, too, self-interest is the motive. "Their only intention in doing them is to adorn their own souls in this world with the praise and honor they expect to get in it, or a reward in the next world" (Bahya, trans. 1973, p. 178). Yet here as well it is incumbent upon us to thank and praise those who do us favors.

Finally, "whoever does a favor for the weak and suffering, out of compassion, does it only in order to save himself the pain of being sorry for the object of his compassion, in the same way as a man would treat his own pain" (Bahya, trans. 1973, p. 178). Still, such a benefactor deserves gratitude from the beneficiary.

Bahya was not interested in explaining why we should feel gratitude toward these five types of benefactors. He took it for granted—on the basis of scriptures that he cited, reason, or accepted social convention—that the beneficiary is under such an obligation. The argument he was leading up to is

that if we are obligated to feel gratitude toward, to thank, and in some relationships to be obedient to our benefactors, even though they are acting out
of self-interest, how much more are we under an obligation to feel gratitude
toward, to thank and be obedient to, God. "How much, then, should a man
obey, praise and thank the Creator of all benefaction and benefactors, whose
beneficence is infinite, permanent and perpetual, done neither for His own
benefit nor for driving away misfortunes, but his all-loving kindness and grace
towards men" (trans. 1973, p. 178).

What is surprising in Bahya's analysis is his rather cynical view of humans. He did not ascribe to them any altruistic motives. In his perspective,
egotistical concerns underlie even the compassion that we feel and act upon
in our relationship with others. Nor did he consider situations in which the
weak, the poor, and those of lower social status confer favors on the strong,
the wealthy, and the powerful. Of course, in those cases, it would be even
easier to suspect ulterior motives, because such benefactors could later be rewarded by their beneficiaries. Perhaps Freud and "selfish-gene" theorists
would agree with Bahya's pessimistic view of human nature, but other psychologists might be more sanguine about our motives for doing good to others, at least sometimes. It is possible that Bahya was exaggerating human egotism because it strengthened his case for gratitude to God, as long as we
accept his premise that, notwithstanding the egotism of the benefactor, the
beneficiary incurs the obligations of gratitude.[5]

In his attempt to convince his audience as to why they should be grateful
to God, Bahya argued that even when we act in ways that confer benefits on
us, it is really God who is the benefactor, with people acting as the medium
through which he implements his will to do us good. "It is not in the power of
the wealthy to pay even one farthing to anyone unless it has been predeter-
mined by God" (trans. 1973, p. 249). Once people realize this, "they would
not put their hope in anybody but God, and would not honor anybody but
those men to whom He has given praiseworthy virtues, for they deserve
God's honor" (p. 249). The point Bahya wanted to make is that we should
not be fawning and obsequious to the wealthy or the powerful. As he elaborated, "When a man is driven by necessity to ask a favor of somebody above
or below him, he should rely on God to grant him the favor, while making the
other person the means of getting it, as one cultivates the soil and sows it as a
means of getting one's livelihood. If God so wishes, He makes the seeds grow,
prosper, and thrive, so it is not the soil that should be thanked, but God alone,
for if He does not wish to give man his sustenance by it, the soil grows nothing, or, if it does grow, it is later afflicted with some misfortune, and the soil is
not to blame" (p. 253).

In his zeal to see God alone as the ultimate source of the good we receive
in life, Bahya, in effect, weakened the claim on us for gratitude to the humans

who bestow favors on us, because they are mere instruments of God's benevolence. It is evident that Bahya sensed this problem, because he said, "It is made clear . . . that in doing favors for others, men's only intention is first of all to benefit themselves, then to adorn their own souls in this world or the next, or to save themselves from suffering, or to increase their wealth. Nevertheless, this does not mean that they should not be thanked, feared, loved and rewarded accordingly" (trans. 1973, p. 178).

In a later section of the book, Bahya noted, "If his request [for a favor of somebody] is answered . . . he should thank God, who fulfilled his need, and he should also thank the man through whom it was done, for his good intention and benevolent heart, and because God chose him to be the means of his welfare. It is known that God does good most of the time through pious men" (trans. 1973, pp. 249–250).

What most concerned Bahya in this latter section of this treatise (entitled "On the Reliance Upon God Alone") was getting us to put our trust exclusively in God and not in mortals. Our natural tendency is to thank the human benefactor, to be grateful to him or her, to perhaps act toward that person in a fawning manner, and to forget God's role in the causal chain of benefaction. Therefore, Bahya emphasized God's will behind all acts of human benevolence.

One problem with this argument of Bahya's for gratitude to God is that the more you ascribe the benefaction to God, the less of it you ascribe to humankind. Therefore, as we reflect on the relationship between the theological idea of gratitude and thanksgiving to God on one hand, and gratitude and thanksgiving to humans on the other, we should not assume that the latter is an obvious derivation from the former. On the contrary, the opposite might be the case—the more you owe God, the less you owe humans. Of course, in the totality of the ethical and moral teachings of Bahya and of Judaism in general, as we have seen and will see even more, gratitude and thanksgiving owed to human benefactors is a very important value. That does not necessarily mean, however, that the two values are always congruent with one another.[6] A fruitful area for research on gratitude would be to examine how this tension plays out in the actual experience of people. For example, who tends to be more grateful to human benefactors such as foundations that support research? Is it the devout believer in God's omnipotence and benevolence, who views granting agencies as God's medium but not the ultimate source of funding? Or is it the atheist, who has no one to thank for a foundation's beneficence other than the organization's founder and its staff?

In concluding our discussion of Bahya, we should bear in mind that, for him, gratitude to God had multiple implications, such as love for God, humility, and obedience. In our contemporary culture, we do not look with great favor on obedience, to authority or to parents and teachers (Seligman, 2000). In biblical covenant theology, as we saw, thankfulness to God imposed the obligation to obey his commandments. This theme continues in postbiblical Judaism, from the Talmudic period through the Middle Ages, and Bahya is but one exemplar of the pervasive claim made by all Jewish theologians, rabbis, and devotional writers—that God's law must be scrupulously obeyed, out of gratitude to and love for him. The close nexus between gratitude, love, and obedience is carried over into Judaism's teachings about children's obligations toward their parents, to which we now turn.

GRATITUDE TO PARENTS

Honoring, revering, and taking care of parents is a very important obligation in Judaism, not surprisingly, inasmuch as it is one of the Ten Commandments (Exodus 20:12; Deuteronomy 5:16) and is repeated many times in the Hebrew Bible (e.g., Leviticus 19:3; Deuteronomy 21:18–21; numerous passages in the book of Proverbs). Why must we do so? Many reasons are offered for this obligation, one of which is that children should be grateful to their parents (Blidstein, 1975, pp. 8–19). Grateful for what? Most obviously, the parent created the child, giving it life. Beyond that, however, the parent nurtured, educated, provided for, and labored for the child.

Moreover, the rabbis and the later moralists, such as Bahya, did expect that "the gratitude shown parents will lead one to gratitude toward God. In this they are true to the biblical demand projected in Deuteronomy 32:6— 'Do you thus requite the Lord? . . . Is he not the Father who created you?'— and elsewhere—'If I am a father where is the honor that is mine?' (Malakhi 1:16)" (Blidstein, 1975, pp. 10–11).

Rabbi Aharon HaLevi of the thirteenth century, to whom is attributed the influential *Sefer HaHinukh* (*Book of Education*), combines both effects of observing the mitzvah (commandment) of honoring parents:

> Among the concepts inherent in this mitzvah is the fact that it is proper for an individual to acknowledge and repay with kindness those who performed kindness for him. He should not be a vile individual who fails to recognize or to acknowledge one's kindness, for this is an utterly evil and abominable trait, in the eyes of God and man. . . . When the individual shall accept this trait upon himself, he will, as a result, acknowledge the kindness of the Almighty, who was the cause of his creation . . . who brought him into the light of the world, and provided for all his needs all the days of his life, and who formed him, and perfected his limbs, and endowed him

with a soul and with intellect and understanding. (as cited by Fendel, 1986, p. 226)

A theme that runs throughout the *Sefer HaHinukh* is that the practice of virtuous behavior inculcates the virtue as a stable trait of character. Therefore there is a feedback loop with respect to gratitude as a general trait, and the mitzvah of honoring parents. You should honor your parents because the virtue of gratitude obligates you to do so, and if you do so, this will reinforce in you the trait of gratitude in general, with respect to other human beings and with respect to God.[7]

The obligation of filial piety did not rest exclusively on the claim of gratitude owed by children to parents, for the rabbis and later moralists were aware that there were reasonable refutations to the claim of gratitude in some instances. For one, not every person feels that being alive is a favor. Some people are in a state of perpetual depression or chronic pain and suffering, and a few even commit suicide. Moreover, as a few talmudic statements remind us, parents often engage in sexual relations for the pleasure it provides and not necessarily out of a desire for the child who is conceived as a result. And as Bahya maintained, parental nurturing is either egocentric or built into human nature. Notwithstanding these observations and reservations, gratitude to parents was an important pillar of the Judaic obligation to honor, obey, and care for one's father and mother.

GRATITUDE TO TEACHERS

Just as we are obligated to be grateful to and honor our parents, so are students obligated to be grateful to and honor their teachers. The Mishnah teaches:

If one's father and one's teacher [interpreted by the Talmud to mean one's primary teacher of Torah] have both lost an article [and a person has time to retrieve and return only one of the two], the lost article of the teacher has priority over the lost article of the father. For his father brought him into this world but his teacher who taught him wisdom brings him into the world to come . . . if his father and his teacher were both in captivity he should first redeem his teacher and then his father. If, however, his father is a scholar [presumably from whom he has also learned Torah], he should first redeem his father and afterwards his teacher. (*Mishnah*, Bava Metzia 2:11)

In other words, the gratitude that one should have for the teacher who bequeaths spiritual and eternal life, and the honor due that teacher, is even greater than the gratitude one must have for the biological parents who bequeathed physical existence. This ruling tells us also that gratitude is not just a feeling or an attitude but that it imposes behavioral and financial obligations.

GRATITUDE AND THE INTENTION OF THE BENEFACTOR

Earlier we suggested that one explanation for the Biblical admonition to the Israelites that they not abhor the Egyptians was because, even though they suffered oppression from the Egyptians, the Israelites also benefited by living in their land. Whether or not this interpretation is plausible, it does raise an interesting question about gratitude. Do I owe gratitude to someone from whom I benefit even though he had no intention of doing me good or, in a more extreme case, even intended to do me evil? In other words, is it the intention that counts or the outcome?[8]

The Talmud alludes to this question in the context of the rabbinic imagining of the day of final judgment of the nations of the world. God will ask the Romans and the Persians (two nations that conquered, and in certain periods oppressed, the Jews), what good deeds have you done? They will answer, ingenuously, that they built marketplaces, bathhouses, and bridges; created economies flourishing with gold and silver; conquered cities; and pursued wars, all so that Israel would be able to engage in the study of Torah. God will respond to them, "Fools, all that you did you did for your own sakes, marketplaces for prostitutes, bathhouses to give you pleasure . . . , bridges so that you can collect tolls, and cities for taxes" (*Babylonian Talmud*, Tractate Avoda Zarah, p. 2b). One theme of this passage seems to be that the rabbis were aware that these empires, as oppressive and cruel as they often were, still created impressive civilizations and infrastructures from which the Jewish people, like everyone else in their empires, benefited, and perhaps these should count as merits in their behalf on judgment day. The author of this particular passage rejected this view, although the very raising of the question suggests perhaps that other Jews were more appreciative of some of the Persian and Roman contributions. They felt that, whatever the Persians' and Romans' egotistical intentions or the wicked uses to which their products were put, these products did provide economies and sophisticated societies that provided Jews certain benefits, enabling them to study Torah with greater ease than might have been possible in more primitive civilizations. The rabbinic view, in this passage at least, was that what counts is good intentions, which the Persians and Romans did not have. The imagined discourse between God and the gentile empires is explicitly formulated, not in terms of whether they are owed gratitude and appreciation, but in terms of whether they have earned any merit for good deeds, which should affect divine judgment. But the concept of reward for meritorious deeds is often conceptually close to the notion of gratitude, as we saw with Rahab. An action that is considered meritorious because it benefited me is one that I should reward, if I can, out of gratitude for it.

Apropos of the mixed feelings of some Jews toward the Roman Empire, an interesting research question to pursue would be how the emotion of gratitude interacts with other, hostile emotions toward the benefactor. Under what conditions would the gratitude prevail over the enmity, and vice versa? This is an issue, for example, that might be faced by children with parents who both nurture and abuse them.

WHEN GRATITUDE IS DANGEROUS

Sometimes gratitude can be dangerous and result in immoral or unethical behavior.[9] The rabbis of the Talmud, who often functioned as judges, were particularly sensitive to the pernicious effect that ingratiation can have on judicial objectivity, even unconsciously. In their discussions of the sin of bribery they elaborated on the notion of bribery by way of words or deeds, which, unlike outright attempts to bribe someone with money, might have insidious effects of which the recipient is even unaware. Therefore, judges in particular had to be hypersensitive to whether a litigant had in some way done them a favor or even just praised or honored them, such that they might be biased in judgment as a result. Receiving a favor or an honor naturally engenders a feeling of gratitude toward the one who bestowed it, and a judge might be uncomfortable ruling against that person because of appreciation for the favor or honor. Here I cite one of numerous anecdotes recorded in the Talmud on this theme: "A man rented the garden of Rabbi Yishmael [a judge]. This man used to bring him every Friday a basket of fruit [to which Rabbi Yishmael was entitled]. On one occasion he brought it on Thursday, and when [Rabbi Yishmael] asked him why, he replied, 'I have a lawsuit, and I thought that while I was on my way here, I would bring the fruit to you.' The Rabbi would not accept them, and said to him, 'I am disqualified from being your judge'" (Montefiore & Loewe, 1960, p. 390).

In this case, the litigant did not offer Rabbi Yishmael a gift, because, as the owner of the garden, Rabbi Yishmael was entitled to the basket of fruit. All he did was bring it a day earlier than usual, which was a very minimal benefit. Moreover, his ostensible motive in doing so, and maybe his true motive as well, was not to do Rabbi Yishmael a favor, but to save himself the trouble of going to Rabbi Yishmael's house the next day. Yet Rabbi Yishmael feared that this slight "favor" could influence him in favor of this litigant, and so he disqualified himself. The story continues: "He [Rabbi Yishmael] appointed two other Rabbis to judge the case; he walked up and down while the case was going on, and thought, 'If the man wished, he could bring forward such and such arguments.' And he [Rabbi Yishmael] said, 'May those who take bribes perish! If I, who did not take a bribe, have had these thoughts, how much worse would have been the thoughts of those who had taken a bribe" (Montefiore & Loewe, 1960, p. 390).

Rabbi Yishmael found himself automatically conjuring up arguments that would bolster the case of the litigant who had brought him the basket of fruit a day earlier than usual. Presumably, there were other arguments that could have been thought up to buttress the case of his opponent, but these didn't occur to Rabbi Yishmael. This made him aware of how the gratitude engendered by a favor can subtly distort a judge's attitude, which led him to vehemently proclaim a curse against those judges who did in fact accept concrete favors, let alone actual bribes, from litigants.

WHY BE GRATEFUL?

It is hard to conceive of a human society in which gratitude and its consequences do not play important social roles, and Judaism takes it for granted that we owe a debt of gratitude to benefactors, whereas it debates some of the specifics of this obligation. Although several theological and rational grounds for the obligation of interpersonal gratitude are invoked in Jewish religious literature, perhaps that obligation is best subsumed under the commandment to love your neighbor as yourself. Just as you would want to be appreciated, thanked, and in some cases rewarded for the efforts and resources you expended on someone else, you in turn have the same obligation of gratitude toward others.[10]

Among the effects of an attitude of gratitude that have often been posited and observed are that it has positive effects on one's personality, and that it has social consequences that go beyond the specific relationship of the beneficiary to the benefactor. Gratitude often nurtures generalized compassionate and altruistic behavior, and it acts as a social adhesive (Fredrickson, chap. 8, this volume; McCullough et al., 2001; McCullough and Tsang, chap. 7, this volume; Schimmel, 1997, p. 208; Schimmel, 2002). Fredrickson for example, in her examination of the relationship between gratitude and the positive emotions, writes that "grateful people appear creative as they formulate actions that promote the well-being of other people, including, but not limited to, the original benefactor. So gratitude appears to broaden people's modes of thinking as they creatively consider a wide array of actions that might benefit others. . . . Although grateful individuals most typically act prosocially simply to express their gratitude, over time the actions inspired by gratitude build and strengthen social bonds. . . . Moreover, people who regularly feel grateful . . . are likely to feel loved and cared for by others" (chap. 8, this volume, p. 151).

There is a close connection between gratitude and humility (Emmons and Shelton, 2002; Schimmel, 1997; Solomon, this volume). Humility is among the highest of Jewish moral values. One who is humble rather than arrogant tends to appreciate how much he or she owes to others—God or humans—for which he or she is grateful, and this gratitude will instill a desire to continue the chain of benefaction by helping others in need.

The close relationship between the Jewish values of humility, gratitude, and caring for the welfare of others is beautifully reflected in a letter shared with me by a Jewish friend who knew that I was writing a paper on gratitude. It was written to him and his wife by their college-age child, who for several years had been involved in community service and other benevolent activities, especially in several impoverished Latin American countries. The youngster, reflecting on praise he had received for his altruistic endeavors, wrote:

> We all want so much, when we are brave enough, to let people know how much they give us. The challenge is to be able to do that all the time and not to pretend that strength comes just from within. I think that you guys taught me that very well by bestowing so much love upon me. So it became natural to me to reflect and realize that the good parts of my personality really came about as a result of the investments that other people made in me. Which is why I find it funny when people think that my passion for helping others is somehow this intrinsic thing that came about upon its own and that I am its creator and deserve most of the accolades for it. Get real. Just go back to Mason Rice [the public elementary school this young man had attended, which emphasized the value of helping others], and "Ethics of the Fathers" [a second-century Jewish treatise on ethics and piety that he had studied in Hebrew school] and swinging quarters for kaparot over my head [a Jewish custom performed on the day before the Day of Atonement, in which the individual sets aside money for charity and symbolically swings it around his head while expressing the idea that charity given to the poor can atone for some sins] for the source. I'd be far happier if people talked about how amazing the Newton Public Schools are than if they said nice things about me. Or if people stopped to think that there are sources for everything: Jessie Timberlake [a particularly inspiring high school Spanish teacher] for my passion for Spanish and ability to speak. I'm not especially talented, I just had amazing teachers and parents who believed and believe in me.

Notes

1. In fact, Job sometimes argued that he would have preferred never to have been born than to exist and endure the suffering and tragedies that were his lot (e.g., Job 3). These sentiments express sorrow, rather than gratitude to God, for having been given life. But there were more experiences in Job's existence than just tragedy and suffering, and to the extent that these were valued by him, gratitude for them was possible, even though it was not emphasized because they were eclipsed by his pain.

2. Psalms of thanksgiving, for example, Psalms 6, 9, 10, 13, 18, 22, 28, 30, 31, 34, 36, 40, 41, 66, 67, 111, 118, 138, 144.

3. Another explanation offered is that the *dayenu* song was a conscious Jewish response to the Christian accusation that the Jews were ingrates, a people lacking the virtue of gratitude. An early Christian diatribe against Jews, by Melito of Sardes, included the following: "Israel the ungrateful . . . How much did you value the ten plagues? How much did you value the nightly pillar and the daily cloud, and the crossing of the Red Sea? How much did you value the giving of manna from heaven and the supply of water from a rock, the giving of Torah at Horeb, and the inheritance of the Land?" (Eric Werner, cited in Yuval, 1999, p. 104).

The *dayenu* prayer responds to this accusation by saying that Israel did indeed feel deep gratitude for God's favors, so much so that, even if he had bestowed on them only one, or only two, or only three (and so on) of the 14, they would have felt that what had been given was sufficient for them to be grateful to him.

4. Zechariah Fendel, 1986, pp. 223–224. See Fendel's notes for the original midrashic sources.

5. One may well wonder, if indeed the five categories of benefactors are motivated by self-interest, whether perhaps we needn't feel gratitude toward them. Bahya himself began his analysis by saying that we need feel gratitude only when the benefactor acted out of good intentions toward us. Perhaps, for Bahya, one who acts out of self-interest can at the same time have good intentions toward the beneficiary, albeit not primarily altruistic ones, and thus be entitled to the gratitude of the recipient. This is what he seems to have said in the passage quoted from pages 249–250 (Bahya, trans. 1973).

6. This isn't the only instance in which a theologically grounded ethics generates, at least on the surface, self-contradictions. For example, why support the poor or heal the sick if God determines who is poor and who is sick? Why should I try to change what God willed? Similarly, with respect to the theological problem of divine omnipotence and human free will, the more power you ascribe to God, the less freedom you leave for humans.

7. Some medieval and contemporary Jewish moralists claim that the obligation to honor and care for parents is itself a means for the inculcation of gratitude as a more general interpersonal ethical norm (see, for example, Fendel, 1986, pp. 224–225). Blidstein (p. 10), however, notes that he has not located a rabbinic source that explicitly makes this claim.

8. Bahya Ibn Pakuda (trans. 1973) discussed this in contrasting the divine benevolence of grace with the human benevolence of self-interest.

9. Compare with Michael E. McCullough and Jo-Ann Tsang, chapter 7, this volume.

10. This, of course, then leaves us with the question, why do I have an obligation to love others as myself? That, however, is a different and much broader theme that goes beyond the purview of this chapter.

References

The Babylonian Talmud. London: Soncino Press, 1960.

Birnbaum, P. (1949). *Daily prayer book*. New York: Hebrew Publishing.

Blidstein, G. (1975). *Honor thy father and mother: Filial responsibility in Jewish law and ethics*. New York: Ktav Publishing.

Emmons, R. A., & Shelton, C. S. (2002). Gratitude and the science of positive psychology. In C. R. Snyder & S. J. Lopez (Eds.), *Handbook of positive psychology* (pp. 459–471). New York: Oxford University Press.

Fendel, Z. (1986). Gratitude and thanksgiving. In Z. Fendel, *The ethical personality* (pp. 219–254). New York: Hashkafah Publications.

The Holy Bible: Containing the Old and New Testaments with the Apocryphal/Deuterocanonical books: The new revised standard version. (1989). New York: Oxford University Press.

Ibn Pakuda, B. (1973). *The book of direction to the duties of the heart* (M. Mansoor, Trans.). London: Routledge & Kegan Paul.

Levenson, J. D. (1985). *Sinai and Zion: An entry into the Jewish Bible*. Minneapolis, MN: Winston.

McCullough, M. E., Kilpatrick, S. D., Emmons, R. A., & Larson, D. B. (2001). Is gratitude a moral affect? *Psychological Bulletin, 127*(2), 249–266.

The Mishnah; translated from the Hebrew, with introduction and brief explanatory notes, by Herbert Danby. (1933). Oxford, UK: Clarendon Press.

Montefiore, C. G., & Loewe, H. (Eds. & Trans.). (1960). *A rabbinic anthology*. Philadelphia: Jewish Publication Society.

Passover Haggadah. (1977). New York: Mesorah Publications.

Schimmel, S. (1997). *The seven deadly sins: Jewish, Christian and Classical reflections on human psychology*. New York: Oxford University Press.

Schimmel, S. (2002). Charity in Jewish tradition and experience. In S. Schimmel, *Responsibility to the vulnerable in Jewish tradition*. Manuscript in preparation.

Seligman, A. B. (2000). *Modernity's wager: Authority, the self, and transcendence*. Princeton, NJ: Princeton University Press.

Yuval, I. J. (1999). Easter and Passover as early Jewish-Christian dialogue. In P. F. Bradshaw & L. A. Hoffman (Eds.), *Passover and Easter: Origin and history to modern times*. Notre Dame, IN: University of Notre Dame Press.

4   The Blessings of Gratitude

A Conceptual Analysis

Robert C. Roberts

GRATITUDE AND WELL-BEING

Our intuitions suggest that gratitude is on the side of happiness and well-being, in contrast to emotions such as anger, anxiety, envy, and *schadenfreude*, which strike us as on the side of misery and dysfunction, despite the occasional pleasures some of them afford. This statement invites immediate qualification on at least two counts. For one thing, *whose* intuitions suggest that gratitude is on the side of happiness? I said "our intuitions," meaning yours and mine, but to include you may be presumptuous. Aristotle, for one, would have reservations about being included, because he thought of the grateful attitude as demeaning: It puts its subject in glad acceptance of the debtor position—not a position noble natures gladly accept (see Aristotle, trans. 1980, bk. 4, chap. 3). The mere fact that gratitude usually feels good did not impress Aristotle in its favor. Epicurus (trans. 1987a, 1987b) regarded gratitude as a vice because it is a disposition of neediness and entails susceptibility to fear. These ancient psychologists' conceptions of well-being traded on contestable suppositions about normative human nature, and so does ours—as indeed any conception of well-being does. If so, the question of whether, or how much, gratitude contributes to well-being may not be straightforwardly decidable by empirical science. It will *seem* to be so decidable in contexts where researchers and their readers share the relevant suppositions about human nature.

For another thing, most emotion types have both good and bad, both functional and dysfunctional, instances. Our initial intuitions may tell us that anger is a bad emotion, but a little further reflection may convince us that we would not want to rule it out of human life if we could (we can't). Anger is sometimes on the side of justice and the noble heart. Likewise, gratitude may sometimes be fawning or misconceived. These qualifications introduce considerations that we will need to address in our examination of the value of gratitude. But despite these needed qualifications, I offer conceptual support for the intuition mentioned in my first sentence: That gratitude is indeed on the side of well-being.

What do I mean by *conceptual* support? I mean *conceptual* as contrasted with *empirical*. My approach is to think with you about what gratitude is, to offer what philosophers call a conceptual analysis of gratitude, and then to use that analysis to show how gratitude as a virtue relates to some emotion dispositions that most would agree constitute or promote unhappiness—resentment, regret, and envy. Because of facts about the conceptual structures of these emotions and the vices they may express, these emotions are in tension with gratitude in various ways, so that the disposition to feel gratitude tends to reduce the dispositions to each of the other emotions and to replace it with something happier. As we explore the conceptual relationships between gratitude and each of these emotion types, I identify a number of ways that gratitude contributes to human well-being. I hope this discussion clarifies issues and suggests research agendas for those who are more empirically minded. Such empirical research will have presuppositions that the philosopher can help to make explicit; so empirical research cannot settle all questions in this domain. But it can in principle settle questions in a hypothetical mode. Assuming a certain picture of normative human nature, it might be able to establish that gratitude promotes human well-being by mitigating dispositions to resentment, regret, and envy.

WHAT IS GRATITUDE?

Let us distinguish episodes of gratitude from the disposition of gratitude. At the moment when it dawns on you how far out of her way your colleague went to enable your vacation to coincide with your mother's 90th birthday, you are struck with a feeling of gratitude. Let us call this episode an emotion and note that the emotion occurs at a given moment, endures for a while, and then subsides, giving place to other mental episodes: You're worried about catching the 5:30 train, you're angry at the passenger who sits astride two seats, oblivious that you are standing uncomfortably. But later in the evening, the feeling of gratitude occurs again as you reflect on what your colleague has done for you.

The disposition of gratitude, by contrast, does not occur at particular moments in the course of your day or week but may be a trait of your character. Short-term dispositions, such as moods, are not traits of character, but in this chapter, I am talking about longer-term dispositions. If you have gratitude in this way, you are formed, as a person, in such a way that you are prone, over a fairly long stretch of your life, to episodes of gratitude on certain kinds of occasions or when contemplating certain situations. People are all more or less equally disposed to shiver when the temperature of the air contacting their skin drops to 40°F. But we are not equally disposed to experience episodes of gratitude when others go out of their way to help us. Some people regard such beneficent treatment as their due, and so they take it for granted. Others resent it, as reducing their dignity or indebting them uncomfortably. Some people may not much notice others' beneficence. I suppose most adult people have some disposition to feel grateful; that is, under some conditions they will feel the emotion. But we single out some people as having the trait of gratitude and others as lacking it, inasmuch as those in the former group are more prone to the emotion, are prone to respond with gratitude to a wider range of beneficent actions, and are more likely to notice beneficence on the part of others—in particular, they are more likely to respond to it with the emotion of gratitude rather than with alternative emotions such as resentment and shame. Because, when we attribute the disposition of gratitude to people, we are probably attributing a virtue to them, we are also usually supposing that their gratitude fits the situations to which it is directed: Their gratitude is seldom silly, trivial, exaggerated, or poorly aimed.

Watkins (chap. 9, this volume) distinguishes very clearly between episodic and trait gratitude. In her broaden-and-build theory of the positive emotions, Fredrickson (chap. 8, this volume) predicts that experienced episodes of gratitude tend to build not only social bonds but also a personal disposition to think creatively about how to repay benefactors and benefit others and a disposition to put these thoughts into action, as well as dispositions to other positive emotions and the ability to cope during hard times. Hursthouse (1999, p. 11) suggests that although gratitude is a virtue, it seems nonstandard because it fits awkwardly the paradigm of a virtue as a trait or state of character. I think the present chapter shows how gratitude fits the paradigm without awkwardness.

Christians think that a strong disposition to feel gratitude is a virtue; Aristotle demurred. But Christians do not think that all situations equally warrant gratitude. If a person feels very strong gratitude for monetary favors (say, stock market tips) that are not particularly needed (i.e., that person already has all the money he or she needs) but feels no gratitude to his or her parents for providing the really good things of life, the Christian is not likely to attribute the virtue of gratitude to that person. It is true that such a person has some gratitude, and that is good, as far as it goes. But because it is a misguided or trivial gratitude, it is not worthy to be called a virtue and does not contribute much to that person's real well-being, assuming the perspective of Christian judgment. To have the virtue of gratitude is to be disposed, as Aristotle might have said (see Aristotle, trans. 1980, bk. 2, chap. 6), not just to be grateful, but to be grateful in the right way, to the right people, for the right things.

One of the ways virtues can go wrong is illustrated by Schimmel's (chap. 3, this volume) story about a Rabbi Yishmael, who received a small favor from a man whose case of litigation Rabbi Yishmael was to judge the following day. The rabbi refused to judge the case because he knew himself well enough to know that his gratitude for even this small favor would prompt him to give his benefactor unfair advantage. He saw that in cases like this his justice would be compromised by his gratitude, so his feeling of gratitude would have something not right about it. Perhaps we can imagine a person in whom the balance of the virtues is so perfect that in situations like Rabbi Yishmael's, the more important virtue in any situation always weighs more heavily. This is to imagine a very virtuous person indeed!

Let us now try to say more precisely what the emotion of gratitude is. If we can do this, we will get a clearer conception of the disposition, because the disposition is defined in terms of the episode. I have proposed (Roberts, 1988, 2003) that episodic gratitude is a concern-based construal in which the subject construes the situation in the following terms. He or she construes himself or herself (the beneficiary) as the recipient of some good (the benefice) from a giver (the benefactor). The formulation in the previous sentence makes the subject the focus of the construal, but this is not necessary. The focus can be the benefice, in which case the subject construes the benefice as coming to himself or herself from the benefactor; or the focus can be the benefactor, so that the subject construes the benefactor as giving the benefice to himself or herself (the beneficiary). In any of these cases, the construal has three major terms: the benefice, the beneficiary, and the benefactor, and whichever term is the focus of the construal is construed according to the other two.

But this is not the end of the story, because construals can meet these conditions without being episodes of gratitude. For one thing, if the beneficiary construes the benefice as his or her legal or moral due, rather than as a gift, the construal will not be gratitude. Revert to your beneficent colleague. If, in your view, it is the colleague's duty to secure you the best possible vacation time and in doing so she does no more than her duty, then your feeling about her action will not be gratitude. Also, if you construe the benefactor as inadvertent or maliciously advertent in the bestowal of the benefice, the episode is not gratitude. For example, you construe her as having enabled your vacation to coincide with your mother's 90th birthday, but you interpret this benefice as coming to you by inadvertence from her: She was not thinking about you at all, but just manipulating vacation times for some other purpose. Or, in another scenario, your colleague intends that your vacation will coincide with your mother's birthday, but you take her thinking to be this: If I can make S's vacation coincide with his mother's birthday, it will ruin his vacation, because he will feel obliged to visit his mother, which is the last thing he would want to do with his vacation time. Again, if you construe your situation in this way, you will not be grateful to the person who made this possible—even if you are in fact delighted to spend the vacation with your mother.

(Notice that I put these conditions for gratitude in terms of construal, and not in terms of either the actual character of the situation or the subject's beliefs. You could be grateful to your colleague even if she was only doing her duty toward you and not being at all generous in giving you the best vacation time—provided that you *construed* her as being generous. Furthermore, you might even believe that she was only doing her duty and still feel gratitude toward her, if only you have an impression of her as acting generously. Like our visual perceptions, our emotions do not always correspond perfectly with our beliefs; we don't always believe our eyes, and sometimes we don't believe our emotions, either. We can feel guilty even when we do not believe ourselves to be guilty, and anxious even when we do not believe ourselves to be threatened in any way.)

So the beneficiary has to construe the benefactor's conferral of the benefice as *benevolent*—that is, as intending the beneficiary's benefit for the sake of the beneficiary (see Berger, 1992). This condition raises a question about our initial formulation, which included reference to a benefice and a benefactor. Can the benefice and benefactor drop out, if only the subject construes the would-be benefactor as benevolently undertaking to benefit him? Might you be grateful to your colleague for going out of her way to secure you a vacation at the time of your mother's birthday, even if she fails miserably to bring about this happy result? I think so, and this fact shows something important about gratitude, even though this kind of case is clearly derivative and deviant. It shows that what the grateful person cares about is not solely the benefice as a good abstracted from the relationship with the benefactor; he may care just as much or more about the attitude of the benefactor—namely, that he is benevolent toward him. The benefice is imbued, in the subject's gratitude, with special value by its being a benefice *of this bene-*

factor and a benefice *intended by the benefactor for this beneficiary.* The grateful person warms to the relational implications of the benefactor's benevolence.

Indeed, one of the conditions for gratitude is the subject's concern for the benevolent bestowal of the benefice by this benefactor *in particular.* Consider again the case of your colleague's effort on behalf of your vacation. Let us say that you construe the timing of your vacation as a genuine benefit and her action in securing it as benevolently motivated, but you do not want to receive this benefit *from her* (perhaps she is in love with you and you do not want that kind of relationship with her). In that case, too, you will not be grateful to her. Gratitude involves a construal of oneself as indebted to the benefactor for the benefice and so bound to the benefactor in a way that people—even dispositionally grateful people—do not always want to be indebted and bound. But if a person is grateful to his benefactor for the benefice, then he is glad (gratified) to be so indebted and bound and will want to express this indebtedness by a return of a sort—not by a return in strict justice, as a tit-for-tat payment for goods received, but by a token return that acknowledges the indebtedness and bond, and the beneficiary's gladness in the benefice and the indebtedness and bond.

My analysis of gratitude as a three-term construal has stressed the benefactor term: To be grateful is to be grateful *to someone.* Furthermore, the analysis implies that the benefactor must be construed as a responsible agent—in all probability a somewhat grown human being, or God. I am aware that we sometimes speak of being grateful with no such benefactor in view. For example, an atheist might say, "I'm so grateful that it didn't rain on our picnic." Here, *grateful* just seems to mean *glad,* and much of the foregoing analysis would not apply to the emotion. Someone who was strongly inclined to feel gratitude in this sense would not necessarily have the interpersonal dispositions that I have attributed to gratitude; we might just say that he or she thinks positively or looks on the bright side. I think that people who use the word *gratitude* for this emotion and this trait are speaking loosely and even misleadingly. It would be better to use the other expressions that I have suggested, and to reserve *gratitude* for the three-term construal. It does sometimes happen that people feel genuine gratitude to nonpersonal causes of benefits such as luck or fate or the universe or evolution, but when they feel this they are personifying the nonpersonal cause—seeing it as wishing them well and intending their benefit. If they know that fate or evolution is not in fact wishing them well and intending their benefit, their emotion will be irrational, in a mild and harmless sort of way. This is analogous to the joy that we can sometimes feel merely by imagining ourselves to have won the lottery. To say that emotions are construals is not to say that the subject of the emotion always believes the content of the emotion. It is only to say that he or she is undergoing an impression in terms of that content. We have many impressions that we do not believe.

Let us now boil down our little harvest of insights to a set of conditions for gratitude as an emotion episode. For reasons given earlier, these are not all strictly necessary conditions; but it seems to me that they are jointly sufficient conditions for gratitude, when we add in the references to caring or concern. Remember that I said earlier that emotions are *concern-based* construals; it is crucial that the various terms of the construal be integrated or synthesized with the concerns that are required to make the emotion a genuinely evaluative and motivating perception. (See Roberts, 2003, sec. 2.7.) I formulate the conditions as forms of propositions held by the subject of the emotion. "I am grateful to S for X" can be analyzed as follows:

1. X is a benefit to me (I care about having X).
2. S has acted well in conferring X on me (I care about receiving X from S).
3. In conferring X, S has gone beyond what S owes me, properly putting me in S's debt (I am willing to be in S's debt).
4. In conferring X, S has acted benevolently toward me (I care about S's benevolence to me, as expressed in S's conferral of X).
5. S's benevolence and conferral of X show that S is good (I am drawn to S). (Or: S's goodness shows that X is good and that, in conferring X, S is benevolent.)
6. I want to express my indebtedness and attachment to S in some token return benefit.

GRATITUDE AND OTHER POSITIVE EMOTIONS

Positive emotions are those that have pleasant affective valence, as in contrast with negative emotions, which are uncomfortable or painful for the subject. The number of positive emotion types that modern English honors with names of their own is much smaller than the number of named negative emotions. Examples of positive emotions are joy, hope, relief, admiration, pride, and—in one rather limited sense of the word—love. For scientific purposes, gratitude must not be lumped together indiscriminately with other positive emotions. We should not assume that because these emotions share positive valence, they must share other properties. The kind of analysis that I have just given of gratitude can be given of any emotion, and to do so is to lay out, in some detail, the differences among the types. This is not the place for a detailed accounting of the differences among the positive emotions, but I can indicate roughly what some of them are, by way of illustrating my point.

(For a detailed account of the differences among about 70 distinct emotion types, see Roberts, 2003, chap. 3.)

We have seen that gratitude is about givers, gifts, recipients, and the attitudes of giver and recipient toward one another. It is a deeply social emotion, relating persons to persons in quite particular ways. Joy, by contrast, has none of this structure. Instead, it is a construal of some situation as good, as satisfying some concern of the person. For example, to rejoice in the good weather on the day of our picnic is simply to construe it as wonderful, as satisfying a concern for good weather on this occasion, without any question of a giver, nor, consequently, of any gift. Joy involves no sense of being indebted for this good. One might, of course, see the good weather as a gift and oneself as a recipient, but this is not required for joy; and when one does construe the situation in such terms, the joy that one feels is not just joy, but gratitude. Hope is a construal of some possible future good as having a reasonably high probability of eventuating. Nothing about gratitude requires an assessment of future probability, and hope, like joy, is not structured around giver and gift. To feel the positive emotion of relief is to construe some situation as good against the background of a past probability that it would not turn out to be good. Neither joy nor gratitude requires any such background to be perceived in the situation. Relief is backward-looking, hope is forward-looking, whereas gratitude may be either and need be neither. One kind of admiration is directed toward persons (though one can admire a beautifully smooth stone from the shore of Lake Superior without any thought of some admirable craftsman). Admiration of persons is a construal of them as excellent in some way that one cares about, but they are not necessarily construed as givers. Again, one *might* admire a person as a giver—as an unusually excellent giver. But this is quite different from being grateful to that person; to be grateful to him or her is to construe that person as a giver to oneself, but one can admire an excellent giver who has never given one anything. When feeling pride, one construes as excellent something whose excellence one cares about in part because of its enhancement of one's own value by association (one did it, or it is one's child, or one owns it, or it belongs to one's country, and so on). Again, givers, gifts, and recipients and their qualities and relations may be far from the picture.

I have given a rather detailed conceptual analysis of gratitude because we are trying to kindle a science of gratitude, and because if we are going to have a science of something, we had better have a pretty clear idea what that thing is and be careful not to confuse it with other things that may be a little bit like it. Gratitude is scientifically interesting not just because it is a positive emotion, but also because of the very distinctive character it has as a positive emotion. One of the most important questions we all want to ask about gratitude is how it is connected with human well-being, and this question must be asked with a clear idea of gratitude's distinctive structure. Let us turn to that question.

HOW GRATITUDE BLESSES

In this section I explore the life-blessing properties of gratitude as a virtue. I examine three emotion dispositions that seem indictable as sources or forms of unhappiness and investigate how gratitude partially dispels, mitigates, or substitutes for them.

Resentment

Note a remarkable symmetry between resentment and gratitude. I was first alerted to this symmetry by Martha Nussbaum's discussion of Epicurus (1994, pp. 242–250), who noted the structural similarity between anger and gratitude. Adam Smith (1790/1969, pt. 2, sec. 1, pp. 136–153) also exploited this symmetry. Resentment and gratitude seem to be mirror opposites of one another. We can almost generate a list of the conditions of resentment by consulting the conditions for gratitude, substituting harms for benefits and offenses for graces, and making a few prepositional and verbal adjustments. On analogy with "I am grateful to S for X," "I resent S for X" can be analyzed as follows:

1. X is a harm to me (I care about avoiding X).
2. S has offended in committing X against me (I desire not to receive X from S).
3. In committing X against me, S has violated what S owes me, by S's offense putting himself or herself in my debt (I dislike S's being in my debt).
4. In doing X, S has acted malevolently (or negligently) toward me (I care about S's malevolence [or negligence] toward me, as expressed in S's doing X).
5. S's malevolence [or negligence] and doing of X show that S is bad (I am repelled by S). (Or: S's badness shows that X is bad and that in doing X, S is malevolent [or negligent].)
6. I want to express S's indebtedness to me and my revulsion toward S in some return harm.

Just as gratitude is structured by three major terms, the beneficiary, the benefice, and the benefactor, resentment is structured by three major terms that we might call the maleficiary, the malefice, and the malefactor. (Two of these are canonical English words, but I am afraid I had to coin *maleficiary*.) One asymmetry between the two emotions is indicated by the bracketed negligence that occurs twice. The resentful person does not necessarily ascribe malevolence to his malefactor; mere negligence can be sufficient as the responsible source of harm. But the resenter sees such negligence as attitudinal dereliction—as a lack of due regard. Another asymmetry is that the return harm that the resenter wants is not a token: The resenter really wants to get even, whereas the grateful person has no intention of getting even but wants to express, in his or her "payback," a continuing indebtedness in which he or she takes pleasure. This accounts too for the asymmetry indicated by Item 3 in the list: The resenter dislikes the offender's being in his or her debt (which equals the offender's being ahead of the resenter, in the give-and-take) and thus wants to "right" the situation, whereas the grateful person is not averse to being and remaining indebted to the benefactor.

People sometimes feel that my analysis of resentment and anger is too harsh, because I take it to be an essential mark of these emotions that the subject wants to inflict a harmful payback on the offender. Doesn't a resenter sometimes just want to signal to the offender, in a friendly or neutral way, that he or she should back off and not commit the offense again? (This would be a payback as deterrent, rather than as punishment.) I will not be able to convince the skeptical reader here, but I will point out that we are strongly inclined to deny attributions of vengeful motives to ourselves. We realize how nasty they are and don't like to think of ourselves as the subjects of them. This is our natural desire to be justified at work. Also, when I speak of a return harm, I do not insist on anything very momentous. A dirty look or a little accusatory twist in one's voice may give the resented party all the payback that one desires. But I do think that the desire for revenge is built into anger and resentment. (For a fuller defense of this claim, see Roberts, 2003, sec. 3.3, and especially sec. 3.3e.)

Gratitude is a pleasant emotion and resentment is for the most part an unpleasant one, but this is a very small part of the blessedness of gratitude and the misery of resentment. Much of that blessedness and misery stems from the social implications of these essentially social emotions. We tend to respond in kind to gratitude and resentment that is directed to us. If someone is grateful to me for some favor I have done him or her, my attitude toward that person will probably be all the more favorable. I will be inclined to do that person further favors, to respond to his or her goodwill with my own goodwill. That person will seem good to me, and worthy of further benevolent attention. He or she in turn is likely to respond again with goodwill, and the cycle of benevolence and helpfulness continues. By contrast, if someone resents what I have done, I will tend all the more to resist that person, to see him or her as an adversary and perhaps as an offender who deserves harm.

And a cycle of malevolence and mutual thwarting ensues. I have spoken of tendency and probability here, for these reactions are not necessary. It is possible to respond to gratitude with horror or offense, especially if the gratitude seems fawning; and one may respond to resentment with amusement, alarm, compassion, or other responses. Still, the tendencies are there, and they are significant in explaining the blessings of gratitude and the miseries of resentment.

If my last point is true, then gratitude tends to bind us together in relationships of friendly and affectionate reciprocity, whereas resentment tends to repel us from one another, or to bind us in relationships of bitter and hostile reciprocity. As noted at the beginning of this chapter, not every instance of gratitude is good, nor is resentment always bad: Situations can call for alienation and enmity. But on the whole or in general, if friendly reciprocity is an important part of human well-being and hostile reciprocity or social isolation an important part of ill-being, then well-being is served by a proneness to gratitude, and misery and dysfunction by a proneness to resentment.

Virtues and vices are pronenesses. The virtue of gratitude is a readiness or predisposition to respond to the actions of others by seeing the goodness and benevolence in them, and consequently desiring to return acknowledging tokens of benefit. It is a psychological condition of sensitivity to benefices, benefactors, and benevolence—perhaps even to the fault of ascribing such things on too little evidence and being prone to exaggerate. There is something generous about the virtue of gratitude. This generosity is also manifest in an openness to receive benefices from others, a willingness to be indebted to them. The resentful person (that is, someone who has the vice of resentment) is quick to notice offenses and to find people to blame for them, looks for things to resent, and has a hair-trigger readiness to notice offenses and take offense at them. And once the resentful person has been offended by someone, he or she doesn't want to let go the alienation but instead treasures it in his or her heart. (I admit that the generosity of gratitude requires a qualification of the point I made earlier, that if the disposition to gratitude is a virtue, it is a disposition to get the situations to which it is a response *right*.)

The grateful person's willingness to be indebted to others may require humility (Roberts & Wood, 2003) and forgivingness (Roberts, 1995). For we are often closed to being indebted to others by a sense of our superiority to them and a desire to maintain that position of superiority, or by resentment against them: We don't want to receive anything good from them because we insist on their badness and their worthiness to be shunned. In Komter's discussion of Melanie Klein (Komter, chap. 10, this volume), she points out that some persons have much more of the trait of gratitude than others. And yet in her discussion of Marina Tsvetajeva, she seems to accept the Russian poet's claim that a certain degree of dependency simply makes gratitude impossible because of the sense of inferiority it entails. Because of her opposition to the Bolshevists, Tsvetajeva was forced to live with her two small children in one icy room at her parents' house and to receive occasional handouts from her friends and acquaintances. She was unable to construe these gifts in terms of gratitude, but instead saw the giving as a mechanical transaction between an impersonal hand (the giver's) and an impersonal stomach (the recipient's). In fact, the transaction was worse than impersonal in Tsvetajeva's mind; it was an offense, and her response was resentment. But if Klein is right and gratitude is a virtue that can have deeper or shallower roots in a personality (see also Watkins, chap. 9, this volume), then a person with more of the virtue might respond, even in Tsvetajeva's difficult situation, with feelings of gratitude to her benefactors. Such a person would generously see beyond the humiliating inequality between beneficiary and benefactor and would thus be able to see the actors as persons.

A certain proneness to resentment is required if a person is to respond with this emotion to those situations that really call for it. But such a proneness is not the *vice* of resentment. It is possible for a person to resent some things and be grateful for others; the well-functioning person will be in just this condition. I am arguing that the virtue of gratitude rules out, or at least mitigates, the vice of resentment. Because of the symmetrical opposition between resentment and gratitude as emotions, the corresponding dispositions will tend to exclude one another. It seems unlikely that a person would be very appreciative of the good things that others contribute to his or her life, strongly sensitive to benevolent motives in people, and quite willing to be indebted to a fairly wide range of others—and at the same time intensely on the lookout for harms to himself or herself, very ready to attribute malevolence and negligence to others, and inclined to bear grudges against those who harm him or her, even in small ways. Even if such a contradictory personality is to be met with from time to time, I should think that the virtue tends to exclude the vice, and vice versa. This thesis could be empirically investigated.

Regret

Regret is another emotion that is often a source or form of unhappiness. In regret, some action, event, or state of affairs is construed as unfortunate and contrasted with some more propitious alternative that might have been. For example, one dwells on some action, such as a bad investment, or some circumstance, such as a war that prevented one's finishing high school, and can't get out of one's mind the better but no longer possible alternative: If only I had waited a week, I would have seen that the investment was a bad idea; if only the war hadn't intervened, I'd be a success now. Everyone has passing regrets, and some things should be regretted; the inability to regret would not be a mark of well-being, but of its opposite. Damasio's (1994, chap. 3) patient Elliot is like this, and he is a wreck of a person for this very reason. Hursthouse (1999, pp. 44–48) points out that regret may be what the well-functioning person feels when he or she has virtuously chosen the lesser of two bad courses of action; and Landman (1993) stresses the positive role of regret in practical reasoning and the process of maturation. But regret can come to dominate a person's consciousness of his or her life and can thus assume something like the status of a character trait. Or at any rate, a person can be subject to relatively long-lasting and exaggerated regrets. This kind of unhappiness is nicely sketched by a character in John Edgar Wideman's *Brothers and Keepers* (1984):

> We have come too far to turn back now. Too far, too long, too much at stake. We got a sniff of the big time and if we didn't take our shot wouldn't be nobody to blame but ourselves. And that's heavy. You might live another day, you might live another hundred years but long as you live you have to carry that idea round in your head. You had your shot but you didn't take it. You punked out. Now how a person spozed to live with something like that grinning in his face every day? You hear old people crying the blues about how they could have been this or done that if they only had the chance. How you gon pass that by? Better to die than have to look at yourself every day and say, Yeah. I blew. Yeah, I let it get away. (p. 152; as quoted in Landman, 1993, p. 11)

The unfortunate action, omission, or circumstance, embittered by the specter of its good but impossible twin, hangs over one's consciousness like a cloud or mires one's gait like a slough of despond.

The constitutionally grateful person has a shield against such debilitating regrets because he or she is inclined to dwell on the favorable, rather than the regrettable. As noted earlier, as an emotion, gratitude is a perception of benefits and benevolence; a person with gratitude-readiness will tend to see what is good in situations and to notice less what is bad. The kind of unfortunate actions and events that make the constitutionally regretful person miserable may have occurred in the grateful one's life as well, but the grateful person can move on from them, because his or her mind is tuned to happier things. Religion can have this effect. Søren Kierkegaard, one of the great Christian psychologists, has the following prayer: "We would receive all at Thy hand. If it should be honor and glory, we would receive them at Thy hand; if it should be ridicule and insults, we would receive them at Thy hand. O let us be able to receive either the one or the other of these things with equal joy and gratitude; there is little difference between them, and for us there would be no difference if we thought only of the one decisive thing: that it comes from Thee" (LeFevre, 1956, Prayer 55).

Trading on Propositions 4 and 5 of our gratitude analysis, Kierkegaard is here praying to become constitutionally grateful in virtue of a Christian theology: that everything that comes from the hand of God must be good, whether or not it seems so to the natural mind, *because* it comes from God who is benevolent. A gratitude to God that carried the rider, "of the things you give me I shall be the judge of what is good and what is bad," and that was thus a conditional gratitude would contain a hidden arrogance—an insult to God. And this would be so, no matter how heartfelt or sincere the emotion was. This is another example of gratitude that is not virtuous. Such gratitude would not be in the service of well-being. (But note that the judgment I have just made depends on a Christian understanding of God and human nature. As I noted earlier, the concept of well-being is essentially contested.) Kierkegaard saw his own life as a discipline whose goal was to have this spiritual shape, this power of seeing his situations. This is not to say that everything that happens is good: Sin is not good, and it certainly happens. But many of the things that seem bad to us, such as lost opportunities and ridicule and insults, may actually be good and will be so if they are part of God's providential care of us. And, regrettable though our sins are, even they are not tragic but have been covered by Christ's atoning work, the very highest expression of God's benevolence to us. So that, although we do not give thanks for our sins, we do give thanks for something closely related to our sins—namely, God's forgiveness of them. Thus the well-formed Christian is constitutionally thankful, with a gratitude that transcends and levels the circumstances of his or her life, for he or she is disposed to give thanks in all circumstances (I Thessalonians 5:18). This constitutional thankfulness is an important aspect of well-being, conceived as the Christian tradition conceives well-being. The reference of Christian gratitude to God, who is eternal and eternally benevolent, makes it a more powerful resistance to gnawing regret than any gratitude with merely finite references can do.

Brother David Steindl-Rast has proposed (chap. 14, this volume) that the study of gratitude be divided into two different subjects: *thankfulness*, which has roughly the structure that I have been attributing to gratitude, and *gratefulness*, which is a "precognitive thrill of being," an overwhelming generalized objectless joie de vivre that he takes to be common to all the religions. *Gratefulness*, by his account, is not *to* anybody or *for* anything. He thinks that this experience is even more important to study than what I have been calling gratitude, for two reasons. First, it is common, he thinks, to all the religions, as well as to nonreligious people, while nevertheless being a religious experience. So it has a wonderful ecumenical unifying potential;

stressing it as the highest kind of experience promotes tolerance and understanding among people of widely differing worldviews. But perhaps even more important, it solves the spiritual problem of evil that seems to beset three-term construal gratitude in religious contexts. Brother David thinks that if I am grateful *to* God *for* my blessings, then I will be let down when my blessings are taken away from me. In that case I am almost certain to confront times when I must, in logical consistency, hate God for my misfortunes and thus miss the blessings of gratitude. No experience that is so subject to the vicissitudes of life as gratitude, conceived as a three-term construal, can be a basic religious attitude, because then it applies only to some people some of the time.

Brother David is right in thinking that the religious person must have a way of transcending the immediate vicissitudes of circumstance. It is not consistent with the Christian life to be grateful to God only when things suit me, and to become ungrateful or angry at him in times of adversity. But Christianity achieves this transcendence without abandoning gratitude as a three-term construal. It does so, instead, by providing a transcendent content for the three-term construal. The center of Christianity is the person of Jesus Christ as the unique and eternal Son of God, his work of atonement for sin in his sacrificial death, and his resurrection from the dead that assures believers of eternal (morally clean) life in him. It is this unchanging fact, this highest of all possible blessings, for which the Christian thanks God in all circumstances. In good fortune the Christian is grateful to God for worldly blessings as tokens of God's goodness as it is manifested in the person and work of Jesus Christ. In bad fortune the Christian is still grateful to God for the person and work of Christ, which is taken as assurance that God loves him or her and that all will be well. This circumstantial transcendence characteristic of the Christian virtue of gratitude is expressed by the little phrase *above all* in the Prayer of General Thanksgiving of the Episcopal *Book of Common Prayer* (1979):

> Almighty God, Father of all mercies,
> We thine unworthy servants
> do give thee most humble and hearty thanks
> for all thy goodness and loving-kindness
> to us and to all men.
> We bless thee for our creation, preservation,
> and all the blessings of this life;
> but above all for thine inestimable love
> in the redemption of the world by our Lord Jesus Christ,
> for the means of grace, and for the hope of glory. (p. 58)

If the virtue of gratitude is the disposition to feel grateful to the right person, for the right thing, at the right time, then Christian gratitude is the disposition "above all" to feel grateful to God for the gift of his Son, at all times. And this orientation to the Father and the Son affects one's emotional sense of all the ordinary blessings, as well as the tribulations, of daily life. It gives one a distinctive Christian wisdom, a power of discrimination, in which the category of blessings expands and the remaining evil is held in the perspective of God's greatest gift.

Aristotle rejected gratitude as a virtue in the most virtuous of all possible human beings, his "great-souled" man. It is instructive to contrast his claim, and its metaphysical background, with Christians' assertion of the virtue of gratitude, and *its* metaphysical background. Aristotle's objection was that gratitude undermines the great man's status: "And he is the sort of man to confer benefits, but he is ashamed of receiving them; for the one is the mark of a superior, the other of an inferior" (Aristotle, trans. 1980, bk. 4, chap. 3, p. 92). To receive benefits gladly from the hand of another, as the grateful person does, is to admit inferiority in the form of the debtor position. Aristotle did not have any notion of human beings as essentially the recipients of life and all its supports from a personal creator God. But for Christians, human beings are essentially debtors—not only to God, but to fellow human beings as well. Christians are likely to emphasize how we all start in a weak and dependent position, owing our very life and well-being to others and, if we live long enough, end in such a condition as well. (A useful recent discussion is MacIntyre, 1999.) Because of this picture of human nature, the Christian tradition finds nothing degrading in being recipients and in fact makes a virtue of acknowledging our status as recipients, with heart and voice. Such acknowledgment is a deep part of worship and is a proper attunement to our nature and the nature of our universe. As such, it is an important aspect of our well-being.

The Christian gratitude that I have discussed here is transcendent in the sense that it is a grasp of blessings and sufferings that transforms them all from a perspective that is above the world. It is an emotion that, by virtue of its theological formation, gives the believer a certain personal independence from the ordinary vicissitudes (fortune and misfortune) that naturally attend human life. Several other emotion types have this feature of taking a perspective that is beyond or above the world. Heidegger (trans. 1961) discussed a kind of awe or wonderment in which the subject takes a stand outside the world of beings and feels the strangeness of there being anything (a universe at all) rather than nothing. Heidegger (trans. 1962) also discussed a transcendent form of anxiety in which what one construes as threatening is nothing within the world. Wittgenstein (1965) discussed a feeling of absolute safety that has an analogous structure, in which one feels safe *no matter what happens* (death, disease, injury, loss of social status, etc.). Schleiermacher's (trans. 1963; see Proposition 4.3) feeling of absolute dependence, in which the subject feels a pure nonreciprocal receptivity of influence from beyond the universe taken as a whole, is another example. (All of these emotions are discussed in some detail in Roberts, 2003, sec. 3.11.) Perhaps the emotion that Brother David Steindl-Rast calls *gratitude*, in contrast to *thankfulness*, is another such transcendent emotion. But it seems quite wrong, and potentially confusing, to call that emotion gratitude, because it deviates so much from the three-term construal that the rest of the world calls gratitude. (The reader might consider, while reading the other chapters in this book, whether the authors are not talking about an emotion that is structured by the ideas of a giver, a gift, and a recipient.) No doubt Brother David's emotion has something in common with Christian gratitude: It is transcendent, and it is positive. But this is not enough to make it gratitude.

Envy

In the Christian tradition, envy is an emotion of ill repute, and the reasons take us back to fundamentals of the Christian conception of human well-being. Resentment and regret are sources of unhappiness if they are overdone, but both have good instances and we would not want to be without *some* disposition to them. Envy, by contrast, is condemned without qualification in the Christian tradition. It is one of the seven deadly sins, and it seems that we could get along very well without it. What is envy?

Consider Invidia, who envies Grace her beauty and intelligence. Grace is pretty much unaware of Invidia's attitude; she dresses simply and speaks unpretentiously and does not exploit her advantages to anybody's detriment. But her excellence speaks for itself, and no matter how modestly Grace comports herself, Invidia often thinks, "I wish she'd look ugly or say something stupid at least *once in a while*." She dislikes Grace for her excellences and enjoys fantasies of bad things happening to her, because whenever she is around Grace, she feels small and worthless. Invidia would like to see Grace brought down to Invidia's own size.

Envy is unhappy in a couple of obvious ways. As a dissatisfaction with what one has or is, it is uncomfortable. And it is the more deeply distressing in being a dissatisfaction *with oneself*; envy is a form of self-alienation and self-hatred. It also bespeaks ill-being in less obvious ways. Envy assumes a perverse conception of value. It says, as it were, "The good is my being better than somebody else or somebody's else's being worse than I; the bad is my being inferior to somebody else or somebody's being superior to me." Envy cannot accept with equanimity the superiority of others who are in one's general sphere (it may have no trouble accepting the superiority of others who are far outside one's sphere: the wealth of Bill Gates, the power of the

U.S. president, the beauty of Helen Hunt—or even the power of one's boss). Thus envy's conception of a benefit is that of something that gives me a competitive edge; a benefit is something with me-up/you-down potential. Part of the reason the Christian tradition is so hard on envy is that it is based in this perverse conception of value: It is deeply false to human nature and the nature of the universe, a distortion of reality.

Yet another way in which envy undermines our well-being is through the effect that it has on relationships. If Invidia's envy of Grace is very strong, they cannot be friends; and even if it is a weak or fleeting envy, it will to some extent degrade any friendship they may have. The envious person is hostile to those regarded as successful competitors for status and worth, and he or she is contemptuous and gloating toward those regarded as unsuccessful competitors. Furthermore, actions that are motivated by envy will express such attitudes, and to whatever extent these come to be known by the persons to whom they are directed, the relationship will tend to be degraded from that direction, too. It is true that some people like to be envied: If Grace were less loving, she might take Invidia's envy as a cue to triumph over her in her heart. But such a "positive" emotion would hardly promote Grace's well-being or the well-being of her relationship with Invidia.

Like resentment and regret, envy is in some ways the reverse of gratitude, so that the disposition to gratitude tends to rule out the disposition to envy and thus to reduce episodes of envy. The deeply grateful person will participate less, or even not at all, in the miseries of envy. In the first place, the virtue of gratitude is a disposition to be satisfied with what one has and is; it is an eye for benefits already received. If Invidia were a grateful rather than an envious person, she would focus not on the ways she falls short of Grace's excellences, but on the abilities and endowments that she herself possesses. In the second place, she would value her abilities and endowments (as well as the other blessings of this life) not as perches from which to look down on the inferior or as a means of being on a level with those who threaten to be her superiors, but first in a more direct, intrinsic way, and second as gifts of a Giver and tokens of his benevolence.

Let's say Invidia is a talented musician. If she is an envious person, she will tend to think competitively about her abilities. She may think, "I'm not as beautiful as Grace, and she's a better talker than I am, but I'm a better musician. So I'm okay after all." Thus for her, a significant part of the value of being a good musician is to bring her up to the level of people like Grace, to make her viable in the competition for self-worth. But if gratitude is one of Invidia's dominant character traits, she will tend to see things differently: She will be freer to value her musical excellence for its own sake, because music is a wonderful thing and making music a great delight. Furthermore, she will be inclined to thank *somebody* for it. She may thank her parents and teachers for their contributions to her musical education, but this may prove less than satisfactory when she comes to think about the talent itself. And so we see again that gratitude has a natural religious tendency—the tendency to posit a Benevolence to whom thanks of a more radical kind can be directed. (See Nakhnikian, 1961, pp. 157–159.) Just as this alternate Invidia values her musical education in part as a binding medium between her and those who provided the education, so she values her talent and her teachers in part as a binding medium between herself and God. The grateful person looks with welcoming eyes for personal debts.

Thus the third way that the spirit of envy and the spirit of gratitude tend to exclude one another is as follows: The envious person is averse to being in a position of inferiority, and so indebtedness is not his or her "thing," whereas the grateful person is content to be in the one-down position of owing an ongoing, unrepayable debt to another, a debt to which he or she gives expression not by paying it off, but by acknowledging it with tokens of gratitude. Thus a real test of the virtue of gratitude is whether Invidia will be able to feel gratitude toward Grace when an occasion arises. Imagine that Grace gives Invidia significant help with some writing that Invidia is working on. If she can feel genuine gratitude to Grace—a person who is superior to her in obvious ways, and yet within her sphere—for this grace, then she is well on the way to deserving her name no longer. Because envy essentially resists inferior status, this disposition to be joyful in the "inferior" position of recipient, and to be bound on these terms in affection to the "superior" one, is a successful antidote to envy. Christians are not slavish in such gratitude to their human benefactors, because of their view that all humans are equally dependent on God and positioned as recipients of His grace. They are, however, slavish (radically worshipful) toward God.

Envy and gratitude, as traits of character, are systemic dispositions to evaluative construal and action. They are ways of reading situations in relation to the self, ways of reading the self, ways of reading others. And the terms in which they read or construe situations are opposed to one another. Gratitude reads situations in terms of good-hearted givers, of gifts, of good indebtedness and the fellowship of willing subordination; envy reads them in terms of competitors for a self-worth that is contingent on superiority and threatens the alienation of unwilling subordination and triumphant superordination. The one is, by the standards of Christianity and many other frameworks, a happy and fitting system of construals, the other a dysfunctional distortion of self and other.

Traits like the envy disposition and the gratitude disposition are aspects of personality, along with other aspects. The fact that most people have some of both dispositions shows that the traits are not strictly incompatible, and I have not claimed that they are. I claim, instead, that they are in tension with one another and tend to rule each other out. The thesis, then, is that persons who are strongly disposed to envy will tend to be weakly disposed to gratitude, and vice versa. This thesis could and should be tested empirically.

CONCLUSION

By exploring the conceptual relationships between gratitude, on the one side, and several unhappy emotions, on the other, we have discerned a number of ways that gratitude, as a virtue, enhances or protects happiness and well-being. Grateful people tend to be satisfied with what they have and so are less susceptible to such emotions as disappointment, regret, and frustration. People who believe in God as He is conceived in Christianity have an even more powerful resource for transcending many of the circumstances that disappoint, frustrate, and anger most of us. In consequence, grateful people, whether religious or not, will be less prone to emotions such as anger, resentment, envy, and bitterness, that tend to undermine happy social relations. But the virtue of gratitude is not only a prophylactic against such corruption of relationships; it also contributes positively to friendship and civility, because it is both benevolent (wishing the benefactor well) and just (giving the benefactor his or her due, in a certain special way). The justice of gratitude can be plausibly argued to be metaphysical—a kind of attunement to one's basic human nature and the nature of the universe—because we are in fact dependent recipients of good things, both from some of our fellow human beings and from God. Such attunement is a realization of human nature and thus maturity, fulfillment, well-being.

I have investigated gratitude's happiness-making properties with respect to three significant emotional sources of unhappiness and dysfunction—resentment, regret, and envy. These are not the only emotional sources of unhappiness. Along similar lines one could investigate anxiety, despair, jealousy, shame, guilt, and no doubt other sources. Such investigations would probably reveal more of gratitude's happiness-making properties, as well as repeating several of the points I have made in this chapter.

References

Aristotle. (1980). *Nicomachean ethics*. Translated by D. Ross, revised by J. L. Ackrill & J. O. Urmson. Oxford, UK: Oxford University Press.

Berger, F. R. (1992). *Gratitude*. In J. Deigh (Ed.), *Ethics and personality: Essays in moral psychology* (pp. 245–256). Chicago: University of Chicago Press.

Book of common prayer. (1979). New York: Church Hymnal Corporation.

Damasio, A. (1994). *Descartes' error*. New York: Avon Books.

Epicurus. (1987a). *Key doctrines*. In A. A. Long & D. N. Sedley, *The Hellenistic philosophers: Vol. 1*. New York: Cambridge University Press.

Epicurus. (1987b). *Letter to Heroditus*. In A. A. Long & D. N. Sedley, *The Hellenistic philosophers, Vol. 1*. New York: Cambridge University Press.

Heidegger, M. (1961). *An introduction to metaphysics* (R. Manheim, Trans.). Garden City, NY: Anchor Books.

Heidegger, M. (1962). *Being and time* (J. Macquarrie & E. Robinson, Trans.). New York: Harper & Row.

Hursthouse, R. (1999). *On virtue ethics*. Oxford, UK: Oxford University Press.

Landman, J. (1993). *Regret: The persistence of the possible*. New York: Oxford University Press.

LeFevre, P. D. (Ed.). (1956). *The prayers of Kierkegaard*. Chicago: University of Chicago Press.

MacIntyre, A. (1999). *Dependent rational animals: Why human beings need the virtues*. Peru, IL: Open Court.

Nakhnikian, G. (1961). On the cognitive import of certain conscious states. In S. Hook (Ed.), *Religious experience and truth* (pp. 156–164). New York: New York University Press.

Nussbaum, M. (1994). *The therapy of desire*. Princeton, NJ: Princeton University Press.

Roberts, R. C. (1988). What an emotion is: A sketch. *Philosophical Review, 97*, 183–209.

Roberts, R. C. (1995). Forgivingness. *American Philosophical Quarterly, 32*, 289–306.

Roberts, R. C. (2003). *Emotions: An essay in aid of moral psychology*. New York: Cambridge University Press.

Roberts, R. C., & Wood, W. J. (2003). *Humility and epistemic goods*. In M. DePaul & L. Zagzebski (Eds.), *Intellectual virtue: Perspectives from ethics and epistemology*. New York: Oxford University Press.

Schleiermacher, F. (1963). *The Christian faith* (H. R. Macintosh & J. S. Stewart, Eds.) [English translation of the second German edition]. New York: Harper & Row.

Smith, A. (1969). *The theory of moral sentiments*. Indianapolis, IN: Liberty Classics. (Original work published 1790)

Wittgenstein, L. (1965). A lecture on ethics. *Philosophical Review, 74*, 3–12.

PART II

Social, Personality, and Developmental
Approaches to Gratitude

PART II

5 Gratitude in Modern Life

Its Manifestations and Development

Dan P. McAdams and Jack J. Bauer

Gratitude seems out of fashion in modern life. It is not that modern people do not know how to be grateful. Nor is it true that we rarely express gratitude for acts of kindness and other good things that come our way. After all, parents still teach their children to say please and, especially, thank you. And U.S. citizens take a day off in November to get together with their families for feasting and football viewing, ostensibly for the purpose of thanksgiving. But when was the last time you were really impressed by a heroic act of gratitude? When was the last time that a national leader made news by suggesting that the key to future prosperity and happiness is being thankful for what we have? How many self-help books, inspirational speeches, or television talk shows urge us on to higher and greater levels of thankfulness?

Gratitude has so little cachet in modern life that it does not even warrant a footnote in William J. Bennett's (1993) authoritative and popular *Book of Virtues*. Drawing from a wide range of traditions, Bennett brought together inspiring moral stories illustrating ten human ideals: self-discipline, compassion, responsibility, friendship, work, courage, perseverance, honesty, loyalty, and faith. Why not gratitude? One could argue that gratitude is subsumed under one or two of Bennett's top 10 (say, faith?). Or one might suggest that, important though it may be, gratitude does not inspire great moral stories. But it is hard to dismiss easily a third line of reasoning concerning gratitude's second-tier status in modern life. That line goes something like this: Gratitude is nice, but nice is not enough.[1]

Nice is not enough for meeting the most pressing psychological and social demands of modern life. Nice won't get you a good job, a decent income, a loving spouse, happy children, a valued place in the community—to say nothing of fame, fortune, or personal fulfillment. As heir to the Enlightenment, cultural modernity values autonomy, achievement, efficient productivity, creative innovation, clear-headed rationality, and the expansion and actualization of the self (Giddens, 1991; Taylor, 1989). In a softer and more interpersonal vein, modern life also holds up romantic love, marital commitment, close friendships, care of children, and civic responsibility as ennobling ideals that enrich life and contribute to the well-being of society writ large (Bellah, Madsen, Sullivan, Swidler, & Tipton, 1985). Although gratitude is not inimical to any of these pursuits, one is hard pressed to see how it is explicitly integral to many of them.

The modern response to gratitude may even shade from mild but unenthusiastic endorsement to occasional ambivalence. In the modern market economy, one does not expect to pay for goods and services with gratitude. It is surely nice if the customer offers token or even heartfelt words of thanks to the salesperson at the close of their negotiations, but the customer must still expect to write a check for that newly purchased home appliance. Gratitude will not yield even a dime of discount. Excessive gratitude may be viewed as ingratiating. When a person offers repeated and effusive thank yous, the beneficiaries may begin to wonder what the grateful individual really wants.

Furthermore, gratitude sometimes hints at darker and more insidious social messages. Gratitude may be seen as a trait that keeps those who have little from wanting too much. Seneca, the great Roman Stoic, held gratitude up as the parent of all virtues (Harpham, chap. 2, this volume), even to the extent that slaves should feel gratitude toward their masters (and masters to their slaves). For Thomas Aquinas and the medieval Christian church, debts of gratitude helped to keep order in the great chain of being, wherein humankind owed gratitude to God, peasants to their lords, lords to their kings, wives to their husbands, children to their parents, recipients to their benefactors, and so on (Harpham, chap. 2, this volume). The modern, egalitarian ear may hear echoes of feudalism, colonialism, and oppressive hierarchy in traditional paeans to gratitude. In the restless and ever-striving modern world, we are rightly suspicious of messages that urge us to sit back and simply be content with the status quo.

To find the clearest and most compelling narratives of gratitude, therefore, we may need to look beyond the discourses of cultural modernity to those more traditional, even ancient, sources that we associate with religion and philosophy. In these older texts, and in some enduring religious practices, we find a stronger and less ambivalent recognition of the importance of gratitude. In considering, then, the manifestations and development of gratitude in modern life, this chapter begins with premodern texts and practices in the Judeo-Christian tradition, to put gratitude into a broader cultural and historical context. In that gratitude, despite its cloudy status in the modern world, is universally endorsed in all of the world's great religious traditions, we next consider the possibility that a tendency toward gratitude is, in some fundamental sense, part of human nature itself. Building on ideas, then, from ancient cultural texts and human evolution, we take a developmental tack to trace the possible origins of gratitude in the cognitive and social realities of childhood and the eventual development of gratitude across the human life course. Finally, we return to the issue of gratitude in modern life by describing recent research that traces themes of gratitude in the mythic life stories that enable modern adults to make sense of their lives.

WESTERN CULTURAL ROOTS: CANONICAL TEXTS AND PRACTICES

If the source texts for Christianity and Judaism are to be believed, ingratitude is what got us into trouble in the first place. Schimmel (chap. 3, this volume) points out that in Genesis, Adam never thanked God for the gift of a helpmate but rather blamed God for having made a woman who led him into sin. Creation's bounties were never enough for the original couple in Eden. Gratitude fits best with a humble approach to living (Emmons & Crumpler, 2000), but humility was nowhere to be seen in Adam and Eve's defiant quest to be as great and to know as much as God. Yet it is that defiant stance—that Faustian urge to assert the self over and against the natural constraints of the cosmos— that may define humankind so clearly and tragically, Genesis seems to suggest. This oh-so-inevitable and supremely natural original sin comes to shape humankind's relationship with God, a relationship that will always be contentious as long as humans act like humans (and God like God).

The problem of gratitude is a recurrent theme throughout the Pentateuch and through much of what Christians call the Old Testament. As Genesis tells it, the world's first murder stemmed directly from a problem in gratitude. The two sons of Adam and Eve chose different modes for expressing their thanksgiving to God. Abel offered the firstborn lamb as his burnt sacrifice to God, but Cain offered the produce of the earth. God was displeased with Cain's offering. So distressed was Cain by God's rebuff that he killed his brother. Later, in the book of Leviticus, God provided the Israelites with elaborate instructions on the preparation of burnt offerings. It was important that they get this right, that their thanks to God be offered in a way that was pleasing to the Lord. (The Latin root for gratitude is *gratus*, which means "pleasing.") Leviticus 1:9 notes that the priest "is to wash the inner parts and the legs [of the young bull] with water, and the priest is to burn all of it on the altar. It is a burnt offering, an offering made by fire, an aroma *pleasing* to the Lord" (*Jerusalem Bible*, emphasis added).

The Old Testament's burnt offering links gratitude to *forgiveness*. By offering these burnt gifts to God, the Israelites received atonement for their transgressions. (It is worth considering the possibility that gratitude and forgiveness spring from the same psychological sources—see McCullough & Worthington, 1999.) The celebrated but ephemeral idealized dynamic between humans and God in the Old Testament was that of a humble people who offered sincere thanks to their Almighty Creator and received forgiveness for their mistakes, including their sins of ingratitude, in return. Indeed, the Israelites seemed to be in constant need of forgiveness, and time and again, God was *displeased* with them. Described repeatedly as a stiff-necked and stubborn people, God's chosen often failed to show their Creator and Protector the gratitude that He feels He deserves (Miles, 1995). Worse yet, they sometimes expressed gratitude to the wrong gods, a sin for which they suffered tremendously. In the books of First and Second Kings especially, the people of Israel and Judah repeatedly forgot that the God of Abraham and Isaac, the God who rescued them from the Egyptians and parted the Red Sea, the one who led them to the Promised Land after 40 years in the wilderness— that particular God should be the one and only object of their gratitude. Instead, they repeatedly took on the ways of competing tribes in Palestine, intermarrying with them and worshipping their gods. And every time, their most-jealous-of-all God punished them severely for their ungratefulness.

Gratitude is a problem in the New Testament, too. The ultimate ingrate, Judas Iscariot, failed to appreciate the gifts that Jesus had to offer and instead betrayed his friend for money. Rather than thank the humble carpenter for his ministry to the poor and the sick, the religious authorities of the day viewed Jesus as a threat and plotted to do him in. In less dramatic venues, furthermore, the New Testament tells stories in which gratitude works well, and stories in which it does not. Listen to Jesus' parable of the Pharisee and the Publican:

> Two men went up to the Temple to pray, one a Pharisee, the other a tax collector. The Pharisee stood there and said this prayer to himself, "I thank you, God, that I am not grasping, unjust, adulterous like the rest of mankind, and particularly that I am not like this tax collector here. I fast twice a week; I pay tithes on all I get." The tax collector stood some distance away, not daring even to raise his eyes to heaven; but he beat his breast and said, "God, be merciful to me, a sinner." This man, I tell you, went home at rights with God; the other did not. For everyone who exalts himself will be humbled,

but the man who humbles himself will be exalted. (Luke 18: 10–14, *Jerusalem Bible*)

In this instance, by mixing gratitude with a plea for forgiveness, the lowly and hated tax collector uttered the right kind of thanksgiving prayer, a prayer that reinforces humility.

In Judaism and Christianity both, simple prayers of thanksgiving are exalted as paragons of gratitude. Even to this day, virtually all Christian denominations build into their religious services a structured time for prayers of thanksgiving to God. In the liturgy of the Lutheran Church, once the offering and the communion bread and wine are brought forward to the altar, the minister enunciates what the *Lutheran Book of Worship* (1978, p. 68) calls "the Great Thanksgiving":

Minister: The Lord be with you.
Congregation: And also with you.
Minister: Lift up your hearts.
Congregation: We lift them to the Lord.
Minister: Let us give thanks to the Lord our God.
Congregation: It is right to give him thanks and praise.
Minister: It is indeed right and salutary that we should at all times
               and in all places offer thanks to the Lord.

What follows in the liturgy is the story of what all Christians should be thankful for: that God "filled all creation with light and life," for example, that "through Abraham you promised to bless all nations," that "at the end of all ages you sent your Son, who in words and deeds proclaimed your kingdom and was obedient to your will, even to giving his life" (*Lutheran Book of Worship* (1978, p. 69). Be thankful. Accept the gifts you have been given. The key idea in the Protestant Reformation, Luther's deep insight, was that the only thing that Christians need to do is to accept by *grace* the gift of Christ's love (Erikson, 1958). Entering the Kingdom of God is all about justification by faith through grace, not a reward for good works, though surely good works are good. Grace and gratitude spring from the same Latin root, *gratus*. For God and for human beings, accepting gifts and giving thanks are to be among the most *pleasing* of human endeavors.

EVOLUTION AND HUMAN NATURE

Contemporary thinking regarding human evolution underscores the importance of pleasing social interactions. One point on which both religious and scientific sources agree is that human beings are by nature social animals.

Having evolved to live in small hunting and foraging groups, humans are now equipped to develop a wide range of behavioral adaptations that promote cooperative group living (Hogan, Jones, & Cheek, 1985; Pinker, 1997; Tooby & Cosmides, 1992). Indeed, some of these same characteristics may be found in other primates as well, as de Waal (1996) and Bonnie and de Waal (chap. 11, this volume) have documented. De Waal has argued that human beings have evolved to exhibit such sympathy-related traits as attachment and cognitive empathy, to establish and respect prescriptive social rules, to reciprocate in kind (be it an act of kindness or revenge), and to engage in behaviors and to formulate mental strategies that promote *getting along* with each other. These four tendencies and capacities—that is, (1) sympathy-related traits, (2) norm-related characteristics, (3) reciprocity, and (4) getting along—form something of an evolutionary foundation for human morality, de Waal has argued. In this context, it is reasonable to suggest that showing gratitude and expecting it from others might qualify as an evolved behavioral adaptation, rooted in reciprocity and designed to facilitate getting along.

Beyond the gratitude expressed to a higher power in prayer and offering lie the more mundane expressions such as "Thank you," "I appreciate that," "I am very grateful to you for assisting me," "I hope I can return the favor some day," and so on. These humble, everyday expressions serve to warm up interpersonal relationships and build positive regard for other people. Acts of gratitude are well designed to affirm episodes of reciprocity in social life (Simmel, 1908/1950; Trivers, 1971). By thanking another person for what he or she has done or intended, an individual is signaling an understanding that the two have now completed a (usually pleasing) reciprocal exchange, and the door is opened to the possibility of new and mutually pleasing exchanges in the future. For this kind of reason, Adam Smith (1790/1976) designated gratitude a crucial moral sentiment (Harpham, chap. 2, this volume). Indeed, anything that promotes pleasing mutual exchanges between human beings is likely to promote the social good. More important from the standpoint of evolution, furthermore, is that the individual who is capable of gratitude, who is blessed with the propensity to engage others in gracious ways, may find that his or her standing in the group is ultimately enhanced, contributing ultimately to inclusive fitness. Put simply, the capacity to experience and express gratitude in groups may give an individual an adaptive advantage, positioning him or her well for survival and reproductive opportunities in life. Gratitude may be grouped, therefore, in the same family as kin selection and reciprocal altruism—evolved adaptations that have proven so useful for fitness in group living that they have become, more or less, foundational features of human nature.

In an authoritative review, McCullough and his colleagues (McCullough, Kilpatrick, Emmons, & Larson, 2001; McCullough & Tsang, chap. 7, this volume) have concluded that gratitude functions as a moral emotion. Like guilt and empathy, a feeling of thankfulness may serve as a moral barometer, a moral motive, and a moral reinforcer. As a barometer, gratitude provides a reading of the moral significance of a situation, signaling a perception that one has been the beneficiary of another person's moral actions. As a moral motive, gratitude urges the grateful person to respond in gracious and prosocial way. As a moral reinforcer, gratitude functions as a social reward and continues to encourage moral action in a social community. Lazarus and Lazarus (1994) argued that gratitude is an empathic emotion associated with the core relational experience of recognizing and appreciating an altruistic gift. Fredrickson (chap. 8, this volume) groups gratitude with other basic positive emotions, all of which serve to broaden people's thought and action patterns and build their enduring personal resources. Consistent with all of these theories is the general idea that human beings are predisposed to feel gratitude in certain social situations, that this predisposition has evolved to serve the individual (and the group) well, and that gratitude works together with a complex array of evolved human adaptations to broaden and build pleasing and mutually beneficial exchanges among individuals in ongoing social communities.

DEVELOPMENT OF GRATITUDE IN CHILDHOOD AND ADOLESCENCE

At what point in the developmental course of life do human beings first feel gratitude? An obvious candidate is the early attachment experience—the bond of love developed between the infant and caregivers (Bowlby, 1969). A cardinal criterion of secure attachment in one-year-olds is the joyful reunion with the caregiver after a brief separation. In the standard laboratory paradigm used by developmental psychologists to assess individual differences in attachment among one-year-olds, the securely attached infant shows joy and excitement when the mother returns to the room after 3 to 6 minutes away (Ainsworth, Blehar, Waters, & Wall, 1978). The mother easily assuages the child's separation anxiety and provides a secure base from which the infant can explore the world. Is it stretching credulity to suggest that the child feels gratitude in this reunion scene? By contrast, insecurely attached infants show a kind of ingratitude, one could argue, as they avoid mother or resist her overtures once she returns from her brief stay away. In writing about the attachment bond, Erikson (1963) suggested that the development of basic trust in the first year leaves behind a lifelong psychological legacy of hope. Early experiences of gratefulness for the loving care shown by caregivers might pave the way for hopeful expectations of future benevolences, reinforcing an unconscious worldview underscoring hope and trust.

Although early attachment experiences may contain some of the elements of primitive gratitude, one key piece may still be missing. As McCullough and Tsang (chap. 7, this volume) and others have suggested, gratitude is certainly an emotion, but it is an emotion with an attribution. Typically, we are grateful to someone, for something. More complex perhaps than distress, anger, joy, excitement, and sadness, gratitude appears to be rather more like such social emotions as guilt and shame—feeling complexes that assume some consolidation of a sense of self as a causal agent in the world and some understanding that others are causal agents as well (Izard, 1977; Lewis, 1990). It is not until they have reached the second year of life, research suggests, that children show clear signs of consolidating what William James (1892/1963) called a sense of the subjective self, a basic sense of "I" (Howe & Courage, 1997; Kagan, 1994). At this time, children first come to own their experiences, to apprehend what they do, think, and feel as belonging to them. The consolidation of subjectivity—that basic sense of I-ness—paves the way for what Dennett (1987) calls the *intentional stance* in human experience. It seems that one prerequisite for the full experience of gratitude is the apprehension of oneself (and eventually others) as an intentional agent (Tomasello, 2000), for gratitude assumes some basic understanding that human agents intend to do things over time, for which one may feel some sense of gratefulness.

In the third and fourth years of life, children continue to develop a sense of themselves and of others as intentional agents in the world. They come to understand their own actions and the actions of others as the results of human intentions. By the time they are 3, children have developed a primitive desire psychology, the first incarnation of what some developmentalists call an internalized *theory of mind* (Baron-Cohen, 1995; Wellman, 1990). At this time, they implicitly know that people do things because they want to, because they desire to do them. A bit later, children add a belief psychology to their theory of mind, knowing now that people, as intentional agents, not only act in accord with what they want but also act in response to their own beliefs.

As a complex social emotion, then, the full experience of gratitude requires an internalized theory of mind, something that we do not see before the age of about 4. Children can feel and express gratitude toward others when, and only when, they understand that other people (like themselves) are intentional beings whose behavior is motivated by desire and belief. In a random universe without motivated actors—the psychological universe that some researchers believe characterizes the experiences of autistic children (Baron-Cohen, 1995)—gratitude is impossible. For example, Sir Isaac Newton did not thank the apple for falling on his head, even if it did stimulate his insights on gravity (if legend is to be believed), because the apple did not intend to do so. The apple had no intention, no desire or belief. (Newton may have thanked God for his good fortune, but in that case he would have attributed intentionality to God.) The emotional experience of gratitude requires the cognitive resources that come with an internalized theory of mind, for we can only be grateful for mindful behavior on the part of others. Indeed, it is mainly for their mindfulness itself—for their desire, belief, or both—that we feel any gratitude at all. People can even be thankful for the good intentions of others, even if those intentions do not translate into explicit behavior. "It's the thought that counts," we often say, suggesting that we are grateful for a person's intentions, even if the behavioral consequences did not work out perfectly well.

Psychological research suggests that children's expression and comprehension of gratitude follows an upward developmental course through middle childhood (Baumgartner-Tramer, 1938; Graham, 1988). Gleason and Weintraub (1976), for example, found that few children (about 21%) younger than 6 years of age expressed thanks to adults who gave them candy, whereas most children (more than 80%) of 10 years or older expressed gratitude in the same situation. The link between attributions of responsibility for positive outcomes, the experience of gratitude, and the desire to do good to one's benefactor may solidify in the early elementary school years (Weiner & Graham, 1988). In addition, parents, teachers, and other socializing agents typically encourage elementary school children to make public and regular expressions of gratitude, especially in response to overtures and help provided by adults.

Moving from childhood into adolescence, the tendency to experience and express gratitude may develop in concert with a host of personal and environmental factors. Common sense and personal experience suggest that the quality of family life and sibling relationships, the effects of peers and the media, the influence of schools and churches, and the overall level of civility that characterizes a child's social world all play some role in the development of gratitude. Along with inborn temperament traits, these environmental factors may help to determine individual differences in the extent to which young persons characteristically feel gratitude in daily life and behave in ways suggestive of gratitude. The young person's developing self-understanding, furthermore, may have implications for gratitude as well. Whereas the 7-year old can thank a teacher for showing her how to write her name, the 17-year old can feel gratitude for a teacher's showing her how to live a good life. Theories of self-understanding suggest that, as individuals move through late childhood and adolescence, they come to see themselves and others in progressively more complex and nuanced ways (Damon & Hart, 1982; Westenberg, Blasi, & Cohn, 1998). In adolescence, these theories suggest, individuals are able to understand and evaluate their own lives and the lives of others in terms of characterological traits, unique developmental histories, and their dynamic positionings in complex and evolving social systems. It is conceivable, therefore, that for some people in adolescence and beyond gratitude's aim might even move beyond thankfulness toward individual persons to include more inclusive and abstract targets of gratefulness. People may feel grateful toward groups, organizations, systems, or even ideals. The question of gratitude's scope as it relates to developmental maturity is a promising arena for future research.

OCCUPATIONAL AND IDEOLOGICAL IDENTITY: SOME PRELIMINARY FINDINGS

In Erikson's (1963) well-known theory of psychosocial development, the primary task of late adolescence and young adulthood is the negotiation of *identity*. At this time in the life course, Erikson maintained, the young person coming of age in a modern society confronts the questions, Who am I? and How do I fit into the adult world? Among the many identity challenges facing the individual at this time are those associated with occupation and ideology (Marcia, 1980). How do I make my way through the world of work? What is my niche in the economy? And what do I believe to be true and good in my life? With respect to the last question, ideological concerns may subsume political, ethical, and religious issues. When it comes to the individual's efforts to negotiate issues such as career choice and religious ideology, for example, research has paid virtually no attention to the role of gratitude.

Although people living in modern societies are likely first to confront seriously occupational and ideological issues in late adolescence and young adulthood, these identity concerns are not typically resolved once and for all at that time. Instead, people may renegotiate their identity commitments and orientations across the adult life course, as circumstances change and opportunities arise. This is especially true in the realm of occupation, because the normative expectation today is that adults may change jobs, and even careers, many times before retirement (Sterns & Huyk, 2001). Although it is significantly less common, individuals may also experience important changes in their personal belief systems or religious ideologies after the late-adolescent years.

We recently collected open-ended narrative data from 67 adults, ranging in age from 25 to 73 years (mean = 40.4), who reported that they had recently undergone a voluntary life transition in either occupation ($n = 40$) or religion ($n = 27$). Each participant told the story of his or her voluntary transition by responding in writing to a series of open-ended questions. These rich qualitative responses can be analyzed in many different ways. For the purposes of the current inquiry, our interest is in the extent to which the participants reported a feeling of gratitude as part of their transition experience.

Each participant described his or her identity transition story in terms of six scenes and parts. Each provided lengthy written descriptions of (1) how he or she made the decision to change career or religion, (2) efforts to put the decision into practice, (3) a conflict experienced in making the change, (4) the role of a significant other person in the identity change, (5) how the change in career or religion influenced other aspects of life, and (6) his or her anticipation of how this change may play out in his or her life in the near future. For each of the six written accounts, the participant described what happened, where and when it happened, who was involved, and what he or she was thinking and feeling at the time. In addition to the narrative accounts of voluntary life transition, each participant completed self-report measures of psychological well-being.

We coded the narrative accounts for overt expressions of gratitude, such as "I was grateful" and "I'm thankful to her." Only the most overt expressions of gratitude were coded. Emotionally positive comments such as "I enjoyed working with him" or "We were good together" were not considered clear examples of gratitude. Each narrative episode, then, was coded dichotomously, as either expressing gratitude (score = +1) or not (score = 0). We then added the total number of episodes containing a gratitude example per participant, to arrive at a total gratitude score.

Expressions of gratitude were relatively rare in our data. For the entire sample, the average score on gratitude was 0.46, suggesting the appearance of one instance of gratitude (across all six vignettes) for every two participants on the average. Instances of gratitude, however, were significantly more common among those describing a religious change ($M = 0.74$, $SD = 1.02$) as compared with those describing a change in career ($M = 0.28$, $SD = 0.55$): $t (1, 65) = 2.41$, $p < .05$). In other words, religion changers were more likely to offer explicit thanks to somebody else (or to God) in their accounts of voluntary life transitions than were individuals who described a change in career. It is interesting that those career changers who did underscore gratitude in their narratives of change tended also to report high levels of psychological well-being ($r = +.50$, $p < .001$), well-being measured as a composite of two different self-report scales (Diener, Emmons, Larson, & Griffen, 1985; Ryff & Keyes, 1995). By contrast, gratitude was unrelated to well-being among religion changers ($r = .01$). Examining the role of other content themes in the narrative accounts, furthermore, we discovered that gratitude was a stronger predictor of well-being among career changers than was any other thematic index, including narrative measures of personal agency (or power) and of feelings of communion (or intimacy).

Although these findings are preliminary and in need of replication, our small study suggests that gratitude may play an important role in identity change. People who have recently undergone an important spiritual change in their lives are wont to express thanksgiving for that change to other people, or to God. People who have recently undergone an important career change are somewhat less likely to do so, but when they do describe accounts of thankfulness, they tend also to report especially high levels of satisfaction with their change and overall well-being. With respect to this latter finding, it is interesting to note that the empirical literature on career change makes virtually no mention of the role of gratitude. Career changes are often assumed to be an individualistic pursuit, primarily centered on one's personal fulfillment or income. Our data suggest that gratitude may play a surprisingly important role in successful and satisfying career changes. Indeed, important identity changes often occur in a complex interpersonal context in which pleasing and fulfilling interactions with other people become prime determinants of how a person ends up making his or her way through the world from one occupational or ideological niche to another.

MIDLIFE AND BEYOND: GRATITUDE, GENERATIVITY, AND INTEGRITY

If identity represents a psychosocial challenge that first arises in late adolescence and young adulthood, what Erikson (1963, 1969) called *generativity* poses the primary developmental task for midlife. Generativity is the adult's concern for and commitment to promoting the well-being of the next generation through parenting, teaching, mentoring, leadership, and other activities and involvements in which adults seek to leave a positive legacy for the future (Erikson, 1969; Kotre, 1984; McAdams, 2001; McAdams, de St. Aubin, & Logan, 1993). In work, family life, civic and community activities, religious involvements, and other arenas of commitment, adults often aim to contribute to the social good and to the development of future generations. Generative adults find ways to be creative and productive in their lives, and they hope that the fruits of their labors will redound positively to their children, their children's children, and future generations more generally. Failures and frustrations in generativity may be experienced as a sense of stagnation, such as when the adult feels that he or she is stuck and unable to be productive, or as overwhelming self-absorption, as when one's attention and energy are directed mainly at the self rather than others (Erikson, 1969; Snarey, 1993). Research suggests that generativity is an important marker of psychosocial adaptation and maturity in the midlife years (de St. Aubin & McAdams, 1995; Keyes & Ryff, 1998; McAdams, 2001).

There is indirect but compelling evidence to suggest that gratitude plays an important and underappreciated role in the lives of highly generative adults. The most relevant research in this regard has examined the *life stories* that highly generative adults construct to make sense of their past, present, and future (Mansfield & McAdams, 1996; McAdams & Bowman, 2001; McAdams, Diamond, de St. Aubin, & Mansfield, 1997). In this research, midlife adults who scored extremely high on self-report and other assessments of generativity are interviewed and asked to tell the stories of their lives according to a standardized life-narrative format (McAdams, 1985, 1993). The life stories they tell are then compared with those told by a matching group of adults who scored relatively low on measures of generativity. Interviews are transcribed and subjected to a series of reliable and objective content-analytic strategies. Life-narrative research of this sort assumes that the narratives people tell about their lives are imaginative reconstructions of the past and anticipations of the future, suggestive of the self-defining personal myth that a person is working on in his or her life (Josselson & Lieblich, 1993; McAdams, 1996; Rosenwald & Ochberg, 1992). Such personal myths function psychologically to provide modern life with some semblance of order and purpose (Bruner, 1990; McAdams, 1985). The main research question, then, is how do highly generative and less generative adults make narrative sense of their lives? To what extent do they understand who they are and how they fit into the world in contrasting mythic ways?

Compared with their less generative peers, highly generative adults tend to construct their life stories around what we have called a *commitment story* (Colby & Damon, 1992; McAdams et al., 1997; Tomkins, 1987). The commitment story consists of five narrative themes: (1) early advantage, (2) suffering of others, (3) moral steadfastness, (4) redemption sequences, and (5) prosocial goals for the future.

In the prototypical commitment story, the protagonist comes to believe early on (in childhood) that he or she has a special advantage (e.g., a family blessing, a special talent, a lucky break) that separates him or her from others. The highly generative adult, therefore, tends to reconstruct the past in such a way as to identify a blessing or advantage that he or she enjoyed at an early age. This early advantage stands in sharp contrast to the realization, again in early childhood, that other people suffer—that "I am blessed, but others are not so fortunate." Thus, compared with less generative adults, highly genera- tive adults are significantly more likely to recall and describe scenes from childhood in which they became aware of the suffering or misfortune of other people. The clash between (1) early advantage and (2) suffering of oth- ers sets up a tension in the story and motivates the protagonist to see himself or herself as called or destined to be of good use to other people. As a result, the protagonist comes to articulate a clear and convincing system of personal beliefs, sometimes rooted in religion and sometimes not, that continues to guide his or her behavior through the course of life, which is (3) moral stead- fastness. Compared with less generative adults, highly generative adults tell a story of continuity and certainty in moral beliefs—they have known what is right since very early in their lives, they have organized their beliefs into a co- herent system that centers their life strivings, and they have continued to hold to this belief system ever since, recalling few periods of strong doubt or significant change in their beliefs. Moving ahead with the confidence of early blessing and steadfast belief, the protagonist of the commitment story en- counters an expectable share of personal misfortune, disappointment, and even tragedy in life, but these bad events often become transformed or re- deemed into good outcomes, which are (4) redemption sequences. Thus, bad things happen, but they often turn into good things, whereas when good things happen, they rarely turn bad. Looking to the future with an expanded radius of care, the protagonist sets goals that aim to benefit others, especially those of the next generation, and to contribute to the progressive develop- ment of society as a whole and to its more worthy institutions—that is, (5) prosocial goals for the future.

Among other things, the commitment story is a narrative of thanksgiv- ing. The narrator begins by showing that he or she was lucky in some way, blessed, specially chosen for good things. Perhaps highly generative people *are* luckier, more blessed; or perhaps they manage to construe their lives— past, present, and future—in narrative ways that underscore the blessings they have received. The idea of a redemption sequence, furthermore, con- nects readily to gratitude. In a redemptive scene, something bad happens (say, the protagonist fails in some way, loses a loved one, suffers in some man- ner), but something good comes out of it all to redeem the sequence. Al- though people may not typically express gratitude for misfortune in life, it is very common among highly generative adults to remark how thankful they are about the redemptive move in the story. A man loses his job, but as a re- sult of this he reprioritizes his life to put his family first and is thankful for having been given this opportunity. A woman divorces her abusive husband, but in what follows, her friendships are strengthened and her self-esteem rises, and she is grateful to those around her who have helped her develop in this way. In redemptive sequences, we are reminded of the famous verse: "I once was lost, but now am found; was blind, but now I see." Redemption can summon amazing grace, abundant gratitude.

The very concept of generativity, moreover, can be seen as an outgrowth of gratitude. Many highly generative adults will remark that, now that they are in their 40s or 50s or 60s, it is time in their lives to give something back, to nurture and take care of the world, for others have been good enough to do that for them (McAdams, 2001). Among the most generative adults, the desire to express gratitude for the benefits they have enjoyed in life, or even for life itself, becomes something of a credo in their life stories, illustrated in how they remember the past and in what they see as their goals for the future. It may indeed be from the most generative adults in modern societies that we are most likely to hear life stories in which protagonists live in an aura of pervasive thankfulness—a kind of pan-gratitude that extends beyond specific personages and personified agents to humankind writ large. As described by Komter (chap. 10, this volume), gratitude may sometimes take the form of a thankfulness for mere existence itself. In life narratives, this kind of experience may be expressed by adults who are deeply involved in caring for and contributing to the well-being of future generations. Such experiences may also be related by older people who have moved on to what Erikson (1963) viewed as the last stage of the human life course—what he called *ego integrity versus despair.*

Erikson suggested that, in the last years, the elderly man or woman may look back on life with a mixture of acceptance and rejection. Ego integrity is, in large part, a gracious acceptance of one's life as something that *was good*, was worth living. Whereas Erikson associated the virtue of wisdom with this last stage, it seems to us that gratitude is at least as central. Ideally, one apprehends life now as a gift, and the existential question becomes Can I accept this gift with thanksgiving? The ultimate test for gratitude may, therefore, await the last years of the human life course—a postgenerative epoch in which men and women are no longer challenged to give something back in gratitude for what they have been given but rather to affirm, one last time, their gratitude as the recipients of life's gifts. Erikson's concept of ego integrity, understood in this way, may strike the modern ear as odd and disconcerting, for it ends up renouncing self-concerns, self-strivings, and even productive work itself. The final challenge in life is simply to be thankful that one has been blessed with life.

At the end of the developmental day, this paradigmatic expression of gratitude—so passive and humble—may be what makes gratitude itself so difficult to experience and express in the modern world, whether we be young or old. This may be why the virtue of gratitude never made William Bennett's (1993) list of the top 10, and why, to find a comfortable way of talking about gratitude, we have to leave the main discourses of modernity and search the ancient sources of religion and faith. Gratitude appears to be so little, so meek, so unassuming, so humble. But we should not be deceived by its appearance.

Note

The writing of this chapter was supported by a grant from the Foley Family Foundation to establish the Foley Center for the Study of Lives at Northwestern University.

1. This chapter was crafted before the September 11, 2001, terrorist attacks on the United States. In the months following the attacks, U.S. citizens expressed gratitude for the heroic efforts of firefighters, volunteers, and many others who gave their time—and in many cases, their lives—to help others. These outpourings of gratitude were both private and public. Indeed, the public displays of gratitude—at funerals, sporting events, in political speeches , and in many other venues—were at levels perhaps unprecedented in recent memory.

References

Ainsworth, M. D. S., Blehar, M. C., Waters, E., & Wall, S. (1978). *Patterns of attachment: A psychological study of the strange situation.* Hillsdale, NJ: Erlbaum.

Baron-Cohen, S. (1995). *Mindblindness: An essay on autism and theory of mind.* Cambridge: MIT Press.

Baumgartner-Tramer, F. (1938). "Gratefulness" in children and young people. *Journal of General Psychology, 53,* 53–66.

Bellah, R. N., Madsen, K., Sullivan, W. M., Swidler, A., & Tipton, S. M. (1985). *Habits of the heart.* Berkeley: University of California Press.

Bennett, W. J. (1993). *The book of virtues.* New York: Simon & Schuster.

Bowlby, J. (1969). *Attachment.* New York: Basic Books.

Bruner, J. (1990). *Acts of meaning.* Cambridge, MA: Harvard University Press.

Colby, A., & Damon, W. (1992). *Some do care: Contemporary lives of moral commitment.* New York: Free Press.

Damon, W., & Hart, D. (1982). The development of self-understanding from infancy to adolescence. *Child Development, 53,* 841–864.

Dennett, D. (1987). *The intentional stance.* Cambridge: MIT Press.

de St. Aubin, E., & McAdams, D. P. (1995). The relations of generative concern and generative action to personality traits, satisfaction/happiness with life, and ego development. *Journal of Adult Development, 2,* 99–112.

de Waal, F. (1996). *Good natured: The origins of right and wrong in humans and other animals.* Cambridge, MA: Harvard University Press.

Diener, E., Emmons, R. A., Larson, R. J., & Griffen, S. (1985). The satisfaction with life scale. *Journal of Personality Assessment, 49,* 71–75.

Emmons, R. A., & Crumpler, C. A. (2000). Gratitude as human strength: Appraising the evidence. *Journal of Social and Clinical Psychology, 19,* 56–69.

Erikson, E. H. (1958). *Young man Luther.* New York: Norton.

Erikson, E. H. (1963). *Childhood and society* (2nd ed.). New York: Norton.

Erikson, E. H. (1969). *Gandhi's truth: On the origins of militant nonviolence.* New York: Norton.

Giddens, A. (1991). *Modernity and self-identity: Self and identity in the late modern age.* Stanford, CA: Stanford University Press.

Gleason, J. B., & Weintraub, S. (1976). The acquisition of routines in child language. *Language in Society, 5,* 129–136.

Graham, S. (1988). Children's developing understanding of the motivational role of affect: An attributional analysis. *Cognitive Development, 3,* 71–88.

Hogan, R., Jones, W., & Cheek, J. (1985). Socioanalytic theory: An alternative to armadillo psychology. In B. R. Schlenker (Ed.), *The self and social life* (pp. 175–189). New York: McGraw-Hill.

Howe, M. L., & Courage, M. L. (1997). The emergence and early development of autobiographical memory. *Psychological Review, 104,* 499–523.

Izard, C. E. (1977). *Human emotions.* New York: Plenum.

James, W. (1963). *Psychology.* Greenwich, CT: Fawcett. (Original work published 1892)

Jerusalem Bible: Reader's edition. (1968). Garden City, NY: Doubleday.

Josselson, R., & Lieblich, A. (Eds.). (1993). *The narrative study of lives.* Thousand Oaks, CA: Sage.

Kagan, J. (1994). *Galen's prophecy.* New York: Basic Books.

Keyes, C. L. M., & Ryff, C. D. (1998). Generativity in adult lives: Social structural contours and the quality of life consequences. In D. P. McAdams & E. de St. Aubin (Eds.), *Generativity and adult development: How and why we care for the next generation* (pp. 227–263). Washington, DC: APA Press.

Kotre, J. (1984). *Outliving the self: Generativity and the interpretation of lives.* Baltimore: Johns Hopkins University Press.

Lazarus, R. S., & Lazarus, B. N. (1994). *Passion and reason: Making sense of our emotions.* New York: Oxford University Press.

Lewis, M. (1990). Self-knowledge and social development in early life. In L. Pervin (Ed.), *Handbook of personality: Theory and research* (pp. 277–300). New York: Guilford Press.

Lutheran book of worship. (1978). Minneapolis, MN: Augsburg.

Mansfield, E., & McAdams, D. P. (1996). Generativity and themes of agency and communion in adult autobiography. *Personality and Social Psychology Bulletin, 22,* 721–731.

Marcia, J. E. (1980). Identity in adolescence. In J. Adelson (Ed.), *Handbook of adolescent psychology* (pp. 159–187). New York: Wiley.

McAdams, D. P. (1985). *Power, intimacy, and the life story: Personological inquiries into identity.* New York: Guilford Press.

McAdams, D. P. (1993). *The stories we live by: Personal myths and the making of the self.* New York: Morrow.

McAdams, D. P. (1996). Personality, modernity, and the storied self: A contemporary framework for studying persons. *Psychological Inquiry, 7,* 295–321.

McAdams, D. P. (2001). Generativity in midlife. In M. E. Lachman (Ed.), *Handbook of midlife development* (pp. 395–443). New York: Wiley.

McAdams, D. P., & Bowman, P. J. (2001). Narrating life's turning points: Redemption and contamination. In D. P. McAdams, R. Josselson, & A. Lieblich (Eds.), *Turns in the road: Narrative studies of lives in transition* (pp. 3–34). Washington, DC: APA Press.

McAdams, D. P., de St. Aubin, E., & Logan, R. (1993). Generativity among young, midlife, and older adults. *Psychology and Aging, 8,* 221–230.

McAdams, D. P., Diamond, A., de St. Aubin, E., & Mansfield, E. (1997). Stories of commitment: The psychosocial construction of generative lives. *Journal of Personality and Social Psychology, 72,* 678–694.

McCullough, M. E., Kilpatrick, S. D., Emmons, R. A., & Larson, D. B. (2001). Is gratitude a moral affect? *Psychological Bulletin, 127*(2), 249–266.

McCullough, M. E., & Worthington, E. L., Jr. (1999). Religion and the forgiving personality. *Journal of Personality, 67,* 1141–1164.

Miles, J. (1995). *God: A biography.* New York: Vintage Books.

Pinker, S. (1997). *How the mind works.* New York: Norton.

Rosenwald, G., & Ochberg, R. L. (Eds.). (1992). *Storied lives: The cultural politics of self understanding.* New Haven, CT: Yale University Press.

Ryff, C. D., & Keyes, C. L. M. (1995). The structure of psychological well-being revisited. *Journal of Personality and Social Psychology, 69,* 719–727.

Simmel, G. (1950). *The sociology of Georg Simmel* (K. H. Wolff, Ed. & Trans.). Glencoe, IL: Free Press. (Original work published 1908)

Smith, A. (1976). *The theory of moral sentiments* (6th ed.). Oxford, UK: Clarendon Press. (Original work published 1790)

Snarey, J. (1993). *How fathers care for the next generation: A four-decade study.* Cambridge, MA: Harvard University Press.

Sterns, H. L., & Huyk, H. (2001). The role of work in midlife. In M. E. Lachman (Ed.), *Handbook of midlife development* (pp. 447–486). New York: Wiley.

Taylor, C. (1989). *Sources of the self: The making of the modern identity.* Cambridge, MA: Harvard University Press.

Tomasello, M. (2000). Culture and cognitive development. *Current Directions in Psychological Science, 9,* 37–40.

Tomkins, S. S. (1987). Script theory. In J. Aronoff, A. I. Rabin, & R. A. Zucker (Eds.), *The emergence of personality* (pp. 147–216). New York: Springer.

Trivers, R. L. (1971). The evolution of reciprocal altruism. *Quarterly Review of Biology, 46,* 35–57.

Tooby, J., & Cosmides, L. (1992). The psychological foundations of culture. In J. Barkow, L. Cosmides, & J. Tooby (Eds.), *The adapted mind: Evolutionary psychology and the generation of culture* (pp. 19–136). New York: Oxford University Press.

Weiner, B., & Graham, S. (1988). Understanding the motivational role of affect: Lifespan research from an attributional perspective. *Cognition and Emotion, 3,* 401–419.

Wellman, H. (1990). *The child's theory of mind.* Cambridge, MA: Harvard University Press.

Westenberg, P. M., Blasi, A., & Cohn, L. D. (Eds.). (1998). *Personality development: Theoretical, empirical, and clinical investigations of Loevinger's conception of ego development.* Mahwah, NJ: Erlbaum.

6   The Gratitude of Exchange and the Gratitude of Caring

A Developmental-Interactionist Perspective of Moral Emotion

Ross Buck

Writing about gratitude at the time of Thanksgiving in the year 2001—following the vicious and devastating September 11 attacks on New York City and Washington, D.C.—takes on a special poignancy. In a cover story for the November 20, 2001, issue of *Time* magazine, Nancy Gibbs pointed out that, strangely, gratitude seems often all the greater at times of grievous loss. We appreciate more what we have left: "We are aware, as if we were truly all one household, of the families who will face an empty chair at the table" (p. 31). Gibbs noted that the tragedy brought people together all around the United States, with many making a special effort to get home for the holiday, often seeking to reconcile personal relationships long gone sour. But, like morality itself, gratitude has a dark side: It is likely that perpetrators of the September 11 horrors had on their lips, at the moment of death, prayers of gratitude.

In the scientific literature, gratitude has usually been conceptualized in terms of exchange (e.g., McCullough, Kilpatrick, Emmons, & Larson, 2001; Tesser, Gatewood, & Driver, 1968). Also, the English word *gratitude* in books of quotations usually deals with exchange. However, at first glance it is difficult to reconcile the notion of gratitude in the exchange sense with its increase at times of disaster. In this regard, it is noteworthy that the poet Edward Arlington Robinson wrote that there are "two kinds of gratitude: the sudden kind we feel for what we take; the larger kind we feel for what we give" (as quoted in Sproul, 1965, p. 314).

Gratitude is defined as a higher level moral emotion involving a constellation of interpersonal/situational contingencies, including the acknowledgment that (a) one has received benefits and (b) one's power is limited (*humility*). As with other emotions, gratitude has experiential and expressive aspects that can be dissociated: One may feel grateful without showing it, and perhaps more commonly, one may express gratitude without feeling it. In line with Robinson's quotation, this chapter distinguishes two sorts of gratitude. First, the *gratitude of exchange* involves a relationship in which the sender of gratitude is a (less powerful) beneficiary receiving something valued, and the receiver is a (more powerful) benefactor who gives up something valued. Implicitly, there is a zero sum, in that the sender accrues benefits and the receiver incurs costs, with the exchange involving the beneficiary humbly giving thanks for the benefits. This exchange process involves issues of equity, reciprocity, and obligation, and it relates to Piaget's (1932/1948) and Kohlberg's (1964) "morality of justice." Second, the *gratitude of caring* relates to Gilligan's (1982) "morality of caring." This kind of gratitude involves a personal relationship associated with love and bonding, and it is different in that giving benefits and receiving benefits are mutually supportive: Literally, the more you give, the more you get. This is Robinson's "larger kind" of gratitude. In the gratitude of caring, all accrue benefits and no one incurs costs; therefore, judgments of exchange, equity, reciprocity, and obligation are not relevant. Finally, it must be acknowledged that gratitude plays a role in the dark side of morality, the morality of subjugation, in which the destruction or humiliation of others is viewed as a moral duty.

A DEVELOPMENTAL-INTERACTIONIST APPROACH TO GRATITUDE

This chapter presents gratitude in terms of a developmental-interactionist theory that analyzes behavior as a consequence of an interaction between phylogenetically structured primary motivational-emotional systems (primes) underlying syncretic cognition associated with *affect*, and analytic cognition associated with language and *reason*.[1] That interaction occurs in a developmental context. The theory conceptualizes social, cognitive, and moral emotions as higher level emotions combining biologically based affects of attachment and expectancy with rational judgments involving interpersonal-situational contingencies (Buck, 1985, 1999). This chapter first discusses basic concepts, including social and cognitive emotions, and considers how they relate to gratitude. It then considers the nature of gratitude in de-

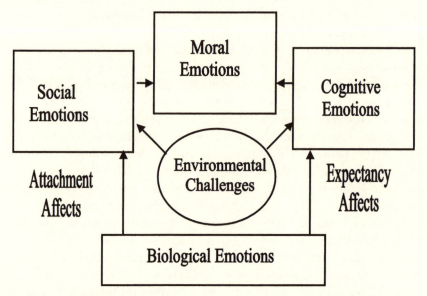

Figure 6.1. Relationships between biologically based attachment and expectancy, judgments of interpersonal and situational contingencies, and higher level social, cognitive, and moral emotions.

tail, and its relationship with other moral emotions, including admiration, respect, and trust. The present view emphasizes that emotion is not only a property of an individual with functions of self-regulation, but also occurs in communicative contexts and has functions of social organization. In this regard, gratitude is inherently dyadic: It involves an implicit communication process between one who gives gratitude and one who receives it.[2]

As noted, higher level emotions combine specific biologically based affects (feelings and desires) and analytic judgments regarding specific environmental challenges or contingencies. Because they involve judgments, higher level emotions require learning to become effectively, appropriately, and competently expressed. There are three sorts of higher level emotions. *Social emotions* combine biological affects associated with attachment (bonding, affection, love) with perceptions of interpersonal contingencies, and they are experienced and expressed in the context of social development. *Cognitive emotions* combine biological affects associated with expectancy (curiosity, attention, interest, involvement) with perceptions of situational contingencies, and they are experienced and expressed in the context of cognitive development. *Moral emotions* combine social and cognitive emotions. That is, they combine attachment and expectancy affects with perceptions of interpersonal-situational contingencies, and they are experienced and expressed in the context of moral development. Moral emotions involve (a) *knowing* the social expectations or rules covering a given situation and (b) *caring* that the rules are followed equitably. The relationships between biologically based attachment and expectancy, perceptions of interpersonal and situational contingencies, and higher level social, cognitive, and moral emotions are summarized in Figure 6.1.

HIGHER LEVEL SOCIAL AND COGNITIVE EMOTIONS

Social Emotions: Combining Attachment and Interpersonal Contingencies

Attachment. The biological aspect of higher level emotions involves affects that, in principle, can be associated with specific neurochemical systems in the brain. The biological aspect of social emotions involves attachment systems that are overlooked in many contemporary theories of emotion (see Buck, 1999; Carter, Lederhendler, & Kirkpatrick, 1997; Panksepp, 1998). Prosocial motivational-emotional attachment systems are associated with such neurochemicals as oxytocin (nurturance), gonadotropin releasing hormone (eroticism) and the endorphins (bonding, play). These provide the emotional basis for two fundamental social motives: the need to be loved and the need to meet or exceed social expectations to gain social approval (Buck, 1988).[3]

Fundamental interpersonal contingencies. Success and failure in fulfilling these motives in the self (P) and comparison other (O) constitute convergences of interpersonal contingencies that underlie four pairs of twin social emotions. Each social emotion associated with the need to meet or exceed expectations has a twin associated with the need to be loved.[4] Relative success of P in exceeding expectations and being loved is associated with the twins that are termed *pride* and *arrogance,* whereas failure is associated with *guilt* and *shame.* Relative success of the comparison O is associated with *envy* and *jealousy,* whereas failure is associated with *pity* and *scorn.* The confluences of interpersonal contingencies with each other and with attachment are seen to be universal and fundamental, whereas the names are intended merely as more or less adequate labels (that of course differ in different languages).

All else being equal, persons who are securely attached are relatively assured of being loved, so they are more focused on meeting or exceeding expectations, whereas persons who are insecurely attached are anxious about being loved (Ainsworth, Blehar, Waters, & Wall, 1978; Bowlby, 1969, 1973,

1980). For these reasons, securely attached persons are more likely to experience *pride*, *guilt*, *envy*, and *pity* in situations in which insecurely attached persons will experience their twins: *arrogance*, *shame*, *jealousy*, and *scorn* (Buck,
1988, 1999; Buck & Vieira, 2002). The social emotions are summarized in
Figure 6.2.

The dynamics of social emotions.   In addition to twins, the present analysis implies that the social emotions are functionally related to each other in other
respects: Each has an *opposite*, a *converse*, and a *reciprocal*. Also, if Person P
feels Emotion X about himself or herself, Comparison Person O will tend to
experience a pattern of *mirror* emotions. These are illustrated in Table 6.1.
For example, all else being equal, proud/arrogant P will tend to pity/scorn
the envious/jealous O, who will feel guilty/ashamed. Proud/arrogant P will
tend *not* to feel guilty/ashamed or to feel envious/jealous of O; likewise, O
will tend not to feel proud/arrogant or to regard proud/arrogant P with
pity/scorn.

These hypotheses about the dynamics of social emotions were tested by
asking participants to rate their own and others' feelings in a series of scenarios designed to elicit social emotions (i.e., "O won the lottery," "O was
dumped by my present lover," "O was jailed for selling drugs to children";

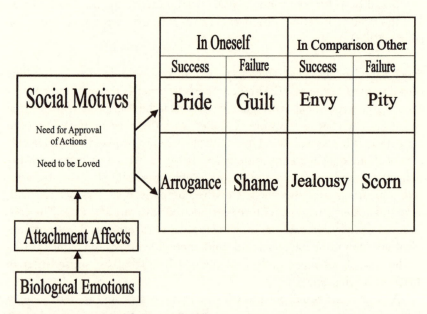

Figure 6.2. Success and failure in fulfilling needs to meet or exceed expectations
and to be loved, in the self and comparison other, constitute convergences of
interpersonal contingencies that underlie eight higher level social emotions.

Table 6.1   Social Emotions and Corresponding Twins, Opposites, Converses, Reciprocals, and Mirrors

	Pride	Arrogance	Guilt	Shame
Twin	Arrogance	Pride	Shame	Guilt
Opposite	Guilt	Shame	Pride	Arrogance
Converse	Envy	Jealousy	Pity	Scorne
Reciprocal	Pity	Scorn	Envy	Jealousy
Mirror opposite	O–Guilt	O–Shame	O–Pride	O–Arrogance
Mirror converse	O–Envy	O–Jealousy	O–Pity	O–Scorn
Mirror reciprocal	O–Pity	O–Scorn	O–Envy	O–Jealousy

	Envy	Jealousy	Pity	Scorn
Twin	Jealousy	Envy	Scorn	Pity
Opposite	Pity	Scorn	Envy	Jealousy
Converse	Pride	Arrogance	Guilt	Shame
Reciprocal	Guilt	Shame	Pride	Arrogance
Mirror opposite	O–Pity	O–Scorn	O–Envy	O–Jealousy
Mirror converse	O–Pride	O–Arrogance	O–Guilt	O–Shame
Mirror reciprocal	O–Guilt	O–Shame	O–Pride	O–Arrogance

Note. Pride, arrogance, guilt, shame, envy, jealousy, pity, and scorn are seen as functionally related: Each has a twin, opposite, converse, and reciprocal. Also, if Person P feels Emotion X about himself or herself, Comparison Person O will tend to experience, or not experience, a pattern of mirror emotions.

Buck & Vieira, 2002). Data (mean correlations) revealed that, as expected, if P reports experiencing a given social emotion, P is

1. likely to report its twin (.66),
2. unlikely to report its opposite (-.61),
3. likely to report its reciprocal emotion directed toward O (.52), and
4. unlikely to report its converse toward O (-.37).

Furthermore, if P reports experiencing a given social emotion, a comparison O is

5. unlikely to report experiencing that emotion or its twin (-.36)
6. likely to report its mirror opposite (.57)
7. unlikely to report its mirror reciprocal (-.57), and
8. likely to report its mirror converse (.85).

These data illustrate overall tendencies that differ when specific twins, opposites, and so on are considered, but they also demonstrate that the basic dynamics of the social emotions function much as expected, although the dynamics might be different if P and O had a personal relationship.

Gratitude and social emotions. As noted previously, gratitude is inherently dyadic, implying a communicative relationship between a sender and a receiver of gratitude. Even though the sender and receiver may never meet, to experience gratitude the sender must perceive a benefit related in some way to the receiver and must experience a lack of power—*humility*—relative to the receiver. The receiver may not be a person at all, but a spiritual being, fate, God, providence, or destiny.

Because gratitude by definition involves a benefit to P, gratitude is more likely to be related to social emotions that imply a relative benefit to P, such as *pride* and *pity*, and is likely to be unrelated or negatively related to *guilt, shame, envy,* and *jealousy.* The question of the relationship between gratitude on one hand and *arrogance* and *scorn* on the other is less clear, but potentially interesting. *Arrogance* and *scorn* do imply a relative benefit to P, but in the present definition they occur only when P is insecurely attached and uncertain of being loved. Such uncertainty may be associated with an inability to respond with *humility*, that is, to perceive and acknowledge that said benefit is related to the power and goodness of someone or something else, so that the gratitude of exchange may be impaired. Furthermore, insecure attachment may imply deficits in the gratitude of caring: P may be uncertain that benefits will accrue from loving or otherwise giving to others. Thus, it may be hypothesized that, all else being equal, gratitude will be weaker in less securely attached persons.

Based on the dynamics of social emotions noted previously, one can hypothesize that gratitude may often be associated with *envy/jealousy* on the part of the sender/beneficiary, because implicitly, the benefactor is comparatively powerful and successful. The psychoanalytic theory of Melanie Klein emphasizes the relationship between gratitude and envy/jealousy, as well as greed (Chiesa, 2001; Klein, 1957, 1998). Correspondingly, the receiver/benefactor may feel *pity* that can turn to *scorn*, because the beneficiary is comparatively less powerful and successful. The dynamics of social emotions would also encourage feelings of *pride/arrogance* on the part of the receiver/benefactor and *guilt/shame* on the part of the sender/beneficiary.

Cognitive Emotions: Combining Expectancy and Situational Contingencies

Expectancy. Just as social emotions are based biologically in attachment systems, cognitive emotions are based biologically in *expectancy systems* responding to rewarding and punishing events in such a way that the individual, through experience, becomes able to obtain the former and avoid the latter (see Depue & Collins, 1999; Rolls, 1999). These systems generate motives to explore and to understand the unfamiliar, termed "SEEKING" by Panksepp (1998), and provide the basis for exploratory or *effectance emotions*—that is, curiosity—that lead to developing *expectancies* associated with situational contingencies (White, 1959). *Curiosity* is defined conceptually as the tendency to explore, and operationally by the range of stimuli that excite exploratory behavior. Curiosity is the affective prime mover motivating exploration during cognitive development, and there is evidence relating novelty and exploratory behavior in mice to opioid peptide levels (van Daal, Jenks, Crusio, Lemmens, & van Abeelen, 1991).

Fundamental situational contingencies. Fundamental situational contingencies classify events as positive, negative, neutral, unexpected, or expected, crossed with whether they are in the future as opposed to occuring now or in the past. Examples of terms associated with combinations of situational contingencies are presented in Table 6.2. As with social emotions, the contingencies, not the labels, are seen to be universal and fundamental. Some of the most fundamental labels of cognitive emotions are associated with labels of biological emotions: for example *happiness, sadness,* and *surprise* are "primary affects" associated with pancultural facial displays (Ekman & Friesen, 1975). It is not surprising that these fundamental situational contingencies would be associated with the evolution of biologically based affects and expressive displays (Tomkins, 1962–1963).

Table 6.2   Labels Associated With Combinations of Fundamental Situational Contingencies

	Future	Actual/Past
Positive	Hope, optimism, trust, certitude, confidence, assurance, faith	Happiness, satisfaction, gratification, fulfillment, comfort, relief, contentment, serenity
Negative	Doubt, distrust, suspicion, skepticism, pessimism, incredulity, cynicism	Sadness, dissatisfaction, frustration, defeat, disappointment, despair, gloom, chagrin
Neutral	Curiosity, interest, concern, commitment, involvement, engagement, attention	Boredom, apathy, unconcern, indifference, coolness, ennui
Unexpected	Uncertainty, insecurity, bewilderment, incertitude, perplexity, hesitation	Surprise, amazement, startle, shock, wonder, astonishment, consternation, awe

Dynamics of cognitive emotions.   Like social emotions, this analysis predicts that, in general, it is likely that emotions to positive events will be experienced together, and less likely that they will be experienced with emotions associated with negative events. Also, there is the possibility of contrast effects across time, so that a negative event following feelings of *hope* and *optimism* may be experienced as more negative than one following feelings of *doubt* and *pessimism*. Moreover, emotions associated with unexpected events could be experienced with either positive or negative feelings.

Gratitude and cognitive emotions.   As gratitude is associated with benefits, it is most likely to be associated with positive actual/past events and the corresponding emotions: *happiness, satisfaction, relief,* and so on. Furthermore, gratitude is likely to be unrelated or negatively related to emotions associated with negative actual/past events: *sadness, frustration, defeat,* etc. Anticipation of future positive or negative events would be associated with the anticipation of being grateful or not, respectively, and it is possible that contrast effects will influence the experience of gratitude. That is, gratitude may be stronger if benefits are realized after a period of *pessimism* and *doubt* compared with a period of *optimism* and *hope*.

MORAL EMOTIONS: COMBINING SOCIAL AND COGNITIVE EMOTIONS

Cognitive emotions involve "hot" expectancy/exploratory affects underlying the development and maintenance of "cold" analytic cognitive understanding of situational contingencies. With human language, learning about situational contingencies is organized linguistically into general expectations or *rules*. The attainment of competence in understanding and dealing with situational contingencies is normally accompanied by competence in dealing with interpersonal contingencies involving attachment; that is, cognitive and social development are ordinarily linked. Attachment feelings and understanding rules combine in the moral emotions involving *caring about fairly following social rules*.

Emotion and Morality

Moral emotions.   The study of moral capacities typically has not involved the analysis of moral emotions. Generally, research has focused on either *moral judgment*, the ability to tell right from wrong, or *moral behavior*, the tendency to act in accordance with moral rules when confronted by situational pressures (Buck, 1988). However, moral judgments and behaviors rarely occur in an affective vacuum; often, judgments of right and wrong are accompanied by strong emotions, both positive (including gratitude) and negative (moral indignation). Indeed, moral feelings are some of the strongest and most persistent motivators of human behavior. Furthermore, although different cultures can and do arrive at different principles of justice, *all do arrive at principles of justice*. These rules make social life possible (Hogan, Johnson, & Emler, 1994). In all cultures, these principles are capable of stirring deep passions.

Biological bases of moral emotions. To recapitulate, there are specific biological bases for both social and cognitive emotions, involving attachment and expectancy, respectively.[5] At the same time, both require experience: Social experience is necessary for the mature expression of social emotions, and cognitive emotions underlie the process of cognitive development by motivating exploration. Both social experience and cognitive development are necessary for the development and mature expression of moral emotions; and moral judgments, behaviors, and feelings do typically change with development. In the present view, social and cognitive development, accompanied and motivated by social and cognitive emotions, are not only *necessary* for the development of morality, they are also *sufficient*. That is, given that a child (a) cares about others and (b) learns about the workings of the world, moral development accompanied by moral emotions is inevitable.

Gratitude and Moral Rules: The Morality of Justice

With the process of cognitive development, *social emotions naturally become moral emotions, insofar as they are aroused by moral judgments*. Moral emotions involve learned expectations about what circumstances *should* result in social emotions of pride, guilt, shame, pity, scorn, and so on. Such expectations are expressed in notions of equity—distributive and retributive justice—that specify how good and bad outcomes, respectively, *should* be meted out (i.e., Homans, 1966).

Moral rules. Rules are defined generally as *social expectations associated with more or less specific interpersonal-situational contexts*. Not all rules are moral rules, which involve considerations of equity and fairness. Rozin (1999) discussed the process of the moralization of rules, noting as an example that in the U.S. moral discourse on tobacco smoking, the harmful effects of second-hand smoke plays a critical role. That is an aspect of smoking that makes the behavior relevant to considerations of fairness and equity: The smoker is harming others as well as the self.

A shared mutual perception that rules are being followed fairly is essential to the smooth functioning of social behavior, particularly if antagonistic relationships are involved. *Justice* is defined here in terms of *following social rules and expectations that result in perceptions of fairness and equity*. Thus, whereas social emotions respond to fundamental interpersonal contingencies, moral emotions respond to *equitable interpersonal contingencies*. Judgments of equity/inequity are learned in the context of social exploration and the attainment of social competence but may differ widely from person to person (i.e., liberals versus conservatives) and from culture to culture. For example, Schweder, Much, Mahapatra, and Park (1997) identified "Big Three" moral codes found in cultures around the world: *autonomy* (emphasizing harm to others), *community* (emphasizing hierarchy and respect), and *divinity* (emphasizing purity). These moral codes specify differing criteria for defining fairness and equity, resulting in different principles of justice.

Civility: Gratitude, admiration, respect, and trust.   The mutual acknowledgment that rules are being followed fairly in a relationship, no matter how difficult and contentious that relationship might be in other respects, is among the most fundamental of affectively loaded moral contexts. The (arguably universal) rule is, If I follow the rules fairly and you follow the rules fairly, we can mutually acknowledge that each of us is acting with civility. (*Civility* is defined here as acting with justice: following rules and meeting social expectations fairly.)

In the present view, gratitude is involved with perceptions of civility and feelings of admiration, respect, and trust in providing an essential lubricant to social interaction. The perception of civility is followed by signals of *gratitude*, which acknowledge receipt of a valuable social commodity—following the rules fairly—resulting in *admiration* one for the other. The result is a relationship of mutual *respect*. The general expectation that another person will follow rules fairly and act with civility is *trust*. This civility-induced gratitude-admiration-respect-trust process is basic to successful social exchange, particularly between potential antagonists. Note that even someone who is hated and despised can be respected and trusted, albeit perhaps grudgingly. Also, note that the *content of the rules is not specified*. They could involve any of the Big Three moral codes identified by Schweder et al. (1997). All else being equal, it probably is easier to agree about what is just from within rather than between moral codes.

As with social and cognitive emotions, the intent here is not to reify terms such as *gratitude, admiration, respect,* or *trust* as involving moral emotions per se. Rather, these words seem best to describe feelings associated with these confluences of equitable interpersonal contingencies. The intent is to demonstrate confluences of equitable contingencies that allow good feelings to occur and to be exchanged, as it were, on a basis perceived to be fair and equitable, without regard to prior personal relationship, kin status, or dominance status. As noted, one can cooperate even with a hated enemy, as long as civility is maintained, and gain a kind of satisfaction from such cooperation.

Gratitude as Communication

As noted, gratitude is associated with separable subjective and display aspects: One may or may not actually feel gratitude when the other acts fairly, but the question of whether and how gratitude is expressed and communicated is a separable issue. In the McCullough et al. (2001) analysis, the communicative function of gratitude was implicit, suggesting that interactions involving expressions of gratitude encourage benefactors to behave morally in future interactions. However, the expression of gratitude can be accomplished effectively without necessarily being accompanied by the experience of true gratitude. As noted, sociopaths may present a convincing façade of expressed gratitude; the same may be true of diplomats.

Gratitude in equal relationships.   Gratitude implicitly involves a communication process between beings differing in status and power as benefactor and beneficiary of something valued. However, gratitude serves important social functions even when it is least obvious: when the relationship is nominally equal, and the benefits exchanged are intangible. In expressing gratitude to another for following the rules fairly, the sender implicitly puts himself or herself in a subordinate position, much like an animal signaling submission.[6] To maintain the equal relationship, it is therefore essential that the receiver reciprocate, expressing gratitude in return. Expressing gratitude serves a critical communicative role in humbly acknowledging that the other is acting fairly and equitably: it is "oil" that, as noted, acknowledges mutual civility and builds trust. The ability to express gratitude with apparent sincerity, and implicitly to invite or compel the other to reciprocate, is perhaps a hallmark of successful diplomacy.

Gratitude in unequal relationships.   When the differences in power and status between beneficiary and benefactor are considerable and the benefits are tangible, expressing gratitude becomes entangled with considerations of dominance and power. As an expression of the recognition that one has received benefits, gratitude is a way for the recipient to acknowledge the benefit while maintaining a sense of integrity and self-worth. In this regard, Seneca wrote in *On Benefits*, "He who receives a benefit with gratitude repays the first installment of his debt" (as quoted in Beck, 1968, p. 131). Gratitude is often pictured as an admirable characteristic (Emmons & Crumpler, 2000). Androcles wrote, "Gratitude is the sign of noble souls" (as quoted in Sproul, 1965, p. 5), and Samuel Johnson stated, "Gratitude is a fruit of great cultivation; you do not find it among gross people" (Boswell, 1785). On the other hand, Aristotle noted, "What soon grows old? Gratitude" (as quoted in Beck, 1968, p. 131). Apparently gratitude works only as the *first* installment of the debt.

Gratitude and hypocrisy.   There are even more cynical accounts of gratitude by those who question whether expressions of gratitude are genuine or instead are used strategically to ingratiate oneself. La Rochefoucauld, whose general take on human morality is captured by the quotation "Our virtues are most frequently but vices in disguise" (as quoted in Beck, 1968, p. 179) wrote in 1665, "The gratitude of most men is merely a secret desire to receive greater benefits (as quoted in Beck, 1968, p. 298). It is interesting that, whereas gratitude is associated with some ambivalence related to whether or not it is genuine, ingratitude is universally excoriated.

Gift giving and gratitude.   The complex interpersonal dynamics associated with gratitude have been investigated in studies of gift giving, which has been described as a double-edged sword (Spandler, Burman, Goldberg, Margison, & Amos, 2000). On the surface, gifts are often offered as simple expressions of gratitude in exchange for benefits, but they can carry hidden meanings that may vary with gender and culture. Spandler et al. suggested that gifts given by patients to psychotherapists can carry hidden messages associated with aggression and dependency, and Lyckholm (1998) discussed ethical issues and complexities in patient-physician gift giving. Gift giving in commercial relationships also carries potential ethical dilemmas, as the line between a gift and a bribe is often difficult to draw, particularly in international business relationships (Reardon, 1986). On the other hand, in less intense personal relationships, gift giving may simply reflect gratitude for perceived benefit. In a meta-analysis of tipping-for-service studies, Lynn and McCall (2000) found relationships between tip size and evaluations of service suggesting that tippers are concerned with equity.

Public versus private expressions of gratitude.   Baumeister and Ilko (1995) found an interesting phenomenon when they compared student accounts of important recent success experiences that were presented as public or private. Results indicated that the public accounts gave many acknowledgments of help received from other persons, whereas the private accounts did not. The authors suggested that the public expressions of gratitude were shallow and perhaps hypocritical: They were a superficial concession to social norms and expectations that did not reflect the true feelings of the students. The notion of gratitude as communicative suggests an alternative explanation: that the students failed to credit others or report feelings of gratitude in a noncommunicative context because it would serve no useful function—there would be no receiver to get the message—and instead simply stated their own contributions. In general, it may be hypothesized that gratitude is not usually expressed in noncommunicative contexts.

Gratitude and Love: The Morality of Caring

The moralities of justice versus caring.   Like McCullough et al. (2001), the foregoing discussion has conceptualized gratitude as an aspect of a process of fair exchange in which the expression and communication of gratitude helps to enable a reciprocal sharing of positive feelings and the eventual establishment of trust. As noted, this analysis is in the tradition of the judgment approach to morality of Piaget and Kohlberg. Piaget analyzed moral development in terms of the cognitive restructuring of social experience. In *The Moral Judgment of the Child* (1932/1948), he applied his methods and theory of cognitive development to study moral judgment by asking children to explain their conceptions of rules in a variety of contexts. From this evidence, Piaget suggested that younger children tend to use an *authoritarian morality* based on the one-sided adult-child relationship, whereas older children used a more *equalitarian morality* that requires experience in peer relationships.

Piaget's observations served as the starting point for studies of moral development by Kohlberg and colleagues, who studied responses to moral dilemmas (for example, judging the morality of a man, Heinz, who stole expensive medicine for his sick wife). These studies supported Piaget in most respects (Kohlberg, 1964). However, one aspect of this research stirred considerable controversy: Women generally did not appear to advance as far as did men, by Kohlberg's criteria. For example, men tended to judge Heinz's actions in terms of his marital and social obligations, whereas women tended to emphasize his love of his wife (Bussey & Maughan, 1982). Some suggested that women have a less well developed sense of moral judgment than men, living up to a stereotyped image of a "good girl" trying to win the affection and approval of others. Carol Gilligan (1982) argued against this interpretation, contending that although women's moral reasoning is typically *different* from men's—emphasizing attachment and caring in the context of real relationships rather than rules, rights and responsibilities abstracted from a meaningful context—it is not less well developed. Gilligan and colleagues (1977, 1982) argued that there are two fundamental moral orientations. The *justice perspective* "draws attention to problems of inequality and oppression and holds up an ideal of reciprocity and equal respect," whereas the *care perspective* "draws attention to problems of detachment and abandonment and holds up an ideal of attention and response to need" (Gilligan & Attanucci, 1988, p. 73).[7]

Gratitude in the morality of caring.   In the morality of caring, the benefits exchanged vis-à-vis the other involve loving and being loved, and the language of exchange is not appropriate. Both loving and being loved are of great value to human beings, who constitute a strongly social species with deep and powerful prosocial emotions that are normally turned on in early attachment relationships (Bowlby, 1969, 1973, 1980). Loving involves giving, and the greater the giving, the greater the benefit received by the giver. As noted, this is Robinson's larger kind of gratitude that we experience for what we give, rather than what we receive.

Such emotional benefits may come to be taken for granted in times of peace and plenty, whereas they are endangered in times of war. The place of gratitude in the morality of caring arguably may explain why gratitude can increase in troubled times. Taken in isolation, the gratitude of exchange would be expected to decline when benefits decline, replaced perhaps by *resentment*. However, the loss of benefits in exchange can make the value of loving and being loved even more appreciated.

Empathy and altruism.   The gratitude for what we give may extend to giving to those who are not in a loving relationship with us. There is considerable evidence that caring, or feeling *empathy* for, a needy person leads to sympathy, compassion, and unselfish tendencies to help: *altruism* (Buck & Ginsburg, 1991, 1997; Eisenberg & Miller, 1987). Batson and Oleson (1991) reviewed the evidence for selfish explanations for altruistic behavior and concluded that the evidence supports the *empathy-altruism hypothesis*: that the expression of needs by others naturally evokes empathic emotions of sympathy and compassion that motivate altruistic responses. They concluded, "The human capacity for altruism is limited to those for whom we feel empathy. . . . It is not that we never help people for whom we feel little empathy; we often do—but, the research suggests, only when it is in our own best interest" (p. 80).

Even though the empathy-altruism relationship appears to be reliably demonstrated, and empathic responses are arguably biologically based and effective in most normally attached persons, it is all too apparent that human beings do not always help others in need. Batson and Oleson (1991) noted that there are "strong forces working against the arousal of empathy. These include anything and everything that makes it difficult for us to attend to or value another person's welfare" (p. 81). Failing to notice the other's needs, or seeing the other as different from ourselves—as one of "them" rather than one of "us"—is common. This brings us to the dark side of morality, and of gratitude.

The Dark Side of Gratitude: The Morality of Subjugation

Schadenfreude.   Exceptions to the empathy-altruism hypothesis go far beyond the failure to help the person in need. Indeed, people can take pleasure in the distress and even agony of others: *schadenfreude* (Ben-Ze'ev, 1992). This is the dark side of morality that underlies Lorenz's (1966) *militant enthusiasm* to bond with friend and to subjugate foe.

Some of the darkest and most violent examples of human behavior stem from the morality of subjugation. From earliest human history, entire peoples have been decimated for the glory of one god or another. The weak have been subjected to witch hunts, lynchings, and pogroms, which not only are socially and morally sanctioned, but encouraged and indeed acclaimed. The organized horror of the Holocaust unfortunately was not an aberration, but an ordinary occurrence in human history in every respect save for its enormous industrial scale and hideous efficiency (see Arendt, 1958). More recent events in Cambodia, Bosnia, Rwanda, Kosovo, East Timor, New York City, and Washington, D.C., give grim testimony that morally approved brutality and atrocity toward out-groups are typical of the human species. Such behavior arguably reveals the essence of evil. At the same time, even such apparently inequitable behavior can be perceived by its perpetrators to be moral. The violent subjugation of an enemy can elicit strong feelings of moral certitude and self-righteousness, and authentic moral gratitude can be felt even in the performance of the most vicious of acts. For example, the suicidal fundamentalist fanatics of the September 11 attacks were by all accounts highly religious men following a strict morality, who may well have died with prayers of gratitude for the suffering of their victims.

Prejudice, authoritarianism, and social dominance orientation.   In *schadenfreude*, the enemy is not viewed as a peer worthy of gratitude, admiration, respect, trust, or even mercy. The individual in the grip of militant enthusiasm tends to hearken back to the authoritarian morality of the child, with its justification of power and expiatory punishment. Love and caring may well be emphasized, but only for the in-group: Friends and allies take on the character of the family, the Children of God, whereas loving and being loved by the in-group may actually be conditioned on participating in the violent destruction of the enemy.

Research on authoritarianism and the social dominance orientation has revealed how members of out-groups may be hated, subjected to prejudice based on stereotypes and other legitimizing myths, and not accorded sympathy or compassion (Adorno, Frenkel-Brunswik, Levinson, & Sanford, 1950; Altemeyer, 1996; Pratto, Sidanius, Stallworth, & Malle, 1994). Often, these tendencies tend to characterize persons who, for one reason or another, feel threatened. The notion that threat increases authoritarian tendencies has been verified both in experiments (Sales & Friend, 1973) and in studies of social archival data (Doty, Peterson, & Winter, 1991; Padgett & Jorgenson, 1982; Sales, 1973). These studies are consistent with Erich Fromm's (1941) thesis that social threat produces feelings of self-doubt, powerlessness, and isolation that can lead to the renunciation of personal freedom and submission to a messianic group with powerful leaders. This is perhaps relevant to our current experience of a rise of religious fundamentalism around the world, from isolated suicidal cults to the highly organized terrorists who attacked the United States on September 11.

The universality of this phenomenon suggests the functioning of basic human qualities: The yearning for a traditional authoritarian morality in response to breakdown of the social order may be a species-typical feature of human nature based on a threat to attachment. Human beings have a strong emotional need to conform to what is expected and valued and thereby to be proud, accepted, and loved. The consequences when rules no longer apply can be devastating: The abilities to act in ways to please others and to win gratitude and affection are founded on these rules, and when they are questioned, this represents a fundamental threat to attachment. In response, the individual may fall back on authoritarian morality—becoming a true believer; finding a new basis of acceptance, affection, and action in a mass movement headed by a strong, charismatic leader (Hoffer, 1951). If the change to authoritarian morality includes the domination of out-groups, the seeds of catastrophe are sown, allowing the moral justification with attendant feelings of gratitude for the most horrific persecution, subjugation, oppression, extermination, and genocide.

CONCLUSIONS

In developmental-interactionist theory, emotion and reason represent two sorts of cognition (knowledge): one involving special-purpose processing based on phylogeny with roots in the simplest of creatures, the other involving general-purpose processing with its most complex and unique expression in human language. These interact in a developmental context. Gratitude, defined generally as a response to receiving benefits with humility, reflects both sorts of processing.

This chapter relates gratitude to specific biological underpinnings in attachment and curiosity, and it distinguishes two kinds of gratitude. In the *gratitude of exchange*, the sender/beneficiary accrues benefits and the receiver/benefactor incurs costs in the context of an intricate web of exchange and obligation. In the *gratitude of caring*, benefits are accrued from the giving of benefits: the ineffable but incomparable benefit of loving and being loved. Furthermore, this chapter presents gratitude as inherently dyadic, implying a communicative relationship between senders and receivers of gratitude, and it distinguishes between experienced and expressed gratitude, noting that gratitude may be effective in enhancing trust even if feigned. Finally, the chapter relates gratitude to social and cognitive emotions involving the receipt of benefits, as well as moral emotions: *admiration, respect*, and *trust*.

A number of specific hypotheses may be based on this analysis. First, because the experience of gratitude requires attachment, biological and developmental factors promoting attachment should promote gratitude as well as other social/moral emotions. Second, gratitude will be experienced and expressed more appropriately with secure as opposed to insecure attachment, and the *experience* of gratitude will not occur without attachment, even though gratitude and other moral emotions may be effectively *expressed* even by sociopaths. Third, because gratitude is communicative, even though it is experienced it may not be expressed in noncommunicative contexts. Fourth, the perception of civility sets off a specific process of moral emotion involving *gratitude, admiration, respect*, and the eventual establishment of *trust*. Fifth, this chapter suggests specific relationships between gratitude, on one hand, and a variety of higher level social and cognitive emotions, on the other.

To summarize the hypothesized role of gratitude in morality, the gratitude of exchange involves reciprocity and mutual respect, and the perception that rules are being followed fairly and equitably (morality of justice). The gratitude of caring is based on devoted attachment and affection and the empathic perception of need (morality of caring). In contrast, the morality of subjugation reserves caring to the in-group. Members of out-groups may be hated, not accorded sympathy or compassion, and viciously attacked with the imprimatur and indeed encouragement of moral justification.

Notes

1. Tucker (1981) distinguished two sorts of cognition. *Syncretic cognition* is holistic, synthetic, and involves right-hemisphere processing. *Analytic cognition* refers to sequential and linear information processing involving the left hemisphere. This dis-

tinction is analogous to those made between "cortico-cognitive" processes based on the hippocampus and neocortex versus "emotional" processing involving the amygdala (LeDoux, 1994; Panksepp, 1994), and "hot" versus "cold" cognitive processing in recent dual-process cognitive theories (Epstein & Pacini, 1999).

2. Many concepts in the social and behavioral sciences are, like gratitude, implicitly dyadic. For example, aggression implies an assailant and victim, empathy a help giver and receiver. A communication perspective often helps to capture the complexity implicit in such concepts.

3. When attachment is absent, these social motives do not exist, and neither do social or moral emotions: This is characteristic of sociopathy. Sociopaths may be socially competent in the cognitive sense, because they may be adept at following social rules and may in fact be interpersonally engaging and charming. William Lyons (personal communication, August, 2000) has remarked that it is quite conceivable that a sociopath could get an *A+* in a seminar on moral philosophy. Because sociopaths are incapable of caring, they are incapable of experiencing gratitude even though they may be adept at hypocritically feigning expressions of gratitude (see discussion in the "Gratitude as Communication" section).

4. The term *comparison other* is used to indicate that the comparison in question is not with someone with whom P has a personal relationship, friendly or unfriendly, secure or insecure. I assume that, when personal relationships are involved, the security of attachment may vary, so P can have a secure attachment vis-à-vis one O and an insecure attachment vis-à-vis another. Therefore, P can experience twin social emotions to the same event (i.e., pride *and* arrogance, guilt *and* shame) depending on the O involved. The role of personal relationships in social emotions is beyond the scope of this chapter.

5. In this view, the biological bases of the moral emotions consist of attachment and expectancy systems. Attachment and expectancy constitute "affective assemblies" in Tomkins's (1982) sense: They are engaged in moral contexts, providing the motivational force—the fire—underlying the sense of justice.

6. Nonverbal displays of gratitude in human beings have not been formally described, but they may involve behaviors similar to submissive displays in animals: head bobbing, bowing, smiling, retreating. Such displays have also been associated with shame and embarrassment (Keltner & Buswell, 1997; Keltner & Harken, 1998; Lewis, 1993), which is consistent with the present analysis because all of these involve similar interpersonal contingencies: The responder is in a position subordinate to the other.

7. It should be noted that, although there may be overall gender differences in the moralities of justice and caring, it is clear that women can attend to justice considerations and men to caring considerations. Discussion of this issue is beyond the scope of this chapter.

References

Adorno, T. W., Frenkel-Brunswik, E., Levinson, D. J., & Sanford, R. N. (1950). *The authoritarian personality*. New York: Harper.

Ainsworth, M. D. S., Blehar, M. C., Waters, E., & Wall, S. (1978). *Patterns of attachment: A psychological study of the strange situation*. Hillsdale, NJ: Erlbaum.

Altemeyer, B. (1996). *The authoritarian specter*. Cambridge, MA: Harvard University Press.

Arendt, H. (1958). *The origins of totalitarianism*. New York: Meridian.

Batson, C. D., & Oleson, K. C. (1991). Current status of the empathy-altruism hypothesis. In M. S. Clark (Ed.), *Review of personality and social psychology: Vol. 12. Altruism* (pp. 62–85). Newbury Park, CA: Sage.

Baumeister, R. F., & Ilko, S. A. (1995). Shallow gratitude: Public and private acknowledgment of external help in accounts of success. *Basic and Applied Social Psychology, 16*(1–2), 191–209.

Beck, E. M. (Ed.). (1968). *Familiar quotations by John Bartlett* (14th ed.). Boston: Little, Brown.

Ben-Ze'ev, A. (1992). Pleasure-in-others'-misfortune. *Iyyun, 41,* 41–61.

Boswell, J. (with S. Johnson). (1785). *Journal of a tour to the Hebrides* [entry for September 14, 1773]. London: Henry Baldwin.

Bowlby, J. (1969). *Attachment and loss: Vol. 1. Attachment*. New York: Basic Books.

Bowlby, J. (1973). *Attachment and loss: Vol. 2. Separation: Anxiety and anger*. New York: Basic Books.

Bowlby, J. (1980). *Attachment and loss: Vol. 3. Loss*. New York: Basic Books.

Buck, R. (1984). *The communication of emotion*. New York: Guilford.

Buck, R. (1985). Prime theory: An integrated view of motivation and emotion. *Psychological Review, 92,* 389–413.

Buck, R. (1988). *Human motivation and emotion* (2nd ed.). New York: Wiley.

Buck, R. (1999). The biological affects: A typology. *Psychological Review, 106,* 301–336.

Buck, R., & Ginsburg, B. (1991). Emotional communication and altruism: The communicative gene hypothesis. In M. S. Clark (Ed.), *Review of personality and social psychology: Vol. 12. Altruism* (pp. 149–175). Newbury Park, CA: Sage.

Buck, R., & Ginsburg, B. (1997). Communicative genes and the evolution of empathy. In W. Ickes (Ed.), *Empathic accuracy* (pp. 17–43). New York: Guilford.

Buck, R., & Vieira, E. (2002, July). *The dynamics of social emotions: Twins, opposites, converses, reciprocals, and mirrors*. Paper presented at the meeting of the International Society for Research on Emotions, Cuenca, Spain.

Bussey, K., & Maughan, B. (1982). Gender differences in moral reasoning. *Journal of Personality and Social Psychology, 42,* 701–706.

Carter, C. S., Lederhendler, I. I., & Kirkpatrick, B. (Eds.). (1997). *Annals of the New York Academy of Sciences: Vol. 807. The integrative neurobiology of affiliation* (pp. 260–272). New York: New York Academy of Sciences.

Chiesa, M. (2001). Envy and gratitude. In C. Bronstein (Ed.), *Kleinian theory: A contemporary perspective* (pp. 93–107). London: Whurr.

Depue, R. A., & Collins, P. F. (1999). Neurobiology of the structure of personality: Dopamine, facilitation of incentive motivation, and extraversion. *Behavioral and Brain Sciences, 22,* 491–569.

Doty, R. M., Peterson, B. E., & Winter, D. G. (1991). Threat and authoritarianism in the United States, 1978–1987. *Journal of Personality and Social Psychology, 61,* 614–628.

Eisenberg, N., & Miller, P. (1987). The relation of empathy to prosocial and related behaviors. *Psychological Bulletin, 101,* 91–119.

Ekman, P., & Friesen, W. (1975). *Unmasking the face.* Englewood Cliffs, NJ: Prentice Hall.

Emmons, R. A., & Crumpler, C. A. (2000). Gratitude as a human strength: Appraising the evidence. *Journal of Social and Clinical Psychology, 19*(1), 56–69.

Epstein, S., & Pacini, R. (1999). Some basic issues regarding dual-process theories from the perspective of cognitive-experiential self theory. In S. Chaiken & Y. Trope (Eds.), *Dual-process theories in social psychology* (pp. 462–482). New York: Guilford.

Fromm, E. (1941). *Escape from freedom.* New York: Holt, Rinehart & Winston.

Gibbs, N. (2001, November 20). Thanksgiving 2001: We gather together. *Time,* 28–41.

Gilligan, C. (1977). In a different voice: Women's conceptions of self and of morality. *Harvard Educational Review, 47,* 481–517.

Gilligan, C. (1982). *In a different voice.* Cambridge, MA: Harvard University Press.

Gilligan, C., & Attanucci, J. (1988). Two moral orientations. In C. Gilligan, J. W. Ward, and J. M. Taylor (Eds.), *Mapping the moral domain* (pp. 73–86). Cambridge, MA: Harvard University Press.

Gray, J. A. (1982a). *The neuropsychology of anxiety: An enquiry into the functions of the septo-hippocampal system.* New York: Oxford University Press.

Hoffer, E. (1951). *The true believer.* New York: Harper.

Hogan, R., Johnson, J., & Emler, N. (1994). A socioanalytic theory of moral development. In B. Puka (Ed.), *Moral development: A compendium: Vol. 2. Fundamental research in moral development* (pp. 303–320). New York: Garland.

Homans, G. C. (1966). *Social behavior: Its elementary forms.* New York: Harcourt, Brace & World.

Keltner, D., & Buswell, B. N. (1997). Embarrassment: Its distinct form and appeasement functions. *Psychological Bulletin, 122,* 250–270.

Keltner, D., & Harken, L. (1998). The forms and functions of the nonverbal signal of shame. In P. Gilbert & B. Andrews (Eds.), *Shame: Interpersonal behavior, psychopathology, and culture* (pp. 78–98). New York: Oxford University Press.

Klein, M. (1957). *Envy and gratitude.* New York: Basic Books.

Klein, M. (1998). Melanie Klein: Tanulmany az irigysegro [Melanie Klein: Study on envy and gratitude]. *Psychiatria Hungarica, 13*(3), 269–280.

Kohlberg, L. (1964). Development of moral character and moral ideology. In M. L. Hoffman & L. W. Hoffman (Eds.), *Review of child development research* (vol. 1, pp. 383–431). New York: Russell Sage Foundation.

Lewis, M. (1993). Self-conscious emotions: Embarrassment, pride, shame, and guilt. In M. Lewis & J. M. Haviland (Eds.), *Handbook of emotions* (pp. 563–573). New York: Guilford.

Lorenz, K. (1966). *On aggression.* New York: Harcourt, Brace & World.

Lyckholm, L. (1998). Should physicians accept gifts from patients? *Journal of the American Medical Association, 280*(22), 1944–1946.

Lynn, M., & McCall, M. (2000). Gratitude and gratuity: A meta-analysis of research on the service-tipping relationship. *Journal of Socio-Economics, 29*(2), 203–214.

McCullough, M. E., Kilpatrick, S. D., Emmons, R. A., & Larson, D. B. (2001). Is gratitude a moral affect? *Psychological Bulletin, 127*(2), 249–266.

Padgett, V. R., & Jorgenson, D. O. (1982, December). Superstition and economic threat: Germany, 1918–1940. *Personality and Social Psychology Bulletin, 8*(4), 736–741.

Panksepp, J. (1994). A proper distinction between affective and cognitive process is essential for neuroscientific progress. In P. Ekman & R. Davidson (Eds.), *The nature of emotion: Fundamental questions* (pp. 224–226). New York: Oxford University Press.

Panksepp, J. (1998). *Affective neuroscience: The foundations of human and animal emotions.* New York: Oxford University Press.

Piaget, J. (1948). *The moral judgment of the child.* Glencoe, IL: Free Press. (Original work published 1932)

Pratto, F., Sidanius, J. Stallworth, L. M., & Malle, B. F. (1994). Social dominance orientation: A personality variable predicting social and political attitudes. *Journal of Personality and Social Psychology, 67*, 741–763.

Reardon, K. (1986). An exploratory study of international business gift customs. *World Communication, 14*, 137–148.

Rolls, J. (1999). *The brain and emotion.* New York: Oxford University Press.

Rozin, P. (1999). The process of moralization. *Psychological Science, 10*, 218–221.

Sales, S. (1973). Threat as a factor in authoritarianism: An analysis of archival data. *Journal of Personality and Social Psychology, 36*, 988–999.

Sales, S., & Friend, K. E. (1973). Success and failure as determinants of level of authoritarianism. *Behavioral Science, 18*, 163–172.

Schweder, R. A., Much, N. C., Mahapatra, M., & Park, L. (1997). The "big three" of morality (autonomy, community, divinity), and the "big three" explanations of suffering. In A. M. Brandt & P. Rozin (Eds.), *Morality and health* (pp. 119–169). New York: Routledge.

Spandler, H., Burman, E., Goldberg, B., Margison, F., & Amos, T. (2000). "A double-edged sword": Understanding gifts in psychotherapy. *European Journal of Psychotherapy, Counseling, and Health, 3*(1), 77–101.

Sproul, K. (Ed.). (1965). *The shorter Bartlett's familiar quotations.* New York: Pocket Books.

Tesser, A., Gatewood, R., & Driver, M. (1968). Some determinants of gratitude. *Journal of Personality and Social Psychology, 9*, 233–236

Tomkins, S. S. (1962–1963). *Affect, imagery, consciousness* (Vols. 1–2). New York: Springer.

Tomkins, S. S. (1982). Affect theory. In P. Ekman (Ed.), *Emotion in the human face* (2nd ed., pp. 353–395). Cambridge, UK: Cambridge University Press.

Tucker, D. M. (1981). Lateral brain function, emotion, and conceptualization. *Psychological Bulletin, 89*, 19–46.

van Daal, J. H., Jenks, B. G., Crusio, W. E., Lemmens, W. A., & van Abeelen, J. H. (1991). A genetic-correlational study of hippocampal neurochemical variation in exploratory activities in mice. *Behavioral Brain Research, 43,* 65–72.

White, R. W. (1959). Motivation reconsidered: The concept of competence. *Psychological Review, 66,* 297–333.

7   Parent of the Virtues?

The Prosocial Contours of Gratitude

Michael E. McCullough and Jo-Ann Tsang

Although gratitude is certainly not the most salient or most frequently experienced emotion in the human emotional repertoire, many people do experience gratitude with some frequency. Sommers and Kosmitzki
(1988) reported that in a sample of 105 U.S. and 40 German adults, approximately 10% and 30%, respectively indicated that they experienced the emotion of gratitude "regularly and often." Moreover, approximately 20% of the
Americans and 50% of the Germans rated gratitude as a useful and constructive emotion. One area of life in which gratitude might be particularly useful
and relevant is the moral realm.

GRATITUDE AS A MORAL EMOTION IN PREVIOUS PSYCHOLOGICAL THEORIZING

Beginning with Cicero (1851), who called gratitude "not only the greatest,
but also the parent of all the other virtues" (p. 139), many students of human
emotion have recognized that grateful feelings have unique and important
functions in the moral and prosocial realm. In *The Theory of Moral Sentiments*
(1790/1976), Adam Smith proposed that gratitude is one of the primary
motivators of benevolent behavior toward a benefactor (see Harpham, chap.
2, this volume, for a review). Smith wrote, "The sentiment which most immediately and directly prompts us to reward, is gratitude" (1790/1976, p.

68). When a benefactor has acted in such a way as to promote the well-being of a beneficiary, gratitude prompts the beneficiary to find ways to acknowledge the gift. Smith proposed that feelings of gratitude are crucial for maintaining a society that is to be based on goodwill. Of course, Smith was well aware that society could function without an economy of gratitude, but he seemed to believe that grateful societies were more attractive than societies of pure utility. In this sense, Smith seemed to consider gratitude to be an important emotional resource for promoting civility and social stability. Smith posited that three psychological factors govern most experiences and expressions of gratitude. Beneficiaries are most likely to feel and express gratitude toward benefactors who (a) intend to benefit them, (b) succeed in benefiting them, and (c) are capable of sympathizing with the beneficiary's grateful feelings.

Emotion theorists in the second half of the twentieth century elaborated on Smith's (1790/1976) theorizing. Simmel (1908/1950) and Gouldner (1960) conceptualized gratitude as a force for helping people maintain their reciprocity obligations. Schwartz (1967) likened gratitude to *inertia*: a force that causes social relationships to maintain a prosocial orientation (just as grudges and resentments help to maintain a negative orientation in relationships that have been troubled by interpersonal transgressions). Trivers (1971), in keeping with the functionalist interpretations of Smith, Simmel, Gouldner, and Schwartz, speculated about the evolutionary functions of gratitude. Trivers viewed gratitude as an evolutionary adaptation that regulates people's responses to altruistic acts. Trivers held that grateful emotions are especially sensitive to the cost/benefit ratio of altruistic acts, with relatively costly benefits eliciting more gratitude.

Cognitive-emotion theorists refined these insights about gratitude by emphasizing the role of cognition in eliciting emotions such as gratitude. For example, Heider (1958) argued that people feel grateful when they have received a benefit from someone who, they believe, *intended* to benefit them. Heider, like Smith, posited that the perceived intentionality of the benefit was the most important factor in determining whether someone felt grateful after receiving a benefit. Other cognitive-emotion theorists such as Weiner (1985); Ortony, Clore, and Collins (1987); and Lazarus and Lazarus (1994) also recognized the moral quality of gratitude. Lazarus and Lazarus, for example, posited that gratitude is one of the "empathic emotions" that are grounded in the human capacity for empathizing with other people. A central aspect of Lazarus and Lazarus's theory is the notion that each emotion is associated with a distinctive dramatic plot or "core relational theme" that helps people to interpret the events that happen to them and to assess their relevance for personal well-being. The core relational theme associated with gratitude is the appreciation of a beneficial, altruistic gift. According to Lazarus and Lazarus, people experience this core relational theme when they empathize with the benefactor's expenditure of effort on the beneficiary's behalf.

GRATITUDE AS A MORAL AFFECT: A FUNCTIONAL MODEL

We concur with previous gratitude researchers in positing that gratitude is a moral and prosocial emotion. In a recent article (McCullough, Kilpatrick, Emmons, & Larson, 2001), we expanded on the prosocial nature of gratitude, detailing three specific prosocial or moral functions that gratitude serves. Namely, the emotion of gratitude functions as a *moral barometer*, a *moral motive*, and (when people express their grateful emotions in words or actions) a *moral reinforcer*. Furthermore, we hypothesized that, because gratitude is so closely tied to moral and prosocial behaviors, personality differences in gratitude would be positively associated with traits that facilitate interpersonal relations, and negatively associated with traits that interfere with maintaining stable, positive relationships (see Roberts, chap. 4, this volume, for details on the distinction between emotional and dispositional gratitude). In this chapter, we elaborate on each of these hypotheses and briefly describe the strength of supporting research evidence.

The Moral Barometer Function of Gratitude

As noted, we have hypothesized that grateful emotions work in the same fashion as does a barometer. A barometer is an instrument that indicates a change in atmospheric conditions, namely, barometric pressure. When the weather changes, the readings on a barometer reflect this change. Previous theorists and researchers have delineated the informational function of affect and emotions (Batson, Turk, Shaw, & Klein, 1995; Epstein, 1984; Schwarz, 1990). Gratitude fills a similar informational function by indicating a certain a particular type of interpersonal transaction—one in which a benefactor contributes to a beneficiary's perceived well-being through some tangible or intangible benefit.

As a moral barometer, gratitude is dependent on social-cognitive input. We posited, as have most other theorists, that people are most likely to feel grateful when (a) they have received a particularly valuable benefit, (b) high effort and cost have been expended on their behalf, (c) the expenditure of effort on their behalf seems to have been intentional rather than accidental, and (d) the expenditure of effort on their behalf was gratuitous (i.e., was not determined by the existence of a role-based relationship between benefactor and beneficiary).

In our review, we concluded that the existing research supports the moral barometer hypothesis quite strongly (Graham & Barker, 1990; Graham, Hudley, & Williams, 1992; Hegtvedt, 1990; Lane & Anderson, 1976; Okamoto, 1992; Okamoto & Robinson, 1997; Overwalle, Mervielde, & De Schuyter, 1995; Tesser, Gatewood, & Driver, 1968; Weiner, Russell, & Lerman, 1979; Zaleski, 1988). Results of one of the earliest studies of the cognitive determinants of gratitude are typical of the sort of evidence that we found for the moral barometer hypothesis. Tesser et al. (1968) studied 126 male and female participants who had read three scenarios in which intentionality, cost, and value of a benefit were systematically manipulated across subjects. Respondents were asked to consider how much gratitude the beneficiary would likely experience under each combination of levels of intentionality, cost, and value. Tesser and his associates found main effects for intentionality, cost, and value: Respondents indicated that they would feel most grateful for a benefit that was (a) rendered intentionally, (b) costly to the benefactor, and (c) valuable to the recipient. Across three different scenarios, the linear combination of these three factors predicted 72% to 85% of the variance in respondents' expectations for the amount of gratitude that they might feel following the receipt of a benefit. Several other studies using both fictional scenarios and autobiographical accounts of gratitude experiences also found that people were most grateful in similar situations, the prototype of which is a situation in which another person intentionally rendered a valuable or costly benefit, or a benefit that was both valuable and costly.

Although people might be motivated by a variety of factors to make public, behavioral expressions of gratitude (grateful emotions being only one of them), studies using behavioral measures of gratitude show that expressions of gratitude and grateful emotions are caused by similar interpersonal factors (Okamoto, 1992; Okamoto & Robinson, 1997). For example, Okamoto and Robinson staged an experiment in which a confederate held the door for another student as they both passed through a doorway. The investigators varied the amount of effort that the confederate expended by varying whether the confederate was coming in or going out of the same door that the participant was entering and whether the confederate allowed the participant to enter the door before the confederate. People were most likely to express gratitude when the imposition on the confederate was highest. The expressions of gratitude also became substantially more formal (i.e., polite) as the level of imposition on the benefactor increased. Thus, the more effort the benefactor appeared to expend on the participants' behalf, the more grateful the participants acted toward the benefactor.

People apparently also experience more gratitude toward benefactors from whom they would not expect benevolence. This finding supports the moral barometer hypothesis function of gratitude because unexpected benevolence probably leads to the attribution that the benevolent action was rendered intentionally. We found evidence for the unexpected benevolence effect in research showing that people experience less gratitude for benefits rendered by someone who is close to them than by someone who is less close to them (Bar-Tal, Bar-Zohar, Greenberg, & Hermon, 1977), and by someone who has more social status and power than they do than by someone who has equal social status and power (Becker & Smenner, 1986; Hegtvedt, 1990; Okamoto & Robinson, 1997).

Our review of the literature also uncovered research that we could not reconcile easily with the moral barometer hypothesis—at least initially. The first challenge was to reconcile the moral barometer hypothesis with research showing that people sometimes experience gratitude in response to good fortune that is not due to the action of other human beings (Graham & Barker, 1990; Moore, 1996; Roseman, 1991; Teigen, 1997; Veisson, 1999; Weiner, Russell, & Lerman, 1979), such as when they achieve good outcomes due to their own effort, God, luck, or chance. To whom is one grateful in these circumstances?

We concluded that perhaps in such cases, people attribute intentionality to nonhuman agents (e.g., God, luck, etc.). If one believes that God, fortune, or luck might have been responsible for a positive outcome, it might be because they attribute causal power to such nonhuman agents. We also considered the possibility that people who claim to experience gratitude in situations in which nonmoral agents are involved (i.e., actors who are not capable of behaving morally) or when they themselves are responsible for the positive outcome actually experience relief, gladness, happiness, or some other pleasant affect but are mislabeling their affective state as gratitude. A third possibility is that experiences that elicit attribution-independent emotions such as happiness and relief activate other positive feelings, including attribution-dependent emotions such as gratitude or pride.

Another empirical challenge to the moral barometer hypothesis was research indicating that perceiving oneself to have received an intentionally rendered, valuable benefit does not necessarily lead to gratitude among young children. We concluded that children come to understand gratitude over the course of several years of development (Baumgartner-Tramer, 1938; Gleason & Weintraub, 1976; Graham, 1988; P. L. Harris, Olthof,

Meerum Terwogt, & Hardman, 1987; Preyer, 1933; Russell & Paris, 1994; Sowa, 1981), and that gratitude does not function reliably as a moral barometer until middle childhood. Such developmental considerations notwithstanding, we concluded that the empirical evidence strongly supports the hypothesis that gratitude is a moral barometer—an emotional response to having received benefits from a person who rendered such benefits intentionally.

The Moral Motive Function of Gratitude

Gratitude may have a second moral function: It may motivate grateful people to behave morally or prosocially themselves. Specifically, we hypothesized that people made grateful by the actions of a benefactor are more likely to contribute to the welfare of the benefactor—or even a third party—in the future. Moreover, we hypothesized that a person who experiences gratitude as the result of a benefactor's prosocial actions is also more likely to inhibit motivations to act destructively toward the benefactor or a third party.

Two studies (Peterson & Stewart, 1996; Graham, 1988) were relevant to the idea that people who have been made grateful by a benefit are more likely to behave prosocially toward the benefactor or other people in ensuing interactions, and both supported the hypothesis (although the evidence was rather indirect). Additionally, research by de Waal on reciprocity in primates demonstrated that chimpanzees (de Waal, 1997) and capuchin monkeys (de Waal & Berger, 2000) behave prosocially toward individuals who have previously provided them a benefit (see also Bonnie & de Waal, chap. 11, this volume). We found only one study (Baron, 1984) that addressed the idea that feeling grateful inhibits people from engaging in destructive interpersonal behavior. Again, this study was supportive of the moral motive hypothesis, but the evidence was indirect at best.

What was most striking to us was how very little research had addressed the moral motive hypothesis, despite its seeming obviousness. Research on reactions to aid and reciprocity—which seem relevant to the motivational value of gratitude—apparently has been dominated by the assumption that the key motive for moral behavior in reciprocity situations is inequity or indebtedness (see Greenberg & Westcott, 1983; Shapiro, 1984). Studies that would permit researchers to examine whether the link between receiving a benefit from a benefactor and the beneficiary's reciprocal behavior is mediated by the beneficiary's gratitude would be particularly valuable. Also, differentiating the unique effects of gratitude as a moral motive from the general effects of positive mood on helping behavior (Carlson, Charlin, & Miller, 1988) would be informative.

The Moral Reinforcer Function of Gratitude Expressions

The third hypothesis proceeding from the moral affect model of gratitude is that expressions of gratitude can reinforce moral behavior. Qualitative researchers have noted that expressions of gratitude can reinforce benevolent actions (Bennett, Ross, & Sunderland, 1996; Bernstein & Simmons, 1974). Conversely, people evaluate ungrateful individuals quite unfavorably (Stein, 1989), and therefore may be less inclined to help ungrateful people in the future.

Experimental data show that benefactors who are thanked for their efforts in rendering benefits to a beneficiary are willing to give more and work harder on behalf of others than are benefactors who have not been thanked for their prior efforts. R. D. Clark (1975); Goldman, Seever, and Seever (1982); and Moss and Page (1972) all found that adults who were thanked for giving a confederate directions were much more likely to help another confederate in the near future—a person who dropped his or her books in the street, for instance—than were benefactors who were rebuked for giving help to the first confederate (but see M. B. Harris, 1972, for a failure to replicate). Also, participants who were thanked for accepting electric shocks for a confederate continued to receive shocks for the confederate at a higher rate than were subjects who were not thanked initially (McGovern, Ditzian, & Taylor, 1975).

Applied researchers also have found that expressions of gratitude can reinforce moral behavior. H. B. Clark, Northrop, and Barkshire (1988) attempted to increase the frequency with which case managers visited their adolescent clients in a residential treatment program. During a 20-week baseline observation period, 43% of the adolescents were visited weekly by their case managers. After the observation period, the residential units began to send thank-you letters to case managers after they visited their clients. During the 20-week period during which the residential units sent thank-you notes, nearly 80% of clients were visited by their case managers each week. During a 10-week reversal period (during which no thank-you letters were sent following visits), the rates of weekly visitation dropped back to roughly their initial levels (i.e., approximately 50% of clients were visited weekly).

Other field experiments indicate that the reinforcement effects of gratitude expressions extend into the economic arena. Restaurant bills on which the server writes "thank you" produce tips that are as much as 11% higher (Rind & Bordia, 1995) than do bills without expressions of gratitude. Also, including thank-you notes in mail surveys typically increases response rates (Maheux, Legault, & Lambert, 1989). In addition, some evidence suggests that people who are high in need for approval may be especially prone to behave in such prosocial fashions when reinforced for moral or prosocial actions they have already enacted (Deutsch & Lamberti, 1986).

Thus, we found substantial support for the moral reinforcer hypothesis. People who have been the recipients of sincere expressions of gratitude are more likely to act again in a prosocial fashion toward their beneficiaries. Also, people are more likely to behave prosocially toward third parties after having received sincere thanks from someone on whom they have already conferred a benefit. The effects of gratitude as a moral reinforcer, of course, would not have surprised early theorists such as Adam Smith (1790/1976) and twentieth-century theorists such as Georg Simmel (1908/1950). They believed that experiencing and expressing gratitude were crucial for positive human relations. Conceptualizing gratitude as an emotion that strengthens people's social resources is also consistent with recent formulations of the functions of positive emotions in general (Fredrickson, 1998).

Gratitude and Prosocially Relevant Personality Traits

The fourth hypothesis related to the moral affect theory is that gratitude is related to personality variables that are linked with prosocial emotion and behavior. This hypothesis is supported by three relevant studies. First, Saucier and Goldberg (1998) reported that the Big Five personality traits (openness to experience, conscientiousness, extraversion, agreeableness, and neuroticism) accounted for approximately 16% of the variability in a measure of gratitude consisting of adjectives including *grateful* and *thankful* ($R = .40$). People who rated themselves (or others) as particularly grateful also rated themselves (or those whom they were rating) as higher in agreeableness ($r = .31$). Agreeableness is actually a higher order personality factor that subsumes a variety of prosocial traits such as empathy, trust, and willingness to forgive. People who are rated high in agreeableness tend to do well in social relationships, and their relationships are characterized by less conflict and greater adjustment (Graziano, Jensen-Campbell, & Hair, 1996). It is of interest that gratefulness ratings also were correlated negatively ($r = -.24$) with openness. The correlations with the other Big Five constructs (conscientiousness, extraversion, and neuroticism) were nearly zero.

Gratitude appears also to be inversely related to narcissism, which is a higher order construct subsuming traits such as grandiosity, entitlement, selfishness, and denigration of others. Farwell and Wohlwend-Lloyd (1998) examined the association of gratitude and narcissism—as measured with Raskin and Hall's (1979) Narcissistic Personality Inventory—in the context of a laboratory-based interdependence game. Participants completed a bogus assessment of creativity. Participants were told that their performance on the creativity test would be combined with the score of a randomly assigned partner and that the resulting aggregate performance would be compared with the scores of other randomly assembled pairs of participants. After completing the bogus creativity task, participants completed the Narcissistic Personality Inventory. Then the experimenter ostensibly scored each participant's performance on the creativity task and aggregated it with data from another respondent. The experimenter then told each participant that his or her dyad had scored better than 85% of the other dyads, and that his or her performance differed from the performance of his or her partner.

Then participants completed several measures of their feelings regarding their own performance ("happy," "proud," and "competent") and two measures of their feelings regarding their partners ("liking" and "gratitude"). These latter two measures were combined into a single index. Narcissism was inversely related to scores on this two-item measure of liking and gratitude toward the partner, $r (54) = -.23$, $p < .05$, suggesting that narcissistic people may experience less gratitude for the actions of their relationship partners than do less narcissistic individuals.

McCullough, Emmons, and Tsang (2002) developed a measure of dispositional gratitude, the GQ-6. They found that the grateful personality was related to a number of different interpersonal traits and behaviors. In both college-student and nonstudent samples, the GQ-6 was positively correlated with self-reported forgiveness, as well as with peer reports of participants' prosocial traits and behaviors. In contrast, the GQ-6 was negatively correlated with envy. Additionally, multiple regression analyses showed that agreeableness predicted unique variance in both self- and peer-ratings of the GQ-6.

The scant data therefore indicate that individual differences in gratitude are related to individual differences in personality factors that have typically been linked to prosocial emotions and behavior, namely, high agreeableness and forgiveness, as well as low narcissism and envy. Further research on the personality correlates of gratitude will help to uncover the prosocial traits of the grateful individual.

QUESTIONS REGARDING THE MORAL AFFECT MODEL OF GRATITUDE

Our review of the existing literature led us to conclude that gratitude does indeed possess moral or prosocial qualities. As a moral barometer, gratitude indicates that someone has been the recipient of another person's benevolence. As a moral motive, gratitude prompts a beneficiary to find ways to behave prosocially toward his or her benefactor, or toward others. As a moral reinforcer, expressions of gratitude cause benefactors to persist in behaving in a benevolent fashion toward other people. Finally, gratitude appears to be linked to traits such as agreeableness, prosociality, narcissism, and envy, which have been identified has having distinctly moral or prosocial features. However, the moral affect model of gratitude raises questions about the very nature of gratitude that might be worth elaborating or clarifying.

Moral, Prosocial, or Both?

One of the first questions regarding our conceptualization of gratitude as a moral affect relates to our use of the term *moral*. Clearly, people feel grateful when they perceive that another person has intentionally acted in a way to improve their well-being, but one might question whether such situations necessarily have anything to do with morality. As discussed in our previous article (McCullough et al., 2001), some situations that might involve gratitude may seem amoral—or actually *immoral*—from an outsider's perspective. The world of organized crime teems with excellent examples of such situations.

Consider, for example, a merchant who sells illegal firearms to underworld figures. He or she might be grateful for a new customer's business, which presumably would contribute to the merchant's well-being, even though shopping in a particular store versus any other store (or no store at all) probably would not be judged as having much moral valence in an absolute sense (e.g., by an impartial perceiver). Moreover, because the merchant is selling illegal firearms to a criminal, an impartial perceiver probably would conclude that the net effects of the transaction are positively *immoral*. Such judgments of absolute nonmorality or immorality, however, would not change the fact that from the merchant's local perspective, the purchaser's actions rendered a benefit to and promoted the well-being of the merchant. Moreover, depending on the supply of illegal firearms, the number of competitors, and the amount of effort the purchaser expended to purchase the gun, the transaction could possess many of the social-cognitive characteristics that would lead the merchant to feel grateful for the purchaser's business.

Consider also a situation in which a wealthy and powerful crime boss helps a hardworking but financially inept employee avoid family stress and public humiliation by helping the employee out of a serious financial strain. Obviously, the employee would feel extremely grateful to the boss. As a result, when the crime boss asks the employee return the favor by killing an enemy, the employee is more inclined to say yes due to the gratitude experienced for the boss's generosity during his or her time of need. Clearly, in such a situation, gratitude would not be motivating moral behavior, but rather, patently *immoral* behavior, even though the behavior (killing the boss's enemy) is perceived by both parties as benefiting the boss's well-being.

Local and absolute morality. In an earlier article (McCullough et al., 2001), we dispatched with the objection that gratitude does not function as a moral affect in such instances by arguing that gratitude can be a response to *perceived* morality, even if the net effects of that benefit do not comport well with perceivers' prototypes or trained ethicists' judgments of what is moral. We distinguished between *local* and *absolute* perceptions of morality. Thus, we posited that the prototypical social events that elicit gratitude are at least moral in a local sense (the beneficiary perceives himself or herself to have been benefited), even if the benefactor's behavior—or the actions motivated by gratitude—were not moral in an absolute sense.

Gratitude and moral rationalization. We might clarify the contrast between local and absolute morality by referring to the literature on moral rationalization. It is possible that people whose gratitude either derives from or results in immoral behavior engage in one or more processes of moral rationalization that allow them to perceive their benefactors' (or their own) immoral actions as consistent with moral principles. Because people have a need to see themselves as good and moral (e.g., Aronson, 1969; Steele, 1988), they are reluctant to admit that their immoral behavior is in violation of moral principles. Instead, they use mechanisms such as motivated reasoning (Kunda, 1990) to convince themselves that their behavior—or the behavior of their benefactors—is, in fact, moral (Tsang, 2002). In the previous example, although an outside person might judge the murder of the crime boss's enemy as immoral, the grateful employee who committed the murder may have used moral rationalization to convince himself or herself of the morality of that action.

Bandura (1990) outlined a theory of moral disengagement that described several rationalization techniques people might use to deactivate their internalized moral self-sanctions, allowing them to act immorally without realizing that their actions violate their moral principles. Methods of moral disengagement include (a) reconstruing conduct (whereby an individual transforms immoral actions into moral ones, for example by pointing to a higher cause), (b) obscuring personal agency (whereby an individual might claim that he or she was simply a cog in a larger machine), (c) disregarding negative consequences (whereby an individual selectively avoids the consequences of immoral behavior), and (d) blaming and dehumanizing victims.

Because maintaining a positive self-concept is so psychologically important, both underworld figures in our examples might engage in different methods of moral rationalization that allow them to avoid viewing themselves as willing participants in an immoral activity. For the merchant, perhaps, selling illegal firearms is not immoral because he or she believes the legal system is unfair, or that the cause for which the weapons will be used is a just one. Although bystanders might believe that the sale of illegal firearms, for instance, is immoral, the seller and the buyer of the weapons might not.

Furthermore, it is possible that the gratitude that these underworld figures experience in such situations actually does stimulate the desire to uphold moral principles—the very principles that have formed the basis for much of the Western understanding of morality. The moral principles most relevant to gratitude are reciprocity and equity. Reciprocity is the principle of helping others who help us (Gouldner, 1960; Wilke & Lanzetta, 1982). The related principle of equity is upheld when all participants in a relationship are perceived as receiving equal outcomes relative to their input (Walster, Berscheid, & Walster, 1973). From this point of view, killing the crime boss's enemy is perceived as moral because the henchman allows one moral principle (e.g., equity or reciprocity) to take precedence over another moral principle (e.g., it is wrong to kill people). As a result, the gratitude that these characters experience might be linked to behaviors (their benefactors' or their own) that they perceive to be moral.

Situations in which gratitude results from or leads to immoral behavior does some violence to the moral affect model of gratitude. At the very least, these situations lead to the qualification that some causes and effects of gratitude, although perhaps "prosocial" in nature, are amoral or even immoral. For this reason, it may add clarity to speak of gratitude as a prosocial affect rather than as a moral one. On the other hand, the organized crime examples that we have discussed illustrate that people who experience gratitude can come to perceive immoral actions as being moral, and perhaps the power of gratitude to shape moral judgment and behavior is a topic worthy of study in its own right.

What Are the Appropriate Levels of Analysis for Studying Gratitude?

A second question related to the moral affect theory of gratitude concerns the various levels at which gratitude might be analyzed and studied empirically. One can imagine at least three levels of analysis from which gratitude might be quantified: (a) the dispositional perspective, (b) the benefactor perspective, and (c) the benefit perspective.

The dispositional perspective is the most general perspective from which one might attempt to classify persons. Laypersons use this level of analysis each time they refer to a person as grateful or ungrateful—labels that ostensibly refer to a person's general tendencies to be grateful or ungrateful across a variety of life experiences, benefits, and beneficiaries. An example of measuring gratitude from the dispositional perspective is the study by Saucier and Goldberg (1998), which used a two-item measure of gratitude (consisting of the adjectives *grateful* and *thankful*) to examine the Big Five correlates of gratitude, or our own work on the GQ-6 (McCullough et al., 2002).

From a benefactor perspective, gratitude is understood by observing people's degrees of gratitude for particular persons who have conferred benefits to them in the past. For example, people are typically expected to be grateful to their parents independently of an exhaustive tally of the benefits that their parents have conferred on them. The exact nature of the benefits received in the past is not the main focus. Rather, from a benefactor perspective, the main question is whether (and the degree to which) a person feels grateful *to someone*.

From the benefit perspective, one is interested in the degree of gratitude that a person feels in response to a particular benefit (e.g., paying one's college tuition, allowing one to merge into traffic, taking out the trash) that a particular benefactor (e.g., a father, a stranger on the highway, a roommate) has bestowed. Thus, the question from the benefit perspective is whether a person is grateful *to someone for something*. The benefit perspective is exemplified in the work of Graham (1988) who examined the cognitive factors that shaped whether a child would feel grateful toward another child who chose him or her to be on a sports team.

In this early stage of empirical work on gratitude, it might be useful to remain mindful of these obvious and seemingly trivial distinctions between the various perspectives from which gratitude might be conceptualized and measured. One reason these distinctions might be important is because phenomena related to gratitude at one level of analysis might not emerge at other levels of analysis.

An analogy from research on forgiveness might help to clarify this point, because forgiveness also can be measured at several levels (McCullough, Hoyt, & Rachal, 2000). McCullough et al. (2000) distinguished between forgiveness as measured at the dispositional level (i.e., a person's general tendency to forgive most persons across most transgressions), the relationship-specific level (i.e., a person's general tendency to forgive a single person across most transgressions), and the offense-specific level (i.e., a person's general tendency to forgive a single person for a specific transgression). McCullough and Witvliet (2001) also distinguished between forgiveness as a response to an isolated transgression, a personality disposition, and a character-istic of social units. We have found that the extent to which a person experi-ences empathy for a particular transgressor is strongly related (e.g., r ranging from .50 to .80) to the extent to which the person reports having forgiven the transgressor (McCullough et al., 1998; McCullough, Worthington, & Rachal, 1997). This robust correlation is consistent with theorizing that em-pathy for one's transgressor causes people to forgive (McCullough et al., 1997). However, researchers have found that measures of the propensity to forgive (analogous to the dispositional perspective outlined earlier) are cor-related fairly trivially with measures of empathic disposition (i.e., $r < .20$; Tangney, Fee, Reinsmith, Boone, & Lee, 1999).

Another situation that raises awareness of the importance of being spe-cific about the levels of analysis at which gratitude-related phenomena take place is the fact that associations that occur between two variables measured at the same level of analysis might not be obtained when variables are meas-ured at different levels of analysis. Another example from forgiveness re-search illustrates this point. Snyder, Yamhure, and Heinze (2000) reported that measures of dispositional hope and dispositional forgiveness were mod-erately correlated, but Sandage, Worthington, and Calvert-Minor (2000) found that hope (measured at the dispositional level of analysis) was not cor-related with people's self-reported forgiveness for a specific transgressor. Careful theorizing that takes into account these various levels of analysis will help researchers on the moral and prosocial contours of gratitude to progress more efficiently in developing and testing theory.

CONCLUSION

Perhaps beginning with Cicero, who called gratitude "the parent of the virtues," scholars in the humanities have associated gratitude with morality and prosocial behavior. The limited amount of social scientific research on gratitude that has accumulated over the last century demonstrates these as-sertions to be generally accurate, with some qualifications. To the extent that gratitude causes us to stop and ponder the benevolence of other people, and to the extent to which gratitude actually motivates people to behave proso-cially, gratitude might be thought of as a social resource that is well worth understanding—and perhaps even cultivating—for the development of a so-ciety based on goodwill.

Preparation of this chapter was supported by a grant from the John Templeton Foun-dation, Radnor, Pennsylvania.

References

Aronson, E. (1969). The theory of cognitive dissonance: A current perspective. In L. Berkowitz (Ed.), *Advances in experimental social psychology* (Vol. 4, pp. 1–34). New York: Academic Press.

Bandura, A. (1990). Selective activation and disengagement of moral control. *Journal of Social Issues, 46,* 27–46.

Baron, R. A. (1984). Reducing organizational conflict: An incompatible response approach. *Journal of Applied Psychology, 69,* 272–279.

Bar-Tal, D., Bar-Zohar, Y., Greenberg, M. S., & Hermon, M. (1977). Reciprocity behavior in the relationship between donor and recipient and between harm-doer and victim. *Sociometry, 40,* 293–298.

Batson, C. D., Turk, C. L., Shaw, L. L., & Klein, T. R. (1995). Information function of empathic emotion: Learning that we value the other's welfare. *Journal of Personality and Social Psychology, 68,* 300–313.

Baumgartner-Tramer, F. (1938). "Gratefulness" in children and young people. *Journal of Genetic Psychology, 53,* 53–66.

Becker, J. A., & Smenner, P. C. (1986). The spontaneous use of thank you by preschoolers as a function of sex, socioeconomic status, and listener status. *Language in Society, 15,* 537–546.

Bennett, L., Ross, M. W., & Sunderland, R. (1996). The relationship between recognition, rewards, and burnout in AIDS caregiving. *AIDS Care, 8,* 145–153.

Bernstein, D. M., & Simmons, R. G. (1974). The adolescent kidney donor: The right to give. *American Journal of Psychiatry, 131,* 1338–1343.

Carlson, M., Charlin, V., & Miller, N. (1988). Positive mood and helping behavior: A test of six hypotheses. *Journal of Personality and Social Psychology, 55,* 211–229.

Cicero, M. T. (1851). *The orations of Marcus Tullius Cicero.* Translated by C. D. Younge, Volume III. London: George Bell & Sons.

Clark, H. B., Northrop, J. T., & Barkshire, C. T. (1988). The effects of contingent thank-you notes on case managers' visiting residential clients. *Education and Treatment of Children, 11,* 45–51.

Clark, R. D. (1975). The effects of reinforcement, punishment and dependency on helping behavior. *Bulletin of Personality and Social Psychology, 1,* 596–599.

Deutsch, F. M., & Lamberti, D. M. (1986). Does social approval increase helping? *Personality and Social Psychology Bulletin, 12,* 149–157.

de Waal, F. B. M. (1997). The chimpanzee's service economy: Food for grooming. *Evolution and Human Behavior, 18,* 375–386.

de Waal, F. B. M., & Berger, M. L. (2000). Payment for labour in monkeys. *Nature, 404,* 563.

Epstein, S. (1984). Controversial issues in emotion theory. In P. Shaver (Ed.), *Review of personality and social psychology: Vol. 5. Emotions, relationships, and health* (pp. 64–88). Beverly Hills, CA: Sage.

Farwell, L., & Wohlwend-Lloyd, R. (1998). Narcissistic processes: Optimistic expectations, favorable self-evaluations, and self-enhancing attributions. *Journal of Personality, 66,* 65–83.

Fredrickson, B. L. (1998). What good are positive emotions? *Review of General Psychology, 2,* 300–319.

Gleason, J. B., & Weintraub, S. (1976). The acquisition of routines in child language. *Language in Society, 5,* 129–136.

Goldman, M., Seever, M., & Seever, M. (1982). Social labeling and the foot-in-the-door effect. *Journal of Social Psychology, 117,* 19–23.

Gouldner, A. W. (1960). The norm of reciprocity: A preliminary statement. *American Sociological Review, 25,* 161–178.

Graham, S. (1988). Children's developing understanding of the motivational role of affect: An attributional analysis. *Cognitive Development, 3,* 71–88.

Graham, S., & Barker, G. P. (1990). The down side of help: An attributional-developmental analysis of helping behavior as a low-ability cue. *Journal of Educational Psychology, 82,* 7–14.

Graham, S., Hudley, C., & Williams, E. (1992). Attributional and emotional determinants of aggression among African-American and Latino young adolescents. *Developmental Psychology, 28,* 731–740.

Graziano, W. G., Jensen-Campbell, L. A., & Hair, E. C. (1996). Perceiving interpersonal conflict and reacting to it: The case for agreeableness. *Journal of Personality and Social Psychology, 70,* 820–835.

Greenberg, M. S., & Westcott, D. R. (1983). Indebtedness as a mediator of reactions to aid. In J. D. Fisher, A. Nadler, & B. M. DePaulo (Eds.), *New directions in helping: Recipient reactions to aid* (pp. 85–112). New York: Academic Press.

Harris, M. B. (1972). The effects of performing one altruistic act on the likelihood of performing another. *Journal of Social Psychology, 88,* 65–73.

Harris, P. L., Olthof, T., Meerum Terwogt, M., & Hardman, C. E. (1987). Children's knowledge of the situations that provoke emotion. *International Journal of Behavioral Development, 10,* 319–344.

Hegtvedt, K. A. (1990). The effects of relationship structure on emotional responses to inequity. *Social Psychology Quarterly, 53,* 214–228.

Heider, F. (1958). *The psychology of interpersonal relations.* New York: Wiley.

Kunda, Z. (1990). The case for motivated reasoning. *Psychological Bulletin, 108,* 480–498.

Lane, J., & Anderson, N. H. (1976). Integration of intention and outcome in moral judgment. *Memory and Cognition, 4,* 1–5.

Lazarus, R. S., & Lazarus, B. N. (1994). *Passion and reason: Making sense of our emotions.* New York: Oxford University Press.

Maheux, B., Legault, C., & Lambert, J. (1989). Increasing response rates in physicians' mail surveys: An experimental study. *American Journal of Public Health, 79,* 638–639.

McCullough, M. E., Emmons, R. A., & Tsang, J. (2002). The grateful disposition: A conceptual and empirical topography. *Journal of Personality and Social Psychology, 82,* 112–127.

McCullough, M. E., Hoyt, W. T., & Rachal, K. C. (2000). What we know (and need to know) about assessing forgiveness constructs. In M. E. McCullough, K. I. Pargament, & C. E. Thoresen (Eds.), *Forgiveness: Theory, research, and practice* (pp. 65–88). New York: Guilford.

McCullough, M. E., Kilpatrick, S. D., Emmons, R. A., & Larson, D. B. (2001). Is gratitude a moral affect? *Psychological Bulletin, 127*(2), 249–266.

McCullough, M. E., Rachal, K. C., Sandage, S. J., Worthington, E. L., Jr., Brown, S. W., & Hight, T. L. (1998). Interpersonal forgiving in close relationships: II. Theoretical elaboration and measurement. *Journal of Personality and Social Psychology, 75,* 1586–1603.

McCullough, M. E., & Witvliet, C. V. (2001). The psychology of forgiveness. In C. R. Snyder & S. Lopez (Eds.), *Handbook of positive psychology* (pp. 446–458). New York: Oxford.

McCullough, M. E., Worthington, E. L., Jr., & Rachal, K. C. (1997). Interpersonal forgiving in close relationships. *Journal of Personality and Social Psychology, 73,* 321–336.

McGovern, L. P., Ditzian, J. L., & Taylor, S. P. (1975). The effect of positive reinforcement on helping with cost. *Psychonomic Society Bulletin, 5,* 421–423.

Moore, D. W. (1996). *Americans most thankful for family and health: Young also thankful for career/job.* Unpublished report, Gallup Organization, Princeton, NJ.

Moss, M. K., & Page, R. A. (1972). Reinforcement and helping behavior. *Journal of Applied Social Psychology, 2,* 360–371.

Okamoto, S. (1992). [Linguistic expressions of gratitude (2)]. *Bulletin of the Faculty of Letters of Aichi Gakuin University, 20,* 35–44.

Okamoto, S., & Robinson, W. P. (1997). Determinants of gratitude expressions in England. *Journal of Language and Social Psychology, 16,* 411–433.

Ortony, A., Clore, G. L., & Collins, A. (1987). *The cognitive structure of emotions.* New York: Cambridge University Press.

Overwalle, F. V., Mervielde, I., & De Schuyter, J. (1995). Structural modeling of the relationships between attributional dimensions, emotions, and performance of college freshmen. *Cognition and Emotion, 9,* 59–85.

Peterson, B. E., & Stewart, A. J. (1996). Antecedents and contexts of generativity motivation at midlife. *Psychology and Aging, 11,* 21–33.

Preyer, M. (1933). The linguistic evolution of the 9-year-old child and the reading books. *Gyermek, 25,* 19–20.

Raskin, R. A., & Hall, C. S. (1979). The Narcissistic Personality Inventory. *Psychological Reports, 45,* 159–161.

Rind, B., & Bordia, P. (1995). Effect of server's "thank you" and personalization on restaurant tipping. *Journal of Applied Social Psychology, 25,* 745–751.

Roseman, I. J. (1991). Appraisal determinants of discrete emotions. *Cognition and Emotion, 5,* 161–200.

Russell, J. A., & Paris, F. A. (1994). Do children acquire concepts for complex emotions abruptly? *International Journal of Behavioral Development, 17,* 349–365.

Sandage, S. J., Worthington, E. L., Jr., & Calvert-Minor, D. N. (2000, August). *Hope and forgiveness: Initial correlations, directions for future research, and an intervention with couples.* Paper presented at the 108th annual convention of the American Psychological Association, Washington, DC.

Saucier, G., & Goldberg, L. R. (1998). What is beyond the Big Five? *Journal of Personality, 66,* 495–524.

Schwartz, B. (1967). The social psychology of the gift. *American Journal of Sociology, 73*, 1–11.

Schwarz, N. (1990). Feeling as information: Informational and motivational functions of affective states. In E. T. Higgins & R. M. Sorrentino (Eds.), *Handbook of motivation and cognition: Vol. 2. Foundations of social behavior* (pp. 527–561). New York: Guilford.

Shapiro, E. G. (1984). Help seeking: Why people don't. *Research in the Sociology of Organizations, 3*, 213–236.

Simmel, G. (1950). *The sociology of Georg Simmel.* Glencoe, IL: Free Press. (Original work published 1908)

Smith, A. (1976). *The theory of moral sentiments* (6th ed.). Oxford, UK: Clarendon Press. (Original work published 1790)

Snyder, C. R., Yamhure, L. C., & Heinze, L. (2000, August). *The tranquility trilogy: High forgiveness, high hope, and low hostility.* Paper presented at the 108th annual convention of the American Psychological Association, Washington, DC.

Sommers, S., & Kosmitzki, C. (1988). Emotion and social context: An American-German comparison. *British Journal of Social Psychology, 27*, 35–49.

Sowa, J. (1981). The ability to define moral concepts by the blind and seeing aged from 8 to 15. *Roczniki Filozoficzne: Psychologia, 29*, 123–139.

Steele, C. M. (1988). The psychology of self-affirmation: Sustaining the integrity of the self. In L. Berkowitz (Ed.), *Advances in experimental social psychology* (Vol. 21, pp. 261–302). New York: Academic Press.

Stein, M. (1989). Gratitude and attitude: A note on emotional welfare. *Social Psychology Quarterly, 52*, 242–248.

Tangney, J. P., Fee, R., Reinsmith, C., Boone, A. L., & Lee, N. (1999, August). Individual differences in the propensity to forgive. Paper presented at the annual meeting of the American Psychological Association, Boston.

Teigen, K. H. (1997). Luck, envy, and gratitude: It could have been different. *Scandinavian Journal of Psychology, 38*, 313–323.

Tesser, A., Gatewood, R., & Driver, M. (1968). Some determinants of gratitude. *Journal of Personality and Social Psychology, 9*, 233–236.

Trivers, R. L. (1971). The evolution of reciprocal altruism. *Quarterly Review of Biology, 46*, 35–57.

Tsang, J. (2002). Moral rationalization and the integration of situational factors and psychological processes in immoral behavior. *Review of General Psychology, 6*, 25–50.

Veisson, M. (1999). Depression symptoms and emotional states in parents of disabled and nondisabled children. *Social Behavior and Personality, 27*, 87–97.

Walster, E., Berscheid, E., & Walster, G. W. (1973). New directions in equity research. *Journal of Personality and Social Psychology, 25*, 151–176.

Weiner, B. (1985). An attributional theory of achievement motivation and emotion. *Psychological Review, 92*, 548–573.

Weiner, B., Russell, D., & Lerman, D. (1979). The cognition-emotion process in achievement-related contexts. *Journal of Personality and Social Psychology, 37*, 1211–1220.

Wilke, H., & Lanzetta, J. T. (1982). The obligation to help: The effects of amount of prior help on subsequent helping behavior. *Journal of Experimental Social Psychology, 6,* 483–493.

Zaleski, Z. (1988). Attributions and emotions related to future goal attainment. *Journal of Educational Psychology, 80,* 563–568.

PART III

Perspectives from Emotion Theory

8 Gratitude, Like Other Positive Emotions, Broadens and Builds

Barbara L. Fredrickson

What good is feeling grateful? Certainly people describe experiences of gratitude as pleasant (Mayer, Salovey, Gomberg-Kaufman, & Blainey, 1991; Reisenzein, 1994). Plus, as Roberts (chap. 4, this volume) contends, experiences of gratitude mitigate against aversive experiences such as resentment, envy, and regret. But beyond lifting people's spirits in the moment and signaling the absence of negative emotions, does gratitude have any lasting benefits? Classic and contemporary analyses of gratitude suggest that it does. Reviewing the classic writings and synthesizing them with contemporary empirical findings, McCullough, Kilpatrick, Emmons, and Larson (2001; see also McCullough & Tsang, chap. 7, this volume) suggested that the positive emotion of gratitude has three moral functions: It serves as a moral barometer, a moral motivator, and a moral reinforcer. I concur with their analysis of gratitude as a moral emotion and use this chapter to push the analysis of gratitude's lasting benefits a bit further. To this end, I situate the emotion of gratitude in the context of a broader conceptualization of positive emotions. In doing so, I explore the lasting benefits of people's fleeting experiences of gratitude and other positive emotions—benefits ranging from personal and social development, to individual health and well-being, and community strength and harmony.

CURRENT PERSPECTIVES ON EMOTIONS

A brief review of current perspectives on emotions provides an important backdrop. Working definitions of emotions vary somewhat across researchers. Even so, consensus is emerging that emotions are best conceptualized as multicomponent response tendencies that unfold over relatively short time spans. Typically, an emotion process begins with an individual's assessment of the personal meaning of some antecedent event—what Lazarus (1991) called the person-environment relationship, or adaptational encounter. This appraisal process may be either conscious or unconscious, and it triggers a cascade of response tendencies manifested across loosely coupled component systems, such as subjective experience, facial expression, and physiological changes. Although related, emotions differ from moods in that they are *about* some personally meaningful circumstance (i.e., they have an object), whereas moods are often free-floating or objectless (Oatley & Jenkins, 1996). Emotions also differ from affective traits such as hostility, neuroticism, or optimism: Enduring affective traits predispose individuals toward experiencing certain emotions, and so affective traits and emotional states represent different levels of analysis (Rosenberg, 1998). Whereas other authors in this volume consider gratitude an enduring disposition, virtue, or affective trait (McCullough & Tsang, chap. 7; Roberts, chap. 4), my own conceptualization considers gratitude to be a temporary emotional state.

Current models of emotions typically aim to describe the form and function of emotions in general. Despite this aim, many models are formulated around prototypic and negative emotions such as fear and anger. For instance, key to many theorists' models of emotions is the idea that emotions are, by definition, associated with *specific action tendencies* (Frijda, 1986; Frijda, Kuipers, & Schure, 1989; Lazarus, 1991; Levenson, 1994; Oatley & Jenkins, 1996; Tooby & Cosmides, 1990). Fear, for example, is linked with the urge to escape, anger with the urge to attack, disgust with the urge to expel, and so on. No theorist argues that people invariably act out these urges when feeling particular emotions. But rather, people's ideas about possible courses of action narrow to a specific set of behavioral options. A key idea in these models is that specific action tendencies are what make emotions evolutionarily adaptive: These are among the actions that worked best in getting our ancestors out of life-or-death situations (Tooby & Cosmides, 1990). Another key idea is that specific action tendencies and physiological changes go hand in hand. So, for example, when you have an urge to escape when feeling fear, your body reacts by mobilizing appropriate autonomic support for the possibility of running (Levenson, 1994).

Although specific action tendencies have been invoked to describe the form and function of positive emotions as well, the action tendencies identified for positive emotions are notably vague and underspecified (Fredrickson & Levenson, 1998). Joy, for instance, is linked with aimless activation, interest with attending, and contentment with inactivity (Frijda, 1986). These tendencies, I have argued, are far too general to be called specific (Fredrickson, 1998). They more resemble generic urges to do anything, or to do nothing, than urges to do something quite specific, like flee, attack, or spit. This strategy of squeezing positive emotions into the same theoretical mold as negative emotions has not produced much understanding or appreciation of positive emotions.

THE BROADEN-AND-BUILD THEORY OF POSITIVE EMOTIONS

Noting that traditional models based on specific action tendencies did not do justice to positive emotions, I developed an alternative model for the positive emotions that better captures their unique effects. I call this the broaden-and-build theory of positive emotions (Fredrickson, 1998, 2001), because positive emotions appear to *broaden* people's momentary thought-action repertoires and *build* their enduring personal resources.

I contrast this new theory with traditional models based on specific action tendencies. Specific action tendencies, in my view, work well to describe the form and function of negative emotions and should be retained for models of this subset of emotions. Without loss of theoretical nuance, a specific action tendency can be redescribed as the outcome of a psychological process that narrows a person's momentary thought-action repertoire by calling to mind an urge to act in a particular way (e.g., escape, attack, expel). In a life-threatening situation, a narrowed thought-action repertoire promotes quick and decisive action that carries direct and immediate benefit. Specific action tendencies called forth by negative emotions represent the sort of actions that worked best to save our ancestors' lives and limbs in similar situations.

Yet positive emotions seldom occur in life-threatening situations. Most often, they are experienced when people feel safe and satiated (Fredrickson, 1998). As such, a psychological process that narrows a person's momentary thought-action repertoire to promote quick and decisive action may not be needed. Instead, I have argued (Fredrickson, 1998)—and demonstrated empirically (Fredrickson & Branigan, 2001b)—that positive emotions have a complementary effect: they *broaden* people's momentary thought-action repertoires, widening the array of the thoughts and actions that come to mind. Joy, for instance, appears to broaden by creating the urge to play, push the limits, and be creative, urges evident not only in social and physical behavior, but also in intellectual and artistic behavior. Interest, a phenomenologically distinct positive emotion, appears to broaden by creating the urge to explore, take in new information and experiences, and expand the self in the process. Pride, a distinct positive emotion that follows personal achievements, appears to broaden by creating urges to share news of the achievement with others, as well as to envision even greater achievements in the future. Contentment, a fourth distinct positive emotion, appears to broaden by creating the urge to take time to savor current life circumstances and integrate these circumstances into new views of self and the world. These various thought-action tendencies—to play, to explore, to envision future achievements, and to savor and integrate—represent ways that positive emotions broaden habitual modes of thinking or acting. In general terms, then, positive emotions appear to "enlarge" the cognitive context (Isen, 1987), an effect recently linked to increases in brain dopamine levels (Ashby, Isen, & Turken, 1999).

Whereas the narrowed mindsets of negative emotions carry direct and immediate adaptive benefits in situations that threaten survival, the broadened mindsets of positive emotions, which occur when people feel safe and satiated, are beneficial in other ways. Specifically, I have argued that these broadened mindsets carry indirect and long-term adaptive benefits because broadening *builds* enduring personal resources (Fredrickson, 1998).

Take play, the urge associated with joy, as an example. Animal research has found that specific forms of chasing play evident in juveniles of a species—such as running into a flexible sapling or branch and catapulting oneself in an unexpected direction—are reenacted in adults of that species exclusively during predator avoidance (Dolhinow, 1987). Such correspondences between juvenile play maneuvers and adult survival maneuvers suggest that juvenile play builds enduring physical resources (Boulton & Smith, 1992; Caro, 1988). Play also builds enduring social resources. Social play, with its shared amusement, excitement, and smiles, builds lasting social bonds and attachments (Aron, Norman, Aron, McKenna, & Heyman, 2000; Lee, 1983; Simons, McCluskey-Fawcett, & Papini, 1986), which can become the locus of subsequent social support. Childhood play also builds enduring intellectual resources by increasing levels of creativity (Sherrod & Singer, 1989), creating the theory of mind necessary for empathy and gratitude (Leslie, 1987), and fueling brain development (Panksepp, 1998). Each of these links between play and resource building suggest that play may be essential to child development. Indeed, Panksepp has argued that "youth may have evolved to give complex organisms time to play" (1998, p. 96).

Like the play prompted by joy, the exploration prompted by the positive emotion of interest creates knowledge and intellectual complexity (Csikszentmihalyi & Rathunde, 1998; Izard, 1977; Renninger, Hidi, & Krapp, 1992). Similarly, envisioning future achievements during experiences of pride fuels self-esteem and achievement motivation (Lewis, 1993). And the savoring and integrating prompted by contentment produce self-insight and alter worldviews (Izard, 1977). Each of these phenomenologically distinct positive emotions shares the feature of augmenting individuals' personal resources, ranging from physical and intellectual resources to psychological and social resources (for more detailed reviews see Fredrickson, 1998, 2000a, 2000b, 2001, 2002a; Fredrickson & Branigan, 2001a).

It is important to note that the personal resources accrued during states of positive emotions are durable—they outlast the transient emotional states that led to their acquisition. By consequence, then, the often incidental effect of experiencing a positive emotion is an increase in one's personal resources. These resources can function as reserves to be drawn on later, to improve coping and odds of survival. Indeed, a recent study of elderly nuns found that those who expressed the most positive emotions in early adulthood lived up to 10 years longer than those who expressed the least positive emotions (Danner, Snowdon, & Friesen, 2001; for related findings, see Ostir, Markides, Black, & Goodwin, 2000).

In sum, the broaden-and-build theory describes the form of positive emotions in terms of broadened thought-action repertoires and describes their function in terms of building enduring personal resources. In doing so, the theory provides a new perspective on the evolved adaptive significance of positive emotions. Those of our ancestors who succumbed to the urges sparked by positive emotions—to play, explore, and so on—would have by consequence accrued more personal resources. When these same ancestors later faced inevitable threats to life and limb, their greater personal resources would have translated into greater odds of survival, and in turn, greater odds of living long enough to reproduce. To the extent, then, that the capacity to experience positive emotions is genetically encoded, this capacity, through the process of natural selection, would have become part of our universal human nature. Supporting this evolutionary account, the capacity to experience gratitude and other positive emotions is evident among nonhuman primates as well (de Waal, 1997; de Waal & Berger, 2000; see also Bonnie & de Waal, chap. 11, this volume).

GRATITUDE BROADENS AND BUILDS

In earlier articles and chapters, I have provided detailed analyses of several specific positive emotions, first including joy, interest, contentment, and love (Fredrickson, 1998; for an extended analysis of contentment, see Fredrickson, 2000a), and later, pride (Fredrickson & Branigan, 2001a). These analyses show that each of these phenomenologically distinct positive emotions conforms to the broaden-and-build theory. Recently, Haidt (2000; see also

Haidt, 2003) has provided a detailed analysis of the positive emotion of elevation, arguing that it too conforms to the broaden-and-build theory. In this chapter, I provide a comparable analysis of gratitude, describing the circumstances that tend to elicit gratitude, apparent changes in its associated momentary thought-action repertoire, and the consequences or outcomes of these changes.

Gratitude arises when an individual (beneficiary) perceives that another person (benefactor) or source (e.g., God, luck, fate) has intentionally acted to improve the beneficiary's well-being (for reviews, see Emmons & Shelton, 2002; Lazarus & Lazarus, 1994; McCullough et al., 2001; McCullough & Tsang, chap. 7, this volume). Gratitude, according to Lazarus and Lazarus (1994), also requires the capacity to empathize with others. Beneficiaries experience gratitude, Lazarus and Lazarus suggest, only when they recognize and appreciate that the benefactor has expended effort to give them an altruistic gift. Drawing from McCullough and colleagues' reviews, the momentary thought-action tendency sparked by gratitude appears to be the urge to behave prosocially oneself, either toward the benefactor, toward others, or both (i.e., gratitude functions as a moral motive). I conceptualize this thought-action tendency as broadened rather than narrowed, because it does not appear to steer grateful individuals simply to repay the benefactor in a tit-for-tat fashion or to mimic and reciprocate the benefactor's exact prosocial act (a point also raised by Roberts, chap. 4, this volume). Rather, grateful individuals appear to creatively consider a wide range of prosocial actions as possible reflections of their gratitude. Perhaps reflecting the creativity invested in returning gifts, Komter (chap. 10, this volume) describes how the Maori, a native tribe of New Zealand, reciprocate gifts by making presents of some part of themselves. Although the empirical evidence supporting the motivational function of gratitude is sparse (McCullough et al., 2001), the available studies have supported the claim that the prosocial reciprocity inspired by gratitude is creative. For instance, in a longitudinal study of women who graduated from Radcliffe College, B. E. Peterson and Stewart (1996) found a positive association between being mentored in early adulthood (by people other than parents and significant others) and contributing to the welfare of others in a generative way in midlife, a finding they speculate may be mediated by gratitude. Likewise, in a study of children's beliefs about gratitude, Graham (1988) found a positive association between a child's feeling of gratitude toward a team captain for choosing him or her to play on a sports team and the expectation that the chosen child would later reciprocate by giving the captain a gift. These two findings suggest that gratitude does not lead to mindless tit-for-tat behavior (e.g., you scratch my back, I'll scratch yours). Instead, grateful people appear creative as they formulate actions that promote the well-being of other people, including, but not limited, to the original benefactor.

So gratitude appears to broaden people's modes of thinking as they creatively consider a wide array of actions that might benefit others. Does this particular positive emotion also build psychological and social resources? Theoretical writings on gratitude suggest that it does (again, for a reviews, see Emmons & Shelton, 2002; McCullough et al., 2001; McCullough & Tsang, chap. 7, this volume). Although grateful individuals most typically act prosocially simply to express their gratitude, over time the actions inspired by gratitude build and strengthen social bonds and friendships (see Emmons & Shelton, 2002; Harpham, chap. 2, this volume; Komter, chap. 10, this volume). Gratitude, according to Trivers (1971), fuels reciprocal altruism, which can be viewed as an index of enduring friendships and alliances. (For evidence of gratitude and reciprocal altruism in nonhuman primates, see Bonnie & de Waal, chap. 11, this volume; de Waal, 1997; de Waal & Berger, 2000.) Moreover, people who regularly feel grateful, McCullough and colleagues (2001; McCullough & Tsang, chap. 7, this volume) suggest, are likely to feel loved and cared for by others. So gratitude appears to build friendships and other social bonds. These are social resources because, in times of need, these social bonds can become the locus of consequential social support. In addition to building individuals' social resources, gratitude also appears to build communities' social resources. Smith (1790/1976) held that gratitude helps to maintain a society based on goodwill (see Harpham, chap. 2, this volume; Komter, chap. 10, this volume). And Simmel (1908/1950) suggested that when individuals feel grateful to people whom they do not know personally (e.g., artists, politicians, or poets) for having performed something beneficial for them and others, their gratitude serves to link individuals to society.

Simmel (1908/1950) also suggested that people experience gratitude even when they realize that the gift given to them cannot be reciprocated in any manner (e.g., the gift of life, the gift of the planet). Under these circumstances, gratitude motivates permanent faithfulness and obligation, and, as suggested by Roberts (1991; chap. 4, this volume), a willingness to remain indebted forever, coupled with strong feelings of appreciation. Such lifelong and devoted relationships not only characterize some children's relationships with their parents, but also some believers' relationships with God (Schimmel, chap. 3, this volume). A handful of studies have underscored the centrality of gratitude in spirituality. For example, in a study of nuns and priests, Samuels and Lester (1985) found that gratitude and love were the most frequent of 50 distinct emotions felt toward God. Similarly, a national survey of adults and teens found that 78% of teens and 89% of adults express gratitude to God regularly (G. H. Gallup, cited in McCullough et al., 2001). Colorfully illustrating the important role of gratitude in spiritual practice, Piper (1996) described the weight that God places on gratitude when deciding people's fates:

> When every human being stands before God on the day of judgment, God would not have to use one sentence of Scripture to show us our guilt and the appropriateness of our condemnation. He would need only to ask three questions: (1) Was it not plain in nature that everything you had was a gift, and that you were dependent on your Maker for life and breath and everything? (2) Did not the judicial sentiment in your own heart always hold other people guilty when they lacked the gratitude they should have had in response to a kindness you performed? (3) Has your life been filled with gratitude and trust toward me in proportion to my generosity and authority? Case closed. (Piper, 1996, p. 59)

Analyses of multiple religious traditions reveal that gratitude consistently features prominently. (For a review of the role of gratitude in Judaism, Christianity, and Islam, see Emmons & Crumpler, 2000; for a review that also targets Buddhism and Hinduism, see Carman & Streng, 1989.)

So gratitude, existing theoretical accounts suggest, can be viewed as building a variety of personal and social resources. It builds and strengthens friendships and other social bonds, it builds and strengthens civil communities, and it builds and strengthens spirituality. Drawing more directly from the broaden-and-build theory, I add to this list that gratitude also builds people's skills for loving and showing appreciation. That is, to the extent that gratitude broadens people's momentary thought-action repertoires, it prompts them to stretch themselves to think creatively about how to repay kindnesses. Those creative efforts will yield new ideas about how people might make a gift of themselves (e.g., using expressive touch or words, caring for others in need). Once generated and practiced, these new methods of repaying kindness can become lasting skills in a person's repertoire for expressing love and kindness. So although gratitude motivates people to express their appreciation, people may build up their more general skills for loving through the process of thinking broadly about how to repay kindness.

It is important that all the goods that gratitude builds—close friendships, civil communities, spiritual practices, and skills for loving—are enduring resources in the sense that they function as reserves that can be drawn on in times of need. Those of our ancestors who accrued more of these resources would by consequence have had increased odds of surviving long enough to reproduce.

GRATITUDE AND OTHER POSITIVE EMOTIONS TRANSFORM INDIVIDUALS

The broaden-and-build theory is not limited to describing the evolutionary significance of positive emotions for our ancestors. It also points to the potential significance that positive emotions have in contemporary society. In particular, the theory underscores the relationship between positive emotions and individual growth and development. Through experiences of positive emotions, individuals can transform themselves, becoming more creative, knowledgeable, resilient, socially integrated, and healthy. Individuals who regularly experience positive emotions, then, are not stagnant. Instead, they continually grow toward optimal functioning. How is this continued growth sustained? Positive emotions provide the fuel, creating a self-sustaining system. In particular, positive emotions generate what I have called an upward spiral toward optimal functioning and enhanced emotional well-being (Fredrickson, 2001; Fredrickson & Joiner, 2002). Positive emotions achieve these beneficial outcomes by broadening individuals' habitual modes of thinking and action.

For example, to the extent that positive emotions broaden the scope of cognition and enable flexible and creative thinking, they also facilitate coping with stress and adversity (Aspinwall, 1998, 2001; Folkman, 1997; Folkman & Moskowitz, 2000; Fredrickson, Mancuso, Branigan, & Tugade, 2000; Lazarus, Kanner, & Folkman, 1980; Tugade & Fredrickson, 2002). Indeed, the broaden-and-build theory implies that if negative emotions narrow the momentary thought-action repertoire and positive emotions broaden that same repertoire, then positive emotions ought to function as efficient antidotes for the lingering effects of negative emotions. In other words, positive emotions should have an *undoing effect* on the lingering aftereffects of negative emotions (Fredrickson & Levenson, 1998; Fredrickson et al., 2000).

The basic observation that positive and negative emotions (or key components of them) are somehow incompatible—or cannot fully and simultaneously coexist—is not new. This has been demonstrated in earlier work on anxiety disorders (e.g., systematic desensitization; Wolpe, 1958), motivation (e.g., opponent-process theory; Solomon & Corbit, 1974), and aggression (e.g., principle of incompatible responses; Baron, 1976). Even so, the mechanism ultimately responsible for this incompatibility has not been adequately identified. Broadening may turn out to be the mechanism. By broadening a person's momentary thought-action repertoire, a positive emotion may loosen the hold that a negative emotion has gained on that person's mind and body by dissipating or undoing preparation for specific action. In other words, negative and positive emotions may be fundamentally incompatible because a person's momentary thought-action repertoire cannot be simultaneously narrow and broad.

One marker of the narrowed thought-action repertoire called forth by negative emotions is heightened cardiovascular activity. Invoking positive emotions following negative emotions, then, should speed recovery from this cardiovascular reactivity, returning the body to more mid-range levels of activation. By accelerating cardiovascular recovery, positive emotions create the bodily context suitable for pursuing the wider array of thoughts and actions called forth.

My collaborators and I have tested the undoing effect by first inducing a high-arousal negative emotion in all participants (i.e., fear or anxiety), and then immediately, by random assignment, inducing either mild joy, contentment, neutrality, or sadness by showing short, emotionally evocative film clips. We predicted that those who experienced positive emotions on the heels of a high-arousal negative emotion would show the fastest cardiovascular recovery. We tested this by measuring the time elapsed from the start of the randomly assigned film until the cardiovascular reactions induced by the initial negative emotion returned to baseline levels. The results support the undoing effect: Participants in the two positive emotion conditions (mild joy and contentment) exhibited faster cardiovascular recovery than those in the neutral control condition, and faster than those in the sadness condition (Fredrickson et al., 2000, Study 1; see also Fredrickson & Levenson, 1998). It is also important that, in another study (Fredrickson et al., 2000, Study 2), we found that the positive and neutral films used in this research, when viewed following a resting baseline, elicited virtually no cardiovascular reactivity whatsoever. So although the positive and neutral films do not differ in what they *do* to the cardiovascular system, they do differ in what they can *undo* in this system. Two distinct types of positive emotions—mild joy and contentment—share the ability to undo the lingering cardiovascular aftereffects of negative emotions, a finding consistent with the idea that positive emotions broaden people's thought-action repertoires.

In subsequent work, my colleagues and I (Tugade & Fredrickson, 2002) have discovered individual differences in people's abilities to harness this beneficial undoing effect of positive emotions. Specifically, we have found that people who score high on a self-report measure of psychological resilience (Block & Kremen, 1996) show faster cardiovascular recovery following negative emotional arousal than do those who score low on this measure. Moreover, this faster recovery is mediated by the positive emotions that highly resilient people bring to the situation. Resilient individuals experience more positive emotions than do their less-resilient peers, both at ambient levels and in response to stressful circumstances. These positive emotions, in turn, allow them to bounce back quickly from negative emotional arousal (Tugade & Fredrickson, 2002). Moving beyond the laboratory, we found that resilient individuals reported fewer symptoms of depression and trauma following the terrorist attacks on the United States of September 11th, 2001. More strikingly, we found that resilient individuals experienced more positive emotions in the midst of this national crisis, and that these positive emotions fully accounted for the relation between resilience and reduced depression (Fredrickson, Tugade, Waugh, & Larkin, 2003). In effect, then, resilient individuals appear to be expert users of the undoing effect of positive emotions.

Further spotlighting the potential role of broadened thinking in the link between positive emotions and improved coping, other studies have shown that people who were bereaved and yet nonetheless experienced positive emotions were more likely to develop long-term plans and goals. Together with positive emotions, having plans and goals predicted greater psychological well-being 12 months after bereavement (Stein, Folkman, Trabasso, & Richards, 1997). Thus, the effects of positive emotions appear to accumulate and compound over time. These emotions not only make people feel good in the present, but they also increase the likelihood that people will function well and feel good in the future. By broadening people's modes of thinking and action, positive emotions improve coping and build resilience, improvements that in turn predict future experiences of positive emotions.

The cognitive literature on depression already has documented a downward spiral in which depressed mood and the narrowed, pessimistic thinking it engenders influence one another reciprocally, leading to ever-worsening functioning and moods, and even clinical levels of depression (C. Peterson & Seligman, 1984). In contrast, the broaden-and-build theory predicts a comparable upward spiral in which positive emotions and the broadened thinking they engender also influence one another reciprocally, leading to appreciable increases in functioning and well-being. (For a complementary discussion of downward and upward spirals, see Aspinwall, 2001.)

Thomas Joiner and I conducted a prospective study to demonstrate that positive emotions do indeed trigger such upward spirals (Fredrickson & Joiner, 2002). In a study of college students, we assessed positive and negative emotions, as well as a concept we call broad-minded coping, at two time points, 5 weeks apart. Our aim was to predict changes in positive emotions and broad-minded coping over time. First, we found that, controlling for initial levels of broad-minded coping, initial levels of positive emotion predicted improvements in broad-minded coping from Time 1 to Time 2. These improvements in broad-minded coping in turn predicted subsequent increases in positive emotions. Next, we found evidence for the reciprocal relations. Controlling for initial levels of positive emotion, initial levels of broad-minded coping predicted improvements in positive emotions from Time 1 to

Time 2. These improvements in positive emotions in turn predicted subsequent increases in broad-minded coping. These findings suggest that, over time, positive emotions and broad-minded coping mutually build on one another, leading to improved coping skills and triggering an upward spiral toward enhanced emotional well-being (Fredrickson & Joiner, 2002).

Upward spirals fueled specifically by the positive emotion of gratitude have also been demonstrated. In a study of the daily emotions, physical symptoms, and health behaviors of college students, Emmons and McCullough (2003, study 1) randomly assigned students to one of three experimental groups. Each week, one group recorded five major events that most affected them during the week. The second group recorded five hassles or stressors that occurred in their lives during the week. The third group recorded five things in their lives for which they were grateful. Results showed numerous beneficial effects unique to participants in the gratitude group: Those who practiced gratitude reported more progress on their goals, fewer physical complaints, more frequent physical exercise, more optimism, and higher overall well-being. So, feeling the pleasant emotion of gratitude in the short run led to more optimal functioning and emotional well-being in the long run.

Studies of the physiological effects of positive emotions closely related to gratitude—namely, appreciation and compassion—suggest that reliable changes in cardiovascular and immune functioning may underlie the upward spiral evident in Emmons & McCullough's (2003) work. In a study comparing heart rate variability in individuals who experienced either anger or appreciation (McCraty, Atkinson, Tiller, Rein, & Watkins, 1995; see also McCraty, chap. 12, this volume), McCraty and colleagues found that appreciation increased parasympathetic activity, a change thought to be beneficial in controlling stress and hypertension. This evidence suggests that gratitude and appreciation might join the set of positive emotions that carry the cardiovascular undoing effect noted earlier (Fredrickson et al., 2000). In related work, the same authors reported that appreciation produces entrainment across various autonomic measures (e.g., heart rate variability, pulse transit time, and respiration rate; McCraty, chap. 12, this volume; Tiller, McCraty, Atkinson, 1996) and that compassion increases immune functioning (McCraty, chap. 12, this volume; Rein, Atkinson, & McCraty, 1995).

GRATITUDE AND OTHER POSITIVE EMOTIONS TRANSFORM ORGANIZATIONS AND COMMUNITIES

So far, I have described how positive emotions, through the psychological mechanism of broadening, can transform people into being more creative, effective, socially integrated, and healthy. In short, positive emotions help people to thrive. I shift now from individuals to social groups, both organizations and communities. The broaden-and-build theory also illuminates ways that positive emotions transform these social collectives, helping them to thrive as well.

First, it is notable that social groups provide recurring contexts in which individuals can experience positive emotions. Many positive emotions have distinctly social origins, and people generally feel good when interacting with others (Watson, Clark, McIntyre, & Hamaker, 1992). Going to work, for instance, gives people reliable social contact that triggers positive emotions. In these ways, groups and organizations can trigger positive emotions in individuals, with all the beneficial repercussions described earlier. But how do positive emotions experienced in groups transform organizations and the broader community?

Organizational and community transformation occurs because each person's positive emotions can reverberate through others. In part, this is because emotions are contagious (Hatfield, Cacioppo, & Rapson, 1993). Experimental studies have shown that one person's expression of positive emotion, through processes of mimicry and facial feedback, can produce experiences of positive emotion in those with whom they interact (Hatfield et al., 1993; Lundqvist & Dimberg, 1995). Organizational leaders' positive emotions may be especially contagious. Studies have shown, for instance, that a leader's positive emotions predict the performance of their entire group (George, 1995). Another and perhaps more critical way that positive emotions spread through groups and organizations is by creating chains of events that carry positive meaning for others.

Take helpfulness as an example. Social psychological experiments have shown that people induced to feel positive emotions become more helpful to others than those in neutral emotional states (for a review, see Isen, 1987). Building on this experimental work, organizational field studies have demonstrated that salespeople who experience more positive emotions at work are more helpful to their customers (George, 1991). This occurs because salespeople experiencing positive emotions are more flexible and creative, and more empathic and respectful (George, 1998). Being helpful not only springs from positive emotional states but can produce positive emotions as well. The person who gives help, for instance, may afterward feel proud of his or her chosen actions. Experiences of pride, I have argued (Fredrickson & Branigan, 2001a), not only create momentary boosts in pleasure and self-esteem, but also prompt people to envision future and more significant achievements in similar domains. Thus, to the extent that helping others brings pride, it may fuel the motivation to help again in the future.

In addition to the positive emotions experienced by the person who gives help, the person who receives help is likely to feel the complementary positive emotion of gratitude. Gratitude, as we have seen, not only feels good, but also produces a cascade of beneficial social outcomes, because it reflects, motivates, and reinforces moral social actions in both the giver and recipient of help (McCullough et al., 2001; McCullough & Tsang, chap. 7, this volume). The feeling of gratitude, McCullough and colleagues argue, reflects or identifies moral action because it surfaces when individuals acknowledge that another has been helpful to them. It motivates moral action because grateful people often feel the urge to repay in some manner those who have helped them. Finally, gratitude reinforces moral behavior because giving thanks or acknowledgment rewards help-givers, making them feel appreciated and more likely to give help in the future.

Added to the positive emotions experienced by the givers and recipients of help, people who merely witness or hear about a helpful interchange may experience positive emotions as well. These onlookers, according to Haidt (2000, 2003), often experience the positive emotion of elevation. The momentary thought-action tendency sparked by elevation, according to Haidt (2000), is a generalized desire to become a better person, and to perform helpful acts oneself. As for gratitude, the thought-action tendency sparked by elevation is broadened rather than narrowed, because it does not steer elevated individuals simply to mimic the helpful acts they have witnessed, but rather to creatively consider a wide range of helpful acts as paths toward becoming more moral people. Experiences of elevation, then, carry the potential to change people as well organizations and communities. To the extent that people act on the urges sparked by elevation, they may reach their goal of becoming better, more moral persons. Also, when others in turn witness the helpful acts inspired by elevation, they too may experience elevation and its beneficial repercussions. As Haidt (2000) put it, "If elevation increases the likelihood that a witness to good deeds will soon become a doer of good deeds, then elevation sets up the possibility for the same sort of 'upward spiral' for a group that Fredrickson (2000a) describes for the individual" (p. 4). As this cycle continues, organizations and communities are transformed to be become ever more compassionate and harmonious.

This analysis, though centered on helpfulness, illustrates how gratitude and related positive emotions might spread through organizations and communities, and how their effects might accumulate and compound at the group level. Complementing this analysis, other research suggests that positive emotions, including gratitude, help to curb organizational conflict by promoting constructive interpersonal engagement (for a review, see Baron, 1993). It is important to note that positive emotions propagate in groups and communities not simply because smiles are contagious (i.e., through facial mimicry), but because positive emotions stem from—and create—meaningful interpersonal encounters. When people act on their experiences of gratitude, for instance, they create meaningful situations for others. The original benefactors may feel reinforced for their initial prosocial acts (McCullough et al., 2001; McCullough & Tsang, chap. 7, this volume), onlookers may feel elevated (Haidt, 2000), and anyone else who receives an altruistic gift may feel gratitude. This socioemotional cycle centered on gratitude could continue indefinitely. In this manner, positive emotions tend to beget subsequent positive emotions. Accordingly, the broaden-and-build theory predicts that positive emotions not only produce individuals who function at higher levels, but also produce organizations and communities that function at higher levels.

Indirect evidence that positive emotions transform organizations and help them to thrive comes from research that links employee engagement to a wide range of organizational outcomes. I have argued elsewhere that measures of employee engagement can be recast as measures of positive emotional experience at work (Fredrickson, 2000c). To the extent that this reframing holds, existing research shows that organizations with employees who experience frequent positive emotions have lower employee turnover, more customer loyalty, higher net sales, and in turn, more profitable financial outcomes (Fleming, 2000a, 2000b; Harter, 2000). Research that expressly traces the effects of gratitude in organizations is clearly needed. Nonetheless, the broaden-and-build theory identifies positive emotions, along with the psychological broadening they engender, as the critical links between the momentary experiences of individual employees and long-range indicators of optimal organizational functioning. Positive emotions transform organizations because they broaden people's habitual modes of thinking and, in doing so, make organizational members more flexible, empathic, creative, and so on. Over time, such broadening builds stronger social connections, better organizational climates, and more effective businesses. The broaden-and-build theory predicts that a wide range of distinct positive emotions—ranging from pride and joy to contentment and gratitude—create and sustain these dynamic processes that keep individuals and organizations developing and thriving.

SUMMARY AND FUTURE RESEARCH DIRECTIONS

Although the broaden-and-build theory of positive emotions did not initially include the emotion of gratitude, the present analysis suggests that gratitude—like joy, interest, contentment, love, pride, and elevation—broadens people's modes of thinking, which in turn builds their enduring personal and social resources. Gratitude, like other positive emotions, appears to have the capacity to transform individuals, organizations, and communities for the better. Although this analysis draws on rich and varied theorizing about gratitude, its foundation of empirical research is comparatively thin. My hope is that the ideas presented here may provide directions for kindling a science of gratitude.

First, future studies could test multiple hypotheses about gratitude drawn from the broaden-and-build theory. For instance, joy and contentment have been shown to broaden people's momentary thought-action repertoires (Fredrickson & Branigan, 2001b). Does gratitude similarly broaden? Does it widen the array of thought and actions that come to mind as grateful individuals creatively consider ways to acknowledge their appreciation?

Second, can feeling grateful be distinguished from feeling indebted? If gratitude is experienced as pleasant and indebtedness as aversive, the broaden-and-build theory predicts that only gratitude would lead to broad and creative thinking about how to repay a gift. In contrast to gratitude's creativity, indebtedness should yield simple tit-for-tat reciprocity reflective of narrowed thinking (e.g., if an invitation to someone's dinner party leaves you feeling unpleasantly indebted, you host your own dinner party, invite that person, and you are even).

A third question for study is whether expressions of gratitude, over time, build and strengthen social bonds. This could be studied in the contexts of friendships, marriages, and work relationships.

Fourth, does gratitude build and strengthen organizations and communities, increasing social harmony? In organizations, does gratitude lead to lower employee turnover, more customer loyalty, higher net sales, or more profitable financial outcomes? In communities, does gratitude lead to more volunteer service, or more helping of those in need? Does it lead to less crime, less littering, or less wasting of natural resources? In nations, does it lead to greater patriotism?

A fifth question is tied more directly to the broadened, creative thinking that I propose is part and parcel of feeling grateful: Does gratitude, over time, build people's skills for loving? Does it build their skills for expressing love and kindness so that, even outside the context of gratitude, people who have been frequently grateful know how to show their love and compassion?

Sixth, do gratitude and other positive emotions mediate the salutary effects of spiritual practices on health? Drawing from the broaden-and-build theory, I have recently sketched a causal model for testing this hypothesis (see Fredrickson, 2002b).

More generally, does gratitude predict future increases in health and well-being? Beyond edging out or undoing negative emotions like resentment, envy, and regret in the present, does gratitude fuel upward spirals that optimize the future? In other words, if you feel grateful today—because it broadens your thinking and builds your social bonds and skills for loving—does this enhance your physical and emotional well-being 6 months from now?

These open empirical questions clearly situate the study of gratitude in the emerging science of positive psychology, with its mission to understand and foster the factors that allow individuals, communities, and societies to flourish (Seligman & Csikszentmihalyi, 2000). The concept of gratitude merits further scientific scrutiny. The more empirical research on gratitude that this volume can inspire, the more benefits we may be able to discover and substantiate. And these lines of inquiry will no doubt have substantial real-world significance: From them, we may learn how gratitude may serve as one of the keys to human flourishing.

My research on positive emotions is supported by grants from the University of Michigan and the National Institute of Mental Health (MH53971 and MH59615), and by an award from the John Templeton Foundation and the American Psychological Association (2000 Templeton Positive Psychology Prize). Portions of this work were presented in Dallas, Texas, in October, 2000, at a symposium on gratitude chaired by Robert Emmons and sponsored by the John Templeton Foundation. I would like to thank Emmons, the Templeton Foundation, and the participants in that symposium for pushing my thinking further on gratitude.

References

Aron, A., Norman, C. C., Aron, E. N., McKenna, C., & Heyman, R. E. (2000). Couples' shared participation in novel and arousing activities and experienced relationship quality. *Journal of Personality and Social Psychology, 78,* 273–284.

Ashby, F. G., Isen, A. M., & Turken, A. U. (1999). A neuropsychological theory of positive affect and its influence on cognition. *Psychological Review, 106,* 529–550.

Aspinwall, L. G. (1998). Rethinking the role of positive affect in self-regulation. *Motivation and Emotion, 22,* 1–32.

Aspinwall, L. G. (2001). Dealing with adversity: Self-regulation, coping, adaptation, and health. In A. Tesser & N. Schwarz (Eds.), *The Blackwell handbook of social psychology: Vol. 1. Intraindividual processes* (pp. 591–614). Malden, MA: Blackwell.

Baron, R. A. (1976). The reduction of human aggression: A field study of the influence of incompatible reactions. *Journal of Applied Social Psychology, 6,* 260–274.

Baron, R. A. (1993). Affect and organizational behavior: When and why feeling good (or bad) matters. In K. Murnighan (Ed.), *Social psychology in organizations: Advances in theory* (pp. 63–88). New York: Prentice Hall.

Block, J. & Kremen, A. M. (1996). IQ and ego-resilience: Conceptual and empirical connections and separateness. *Journal of Personality and Social Psychology, 70,* 349–361.

Boulton, M. J., & Smith, P. K. (1992). The social nature of play fighting and play chasing: Mechanisms and strategies underlying cooperation and compromise. In J.

H. Barkow, L. Cosmides, & J. Tooby (Eds.), *The adapted mind: Evolutionary psychology and the generation of culture* (pp. 429–444). New York: Oxford University Press.

Carman, J. B., & Streng, F. J. (Eds.). (1989). *Spoken and unspoken thanks: Some comparative soundings.* Cambridge, MA: Harvard Center for the Study of World Religions.

Caro, T. M. (1988). Adaptive significance of play: Are we getting closer? *Trends in Ecology and Evolution, 3*(2), 50–54.

Csikszentmihalyi, M., & Rathunde, K. (1998). The development of the person: An experiential perspective on the ontogenesis of psychological complexity. In W. Damon (Series Ed.) & R. M. Lerner (Vol. Ed.), *Handbook of child psychology: Vol. 1. Theoretical models of human development* (5th ed., pp. 635–684). New York: Wiley.

Danner, D. D., Snowdon, D. A., & Friesen, W. V. (2001). Positive emotions in early life and longevity: Findings from the nun study. *Journal of Personality and Social Psychology, 80,* 804–813.

de Waal, F. B. M. (1997). The chimpanzee's service economy: Food for grooming. *Evolution and Human Behavior, 18,* 375–386.

de Waal, F. B. M., & Berger, M. L. (2000). Payment for labour in monkeys. *Nature, 404,* 563.

Dolhinow, P. J. (1987). At play in the fields. In H. Topoff (Ed.), *The natural history reader in animal behavior* (pp. 229–237). New York: Columbia University Press.

Emmons, R. A., & Crumpler, C. A. (2000). Gratitude as a human strength: Appraising the evidence. *Journal of Social and Clinical Psychology, 19,* 56–69.

Emmons, R. A., & McCullough, M. E. (2003). Counting blessings versus burdens: An experimental investigation of gratitude and subjective well-being in daily life. *Journal of Personality and Social Psychology, 84*(2), 377–389.

Emmons, R. A., & Shelton, C. M. (2002). Gratitude and the science of positive psychology. In C. R. Snyder & S. J. Lopez (Eds.), *Handbook of positive psychology* (pp. 459–471). New York: Oxford University Press.

Fleming, J. H. (2000a). Relating employee engagement and customer loyalty to business outcomes in the financial services industry. *Gallup Research Journal, 3,* 91–101.

Fleming, J. H. (2000b). Relating employee engagement and customer loyalty to business outcomes in the retail industry. *Gallup Research Journal, 3,* 103–115.

Folkman, S. (1997). Positive psychological states and coping with severe stress. *Social Science Medicine, 45,* 1207–1221.

Folkman, S., & Moskowitz, J. T. (2000). Positive affect and the other side of coping. *American Psychologist, 55,* 647–654.

Fredrickson, B. L. (1998). What good are positive emotions? *Review of General Psychology, 2,* 300–319.

Fredrickson, B. L. (2000a). Cultivating positive emotions to optimize health and well-being. *Prevention and Treatment, 3,* Article 0001a. Retrieved May 12, 2003, from http://journals.apa.org/prevention/volume3/pre0030001a.html

Fredrickson, B. L. (2000b). Cultivating research on positive emotions [Response to commentaries on "Cultivating positive emotions to optimize health and well-being"]. *Prevention and Treatment, 3,* Article 7. Retrieved May 12, 2003, from http://journals.apa.org/prevention/volume3/pre0030007r.html

Fredrickson, B. L. (2000c). Why positive emotions matter in organizations: Lessons from the broaden-and-build model. *Psychologist-Manager Journal, 4,* 131–142.

Fredrickson, B. L. (2001). The role of positive emotions in positive psychology: The broaden-and-build theory of positive emotions. *American Psychologist, 56,* 218–226.

Fredrickson, B. L. (2002a). Positive emotions. In C. R. Snyder & S. J. Lopez (Eds.). *Handbook of positive psychology* (pp. 120–134). New York: Oxford University Press.

Fredrickson, B. L. (2002b). How does religion benefit health and well-being? Are positive emotions active ingredients? *Psychological Inquiry, 13,* 209–213.

Fredrickson, B. L., & Branigan, C. A. (2001a). Positive emotions. In T. J. Mayne and G. A. Bonnano (Eds.), *Emotion: Current issues and future developments* (pp. 123–151). New York: Guilford.

Fredrickson, B. L., & Branigan, C. (2001b). *Positive emotions broaden the scope of attention and thought-action repertoires: Evidence for the broaden-and-build theory.* Manuscript submitted for publication.

Fredrickson, B. L., & Joiner, T. (2002). Positive emotions trigger upward spirals toward emotional well-being. *Psychological Science, 13,* 172–175.

Fredrickson, B. L., & Levenson, R. W. (1998). Positive emotions speed recovery from the cardiovascular sequelae of negative emotions. *Cognition and Emotion, 12,* 191–220.

Fredrickson, B. L., Mancuso, R. A., Branigan, C., & Tugade, M. M. (2000). The undoing effect of positive emotions. *Motivation and Emotion, 24,* 237–258.

Fredrickson, B. L., Tugade, M. M., Waugh, C. E., & Larkin, G. R. (2003). What good are positive emotions in crises? A prospective study of resilience and emotional responding following the terrorist attacks on the United States on September 11th, 2001. *Journal of Personality and Social Psychology, 84*(2), 365–376.

Frijda, N. H. (1986). *The emotions.* Cambridge, UK: Cambridge University Press.

Frijda, N. H., Kuipers, P., & Schure, E. (1989). Relations among emotion, appraisal, and emotional action readiness. *Journal of Personality and Social Psychology, 57,* 212–228.

George, J. M. (1991). State or trait: Effects of positive mood on prosocial behavior at work. *Journal of Applied Psychology, 76,* 299–307.

George, J. M. (1995). Leader positive mood and group performance: The case of customer service. *Journal of Applied Social Psychology, 25,* 778–794.

George, J. M. (1998). Salesperson mood at work: Implications for helping customers. *Journal of Personal Selling and Sales Management, 18,* 23–30.

Graham, S. (1988). Children's developing understanding of the motivational role of affect: An attributional analysis. *Cognitive Development, 3,* 71–88.

Haidt, J. (2000). The positive emotion of elevation [Commentary on "Cultivating positive emotions to optimize health and well-being" by B. L. Fredrickson]. *Prevention and Treatment, 3,* Article 3. Retrieved May 12, 2003, from http://journals.apa.org/prevention/volume3/pre0030003c.html

Haidt, J. (2003). Elevation and the positive psychology of morality. In C. L. M. Keyes & J. Haidt (Eds.), *Flourishing: Positive psychology and the life well-lived* (pp. 275–289). Washington, DC: American Psychological Association.

Harter, J. (2000). The linkage of employee perception to outcomes in a retail environment: Cause and effect? *Gallup Research Journal, 3*, 25–38.

Hatfield, E., Cacioppo, J. T., & Rapson, R. L. (1993). Emotional contagion. *Current Directions in Psychological Science, 2*, 96–99.

Isen, A. M. (1987). Positive affect, cognitive processes, and social behavior. *Advances in Experimental Social Psychology, 20*, 203–253.

Izard, C. E. (1977). *Human emotions.* New York: Plenum.

Lazarus, R. S. (1991). *Emotion and adaptation.* New York: Oxford University Press.

Lazarus, R. S., Kanner, A. D., & Folkman, S. (1980). Emotions: A cognitive-phenomenological analysis. In R. Plutchik & H. Kellerman (Eds.), *Theories of emotion* (pp. 189–217). New York: Academic Press.

Lazarus, R. S., & Lazarus, B. N. (1994). *Passion and reason: Making sense of our emotions.* New York: Oxford University Press.

Lee, P. C. (1983). Play as a means for developing relationships. In R. A. Hinde (Ed.), *Primate social relationships* (pp. 82–89). Oxford, MA: Blackwell.

Leslie, A. M. (1987). Pretense and representation: The origins of "theory of mind." *Psychological Review, 94*, 412–426.

Lewis, M. (1993). Self-conscious emotions: Embarrassment, pride, shame, and guilt. In M. Lewis & J. M. Haviland (Eds.), *Handbook of emotions* (pp. 563–573). New York: Guilford.

Levenson, R. W. (1994). Human emotions: A functional view. In P. Ekman & R. Davidson (Eds.), *The nature of emotion: Fundamental questions* (pp. 123–126). New York: Oxford University Press.

Lundqvist, L. O., & Dimberg, U. (1995). Facial expressions are contagious. *Journal of Psychophysiology, 9*, 203–211.

Mayer, J. D., Salovey, P., Gomberg-Kaufman, S., & Blainey, K. (1991). A broader conception of mood experience. *Journal of Personality and Social Psychology, 60*, 100–111.

McCraty, R., Atkinson, M., Tiller, W., Rein, G., & Watkins, A. D. (1995). The effects of emotions on short-term power spectrum analysis of heart rate variability. *American Journal of Cardiology, 76*, 1089–1093.

McCullough, M. E., Kilpatrick, S. D., Emmons, R. A., & Larson, D. B. (2001). Is gratitude a moral affect? *Psychological Bulletin, 127*, 249–266.

Oatley, K., & Jenkins, J. M. (1996). *Understanding emotions.* Cambridge, MA: Blackwell.

Ostir, G. V., Markides, K. S., Black, S. A., & Goodwin, J. S. (2000). Emotional well-being predicts subsequent functional independence and survival. *Journal of the American Geriatrics Society, 48*, 473–478.

Panksepp, J. (1998). Attention deficit hyperactivity disorders, psychostimulants, and intolerance of childhood playfulness: A tragedy in the making? *Current Directions in Psychological Science, 7*, 91–98.

Peterson, B. E., & Stewart, A. J. (1996). Antecedents and contexts of generativity motivation at midlife. *Psychology and Aging, 11,* 21–33.

Peterson, C., & Seligman, M. E. P. (1984). Causal explanations as a risk factor for depression: Theory and evidence. *Psychological Review, 91,* 347–374.

Piper, J. (1996). *Desiring God: Meditations of a Christian hedonist.* Sisters, OR: Multnomah.

Rein, G., Atkinson, M., & McCraty, R. (1995). The physiological and psychological effects of compassion and anger. *Journal of Advancement in Medicine, 8,* 87–105.

Reisenzein, R. (1994). Pleasure-arousal theory and the intensity of emotions. *Journal of Personality and Social Psychology, 67,* 525–539.

Renninger, K. A., Hidi, S., & Krapp, A. (Eds.). (1992). *The role of interest in learning and development.* Hillsdale, NJ: Erlbaum.

Roberts, R. C. (1991). Mental health and the virtues of community: Christian reflections on contextual therapy. *Journal of Psychology and Theology, 19,* 319–333.

Rosenberg, E. L. (1998). Levels of analysis and the organization of affect. *Review of General Psychology, 2,* 247–270.

Samuels, P. A., & Lester, D. (1986). A preliminary investigation of emotions experienced toward God by Catholic nuns and priests. *Psychological Reports, 56,* 706.

Seligman, M. E. P., & Csikszentmihalyi, M. (2000). Positive psychology: An introduction. *American Psychologist, 55,* 5–14.

Sherrod, L. R., & Singer, J. L (1989). The development of make-believe play. In J. Goldstein (Ed.), *Sports, games and play* (pp. 1–38). Hillsdale, NJ: Erlbaum.

Simmel, G. (1950). *The sociology of Georg Simmel.* Glencoe, IL: Free Press. (Original work published 1908)

Simons, C. J. R., McCluskey-Fawcett, K. A., & Papini, D. R. (1986). Theoretical and functional perspective on the development of humor during infancy, childhood, and adolescence. In L. Nahemow, K. A. McCluskey-Fawcett, & P. E. McGhee (Eds.), *Humor and aging* (pp. 53–77). San Diego, CA: Academic Press.

Smith, A. (1976). *The theory of moral sentiments* (6th ed.). Oxford, UK: Clarendon Press. (Original work published 1790)

Solomon, R. L., & Corbit, J. D. (1974). An opponent-process theory of motivation: I. Temporal dynamics of affect. *Psychological Review, 81,* 119–145.

Stein, N. L., Folkman, S., Trabasso, T., & Richards, T. A. (1997). Appraisal and goal processes as predictors of psychological well-being in bereaved caregivers. *Journal of Personality and Social Psychology, 72,* 872–884.

Tiller, W. A., McCraty, R., & Atkinson, M. (1996). Cardiac coherence: A new, noninvasive measure of autonomic nervous system order. *Alternative Therapies in Health and Medicine, 2,* 52–65.

Tooby, J., & Cosmides, L. (1990). The past explains the present: Emotional adaptations and the structure of ancestral environments. *Ethology and Sociobiology, 11,* 375–424.

Trivers, R. L. (1971). The evolution of reciprocal altruism. *Quarterly Review of Biology, 46,* 35–57.

Tugade, M. M., & Fredrickson, B. L. (2002). Positive emotions and emotional intelligence. In L. Feldman Barrett & P. Salovey (Eds.), *The wisdom in feeling: Psychological processes in emotional intelligence* (pp. 319–340). New York: Guilford.

Watson, D., Clark, L. A., McIntyre, C. W., & Hamaker, S. (1992). Affect, personality, and social activity. *Journal of Personality and Social Psychology, 63,* 1011–1025.

Wolpe, J. (1958). *Psychotherapy by reciprocal inhibition.* Stanford, CA: Stanford University Press.

9 Gratitude and Subjective Well-Being

Philip C. Watkins

> The test of all happiness is gratitude.
> —G. K. Chesterton (1908/1986, p. 258)

In his struggle to understand the function of praise, C. S. Lewis wrote, "I think we delight to praise what we enjoy because the praise not merely expresses but completes the enjoyment; it is its appointed consummation. It is not out of compliment that lovers keep on telling one another how beautiful they are; the delight is incomplete until it is expressed" (1958, p. 95).

Lewis was not satisfied with the theory that the only function of praise is a return of social reinforcement. The passage just quoted indicates that he believed that the primary motive for praise was that it completes our enjoyment of the blessing. It is as if our enjoyment is incomplete unless some praise or gratitude is expressed to the source of our enjoyment. Here Lewis presented the provocative hypothesis that the expression of gratitude contributes in an important way to human happiness. Chesterton (1908/1986) went even further by suggesting that a genuine expression of gratitude is the test of an authentic happiness.

In my lab, my students and I have followed Lewis's approach to gratitude. Rather than focusing on the social benefits of expressing gratitude (which appear to be clear in the literature; see McCullough, Kilpatrick, Emmons, & Larson, 2001; McCullough & Tsang, chap. 7, this volume), we have investigated the emotional benefits of grateful experience. Although we do not deny the evolutionary and functional importance of gratitude to social life (Bonnie & de Waal, chap. 11, this volume; Komter, chap. 10, this volume; Trivers, 1971), our perspective has been to investigate the functional importance of gratitude to the enjoyment of life.

In his classic text *The Varieties of Religious Experience*, William James observed that "how to gain, how to keep, how to recover happiness is in fact for most men at all times the secret motive of all they do" (1902/1958, p. 76). That this is perhaps the most often quoted text by William James in the last 10 years attests to the growth and acceptance of the study of happiness and subjective well-being (SWB). Because compelling arguments for the importance of the study of SWB have been put forth and largely accepted by the psychological community (e.g., Diener, 1984; Diener, Suh, Lucas, & Smith, 1999; Myers, 1993; Myers & Diener, 1995; Veenhoven, 1988), I do not attempt to recapitulate the grounds for SWB research here. Suffice it to say that SWB is now an important research area in the social sciences, and if gratitude proves to be a significant predictor of happiness, this is a relationship that should not be taken lightly. Again to quote Chesterton, "Pessimism is at best an emotional half holiday; joy is the uproarious labour by which all things live" (1908/1986, p. 364). If indeed gratitude is an important component of "the uproarious labour by which all things live," this relationship deserves to be studied.

In this chapter I argue that gratitude is a significant component of SWB. I follow Diener's (1984) approach to SWB and use the terms *SWB* and *happiness* interchangeably. Diener emphasized three hallmarks of SWB (pp. 543–544). The first rather obvious but often overlooked factor of SWB is that it is subjective. One's own experience of one's happiness is what defines SWB. Second, Diener emphasizes that SWB is not merely the absence of negative factors (such as depression), but a positive measure of a construct. Third, the measurement of SWB should be global, that is, it should cover "all aspects of a person's life" (p. 544). Both happiness and gratitude may be studied as affective traits or affective states. Briefly, an affective state is one's immediate phenomenal experience of an emotion. Conversely, an affective trait describes one's tendency or disposition to experience a particular emotion (for a review of this distinction with regard to gratitude, see McCullough, Emmons, & Tsang, 2002; McCullough et al., 2001). Thus, a person high in the affective trait of gratitude might not experience grateful feelings at any given moment but will be more likely to experience gratitude in response to benefits than most (i.e., he or she will be predisposed to grateful feelings). In this chapter I first describe research that has investigated the relationship between SWB and gratitude as an affective trait. Second, I review the few studies that have attempted to experimentally manipulate the states of gratitude and SWB. I then propose some mechanisms that might explain the relationship between gratitude and SWB, and conclude with a discussion of future research issues and considerations.

SWB AND THE GRATEFUL TRAIT

One of the most surprising results of the first 30 years of SWB research has been how poorly demographic variables have predicted happiness. Variables such as age, intelligence, gender, and material well-being have predicted such a small proportion of the variance of SWB that reviewers have concluded that demographics are largely irrelevant to the SWB issue (DeNeve, 1999, p. 142; for additional reviews see Diener, 1984; Diener et al., 1999; Myers, 1993; Myers, 2000a; Myers & Diener, 1995). However, personality variables have fared much better as predictors of SWB (e.g., DeNeve, 1999; DeNeve & Cooper, 1998). To date, the research has largely affirmed the verse penned by William Cowper: "Happiness depends, as Nature shows, / Less on exterior things than most suppose" (as cited in Tripp, 1970, p. 276).

If personality traits such as extraversion are the best predictors of SWB, might the affective trait of gratitude be an important personality predictor of happiness? To anticipate my forthcoming review, several studies support the idea that the disposition of gratitude is a reliable predictor of SWB.

To my knowledge, two dispositional gratitude measures have been developed. Probably the better developed of the two is the Gratitude Questionnaire (GQ-6), a fairly short measure that appears to have good psychometric properties (McCullough, Emmons, & Tsang, 2002). In my lab we have developed the Gratitude, Resentment, and Appreciation Test (GRAT), which also appears to have adequate psychometric properties (Watkins, Porter, & Curtis, 1996; Watkins, Porter, & Miller, 1997). Both of these measures have been found to have reliable associations with various SWB measures. For example, the GQ-6 and the GRAT are both positively correlated with the Satisfaction With Life Scale (SWLS), one of the most frequently used measures of SWB (Diener, Emmons, Larsen, & Griffin, 1985; Pavot & Diener, 1993). In two studies, McCullough and colleagues (2002) found a strong positive association between the GQ-6 and the SWLS ($r = .53$). In two studies, my students and I (Watkins, Grim, & Hailu, 1999; Watkins et al., 1997) found that the GRAT had a similar relationship with the SWLS ($r = .49$, $r = .50$). Thus, the more grateful individuals report themselves to be, the more they express satisfaction with their lives.

These relationships compare favorably with other personality variables that have consistently been found to correlate with the SWLS. Figure 9.1

demonstrates this graphically by comparing the association of dispositional gratitude with the SWLS with typical relationships demonstrated by other variables. This figure shows that the affective trait of gratitude may need to be taken as a serious player as researchers are investigating personality components of SWB.

Although the SWLS is one of the most commonly used measures of SWB, the authors of this instrument did not intend for it to measure all aspects of SWB. As such, it is primarily tapping the cognitive component of SWB, because individuals are required to make satisfaction judgments about their lives as a whole (Diener et al., 1985; Pavot & Diener, 1993). We must look to other measures to evaluate the contribution of gratitude to the affective component of SWB. McCullough et al. (2002) performed perhaps the most direct test of this relationship when they compared the GQ-6 to the Subjective Happiness Scale (Lyubomirsky & Lepper, 1999). The GQ-6 showed a reliable positive relationship with this measure ($r = .50$). Similarly, we (Watkins et al., 1999) have found the GRAT to have a strong relationship with the Fordyce happiness measure (Fordyce, 1988). Here the GRAT was correlated with the average happiness rating at .49. We (Watkins et al., 1997) also found the GRAT to be associated with elation ($r = .47$) as measured by the Semantic Differential Feeling and Mood Scale (Lorr & Wunderlich, 1988). Furthermore, both the GQ-6 and the GRAT have been shown to be positively associated with positive affectivity ($r = .31$ and $r = .36$, respectively; McCullough et al., 2002; Watkins et al., 1997), as measured by the Positive and Negative Affect Scales (PANAS; Watson, Clark, & Tellegen, 1988). All of these associations were reliable and provide considerable support for the notion that the grateful disposition is also related to the more affective component of SWB. Summarizing the self-report data, two independently developed dispositional gratitude measures have shown very similar positive relationships with various measures of positive emotion and SWB.

Because of the subjective nature of SWB, this area will probably always rely on self-report measures. However, some researchers (e.g., Diener et al., 1999) have also urged the use of non-self-report measures of happiness. For example, Diener et al. (1999) suggested using recall measures as an indirect measure of SWB to compliment findings from self-report measures. Following this lead (see also Seidlitz & Diener, 1993; Seidlitz, Wyer, & Diener, 1997), my students and I compared recall of emotional events with level of dispositional gratitude (Watkins et al., 1999). In this study, participants were asked to recall positive and negative events from their past for 3 minutes each. We created a positive memory bias measure by subtracting the number of negative events from the number of positive events recalled. This constituted our intentional recall variable. As expected, we found that grateful in-

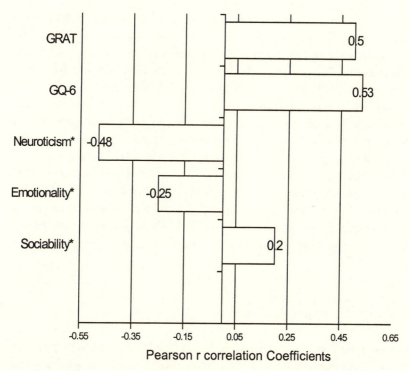

Figure 9.1. Comparison of correlations of gratitude and other personality variables with the Satisfaction With Life Scale.

dividuals were more likely to have a positive memory bias. Because many studies have shown that depression is inversely related to positive memory bias (e.g., Grimm & Watkins, 1998; Watkins, Mathews, Williamson, & Fuller, 1992; for a review, see Blaney, 1986), in a second study we sought to determine if the grateful disposition contributed to positive memory bias independently from depression. Indeed we found that after controlling for depression, the GRAT still reliably predicted positive memory bias (Watkins et al., 1999).

In addition to this relationship with intentional memory bias, we also found that gratitude was positively associated with an intrusive memory bias (Watkins et al., 1999). While completing the recall trials, we asked our participants to check a box at the bottom of the page if a life event of the opposite valence of that which they were trying to recall came to mind. For example, if while attempting to recollect positive events from one's life a negative event came to mind, one would check a box indicating the occurrence of an intrusive memory. As with intentional memory, we found that grateful individuals were more likely to have a positive intrusive memory bias ($r = .32$

and .22 in the two studies). These studies provided two indirect measures of SWB, both of which we found to be related to our trait measure of gratitude.

Another indirect measure of positive affect that has been used is pleasantness ratings of neutral words (Isen & Shalker, 1982; Kuykendall, Keating, & Wagaman, 1988). In a study (Woodward, 2000) recently completed in my lab, the GRAT was found to be positively related to pleasantness ratings of neutral words. This approach circumvents problems associated with self-presentation biases and thus provides important indirect data supporting the hypothesis that the disposition of gratitude is related to happiness.

Another way to skirt the well-known problems with self-report measures is to use informants. McCullough et al. (2002) showed that friends and relatives ratings of participants' level of gratefulness reliably correlated with the participants' own reports of their SWB. Thus, self-report and non-self-report data converge to support the idea that grateful people tend to be happy people.

SWB AND THE GRATEFUL STATE

Although the relationships between the grateful trait and SWB appear to be strong, this research suffers from the same limitations as most SWB research to date. As Diener et al. (1999) correctly note, most SWB research is correlational in nature, as are the studies I have just reviewed to this point relating the grateful trait to happiness. Although it is difficult to see how the grateful disposition could be manipulated in the lab, the correlational nature of the studies reviewed earlier prevents making any causal determinations. The gratitude trait and SWB relationship could be due to gratitude causing happiness in some way, but it could also be that gratitude is something of an epiphenomenal result of being happy. Thus, as Diener and colleagues (1999) have encouraged, experimental studies looking into the relationship between gratitude and SWB need to be conducted.

In the context of attempting to show the benefits of an attitude of dependence, G. K. Chesterton stated that "gratitude produced the most purely joyful moments that have been known to man" (1924/1990, p. 78). Is there any truth to the claim that moments of gratitude are accompanied by happiness? Survey data indicates that most people think so. In a Gallup poll (Gallup Survey Results On "Gratitude," 1998), 95% of respondents said that expressing gratitude made them feel at least *somewhat happy*. In fact, over fifty percent of those in this survey said that expressing gratitude made them feel *extremely happy*. Mayer, Salovey, Gomberg-Kaufman, and Blainey (1991), presented converging evidence that gratitude is a positive affective state. They found that the adjectives *grateful* and *thankful* both loaded on their pleasantness dimension. Furthermore, recent analyses from our lab (Woodward, 2000) have shown that with experimental manipulations of mood, positive affect and gratitude tend to covary. So people commonly associate grateful states with happy states, but does being grateful actually *cause* an improvement of mood? Several preliminary studies suggest that it does.

In my lab, we have conducted several studies attempting to manipulate gratitude to investigate the causal influence of gratitude on mood. Woodward (2000, Study 1) found that she could manipulate gratitude by having individuals focus on things they were thankful for versus anticipated benefits that in fact were not received. Early in fall quarter, students were randomly assigned to one of two conditions. Students either listed activities they were able to do over the summer that they were thankful for, or they listed things they had wanted to do but were unable to. We then asked students to tell us how grateful they were for their summer on a Likert-type scale. Indeed, students in the thankful condition reported more gratitude than those in the envy condition. More important, students in the grateful condition reported less negative affect following the intervention than did students in the envy condition (as measured by the negative affect scale of the PANAS; Watson et al., 1988).

However, in a conceptual replication we failed to find this effect again (Woodward, 2000, Study 2). In this study, early winter quarter, we asked some students to recall gifts received over the holidays that they were thankful for. Another group listed gifts they would have liked to receive but didn't. We found that this manipulation did not affect reported gratitude for the holiday break, and likewise mood was not reliably different between the two groups. There are several explanations that may be offered as to why this manipulation failed. As McCullough et al. (2001) have shown in their review, a number of studies suggest that if a benefit is expected then one tends not to respond with as much gratitude. Because most people expect to receive gifts over the December holidays, they also may not experience much gratitude in response to those gifts. A second possibility is that people tend to be more grateful for experiences and relationships than they do for material blessings. Because we asked our participants to recall material blessings received in Study 2, this may have mitigated any grateful response.

In a study recently completed (Stone & Watkins, 2001), preliminary analyses have shown that subjects in grateful experimental conditions displayed more mood improvement than those in a comparison condition. Participants were randomly assigned to one of four conditions. In the control condition students were asked to write about the layout of their living rooms. The remaining participants were randomly assigned to one of three gratitude conditions. Some participants were simply asked to think about someone they were grateful for, others were asked to write about someone they were grateful to, and finally a group of students was asked to write a letter of gratitude to someone they felt grateful to. All participants were administered the PANAS both before and after the experimental manipulation. Results showed that the students in the grateful conditions reliably displayed a greater increase in positive affect.

A variety of emotional benefits resulting from a simple practice of gratitude have been demonstrated (Emmons & McCullough, 2003). In Emmons and McCullough's first study, students were randomly assigned to one of three conditions. Participants either wrote about five things they were grateful for in the past week (gratitude condition), five hassles from the day (hassles condition), or five events or circumstances that affected them in the last week (events condition). Participants completed these exercises along with a variety of other measures for 10 weeks. What I find particularly interesting about this study is that Emmons and McCullough included two global appraisal measures in the students' weekly monitoring. One appraisal tapped participants feelings "about their life as a whole during the week" (Emmons & McCullough, p. 380), and a second question asked them about their global expectations for the coming week. As in our studies (Stone & Watkins, 2001; Woodward, 2000), students in the gratitude condition reported being more grateful than those in the hassles condition. Results from the two global well-being measures are more important for our purposes. Participants in the grateful condition felt better about their lives as a whole and were more optimistic about the future than students in both of the other comparison conditions. In addition, those in the grateful condition reported fewer health complaints and even said that they spent more time exercising than control participants did. Thus, a simple weekly intervention showed significant emotional and health benefits.

In their second study, Emmons and McCullough (2003) increased the gratitude intervention to a daily practice over a 2-week period. As in their first study, participants were randomly assigned to one of three conditions. The gratitude and hassles conditions were identical to the first study, but the events condition was changed to a downward social comparison manipulation. In this condition, participants were encouraged to "think about ways in which you are better off than others" (Emmons & McCullough, p. 381). Emmons and McCullough added this condition to control for possible demand characteristics. I found this to be an intriguing comparison condition that could be developed for future gratitude research. However, some research has shown that situations in which we feel that "it could have been worse"— that we could have or should have been worse off—often produce a response of gratitude (e.g., Teigen, 1997). This comparison condition may have inadvertently produced some gratitude responses, thus mitigating any differences seen between the gratitude condition and this comparison condition. Even so, the gratitude condition showed an impressive array of benefits. Although the health benefits from the first Emmons and McCullough study were not evident in this study, participants in the grateful condition felt more joyful, enthusiastic, interested, attentive, energetic, excited, determined, and strong than those in the hassles condition. Again the gratitude manipulation showed a significant effect on the positive affect factor as compared with the hassles condition, but no reliable impact on negative affectivity. In addition, there was some evidence that this daily intervention showed a stronger effect than the weekly practice of the first study.

In a third study, Emmons and McCullough (2003) replicated these effects in adults with neuromuscular diseases. Patients were randomly assigned to a gratitude condition or to a true control condition in which the subjects simply filled out daily experience rating forms. Like those in the previous studies, the gratitude group showed significantly more positive affect and satisfaction with life, but they also showed less negative affect than the control group. Not only did patients in the grateful condition show an advantage in positive affect and life satisfaction in self-reports, but also in the reports of significant others. These studies and those from our lab support the contention that gratitude has a causative influence on subjective well-being.

A CYCLE OF VIRTUE?

In this chapter I have reviewed evidence pointing to a strong relationship between gratitude and happiness. Several studies have shown that grateful people tend to be happy people. I have also reviewed preliminary experimental studies supporting the theory that a practice of gratitude actually increases various positive emotional states. If gratitude, both as state and trait, contributes to happiness, what mechanisms might be involved? Why might gratitude contribute to happiness? In this section I offer some theoretical suggestions regarding the contribution of gratitude to SWB.

One mechanism for the contribution of gratitude to happiness might involve the additional emotional advantages one gains from a benefit when it is perceived to be a gift, that is, a favor that has been given to one for one's benefit. Speaking of the joy that moments of gratitude bring, Chesterton remarked, "All goods look better when they look like gifts" (1924/1990, p. 78). If one perceives a benefit to be gift, is one indeed more likely to enjoy the benefit? Perceiving a positive experience as a gift may be a form of cognitive amplification that enhances positive affect (Diener, Colvin, Pavot, & Allman, 1991). Although to my knowledge there are no data that speak directly to this issue, various studies have shown that if one thinks a benefit was given intentionally for one's benefit, one is more likely to experience gratitude (for a review see McCullough et al., 2001). Presumably, those who are dispositionally grateful should be more likely to perceive benefits as gifts. If good things really are better when perceived as gifts, this could be one way that gratitude directly contributes to states of happiness.

C. S. Lewis (1958) argued that our delight with someone else is "incomplete until it is expressed" (p. 95). Like Chesterton, Lewis argued that our enjoyment of something will be somewhat restrained unless we are allowed to express our appreciation for the benefit. The implication is that gratitude should increase our enjoyment of a blessing. It is as if one action readiness mode of enjoyment is gratitude. Following Lewis, just as it is difficult to resist running when one is afraid, it should be more difficult (if not somewhat aversive) to suppress one's appreciation for a benefit received. As Lewis summarized Aristotle in another passage, "Aristotle has taught us that delight is the 'bloom' on an unimpeded activity" (1963, p. 115). Thus, the "unimpeded activity" of expressing gratitude for a benefit may increase our delight in the good. Following Fredrickson's theory of positive emotions (1998; chap. 8, this volume), we would not expect the thought/action readiness of the enjoyment of a gift to be as specific as that of fear. Thus, although fear may prepare us for flight, enjoyment of benefits may prepare us for a much wider variety of thoughts and activities that may be characterized as expressions of gratitude. Future research could test these ideas, but if Lewis and Chesterton are right, gratitude may have direct emotional benefits that contribute to SWB.

One of the most frequent questions coming from experts of SWB seems to be, If we are so rich, why aren't we happy? (Csikszentmihalyi, 1999). As I touched on earlier, generally speaking, SWB research has shown that happiness can't be bought. In the midst of our increasingly abundant culture, people don't seem to be getting any happier, and some have argued that in fact the misery index is rising (in terms of variables such as depression and suicide rate; e.g., Csikszentmihalyi, 1999; Myers, 2000b). One reason that increases in material blessings do not increase happiness is related to the principle of adaptation (Csikszentmihalyi, 1999; Myers, 2000b). Research from a number of different areas in psychology has shown how humans have an amazing ability to adapt to their ongoing circumstances. In the context of emotion theory, Frijda (1988) referred to this as the "law of habituation". Briefly, this law states that, over time, we tend to get used to our current level of satisfaction. For example, a major league baseball player may not be happy (and perhaps may even feel deprived) with his $500,000-per-year salary, because this has been his salary for the past 5 years, and other teammates are making much more. Frijda believes, however, that one need not be a slave to the law of habituation. He suggested that "Adaptation to satisfaction can be counteracted by constantly being aware of how fortunate one's condition is" (Frijda, 1988, p. 354). This is exactly what a practice of gratitude should accomplish, consistently reminding one of how good their life really is. Therefore another route from gratitude to happiness might be by counteracting the law of habituation (see similar arguments in Emmons & McCullough, 2003).

A third mechanism whereby gratitude contributes to happiness might be by directing attention away from upward social comparisons that lead to feelings of deprivation. McCullough et al. (2002) argue that focusing on blessings one is grateful for directs attention away from making comparisons with others who have more. A number of studies have shown that upward social comparisons lead to less positive affect and more unpleasant feelings such as depression and feelings of deprivation (e.g., Botta, 1999; Cattarin, Thompson, Thomas, & Williams, 2000; Hagerty, 2000; Hennigan et al., 1982). In their study of dispositional gratitude, McCullough et al. (2002) found that gratitude was inversely related to dispositional envy. When an individual is grateful for the greenness of his or her own lawn, he or she is not likely to be looking at the greener grass on the other side of the fence. I should note that the converse likely holds as well; if one's attention is consistently devoted to things one does not have, one will be unlikely to focus on appreciating the blessings one does have. It seems that a fruitful approach for future research would be to investigate how one's disposition of gratitude generally affects one's social comparisons. For example, if given the opportunity, will grateful individuals be less likely to engage in upward social comparisons than those less grateful? Alternatively, in the context of upward comparisons, are grateful people less likely to be affected emotionally (cf. Lyubomirsky & Ross, 1997)?

On a related note, might gratitude assist in delaying gratification? If grateful individuals are more satisfied with the blessings they have, it seems reasonable that they will not have an excessive desire for things they do not have and perhaps cannot afford. I propose that grateful individuals should be more able to delay gratification. This ability might lead grateful individuals to be more able to save resources until they can obtain benefits without falling into debt. Conversely, less grateful individuals who are dissatisfied with their current blessings should be less willing to wait for benefits in life (such as a new car or home, for example), thus mortgaging their future, which it seems would lead to a more unhappy life. Past research has shown that depression is associated with a decreased ability to delay gratification (e.g., Wertheim & Schwarz, 1983), and positive affect inductions have been shown to increase children's ability to delay reward (Fry, 1975; Schwarz & Pollack, 1977; Yates, Lippett, & Yates, 1981). Thus, it seems reasonable to propose that the emotional benefits of gratitude might assist one in waiting for rewards, and this in turn might provide for increased SWB. Again, these proposals could be fruitful avenues for future research.

Another potential mechanism for the gratitude-happiness connection might be that the practice of gratitude serves as an effective coping mechanism (cf. Emmons & McCullough, 2003). If he or she tends to view life as a gift, the grateful person may be able to find benefits even in unpleasant circumstances. For example, many believe that good character is developed through times of difficult life circumstances. Also, grateful persons may be more able to appreciate how difficult situations have reoriented their perspective to reveal what is really important in their lives. If a grateful attitude promotes better coping with stressful circumstances, this should promote long-term SWB. Results from several studies have suggested that gratitude is a common response to stressful situations (e.g., Coffman, 1996; Ventura, 1982; Ventura & Boss, 1983). In a recent study (Watkins, Christianson, Lawrence, & Whitney, 2001), we found that the disposition of gratitude was positively related to two measures of emotional intelligence. Although the GRAT was related to all three scales of emotional intelligence of the Trait Meta-Mood Scale (Salovey, Mayer, Goldman, Turvey, & Palfai, 1995), the strongest association was with the mood repair scale. This evidence supports the idea that gratitude may give one a helpful perspective on life that assists in mood repair following a stressful event.

Recent evidence from Masingale et al. (2001)—a study from the lab of my colleague Russell Kolts—lends more support to the supposition that gratitude may be an effective coping mechanism for dealing with stressful events. In a study investigating posttraumatic stress disorder (PTSD) symptoms in student survivors of trauma, Masingale et al. found that gratitude predicted the level of PTSD symptoms in trauma survivors. Grateful individuals were found to have significantly lower PTSD symptoms than less grateful individuals on two different PTSD scales. Although a prospective analysis would provide stronger evidence for the causal aspects of gratitude for dealing with trauma, this study provides promising evidence that gratitude may be an adaptive way for dealing with difficult life circumstances.

Results from our memory bias studies referred to earlier (Watkins et al., 1999) appear to coincide with this evidence. After recalling positive and negative events, participants rated the emotional impact of the events for the time when the event occurred (*then*) and how recalling the event affected them now (*now*). We used a Likert scale varying from *unpleasant* to *pleasant emotional impact*. We found that although *then* ratings of negative events did not differ between grateful and less grateful individuals, grateful individuals rated the *now* impact as significantly more positive than did less grateful individuals. Thus, time appeared to have more of a healing effect on unpleasant memories for grateful participants. This result supports the idea that a grateful approach to negative life events might help reframe memories of unpleasant events so that they have less aversive emotional impact.

Based on recent results from depression research in mood-congruent memory (Grimm, 2000; Grimm & Watkins, 1998), I have come to the conclusion that accessibility of negative memories is not as important to the maintenance of depression as is the emotional impact of these memories (cf. Teasdale, 1983). I believe the finding that gratitude might help reframe memories of negative events is important to viewing how gratitude might be an adaptive coping response and in turn might be an important component of SWB. One way grateful individuals might reframe unpleasant life events is through the "redemptive sequences" described by McAdams and Bauer in chapter 5 of this volume, whereby bad things turn good (see also McAdams, Reynolds, Lewis, Patten, & Bowman, 2001). McAdams et al. (2001) have shown that individuals whose life stories are characterized by redemptive sequences tend to be more satisfied with their lives. Furthermore, their research has suggested that redemptive life sequences are more predictive of SWB than the emotional tone of all life events related from one's life story. In other words, redemptive stories were more predictive of SWB than was simply the positivity of one's life events. It may be that gratitude promotes the construction of redemptive life sequences because individuals who approach life with an attitude that all of life is a gift will be more likely to find good in bad life circumstances.

A fifth mechanism whereby gratitude might promote SWB is through the accessibility and recollection of pleasant life events. In the depression literature, some have argued that the more negativistic memory bias of depressed individuals might serve to maintain their disorder. For example, Teasdale (1983) has argued that a number of studies support the conclusion that depressed individuals are more likely to recall negative memories. This conclusion is supported by evidence from autobiographical memory tasks (e.g., Grimm & Watkins, 1998; Teasdale & Fogarty, 1979), and from studies using valenced word lists (e.g., Watkins et al., 1992). This mood-congruent memory bias appears to be robust in explicit memory (for a review, see Blaney, 1986) and to be somewhat less consistent in implicit memory (for a review see Watkins, 2002). Teasdale (1983) has argued that because depressed individuals are more likely to recollect unpleasant experiences, this should directly affect their current mood state. In addition, remembering negative life events should activate associations to other aversive memories, thereby increasing the likelihood that these experiences will come to mind and again have an aversive impact on current affect. Furthermore, Teasdale has argued that the tendency to recall more negative experiences should decrease depressive persons' outcome expectancy for mood-repair activities, thereby decreasing their likelihood of engaging in these coping behaviors. In all of these ways, Teasdale has argued that mood-congruent memory should promote the maintenance of depression. Whereas Teasdale has emphasized the recollection of negative memories, it could be argued that it is the lack of accessibility of positive memories that is more important in depression. For example, in our explicit memory research, depressed individuals have not typically recalled more negative information than nondepressed controls. Rather, it has been that controls tend to recall many more positive memories than their depressed counterparts (Grimm & Watkins, 1998; Watkins et al., 1992).

Williams, Watts, McLeod, and Mathews (1988, 1996) explained this cognitive bias in depression by arguing that the depressed condition is associated with mood-congruent elaboration. Elaboration refers to the creation of new associations between representations in memory, and the activation of old associations. Williams and colleagues proposed that depressed individuals are more likely to conceptually elaborate negative information, which promotes better learning of mood-congruent information. Additionally, the tendency for depressives to elaborate negative information should enhance mood-congruent retrieval by providing more associative links to negative memory representations. Although this approach appears to be one of the best accounts of information processing biases in depression, one could argue that it is not so much the elaboration of negative information that characterizes depression as it is the failure to show enhanced elaboration of positive information.

Although it is probably inappropriate to see depression as simply the converse of happiness, most depressed individuals show a low satisfaction with life. Thus, an important aspect of happiness may be the accessibility of positive memories (Seidlitz & Diener, 1993). I propose that gratitude should enhance the retrievability of positive experiences by increasing elaboration of positive information. I submit that this enhanced elaboration should take place both at encoding and retrieval. A more grateful person should be more likely to notice positive aspects in his or her life and thus enhance the encoding of these experiences into memory. Second, if at encoding an individual experiences gratitude in response to a benefit, this by definition should increase the conceptual elaboration of the event representation. Elaborating the event at encoding increases the number of completed retrieval routes to this representation and thereby increases the retrievability of the event (Graf & Mandler, 1984). Third, I submit that grateful individuals should be more likely to recall past benefits from their life and to experience gratitude in response to these blessings. In other words, grateful individuals should be more likely to count their blessings. The very act of recalling positive life events should increase their accessibility. Furthermore, the experience of gratitude in response to these recollections should provide more cognitive elaboration of these positive experiences, thereby increasing their retrievability. Earlier, I described the life events recall study (Watkins, Christianson, Lawrence, & Whitney, 2001) in which we showed that the grateful trait predicts a positive recall bias, after controlling for depression. This result lends some support to the proposition that gratitude increases the elaboration of positive information.

The increased availability of positive life experiences should provide memorial evidence for judgments of SWB, as well as fodder for increased positive affect. Furthermore, it seems that the ability to recall blessings from one's past would assist attempts to cope with unpleasant situations and emotions (Rusting & Dehart, 2000). For example, if in response to a perceived failure, such as a poor test grade, one is able to recall many past compliments and blessings received from others, it seems that this failure would be more tolerable.

Because gratitude is best classified as a positive affect, perhaps these predictions about gratitude's enhancing the elaboration of positive information are not unique. After all, the work of Alice Isen and colleagues has repeatedly shown how positive affect inductions increase the availability of positive information in memory (e.g., Isen, Shalker, Clark, & Karp, 1978; for a review see Ashby, Isen, & Turken, 1999). However, here I make the strong prediction that both a grateful disposition and a practice of gratitude should enhance elaboration of positive information beyond that of mere positive affect. I submit that if an individual receives a benefit, that person will be more likely to recall that benefit if he or she feels grateful in response to the event than if he or she feels merely pleased about the event.

In this and in other areas of gratitude research, I believe it is important to embark on the difficult task of dissociating the effects of gratitude from positive affectivity generally. If the cognitive and affective effects of gratitude are identical to other positive emotions, the construct of gratitude may not contain any unique explanatory power. However, it is important to point out that it is not necessary to demonstrate that gratitude has unique effects above and beyond any previous effects shown to be the result of positive affect inductions. It is only necessary to demonstrate the unique emotional and cognitive effects of gratitude in comparison with positive affect that does *not* involve gratitude. In much of the existing positive affect research, it is not possible to determine if gratitude was involved in the affect inductions. For example, perhaps the most common and reliable positive affect induction procedure used by Isen and colleagues has been the administration of an unexpected gift (Ashby et al., 1999). As McCullough and colleagues (2001) have shown in their review of the gratitude literature, receiving a gift and receiving a gift beyond one's social expectations have both been shown to be conditions in which gratitude responses are likely. Thus, it seems likely that grateful emotion was involved in some of the past research using positive affect inductions. The challenge for future gratitude research is to develop gratitude inductions that clearly contrast with positive affect inductions devoid of gratitude. I believe that Emmons and McCullough (2003) have made an important first step in this direction by attempting to compare a gratitude manipulation with a pride manipulation.

It is also possible that gratitude increases happiness by increasing the actual number of benefits in a person's life. In particular, gratitude could increase happiness by enhancing a person's social benefits. SWB has been shown to be related to the quality of one's friendships in life (Diener et al., 1999; Myers, 2000a), and I propose that gratitude is also related to the quality of one's social contacts. Although I am not aware of any evidence that directly supports this proposed mechanism, a few experimental studies offer indirect support. Several studies have shown that expressing gratitude increases the likelihood of receiving future benefits (Carey, Clicque, Leighton, & Milton, 1976; Crano & Sivacek, 1982; Maheux, Legault, & Lambert, 1989; McGovern, Ditzian, & Taylor, 1975; Rind & Bordia, 1995). In addition, research has shown that individuals failing to show gratitude are not well liked (e.g., McGovern et al., 1975), and by implication grateful individuals should be more likable. However, there is evidence to suggest that when individuals think that someone is expressing gratitude only to garner more benefits, that person is less likely to receive those benefits (Carey et al., 1976). I submit that the expression of gratitude in Lewis's terms—as a completion of one's enjoyment of a benefit—is more likely to be perceived by others as a genuine expression of gratitude, and thus is more likely to garner social benefits. A paradox of gratitude is that, although gratitude results in social benefits, if one expresses gratitude in order to receive these benefits, one is not as likely to realize these rewards. However, in general the evidence supports the proposal that the expression of gratitude often results in social reward, and this may be another reason that gratitude supports long-term SWB.

Finally I would like to suggest that gratitude might increase SWB through the prevention of depressive episodes. In several studies, we have found that depression appears to have a particularly strong inverse association with gratitude that exceeds relationships with other aversive states. In two studies, my colleagues and I (Watkins et al., 1997, 1999) have found that the GRAT is negatively related to depression as measured by the Beck Depression Inventory ($r = -.34, -.54, -.56$). However, it is well known that self-report questionnaires are inadequate measures of the clinical syndrome. Therefore, in another study (Woodward, Moua, & Watkins, 1998), we evaluated the gratitude status of individuals who were diagnosed with the use of a structured clinical interview. We found that clinically depressed individuals showed significantly lower gratitude as measured by the GRAT (almost two standard deviations below our nondepressed controls). This could simply be a consequence of the negativistic biasing of depressed mood. But we also found that nondepressed individuals who had a significant history of depression had reliably lower GRAT scores than nondepressed individuals without a history of depression. This finding leads to the suggestion that a lack of gratitude may be a vulnerability factor for depression.

How might gratitude prevent depression? Many of the mechanisms I have suggested above should also contribute to the prevention of depression. If gratitude provides more focus on and enjoyment of benefits, this seems to contravene depression. To the extent that gratitude helps individuals direct their attention to blessings they have and away from things they lack, this should decrease the likelihood of depression. Stressful events appear to be important precursors of depressive episodes, so if gratitude proves to be an effective coping technique, this should also help to prevent depression. Also, in providing for increased access to positive memories, gratitude could help build more positive cognitions. Although depression treatment approaches have historically emphasized correcting negative thoughts, recently some have encouraged more emphasis on building positive thoughts (e.g., Ingram, Slater, Atkinson, & Scott, 1990; Ingram & Wisnicki, 1988; Lightsey, 1994). A practice of gratitude could help develop a more positive way of thinking about life events, and so assist in the prevention of depression (cf. Fredrickson, 2000). Various depression researchers have proposed that the lack of social rewards (or increased social punishment, or both) is important in the etiology and maintenance of depression. If a grateful disposition actually provides for a more enjoyable social life, this should also help to contravene depression. On a related note, I propose that gratitude may mitigate depression by directing one's attention away from oneself to others. Research has shown that depressed individuals engage in self-focus that exacerbates their dysphoria (for a review, see Ingram, 1990). I submit that a grateful disposition and practice should result in directing one's attention more to others and what they are providing for one, and away from maladaptive self-preoccupation. SWB appears to be determined not just by the frequency of positive emotional events, but also by the proportion of pleasant to unpleasant events (Diener et al., 1999). Gratitude may contribute to long-term SWB by preventing depressive episodes.

Surely there are proposals for mechanisms explaining how gratitude may increase SWB in addition to those I have suggested here. But one might also argue that happiness promotes gratitude. There are good reasons for suggesting this causal link. In evaluating the conditions that produce gratitude, the literature suggests that three perceptions on the part of the gift receiver increase his or her experience of gratitude. First, the receiver must acknowledge the goodness of the gift. Research has shown that the more the receiver values the gift, the more likely he or she is to experience gratitude (e.g., Tesser, Gatewood, & Driver, 1968). Second, if the receiver acknowledges the goodness of the giver, he or she is more likely to feel grateful. Several studies have shown that if the receiver thinks the giver is providing a favor intentionally for his or her benefit, the receiver is more likely to experience gratitude (Graham, 1988; Tesser et al., 1968). Third, the receiver is more likely to feel grateful if he or she thinks that the gift is gratuitous. The more a gift goes beyond the receiver's social expectations, the more likely he or she will be to experience gratitude (e.g., Bar-Tal, Bar-Zohar, Greenberg, & Hermon, 1977; Hegtvedt, 1990).

Research from the positive affect literature suggests that the first two perceptions are more likely if one is happy. Several studies suggest that when positive affect is induced experimentally, people evaluate things more positively. For example, in the classic study by Isen and colleagues (1978), people evaluated their home appliances more positively if they had just been given an inexpensive gift (see also Isen & Shalker, 1982). This evidence suggests that if one is feeling good, one is more likely to recognize the goodness of benefits, thus promoting grateful responses. Second, when one is encouraged to feel better, research suggests that one evaluates others more positively (e.g., Isen, Niedenthal, & Cantor, 1992). If positive emotion encourages positive evaluations of others, this implies that happy people should be more likely to recognize the goodness of the giver in response to a gift. In other words, happy people should be more likely to acknowledge the good intentions of a giver. This too should promote grateful responding. Although the evidence for happiness promoting gratitude is somewhat indirect, future research could investigate more directly whether positive affect inductions result in increased evaluations of the goodness of gifts, increased acknowledgment of good intentions of givers, and in turn whether gratitude is more likely.

Does gratitude cause happiness, or does happiness cause gratitude? I propose that the answer to both questions is yes. Gratitude promotes happiness, but happiness probably increases the likelihood of gratitude as well. I propose that gratitude and happiness operate in a cycle of virtue similar to the "positive loop" suggested by Isen and colleagues (1978). Some authors have proposed that emotional disorders are characterized by vicious cycles (e.g., Teasdale, 1983). Here I propose that gratitude and happiness feed off each other in a more adaptive cycle. Figure 9.2 illustrates this proposal. Those who are more likely to respond with gratitude to life situations should be more happy generally because of enhanced enjoyment of life benefits, enhanced encoding and recollection of positive life events, and other possible

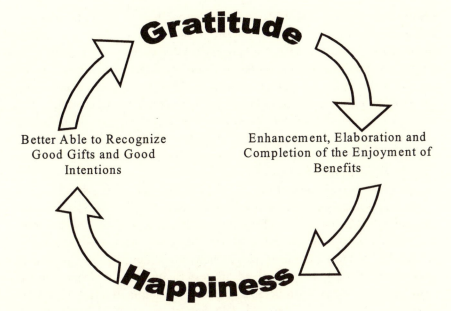

Figure 9.2. Adaptive cycle of gratitude and happiness.

mechanisms that I explored earlier. Positive affect research suggests that happiness enhances the likelihood that one will recognize and interpret life situations as good, and that happy people are more likely to acknowledge the good intentions of others in providing benefits to them. Existing gratitude research suggests that both of these conditions enhance the likelihood of grateful responses. I propose that gratitude promotes happiness, which in turn should promote more gratitude. Obviously, gratitude does not inevitably result in happiness, nor is gratitude the inevitable consequence of happiness. Many factors, including life events and individual differences, may interrupt or enhance this cycle. However, I submit that this cycle may provide a helpful model for understanding the relationship between gratitude and SWB, and I hope that it will energize future research.

ISSUES FOR FUTURE RESEARCH

In the previous theoretical discussion, a number of empirical issues are apparent. In this section I briefly review some additional research issues that I believe to be important for understanding the gratitude-SWB association. First, I believe there are several methodological advancements that would greatly benefit this research. Much of the research reviewed in this chapter has relied on self-report measures. In this regard, the field could be advanced by using measures that are not so directly dependent on self-report. For example, memory and other cognitive measures utilized by cognitive science should prove useful. Another approach would be to compare grateful and less grateful individuals' emotional responses to ambiguous situations. Perhaps psychophysiological measurements would provide useful findings as well. Gratitude research could take advantage of the methodological advances in personality, cognitive, and emotion psychology to go beyond using self-report instruments.

Another important methodological advance would be the development of reliable techniques for inducing gratitude in the lab. In the preceding discussion on SWB and the grateful state, I reviewed several studies that offer suggestions as to how one might proceed in developing these manipulations. This methodological development is important, because to understand some of the ways in which gratitude actually causes changes in mood and cognition, we need to be able to reliably manipulate gratitude in the laboratory. A systematic research program that would identify reliable manipulation techniques should not only provide benefits for other researchers, but should also provide important data on theoretical issues about gratitude. For example, when our two gratitude manipulation studies are compared, it appears that the technique used by Stone and Watkins (2001) was more effective at manipulating gratitude and consequent affect than our earlier techniques that relied on a listing methodology (e.g., Woodward, 2000). Perhaps simply listing things one is thankful for is not as effective in eliciting gratitude as focusing on one significant thing one is thankful for. If future studies bear out this difference, not only does this provide researchers with valuable information about how to best manipulate gratitude in the lab, it also has theoretical implications.

A third empirical issue concerns whether the disposition of gratitude can be changed. Although the studies reviewed earlier suggest that one's grateful state can be manipulated in the lab, by definition the grateful trait should be much more difficult to change. In fact, we have found that scores on the GRAT are not significantly affected by reliable mood induction techniques (Moua, 1998). Not only should the grateful trait be difficult to manipulate in the lab, one could argue that even in more realistic long-term circumstances the grateful disposition is not likely to change. This question is important, because the grateful disposition may have more important consequences for SWB than a few grateful experiences. Implicit in some gratitude research programs is the assumption that by improving gratitude, one can improve one's happiness. However, if enhancing the grateful disposition is as futile as attempting to increase height or change eye color (cf. Lykken & Tellegen, 1996), this goal seems fruitless. Although I propose that the grateful disposition (like other attitudes) is difficult to change, improving one's tendency to respond gratefully should not be impossible. Research that evaluates the question of whether one can change one's grateful disposition over the long run will have important implications for the value of gratitude research for long-term SWB.

Perhaps much of the future research on gratitude could be summed up by the question, How do grateful people think? Because the few emotion theories that deal with gratitude argue that this is a complex emotion (e.g., Lazarus & Lazarus, 1994; Ortony, Clore, & Collins, 1988; Weiner, Russell, & Lerman, 1978), cognitive variables are important to consider. How does a grateful person think about a benefit? In response to a stressful situation, how does a grateful person think about the circumstance? How do grateful people reflect on their past? Is there a difference between grateful memories and memories that are merely pleasant? Are grateful memories represented differently than more generic pleasant memories? The information-processing approach may prove valuable for investigating these questions, and the answers to these questions should provide useful information about how people can improve their grateful dispositions.

CONCLUSIONS

I began this chapter by suggesting that gratitude may directly contribute to emotional well-being. I have reviewed several studies that provide empirical support for this proposal; however, the relationship between gratitude and happiness is far from clear. I have suggested several causal mechanisms whereby gratitude may contribute to SWB. Future research could further investigate these possibilities. Although gratitude could be an important causal agent for states of happiness, it is also possible that gratitude is something of an epiphenomenon of happiness. A third possibility that I have proposed is that gratitude may contribute to happiness, and happiness in turn may make gratitude more likely, resulting in a cycle of virtue. Again, it is my hope that this model will provide direction for future gratitude and SWB research. Whatever the case, the initial evidence provides promising hints that gratitude may be an important component of SWB; indeed, grateful people do tend to be happy people. Perhaps future research will provide additional affirmation for C. S. Lewis's conclusion, "Except where intolerably adverse circumstances interfere, praise almost seems to be inner health made audible" (1958, p. 94).

References

Ashby, F. G., Isen, A. M., & Turken, U. (1999). A neuropsychological theory of positive affect and its influence on cognition. *Psychological Review, 106,* 529–550.

Bar-Tal, D., Bar-Zohar, Y., Greenberg, M. S., & Hermon, M. (1977). Reciprocity behavior in the relationship between donor and recipient and between harm-doer and victim. *Sociometry, 40,* 293–298.

Blaney, P. (1986). Affect and memory: A review. *Psychological Bulletin, 99,* 229–246.

Botta, R. (1999). Television images and adolescent girls' body image disturbance. *Journal of Communication, 49*(2), 22–41.

Carey, J. R., Clicque, S. H., Leighton, B. A., & Milton, F. (1976). A test of positive reinforcement of customers. *Journal of Marketing, 40,* 98–100.

Cattarin, J. A., Thompson, J. K., Thomas, C., & Williams, R. (2000). Body image, mood, and televised images of attractiveness: The role of social comparison. *Journal of Social and Clinical Psychology, 19,* 220–239.

Chesterton, G. K. (1986). Orthodoxy. In D. Dooley (Ed.), *G. K. Chesterton: Collected works* (Vol. 1, pp. 209–366). San Francisco: Ignatius Press. (Original work published 1908)

Chesterton, G. K. (1990). *Saint Francis of Assisi.* New York: Doubleday. (Original work published 1924)

Coffman, S. (1996). Parents' struggles to rebuild family life after Hurricane Andrew. *Issues in Mental Health Nursing, 17,* 353–367.

Crano, W. D., & Sivacek, J. (1982). Social reinforcement, self-attribution, and the foot-in-the-door phenomenon. *Social Cognition, 1,* 110–125.

Csikszentmihalyi, M. (1999). If we are so rich, why aren't we happy? *American Psychologist, 54,* 821–827.

DeNeve, K. M. (1999). Happy as an extraverted clam? The role of personality for subjective well-being. *Psychological Science, 8,* 141–144.

DeNeve, K. M., & Cooper, H. (1998). The happy personality: A meta-analysis of 137 personality traits and subjective well-being. *Psychological Bulletin, 124,* 197–229.

Diener, E. (1984). Subjective well-being. *Psychological Bulletin, 95,* 542–575.

Diener, E., Colvin, C. R., Pavot, W. G., & Allman, A. (1991). The psychic costs of intense positive affect. *Journal of Personality and Social Psychology, 61,* 492–503.

Diener, E., Emmons, R. A., Larsen, R. J., & Griffin, S. (1985). The Satisfaction With Life Scale. *Journal of Personality Assessment, 49,* 71–75.

Diener, E., Suh, E. M., Lucas, R. E., & Smith, H. L. (1999). Subjective well-being: Three decades of progress. *Psychological Bulletin, 125,* 276–302.

Emmons, R. A., & McCullough, M. E. (2003). Counting blessings versus burdens: An experimental investigation of gratitude and subjective well-being in daily life. *Journal of Personality and Social Psychology, 84*(2), 377–389.

Fordyce, M. W. (1988). A review of research on the happiness measures: A sixty second index of happiness and mental health. *Social Indicators Research, 20,* 355–381.

Fredrickson, B. L. (1998). What good are the positive emotions? *Review of General Psychology, 2,* 300–319.

Fredrickson, B. L. (2000). Cultivating positive emotions to optimize health and well-being. *Prevention and Treatment, 3*, Article 0001a. Retrieved May 12, 2003, from http://journals.apa.org/prevention/volume3/pre0030001a.html

Frijda, N. H. (1988). The laws of emotion. *American Psychologist, 23*, 349–358.

Fry, P. S. (1975). Affect and resistance to temptation. *Developmental Psychology, 13*, 519–520.

Gallup survey results on "gratitude," adults and teenagers. (1998). *Emerging Trends, 20*, 4–5, 9.

Graf, P., & Mandler, G. (1984). Activation makes words more accessible but not necessarily more retrievable. *Journal of Verbal Learning and Verbal Behavior, 23*, 533–568.

Graham, S. (1988). Children's developing understanding of the motivational role of affect: An attributional analysis. *Cognitive Development, 3*, 71–88.

Grimm, D. L. (2000). *Involuntary mood-congruent memory bias in depression*. Unpublished master's thesis, Eastern Washington University, Cheney.

Grimm, D. L., & Watkins, P. C. (1998, May). *Time may not heal all wounds*. Paper presented at the 10th Annual Convention of the American Psychological Society, Washington, DC.

Hagerty, M. R. (2000). Social comparison of income in one's community: Evidence from national surveys of income and happiness. *Journal of Personality and Social Psychology, 78*, 764–771.

Hegtvedt, K. A. (1990). The effects of relationship structure on emotional responses to inequity. *Social Psychology Quarterly, 53*, 214–228.

Hennigan, K. M., Heath, L., Wharton, J. D., Del Rosario, M. L., Cook, T. D., & Calder, B. J. (1982). Impact of the introduction of television on crime in the United States: Empirical findings and theoretical implications. *Journal of Personality and Social Psychology, 42*, 461–467.

Ingram, R. E. (1990). Self-focused attention in clinical disorders: Review and a conceptual model. *Psychological Bulletin, 107*, 156–176.

Ingram, R. E., Slater, M. A., Atkinson, J. H., & Scott, W. (1990). Positive automatic cognition in major affective disorder. *Psychological Assessment, 2*, 209–211.

Ingram, R. E., & Wisnicki, K. S. (1988). Assessment of positive automatic cognition. *Journal of Consulting and Clinical Psychology, 56*, 898–902.

Isen, A. M., Niedenthal, P. M., & Cantor, N. (1992). An influence of positive affect on social categorization. *Motivation and Emotion, 16*, 65–78.

Isen, A. M., & Shalker, T. E. (1982). The effect of feeling state on evaluation of positive, neutral, and negative stimuli: When you "accentuate the positive," do you "eliminate the negative"? *Social Psychology Quarterly, 45*, 58–63.

Isen, A. M., Shalker, T. E., Clark, M., & Karp, L. (1978). Affect, accessibility of material in memory, and behavior: A cognitive loop? *Journal of Personality and Social Psychology, 36*, 1–12.

James, W. (1958). *Varieties of religious experience*. New York: Mentor Books. (Original work published 1902)

Kuykendall, D., Keating, J. P., & Wagaman, J. (1988). Assessing affective states: A new methodology for some old problems. *Cognitive Therapy and Research, 12*, 279–294.

Lazarus, R. S., & Lazarus, B. N. (1994). *Passion and reason: Making sense of our emotions.* New York: Oxford University Press.

Lewis, C. S. (1958). *Reflections on the Psalms.* New York: Harcourt, Brace.

Lewis, C. S. (1963). *Letters to Malcolm: Chiefly on prayer.* San Diego: Harcourt Brace Jovanovich.

Lightsey, O. R. (1994). "Thinking positive" as a stress buffer: The role of positive automatic cognitions in depression and happiness. *Journal of Counseling Psychology, 41,* 325–334.

Lorr, M., & Wunderlich, R. A. (1988). A semantic differential mood scale. *Journal of Clinical Psychology, 44,* 33–35.

Lykken, D., & Tellegen, A. (1996). Happiness is a stochastic phenomenon. *Psychological Science, 7,* 186–189.

Lyubomirsky, S., & Lepper, H. S. (1999). A measure of subjective happiness: Preliminary reliability and construct validation. *Social Indicators Research, 46,* 137–155.

Lyubomirsky, L., & Ross, L. (1997). Hedonic contrasts of social comparison: A contrast of happy and unhappy people. *Journal of Personality and Social Psychology, 73,* 1141–1157.

Maheux, B., Legault, C., & Lambert, J. (1989). Increasing response rates in physicians mail surveys: An experimental study. *American Journal of Public Health, 79,* 638–639.

Masingale, A. M., Schoonover, S., Kraft, S., Burton, R., Waring, S., Fouad, B., Tracy, J., Phillips, S., Kolts, R. L., & Watkins, P. (2001, December). *Gratitude and post-traumatic symptomatology in a college sample.* Paper submitted for presentation at the convention of the International Society for Traumatic Stress Studies, New Orleans.

Mayer, J. D., Salovey, P., Gomberg-Kaufman, S. & Blainey, K. (1991). A broader conception of mood experience. *Journal of Personality and Social Psychology, 60,* 100–111.

McAdams, D. P., Reynolds, J., Lewis, M., Patten, A. H., & Bowman, P. J. (2001). When bad things turn good and good things turn bad: Sequences of redemption and contamination in life narrative and their relation to psychosocial adaptation in midlife adults and in students. *Personality and Social Psychology Bulletin, 27,* 474–485.

McCullough, M. E., Emmons, R. A., & Tsang, J. (2002). The grateful disposition: A conceptual and empirical topography. *Journal of Personality and Social Psychology, 82,* 112–127.

McCullough, M. E., Kilpatrick, S. D., Emmons, R. A., & Larson, D. B. (2001). Gratitude as moral affect. *Psychological Bulletin, 127,* 249–266.

McGovern, L. P., Ditzian, J. L., & Taylor, S. P. (1975). The effect of positive reinforcement on helping with cost. *Bulletin of the Psychonomic Society, 5,* 421–423.

Moua, G. (1998). *Gratitude: The mediating factor of mood-congruent memory.* Unpublished master's thesis, Eastern Washington University, Cheney.

Myers, D. G. (1993). *The pursuit of happiness: Discovering the pathway to fulfillment, well-being, and enduring personal joy.* New York: Avon Books.

Myers, D. G. (2000a). The funds, friends, and faith of happy people. *American Psychologist, 55*, 56–67.

Myers, D. G. (2000b). *The American paradox: Spiritual hunger in an age of plenty.* New Haven, CT: Yale University Press.

Myers, D. G., & Diener, E. (1995). Who is happy? *Psychological Science, 6*, 10–18.

Ortony, A., Clore, G. L., & Collins, A. (1988). *The cognitive structure of emotions.* Cambridge, UK: Cambridge University Press.

Pavot, W., & Diener, E. (1993). Review of the Satisfaction With Life Scale. *Psychological Assessment, 5*, 164–172.

Rind, B., & Bordia, P. (1995). Effects of server's "thank you" and personalization on restaurant tipping. *Journal of Applied Social Psychology, 25*, 745–751.

Rusting, C. L., & DeHart, T. (2000). Retrieving positive memories to regulate negative mood: Consequences for mood-congruent memory. *Journal of Personality and Social Psychology, 78*, 737–752.

Salovey, P., Mayer, J. D., Goldman, S. L., Turvey, C., & Palfai, T. P. (1995). Emotional attention, clarity, and repair: Exploring emotional intelligence using the Trait Meta-Mood Scale. In J. W. Pennebaker (Ed.), *Emotion, disclosure, and health* (pp. 125–154). Washington, DC: American Psychological Association.

Schwarz, J. C., & Pollack, P. R. (1977). Affect and delay of gratification. *Journal of Research in Personality, 11*, 147–164.

Seidlitz, L., & Diener, E. (1993). Memory for positive versus negative life events: Theories for the differences between happy and unhappy persons. *Journal of Personality and Social Psychology, 64*, 654–664.

Seidlitz, L., Wyer, R. S., & Diener, E. (1997). Cognitive correlates of subjective well-being: The processing of valenced life events by happy and unhappy persons. *Journal of Personality and Social Psychology, 31*, 240–256.

Stone, T. L., & Watkins, P. C. (2001, May). *Does the expression of gratitude improve mood?* Paper presented at the 81st Annual Convention of the Western Psychological Association, Maui, HI.

Teasdale, J. D. (1983). Negative thinking in depression: Cause, effect, or reciprocal relationship? *Advances in Behaviour Research and Therapy, 5*, 3–25.

Teasdale, J. D., & Fogarty, S. J. (1979). Differential effects of induced mood on retrieval of pleasant and unpleasant memories from episodic memory. *Journal of Abnormal Psychology, 88*, 248–257.

Teigen, K. H. (1997). Luck, envy, and gratitude: It could have been different. *Scandinavian Journal of Psychology, 38*, 313–323.

Tesser, A., Gatewood, R., & Driver, M. (1968). Some determinants of gratitude. *Journal of Personality and Social Psychology, 9*, 233–236.

Tripp, R. T. (1970). *The international thesaurus of quotations.* New York: Harper & Row.

Trivers, R. L. (1971). The evolution of reciprocal altruism. *Quarterly Review of Biology, 46*, 35–57.

Veenhoven, R. (1988). The utility of happiness. *Social Indicators Research, 20*, 333–354.

Ventura, J. N. (1982). Parent coping behaviors, parent functioning, and infant temperament characteristics. *Nursing Research, 31,* 269–273.

Ventura, J. N., & Boss, P. G. (1983). The Family Coping Inventory applied to parents with new babies. *Journal of Marriage and the Family, 45,* 867–875.

Watkins, P. C. (2002). Implicit memory bias in depression. *Cognition and Emotion, 16,* 381–402.

Watkins, P. C., Christianson, P., Lawrence, J., & Whitney, A. (2001, May). *Are grateful individuals more emotionally intelligent?* Paper presented at the annual convention of the Western Psychological Association, Maui, HI.

Watkins, P. C., Grimm, D. L., & Hailu, L. (1999, June). *Counting your blessings: Grateful individuals recall more positive memories.* Paper presented at the annual convention of the American Psychological Society, Denver, CO.

Watkins, P. C., Mathews, A., Williamson, D. A., & Fuller, R. D. (1992). Mood-congruent memory in depression: Emotional priming or elaboration? *Journal of Abnormal Psychology, 101,* 581–586.

Watkins, P. C., Porter, W. T., & Curtis, N. (1996, April). *The attitude of gratitude: Development of a new measure.* Paper presented at the annual convention of the Western Psychological Association, San Jose, CA.

Watkins, P. C., Porter, W. T., & Miller, C. (1997, April). *Gratitude and subjective wellbeing.* Paper presented at the annual convention of the Western Psychological Association, Seattle, WA.

Watson, D., Clark, L.A., & Tellegen, A. (1988). Development and validation of brief measures of positive and negative affect: The PANAS Scales. *Journal of Personality and Social Psychology, 54,* 1063–1070.

Weiner, B., Russell, D., & Lerman, D. (1978). Affective consequences of causal ascriptions. In J. H. Harvey, W. J. Ickes, & R. F. Kidd (Eds.), *New directions in attributional research* (Vol. 2, pp. 59–88). Hillsdale, NJ: Erlbaum.

Wertheim, E. H., & Schwarz, J. C. (1983). Depression, guilt, and self-management of pleasant and unpleasant events. *Journal of Personality and Social Psychology, 45,* 884–889.

Williams, J. M. G., Watts, F. N., McLeod, C., & Mathews, A. (1988). *Cognitive psychology and emotional disorders.* Chichester, UK: Wiley.

Williams, J. M. G., Watts, F. N., McLeod, C., & Mathews, A. (1996). *Cognitive psychology and emotional disorders* (2nd ed.). Chichester, UK: Wiley.

Woodward, K. M. (2000, April). *The effect of gratitude on mood states.* Paper presented at the annual convention of the Western Psychological Association, Portland, OR.

Woodward, K. M., Moua, G. K., & Watkins, P. C. (1998, April). *Depressed individuals show less gratitude.* Paper presented at the annual convention of the Western Psychological Association, Albuquerque, NM.

Yates, G. C. R., Lippett, R. M. K., & Yates, S. M. (1981). The effects of age, positive affect induction, and instructions on children's delay of gratification. *Journal of Experimental Child Psychology, 32,* 169–180.

PART IV

Perspectives from Anthropology
and Biology

10   Gratitude and Gift Exchange

Aafke Elisabeth Komter

In our commonsense thinking about gratitude, we are inclined to think of it as a warm and nice feeling directed toward someone who has been benevolent to us. The definitions of gratitude given in dictionaries confirm this perspective. Although I think that this view contains an important element of truth, it disregards a more fundamental meaning of gratitude. Beneath the warm feelings of gratitude resides an imperative force, a force that compels us to return the benefit we have received. Gratitude has a clearly specified action tendency connected to it, as has also been stipulated by emotion theorists (Lazarus & Lazarus, 1994). This duty to return led the social psychologist Barry Schwartz (1967) to speak of the "gratitude imperative." Why aren't we allowed to look a gift horse in the mouth? Because that would be a sign of ingratitude and of indifference toward the giver, and that is simply disastrous. In Japan the recipient of a gift is not allowed to unpack the gift in the presence of the giver. To Western eyes this may seem an exotic habit, but on closer inspection it contains a very important message about gratitude: By keeping the gift wrapped, the recipient's possible disappointment about the gift and its giver—showing itself in a lack of gratitude—remains hidden. Perhaps this is the Japanese version of our gift horse.

Why is a lack of gratitude felt as something to be avoided by all means? Because gift exchange and the concomitant feelings of gratitude serve to confirm and maintain social ties. Gratitude is part of the chain of reciprocity and as such, it has "survival value": It is sustaining a cycle of gift and counter-gift, and thereby essential in creating social cohesion and community. Gratitude is the oil that keeps the engine of the human "service economy" going, to use Bonnie and de Waal's term (chap. 11, this volume).

But gratitude is not merely a moral coercion; it is also a moral virtue. Gratitude as a virtue is an important aspect of character: the capacity to experience as well as express feelings of being thankful. The fact that someone may be seen as a grateful person indicates that gratitude is a personality asset, a talent, or even a gift that permeates all the social relationships this person is involved in. Lacking this virtue results in ingratitude, which seems to be an enduring personality characteristic as well. People who are regarded as ungrateful incur the risk of becoming isolated and estranged because of their inability to contribute to the essential symbolic nourishment human relationships are fed on, that is, the mutual exchange of gifts connecting people by the bonds of gratitude.

Let us have a closer look at the linguistic meanings of the word *grateful*. In English as well as Dutch, *grateful* has a wider range of meanings than the literal one of being grateful to someone for having received something. The first meaning becomes clear if we speak of a *grateful shade*, where the word is synonymous with salutary or pleasant. In *grateful soil* the word means fertile, able to produce abundance without much outside help. In Dutch we speak of a *grateful task* or a *grateful subject*, indicating that the task or subject promises its own reward without much extra effort required on the part of those dealing with the task or subject (gratitude itself seems to be this kind of grateful subject).

I refrain here from trying to give a full-blown definition of gratitude, because definitions of such multilayered and complex phenomena are bound to be inadequate. What I do, however, is sketch the contours of an "anatomy of gratitude," in an effort to delineate some of its most prominent aspects and meanings. I approach the subject from various angles, starting with the very thing that is given away. Anthropological perspectives on the "spirit of the gift" wanting to be returned to the original donor will be the focus here. The next section moves on to the recipient of the gift. Here gratitude is analyzed from a psychological point of view, as a personality characteristic. How do people develop the capacity to be grateful and express gratitude toward others? Then some more sociological views on gratitude are discussed, changing the focus to the mutual relationship between the recipient and the giver, and the social and cultural impact of gratitude. Reciprocity appears to be the underlying principle behind gift exchange, with the connected feelings of gratitude functioning as the moral cement of human society and culture. Without gratitude, there would be no social continuity, because it fosters and maintains the network of social ties in which we are embedded. In the final section, I attempt to dissect the concept of gratitude by highlighting the various layers of which it is composed.

THE SPIRIT OF THE GIFT

Let us first examine some of the most seminal insights on gifts and gratitude formulated by anthropologists (for an overview, see Komter, 1996a). According to them, one of the main characteristics of gifts is that they should be given and reciprocated. A gift that cannot "move" loses its gift properties. A very clear example is the *Kula*, the ceremonial exchange of gifts by the inhabitants of the Trobriand Islands near New Guinea. Malinowski, who lived among them during World War I, described this ritual in detail in *Argonauts of the Western Pacific* (1922). The *Kula* is a form of exchange on the part of the communities inhabiting a wide ring of islands, which form a closed circuit. Along this route, articles of two kinds constantly travel in opposite directions. Only the long necklaces of red shell move in a clockwise direction, whereas bracelets of white shell move in a counterclockwise direction. After some time, these articles meet articles of the other class on their way and are exchanged for them. It takes between 2 and 10 years for each article in the *Kula* to make a full round of the islands. This practice shows that it is not the articles that count but the exchange itself, the principle of give-and-take, as Malinowski termed it. The important thing is that the *Kula* gifts are kept in motion. If someone keeps a gift too long, he or she will develop a bad reputation. Someone who owns something is expected to share it, to pass it on. Among the Trobriand Islanders, to possess is to give, as Malinowski said.

Another example of a gift cycle can be found in the work of the French ethnologist and sociologist Marcel Mauss. In his famous work, *Essai sur le Don*, or *The Gift* (1923/1990), he described the habits and traditions of the native tribes in New Zealand, the Maori. The Maori have a word, *hau*, that means "spirit," in particular the spirit of the gift. Returning from the forest where they have killed birds, the hunters of these tribes give a part of their game to the priests, who cook the birds at a sacred fire. After they have eaten some of them, the priests have an offering ceremony in which they return the *hau*—in the form of a part of the birds—to the forest, where it is supposed to produce a new abundance of birds to be killed by the hunters again. As in the *Kula*, there is a cycle of gift giving: The forest gives its richness to the hunters, the hunters give it to the priests, and the priests return it to the forest. The ceremony performed by the priests is called "nourishing *hau*," feeding the spirit, a literal form of feedback. The spirit of the gift is only kept alive by returning it to where it came from. By placing the gift back in the forest, the priests treat the birds as a gift of nature.

The key idea of Maori law is that the thing given or received is not inactive. After a thing has been abandoned by the giver, it still possesses something of him or her (*hau*). Through *hau*, the giver has a hold over the recipient because, as Mauss (1923/1990) wrote, "It is the *hau* that wishes to return to its birthplace, to the sanctuary of the forest and the clan, and to the owner" (p. 12). The spirit of the gift remains attached to the chain of beneficiaries until they give back from their own property, "their goods, or from their labor or trading, by way of feasts, festivals and presents, the equivalent or something of even greater value" (p. 12). The legal tie in Maori law, a tie occurring through things, is "one between souls, because the thing itself possesses a soul, is of the soul. Hence it follows that to make a gift of something to someone is to make a present of some part of oneself" (p. 12). Therefore, the recipient of the gift "must give back to another person what is really part and parcel of his nature and substance, because to accept something from somebody is to accept some part of his spiritual essence, of his soul. To retain that thing would be dangerous and mortal." The reason for this is that things do not only come from persons morally, but also physically and spiritually. Gifts exert a magical or religious hold over people. The thing given is invested with life and "seeks to return to . . . its 'place of origin'" (p. 13).

Several scholars of authority have criticized Mauss for his spiritual interpretation of the *hau*. Firth (1929/1959), for example, preferred secular to spiritual explanations. According to him, the fear of punishment or social sanctions is the real reason to fulfill one's obligation to return a gift. These sanctions can include a threat to the continuity of economic relations, or to the maintenance of prestige and power. Another anthropologist, Sahlins (1972), offered an alternative explanation, which is secular as well. Returning to the original text of the Maori legend, he discovered an interesting aspect that Mauss neglected in his rendering of the story. The participation of a third party in the cycle of gift exchange is crucial to Sahlins' conception of *hau*: For a gift to bring increase, it is necessary that a third party causes this increase. In the Maori legend, after having received the birds taken by the hunters, the priests offer some of them to the *Mauri* (a sacred stone acting as a shrine), which can then cause the birds to abound. According to Sahlins, the term *profit* would have been a better translation of *hau* than Mauss's "spirit." Sahlins conceived of *hau* as the "increase power" of the goods of the forest. The ceremonial offering of birds by the priests restores the fertility of the forest. In Sahlins's words, "The *hau* of a good is its yield, just as the *hau* of a forest is its productiveness" (1972, p. 160).

More recently, the French anthropologist Maurice Godelier (1999) reevaluated the various interpretations of *hau*. Godelier interpreted the game the hunters give to the priests as an "offering of thanksgiving in the hope that the forest and the priests will continue acting on behalf of the hunters" (p. 52). According to him, the essential idea in *hau* is that the original donor retains his or her rights to the object he or she has given, regardless of the number of times it changes hands. Here Godelier is paying tribute to the work of the late Annette Weiner (1992), who analyzed the *Kula* ceremonials from the perspective of "keeping-while-giving." She stated that certain categories of objects, in particular sacred objects, are given and kept at the same time because their ownership is inalienable in the end. Objects may circulate, and every person who receives them becomes a donor in turn. But only the original donor has the ultimate rights over the object because his or her ownership is inalienable; the other donors merely enjoy alienable and temporary rights of possession and use, which they transfer when they pass on the object. Following Godelier's view, it is not so much the spirit or the soul of the gift that makes it want to return to its original owner, nor its profit or yield, but rather the owner's inalienable rights to the object, which are known, felt, and respected by the other donors. Godelier made an interesting shift here from explaining the return of gifts on the grounds of properties of the object itself to attributing the cause to characteristics of the recipient, namely, his or her original rights, replacing the animistic and spiritual interpretation with a psychological and personal one.

However interesting Godelier's interpretation in terms of the first donor's rights may be, the spiritual explanation cannot so easily be ignored. In many other tribal communities, there are examples of things that are thought to possess a spirit, to be animated, alive, to have a will of their own, to wish to return to where they originally come from. An animistic way of experiencing things often originates in situations where natural fertility and growth are felt to be important. Lewis Hyde (1983) described a practice among American Indian tribes who depend on the ocean for their primary sustenance, especially the salmon that annually enter their rivers. The salmon are believed to dwell in a huge lodge beneath the sea and to have a human form when they are at home. Only once a year they change their bodies into fish bodies, swim to the mouths of the rivers, and sacrifice themselves to their land brothers as food for the winter. The first salmon in the rivers is welcomed with an elaborate ceremony. The fish is caught, placed on an altar, and laid out before the group with its head pointing inland to encourage the rest of the salmon to continue swimming upstream. According to Hyde,

> The first fish was treated as if it were a high-ranking chief making a visit from a neighboring tribe. The priest sprinkled its body with eagle down or red ochre and made a formal speech of welcome, mentioning . . . how much the tribe had hoped the run would continue and be bountiful. The celebrants then sang the songs that welcome an honored guest. After the ceremony the priest gave everyone present a piece of the fish to eat. Finally . . . the bones of the first salmon were returned to the sea. The belief was that salmon bones placed back into the water would reassemble once they had washed out to sea; the fish would then revive, return to its home, and revert

to its human form. . . . If they were not, the salmon would be offended and might not return the following year with their gift of
winter food. (1983, pp. 26–27)

This beautiful Indian story demonstrates the idea that gifts of nature can
only bear fruit if people show them gratitude in a proper way. The action tendency of gratitude is clearly illustrated in this example. The view that natural
wealth should be treated as a gift is as old as the Old Testament, in which the
first fruits of the earth are perceived as belonging to God. The fertility of the
earth is a gift from God, and in order to continue it, its fruits should be returned to him (Hyde, 1983). Perhaps this religious origin of gratitude also has
an ecological aspect. Throughout history, people have had some sense that it
is wrong to usurp the wealth offered by nature. It was a common practice
among European farmers in the Middle Ages to let their fields rest after they
had intensively cultivated them for some time. It is difficult to separate the
religious awe felt by humans for the abundance of the earth from their feeling that they should not exhaust its resources.

Hyde described another interesting category of gifts in which gratitude
can be seen at work, namely, gifts given at funerals. Gratitude apparently not
only binds the living to nature and to one another, it also connects the living
to the dead. Gifts given at someone's death are part of a general class of
"threshold gifts" that mark the passage from one state into another. By means
of these gifts, the transformation from one identity to another is facilitated.
Often some attributes pertaining to the life of the deceased (human or animal) are inserted into the coffin: Pharaohs are buried with their most valuable treasures and jewelry, and children are accompanied by their most cherished toys on their journey to another state. Many people believe that a
corpse should be buried with gifts intended to help the soul on its journey. If
the dead are not properly laid to rest, they will walk ceaselessly on earth, according to some folk beliefs. Gifts not only help transform the identity of the
once living being into the now dead one, they also express our gratitude to
the deceased, to the fact that we knew them and enjoyed the privilege of
being in their company for a certain period of time.

Hyde spoke of gratitude as a "labor undertaken by the soul" to effect the
transformation after a gift is received. "Between the time a gift comes to us
and the time we pass it along, we suffer gratitude. . . . Passing the gift along is
the act of gratitude that finishes the labor" (1983, p. 47). In this final act, the
true acceptance of the original gift is accomplished. The spirit of the gift has
been kept intact by giving ourselves away: Our ties with people who are or
were dear to us have been renewed and strengthened.

How people react to natural abundance and how they create and maintain mutual bonds by exchanging goods and services can both be interpreted

in terms of the concept of gratitude. Malinowski's principle of give-and-take seems to be based on an underlying feeling of indebtedness to the giver, which we are now inclined to call gratitude. Gifts returned to nature (because nature expects us to do so) and gifts wanting to return to where the original giver lives both seem to indicate an inner feeling of obligation to the outside world that is projected onto that world. That sense of obligation can only be resolved by means of an act of gratitude. Also, the story about the spirit of the gift can be regarded as a metaphor of gratitude. The difference in our modern conception is that gratitude is not thought of as an internal feeling or emotion, but as an external force that compels the recipient to reciprocate. Perhaps this deindividualized and external conception of gratitude derives its compelling force exactly from the fact that it *is* externalized and objectified: Acting in the spirit of gratitude is seen as a generally endorsed obligation that one cannot afford to shirk on penalty of social disapproval and exclusion.

THE RECIPIENT OF THE GIFT

From a psychological point of view, gratitude may be considered a virtue, a personality characteristic or asset. It is something one has to learn, and some people are better equipped to learn it than others. What are the preconditions for developing a capacity to be grateful? In her essay "Envy and Gratitude" (1957/1987), Melanie Klein considered gratitude from a psychoanalytic point of view. She held that envy is the most powerful factor in disturbing feelings of love and gratitude at their root, because it originates in the earliest relation of a child to its mother. This relationship has a fundamental importance for the individual's whole later emotional life, according to Klein. The quality of the mother's earliest breast contact with the child and, more symbolically, of her capacity to represent a "good object" to the child that it can identify with, is of great importance for laying the foundations for hope, trust, and belief in goodness. Any deprivation in this respect—not only the breast's literal failure to provide enough milk, but also (and perhaps more important) the mother's withholding of emotional nourishment—may cause the child to develop a serious emotional impairment in the form of hate, envy, jealousy, or greed. The most significant consequence of this emotional impairment is that the child is deprived of the opportunity to experience enjoyment as a result of being satisfied by the good object. Envy tends to become such a persistent characteristic because it spoils the capacity for enjoyment; enjoyment gives rise to gratitude, and only gratitude can mitigate destructive impulses such as envy and greed.

Only children who have been able to develop a deep-rooted relationship with a good maternal object can build up a strong and permanent capacity for love and gratitude, which can withstand temporary states of envy and hatred. In Melanie Klein's words, "One major derivative of the capacity for love is the feeling of gratitude. Gratitude is essential in building up the relation to the good object and underlies also the appreciation of goodness in others and in oneself. Gratitude is rooted in the emotions and attitudes that arise in the earliest stage of infancy, when for the baby the mother is the one and only object" (1957/1987, p. 187). Just as Freud described the infant's bliss in being suckled as the prototype of sexual gratification, Klein considered these experiences as constitutive for all later happiness. The full gratification of the maternal breast brings about the experience of having received a unique gift from the loved object, a gift that the child wants to keep.

This first gift is the basis of gratitude. The gratitude of being satisfied enables a child to accept and assimilate to the loved primal object, not only as a source of food, but also as a whole person. This is the first sign of basic trust in other people. The more regular the gratification and the more fully it is accepted, the more often the child will experience enjoyment, and gratitude and the wish to return pleasure in its wake. This recurrent experience plays an important role in the capacity to return goodness. Here we can see how gratitude and generosity become connected. Inner wealth makes one able to share gifts with others. As Klein said, "If this gratitude is deeply felt it includes the wish to return goodness received and is thus the basis of generosity. There is always a close connection between being able to accept and to give, and both are part of the relation to the good object" (1963/1987, p. 310).

Klein's theory can be criticized in several ways. One may question her emphasis on the weighty role of the motherly breast in the development of basic personality traits such as envy, jealousy, and greed on one hand and gratitude on the other. Should we interpret her account in a literal way, taking the abundance of the breast as the decisive factor for the development of gratitude, or would a more symbolic reading be more appropriate? The latter is probably the more fruitful option. Even if the motherly breast fails to produce enough milk, other attributes of the primary caring figure such as warmth, attention, closeness, and reactivity to the child may act as symbolic substitutes for the breast. Another possible objection to Melanie Klein's hypotheses is the lack of convincing empirical evidence; the clinical material she adduced to support her ideas may be considered too idiosyncratic, too filtered through her own analytical perspective. Finally, Klein's focus on the lasting impact of the child's very early experiences in relation to the mother on its adult emotional life may be considered exaggerated.

Nonetheless, the idea of a relation between the absence of shortages in motherly dedication and the capacity to enjoy the first gift a child receives from its caretaker (whether it be milk, warmth, or closeness) sounds highly probable. The hypothesis that one should first develop a capacity to enjoy the good things one receives from others before being able to experience gratitude also seems reasonable enough. Finally, the connection between gratitude and generosity, the idea that the capacity to receive and be grateful fosters the desire to return goodness, seems theoretically plausible. The principle of reciprocity that is demonstrated in so many anthropologists' accounts seems to apply at the level of the earliest interactions between mother and child as well. A lack of basic love and care—the first gift—leads to a failing capacity to enjoy, and this in turn impairs the capacity to be grateful, transformed in the return gift. As in all gift relationships, the bond is only kept intact if gifts are returned properly. Both the mother and the child may fail in this respect. In that case the negative side of the principle of reciprocity might come to apply. The less the mother is capable of giving the best of her being to the child, the less responsive and grateful the child will become. An ever more disturbed relationship may develop if the child doesn't give in return, causing the mother to become less responsive as well. Just as the gift of gratitude paves the way for new gifts to be given, a lack of gratitude evokes a diminishing propensity in others to give return gifts.

Whatever the merits of Melanie Klein's conception of how children develop the capacity to experience and express gratitude, it is clear that there are substantial individual differences. Some people are much more able to express genuine gratitude and be generous without compromise than others. Gratitude is a personal virtue that is neither self-evident nor equally distributed among all human beings.

GRATITUDE, RECIPROCITY, AND CULTURE

Gratitude: The "Moral Memory of Mankind"

A sociological view on gratitude would emphasize the interpersonal relationships and social interactions in which gratitude gets shape. Gratitude is always embedded in a relationship between two parties. The capacity to be grateful and generous develops in the context of a social relationship. The primary function of gift giving—creating social ties—is clearly demonstrated in the interaction between mother and child: The bond is only kept alive and intact if there is some degree of positive reciprocity. Gratitude plays a crucial role in establishing and maintaining social relations. At the beginning of the twentieth century, the sociologist Georg Simmel wrote his beautiful essay "Faithfulness and Gratitude" (1908/1950), one of the few texts to directly address the subject of gratitude. He called gratitude "the moral memory of mankind" (p. 388). By mutual giving, people become tied to each other by a web of feelings of gratitude. Gratitude is the motive that moves us to give in return, and thus creates the reciprocity of service and counterservice. Although it has psychological feelings at its base, its main function is social, according to Simmel. Gratitude functions in the chain of reciprocity. Gift exchange and the concomitant feelings of gratitude are at the basis of a system of mutual obligations among people, and as such function as the moral cement of human society and culture. Simmel referred to the role of gratitude in fostering the continuity of social life. Gratitude connects people with what has gone on before and gives them the continuity of interactional life. Simmel conducted a mental experiment by imagining what would happen if every grateful action based on benefits received in the past were suddenly eliminated: Society would definitely break apart. Gratitude not only creates and smoothens interpersonal relationships; it also fulfills important cohesive functions for society and culture as such.

The social nature of the principle of reciprocity is very clear from the fascinating animal research data collected by Frans de Waal (1996). After having offered ample illustrations of chimpanzees sharing and exchanging food, de Waal has asked the crucial question about *why* they do so. In his experiments, he has observed chimpanzees watching a caretaker arrive with bundles of blackberry, sweet gum, beech, and tulip branches. Characteristically, a general pandemonium ensues: wild excitement, hooting, embracing, kissing, and friendly body contact, which he has called a "celebration." De Waal has noted that he considers this a sign indicating the transition to a mode of interaction characterized by friendliness and reciprocity. Celebration eliminates social tensions and thus creates a setting for a relaxed sharing of the food. Perhaps the chimpanzees' basic feeling of delight preceding the sharing of food can be compared with the joy of children receiving the good object from their mother, as described by Melanie Klein. Perhaps celebration and joy are preconditions of the harmonious being together in which the first acts of reciprocity can take place. De Waal's results clearly demonstrate that celebration is followed by a pattern of reciprocal giving and receiving: Those who share with others will also receive from others, and those who are poor givers will be poor recipients as well. Apparently, animals have the mental capacity to keep track of what they have given and received and apply this capacity whenever it is appropriate (see Bonnie & de Waal, chap. 11, this volume).

A sociological pattern of reciprocity is exactly what I found in a study on gift giving in the Netherlands that I conducted in 1993 with the Dutch sociologist Schuyt (Komter, 1996b; Komter & Schuyt, 1993). Gift giving was studied in a random sample of 513 Dutch citizens by means of a questionnaire. In addition to using the questionnaire, we extensively interviewed 99 respondents from Amsterdam and the vicinity. The main and very simple research question was who gives what to whom, and why? Results were analyzed quantitatively as well as qualitatively. Although certain categories of respondents appeared to be greater givers than others—women, younger people, better educated people—reciprocity was the rule in all categories in about the same degree. The principle of reciprocity not only applied to material gifts (presents and money gifts) but also to nonmaterial gifts (offering care or help, offering hospitality; inviting others to stay in one's house or serving dinner to other people). In figure 10.1, the findings related to reciprocity are shown.

Although theoretically one could assume that certain categories of people—for instance, highly attractive or likable people, or people in power—receive more gifts than they give, our data show the opposite pattern: *Everyone* has the feeling of giving more than they receive. Assuming that this finding reflects a factual truth and not some perceptual bias or estimation inaccuracy, then the most plausible explanation is that an important category of gift recipients, children, is not included in the sample. But other interpretations in which some kind of bias is presupposed are possible, too: for example, the role of memory (see Komter 1996b, for a more detailed explanation).

In the in-depth interviews, we asked the respondents how they felt about their giving and receiving. What kind of feelings were accompanying their gifts? From their answers (recorded verbatim), several psychological motives could be distilled. An analysis of the motives underlying forms of nonmaterial giving, such as help and care, showed that various levels of altruism may be involved. A person may offer help because he or she feels a general moral obligation to do so, or simply because the recipient needs it, with-

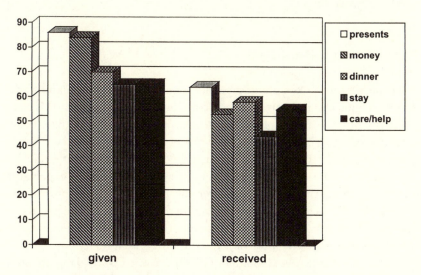

Figure 10.1. Gifts given or received during the past month (presents and dinner) or the past 9 months (money, stay, care); $N = 513$.

out expecting any return. In other cases, however, people make calculations about the "debt balance" in which they are involved: Doesn't the recipient profit too much from their gift giving? Does equivalence exist between what is received and what is given? Sometimes people may feel that they are taken advantage of; their own gift giving has been much more generous compared to what they received, which is clearly felt as unfair. Apparently, gift exchange is not entirely exempt from considerations of costs and benefits, and feelings of gratitude may suffer from this. A next category of motives was more inspired by expectations of reciprocity: I help you, but I expect you to help me if I need it at some time. Most of the reported motives are of this mixed type. Feelings of obligation to return a gift, tit-for-tat-like considerations, and not purely altruistic motives appear to be the main forces behind interpersonal gift giving. The general picture that arises from the motives reported by our respondents is one of "balanced reciprocity" (Sahlins, 1972), in which both giver and recipient expect one another to give in more or less equal proportion and frequency. A disturbed debt balance between giver and recipient may cause a sense of injustice, which in turn may seriously threaten feelings of gratitude. The continuation of the relationship as such may be at risk in such cases.

The psychological motives that we discovered in the in-depth study perfectly reflect the more general sociological pattern of reciprocity found in the larger sample of 513 respondents. As Marcel Mauss observed (1923/1990), gift giving carries its own reward, in that return gifts are the inevitable result. Once again, the founding father of the theory of gift giving has been proved right.

Gratitude, Power, Dependence

Thus far, I have spoken about gratitude as a positive emotion and a social force bringing about community and cohesion. However, gratitude is not always the positive and unproblematic phenomenon we would like it to be, but may be complicated by issues of power and dependence. For instance, the principle of reciprocity can be disturbed if returns are not equivalent. One party may not have enough resources to meet the other's expectations of what counts as proper returns. Power may be involved in reciprocity, causing asymmetry, with one party feeling, or being actually obliged, to give much more than the other. In such cases, gratitude will look different than in situations dominated by more or less symmetrical reciprocity.

The sociologist Alvin Gouldner (1960) was the first to elaborate on the role of power in situations of asymmetrical reciprocity. The respective levels of the resources of giver and recipient should be taken into account, as well as the needs of the recipient and the freedom the giver has to either give or not. Giving may be compelled by other people or by strong normative expectations to do so, thus restricting the spontaneity and the voluntariness of the gift giving. This will probably affect the way gratitude is experienced. Unfortunately Gouldner, like most of his sociological and anthropological colleagues, has not addressed that particular subject.

As is often the case with really fundamental issues, literature offers some interesting insights that are notoriously absent in the social science field. The Russian writer and poet Marina Tsvetajeva (1917/2000), who wrote most of her work just after the Russian Revolution in 1917, had a very uncommon but enlightening view on the vicissitudes of gratitude. She deeply mistrusted the Bolshevist rulers and their oppressive political tactics. This distrust was reciprocal. The Bolshevists regarded Tsvetajeva as a hostile element and obstructed publication of her work, necessitating her to live with her two small children in one icy room at her parents' house. Poverty and hunger made her dependent on alms offered to her by friends and acquaintances from time to time. In this type of situation, gratitude looks quite different from what we are used to. What feelings toward the giver does a poor person have on receiving a loaf of bread, and what kind of expectations does the giver have?

Tsvetajeva (1917/2000) analyzed this example, taken literally from her own life, as follows. It is not a real giver and a real recipient who are the actors here, each with their own person reflected in their actions, but merely a giving hand and a receiving stomach. When a stomach receives bread, this has nothing to do with the personal being of either the giver or the recipient. In the act of exchange, it is merely two pieces of flesh that are involved. It would therefore be absurd for one piece of flesh to demand gratitude from the other. Gratitude, in that case, would degenerate into paid love (prostitution) and be an outright offense to the giver as well as the recipient. As Tsvetajeva said, only souls can be grateful, but only because of other souls. "Thank you for your existence. Everything else is offense" (pp. 200–201). Ultimately only silent gratitude—gratitude not expressed in words or acts—is acceptable, as the mere expression of gratitude already implies some reproach or humiliation for the giver: He or she has something the recipient doesn't have, a painful confrontation between having and not having. The best solution here is to give, to receive, and then to rapidly forget about it, so as to preclude any feelings of gratitude at all; to give and withdraw, to receive and withdraw, without any consequences. In such an unequal power relationship, the moral obligation to express gratitude is derogatory and an obstacle to the development of lasting ties.

In gift exchange, a subtle balance of dependence and independence is involved, causing power and control to be deeply ingrained. Inspired by Simmel, Mauss, and Gouldner, the social psychologist Schwartz (1967) introduced the concept of a "balance of debt" in which the participants in reciprocal gift exchange become involved. Depending on the personal biography and specific psychological makeup, people react differently to this balance of debt. Some have great difficulty receiving help or material goods from others, because they cannot deal with feelings of gratitude or being indebted to another person. The balance of debt may be disturbed in several ways. One means of exercising power is to *keep* another person indebted by way of over-reciprocation. Another offense is returning a gift too quickly. Giving immediately in return can be interpreted as a sign of ingratitude. As Seneca stated, "A person who wants to repay a gift too quickly with a gift in return is an unwilling debtor and an ungrateful person" (as quoted in Gouldner, 1960, note 46, p. 175). A certain period between the gift and the return gift is also needed because the resources to be able to return the gift appropriately have to be found and mobilized. According to Schwartz (1967), the balance of debt should never be brought into complete equilibrium, because "the continuing balance of debt—now in favor of one member, now in favor of the other—insures that the relationship between the two continues, for gratitude will always constitute a part of the bond linking them" (p. 8).

Not only disequilibrium of the debt balance but rivalry as well may disturb the normal development of feelings of gratitude, as is demonstrated by the *potlatch*. Practiced, for instance, by North American Indians, the potlatch is a ceremony of competitive gift giving and the collective destruction of wealth to acquire personal status and prestige. Gift giving in this practice should not be confused with acting on the grounds of a moral obligation to return gifts. What is seemingly an act of gratitude is ultimately one of power and greed.

In the preceding sections, we have seen that gratitude is a personal asset as well as a moral virtue: a capacity one has to learn. Moreover, gratitude has been analyzed as the moral basis of reciprocity. By acting as a moral obligation to give in return, gratitude not only serves to reinforce bonds at the level of social relationships, it is also a means of establishing social cohesion and creating a shared culture. It is important, at this point, to emphasize that indebtedness is not in any way contrary to gratitude, but rather is its moral core.

GRATITUDE DISSECTED

Five general conclusions can be drawn from what has been stated previously. First, a theory of gratitude should integrate its psychological, moral, social and cultural dimensions. Like the gift, gratitude proves to be a truly interdisciplinary subject. Views from anthropology, psychology, and sociology highlight different aspects and add different emphases. Second, gratitude is part of a chain of reciprocity; it is universal and has survival value because it is sustaining a service economy, to use Bonnie and de Waal's (chap. 11, this volume) terms. Third, gratitude is a response to a voluntary gift but is itself imperative: Not showing gratitude when it is appropriate would lead to social disapproval and exclusion. Fourth, gratitude derives its social importance and effectiveness from the moral obligation implied in it. And fifth, gratitude can be a positive as well as a negative force (e.g., in a context of dependency and power inequality), or a combination of the two.

Where do the various reflections on gratitude presented in this chapter bring us? Is it possible to formulate a tentative theory of gratitude that integrates the various insights and pays justice to the richness of the theme? In the anthropological accounts, an animistic view of what we would call gratitude is predominant. Things that are given are thought to have a hold over the recipient because of *hau*; they are experienced as active, as possessing a life of their own, as spirited and having a soul. This spirit causes them to "want" certain things to happen; in particular, they want gifts be returned to where they came from. Another force that causes people to give in return is nature itself. The riches offered by the earth "ask" to be returned in order to restore abundance. The point of departure for a psychological view of gratitude is the recipient, whose capacity to experience the joy generated by receiving gifts is seen as the necessary precondition for gratitude. From a social viewpoint, gratitude is conceptualized as the impulse that leads to mutuality and reciprocity. However, looking at gratitude from a social point of view may also reveal a more negative picture: Power inequality and dependency may be involved, with expressions of gratitude being the result of fear of social sanctions or disapproval. If we focus on the ramifications of ties created by gratitude throughout society, the fundamental societal and cultural value of gratitude becomes clear. All these views have a strong and inescapable force in common that compels recipients to give in return, and it is this mysterious force that lies at the heart of gratitude. The force is alternatively thought to reside in the given object, in nature, in the person of the recipient, or in the social relationship existing between the giver and the recipient. A theory of gratitude should offer us some understanding of the specific nature of this force. Let us, therefore, scrutinize more closely the various layers of this force that are embedded in the views outlined above.

The first layer of gratitude is a spiritual, religious, or magical one. Related to this view is the ecological one, because in either case, the origin of the force asking for restoration of the equilibrium is located outside human beings, in nature or in spiritual essences. At a very fundamental level of human existence, gratitude seems to be the symbolic way of making people understand that they are part of nature, actors in natural cycles of taking riches from the earth and giving back the appropriate returns. Throughout history, people have apparently had some understanding that what nature gives them is influenced by what they give nature. The ecological idea often takes on religious, spiritual, or magical connotations. Whether it is nature, *hau*, or God, the essential concept is gratitude or the need to restore some equilibrium. The notion of a cycle of gifts that have to be kept in motion by passing them on, the idea of abundance returning only if due respect is paid—these representations are indicative of the same basic idea that life can only be safeguarded if we pass on what we have received. To come and remain alive means to give away.

The moral and psychological aspects of gratitude constitute its second layer. Gratitude can be conceived as a feeling of moral indebtedness as a consequence of what has been received. We have seen that this feeling may have its roots in early childhood, where its first manifestation is the experience of a child's joy (comparable to the celebration of de Waal's chimps). Joy is the child's reaction to the first gift of motherly care and love, and it paves the way for gratitude. Although in later life the experience of gratitude may vary according to the extent to which one is dependent on others for the satisfaction of one's needs, the talent for gratitude can be considered an enduring personality trait and a moral virtue. It is interesting that the ability to receive and be grateful seems intrinsically related to its counterpart, the ability to return goodness, or generosity. Whatever the impact of psychological factors, we should bear in mind that from its inception onward, gratitude is embedded in social relationships.

One might say that to give is to live, not only as an individual but also as part of society. Not being grateful ultimately means the discontinuation of social bonds and community life and the termination of individual well-being and satisfaction. This then is the third layer of gratitude, which is the precondition for reciprocity and mutual exchange. As the anthropological literature on gift exchange amply demonstrates, gratitude keeps social relations intact by being the driving force behind the return gifts. Gratitude is the in-between connecting gift and return gift. Together, the three elements of gift, gratitude, and countergift form the chain that constitutes the principle of reciprocity. The social view of gratitude may also involve some negative aspects. Power can seriously threaten the capacity to feel and express gratitude. Giving in return is not always inspired by pure gratitude but can be motivated by a fear of social sanctions or of the discontinuation of profits ensuing from social relationships. Only in more or less equally balanced relationships can gratitude unfold the best of its powers.

Finally, there is the fourth layer, consisting of the societal and cultural meaning of gratitude. As Simmel stated, a culture or society deprived of all acts of gratitude will inevitably break down. Just as gratitude is indispensable in the life of one individual who will face isolation and loneliness if the capacity to feel grateful is impaired, gratitude is also a crucial ingredient of

Table 10.1   Expressions of Gratitude in Experience and Behavior

Manifestations of Gratitude	Layers of Gratitude
• Hau, the "spirit" of the gift, nature expecting returns	• Spiritual/religious/magical/ecological
• Joy and the capacity to receive	• Moral/psychological
• Mutuality, reciprocity; power inequality, fear of sanctions	• Social
• Webs of feelings connecting people	• Societal/cultural

every society and culture. Without the ties created by gratitude, there would be no mutual trust, no moral basis on which to act, and no grounds for maintaining the bonds of community.

Table 10.1 summarizes the various ways in which gratitude may be expressed in people's experience and behavior, as well as the conceptual layers belonging to a particular manifestation of gratitude. The four layers or meanings of gratitude are not mutually exclusive. On the contrary, they are different formulations of the same force of gratitude that compels people to restore the disequilibrium caused by having received a gift, whether from a supernatural power, nature, or a fellow human being. In all of these cases, the failure to reciprocate will act as a boomerang to the recipients themselves, because the fundamental principle underlying gift giving—keeping gifts in motion by passing them on—is not heeded. To conclude with the words of Lewis Hyde (1983), "Those who will not acknowledge gratitude or who refuse to labor in its service neither free their gifts nor really come to possess them" (p. 50).

References

de Waal, F. (1996). *Good natured: The origins of right and wrong in humans and other animals.* Cambridge, MA: Harvard University Press.

Firth, R. (1959). *Primitive economics of the New Zealand Maori.* London: Routledge. (Original work published 1929)

Godelier, M. (1999). *The enigma of the gift.* Cambridge: Polity.

Gouldner, A. W. (1960). The norm of reciprocity: A preliminary statement. *American Journal of Sociology, 25,* 161–178.

Hyde, L. (1983). *The gift: Imagination and the erotic life of property.* New York: Vintage.

Klein, M. (1987). Envy and gratitude. In *Envy and gratitude, and other works 1946–1963* (pp. 176–236). London: Hogarth Press and Institute of Psycho-Analysis. (Original work published 1957)

Klein, M. (1987). On the sense of loneliness. In *Envy and gratitude, and other works 1946–1963* (pp. 300–314). London: Hogarth Press and Institute of Psycho-Analysis. (Original work published 1963)

Klein, M. (1987). *Envy and gratitude, and other works 1946–1963* (Vol. 3). London: Hogarth Press and Institute of Psycho-Analysis. (Original work published 1946–1963)

Komter, A. (Ed.). (1996a). *The gift: An interdisciplinary perspective.* Amsterdam: Amsterdam University Press.

Komter, A. (1996b). Reciprocity as a principle of exclusion: Gift giving in the Netherlands. *Sociology, 30,* 299–316.

Komter, A., & Schuyt, C. J. M. (1993). *Geschenken en relaties* [Gifts and relationships]. *Beleid & Maatschappij, XX,* 277–285.

Lazarus, R. S., & Lazarus, B. N. (1994). *Passion and reason: Making sense of our emotions.* New York: Oxford University Press.

Malinowski, B. (1922). *Argonauts of the Western Pacific.* London: Routledge.

Mauss, M. (1990). *The gift: The form and reason for exchange in archaic societies.* London: Routledge. (Original work published 1923)

Sahlins, M. (1972). *Stone age economics.* London: Tavistock.

Schwartz, B. (1967). The social psychology of the gift. *American Journal of Sociology, 73,* 1–11.

Simmel, G. (1950). Faithfulness and gratitude. In K. H. Wolff (Ed. & Trans.), *The sociology of Georg Simmel* (pp. 379–395). New York: Free Press. (Original work published 1908)

Tsvetajeva, M. (2000). *Ik loop over de sterren: Schetsen, dagboekfragmenten en brieven over de Russische Revolutie* [I walk over the stars: Sketches, diary fragments and letters about the Russian Revolution]. Amsterdam: De Bezige Bij. (Original work published 1917)

Weiner, A. (1992). *Inalienable possessions: The paradox of keeping-while-giving.* Berkeley: University of California Press.

11 Primate Social Reciprocity and the Origin of Gratitude

Kristin E. Bonnie and Frans B. M. de Waal

> If you pick up a starving dog and make him prosperous, he will not
> bite you. This is the principal difference between a dog and a man.
> —(Twain, 1894/1976, p. 122)

Gratitude, defined as an emotional appreciation of and thankfulness for favors received, has been well established as a universal human attribute. Its presence is expressed and felt in different ways by virtually all peoples, of all cultures, in all of society (McCullough, Kirkpatrick, Emmons, & Larson, 2001). Though the phenomenon of gratitude can be evaluated in a wide variety of personal and social contexts, we focus here on gratitude in the context of services rendered and received. Reciprocity—the mutual exchange of favors—encompasses a wide variety of goods and services. The importance of such exchanges in human society is difficult to ignore. "Social equilibrium," sociologist Alvin Gouldner (1960) wrote, "could not exist without the reciprocity of service and return service" (p. 162). But reciprocity is not a uniquely human attribute. "Acts of giving, receiving, and repayment permeate nearly every aspect of human life, and seemingly, the lives of many other species" (Taylor & McGuire, 1988, p. 67). Reciprocal exchanges govern the lives of many social beings, including fish, birds, and mammals.

Imagine, for a moment, what our society would be like without reciprocity and the feelings of gratitude that appear to drive it. Could civilization of any size or composition even exist? Also, try to imagine an intricate web of reciprocal exchange relationships without a mechanism such as gratitude:

Someone does something for you, or gives you something, and this action fails to arouse any form of appreciation. This is equally difficult to imagine. One could thus argue that human society as we know it relies on gratitude as its glue and lubricant. And even if gratitude is arguably a cultural phenomenon, developed over time and passed on through the generations, is not the role of learning more likely that of modifier, not creator, of this particular psychological mechanism? Otherwise, why would gratitude occur in all societies that we know of? And why, as we argue, are there hints of it in animals besides ourselves (referred to in the rest of this chapter as simply *animals*)?

DO ANIMALS SHOW GRATITUDE?

The question of whether or not gratitude can be found in the animal world was taken up over two centuries ago by philosopher and economist Adam Smith. In *The Theory of Moral Sentiments* (1790/1976), Smith focused primarily on the ability of animals to be objects of gratitude, that is, at the receiving end. For example, he observed that animals that have provided companionship and remarkable service to their masters could be the objects of "lively gratitude." Smith, however, was rather conservative in his thoughts on the animal world. "But before anything can be the proper object of gratitude or resentment," he wrote, "it must not only be the cause of pleasure or pain, it must likewise be capable of feeling them" (p. 179). Although he did not elevate animals to the human level, he did distinguish them from inanimate objects. In Smith's mind, the ability to appreciate gratitude could be more clearly interpreted as a spectrum, with inanimate objects—such as a tree providing shade—falling on one end, and humans on the other. Cognitively advanced animals, under Smith's hypothesis, fall somewhere in between. Whereas he suggested that animals may be the subjects of gratitude and may even be capable of feeling the gratitude of others, he only casually alludes to the possibility that animals themselves may be capable of expressing gratitude. Did Mark Twain then go too far when he suggested that a starving dog would express gratitude for human aid?

In any critical examination of animal gratitude, it is useful to consider alternative explanations. Even though we have all heard of (and the authors have personal experience with) pets adopted from a miserable stray existence into the comfort of modern homes, it is impossible to tell if their greater-than-average appreciation (e.g., tail wagging, purring) of our care and food has anything to do with gratitude. The simpler alternative is that, after prolonged deprivation, there is a contrast effect that lasts a lifetime, making these animals show greater-than-average expressions of pleasure at receiving a full bowl of food. In humans, no one would confuse pleasure with gratitude. On the other hand, if the pleasure is expressed in a personal manner, aimed specifically at the individual who delivers it, are not we getting closer to gratitude? Consider, for example, an anecdote recounted by Leuba (1928) about a pair of captive chimpanzees (*Pan troglodytes*): "Two chimps had been shut out of their shelter by mistake during a cold rain storm. They were standing dejected, water streaming down their shivering bodies, when Prof. Köhler chanced to pass. He opened the door for them. Instead of scampering in without more ado, as many a child would have done, each of them delayed entering the warm shelter long enough to throw its arms about his benefactor in a frenzy of satisfaction" (p. 102).

Although only an isolated account of a single pair of chimpanzees, the image is convincing. Chimpanzees do not normally hug their caretakers for no reason. Another account from personal experience by the second author concerns a zoo chimpanzee whom he trained to bottle-feed an abandoned infant of her own species. The following summarizes an earlier description by de Waal (1982):

> During the training phase, the infant remained firmly in human possession even though the adoptive female was extremely attracted to it. The training itself must have been a rather frustrating experience because the female was not permitted to drink from the milk bottle herself: she was asked to insert it through the bars for the infant to suckle on. When, after weeks of training, she performed these actions to our satisfaction, we finally made the transfer, placing the wriggling infant in the straw of a night cage, and letting the female in with her. At first, the adoptive mother intently stared into the infant's face without touching it: in her mind, it belonged to us. She approached the bars where the caretaker and myself sat watching. First she kissed the caretaker, then myself, glancing between the infant and us as if asking permission. We both urged her "Go, pick her up!" Eventually, she did, and from that moment on the female became the most caring and protective mother one could imagine, raising the infant as we had hoped.
>
> Before the adoption, this female and I had no special relation. Since the actual adoption, however, more than twenty years ago, she has showered me with the greatest possible affection. I visit this zoo less than once per year, but she always picks out my face from the crowd, and acts as if I am a long-lost family member. Our training made it possible for her to have this infant as well as some of her own (she suffers from insufficient lactation, hence had lost infants

before this moment), and I am inclined to interpret her exceptional reaction to me as eternal gratitude for the one thing female chimpanzees value above anything else—offspring. (pp. 66–70)

FORMS OF COOPERATION

If gratitude exists in animals, one expects this to apply especially to species with highly evolved cooperation based on cognitive evaluations of costs, benefits, and partnerships. There would be no need for a loner (e.g., a self-sufficient solitary hunter, such as the tiger) to keep received services in mind, let alone associate these services with positive feelings; the occasion to act on such emotions would rarely, if ever, occur. In contrast, the need for such feelings is far greater among animals, such as chimpanzees and many other nonhuman primates, in highly complex and cooperative societies. Thus, the argument here is a utilitarian one, as usual in biology: The functional context of feelings of gratitude is mutual dependence.

Up to this point, however, we have only suggested that gratitude must somehow be involved in reciprocal exchanges involving memory of past events. The basis for our argument is founded in a theory described by Trivers (1971) in "The Evolution of Reciprocal Altruism." Reciprocal altruism (RA) encompasses interindividual exchange of costly acts such that the benefit to the giver is attained only after a significant time delay. It can be described in a nutshell by the following situation. A person comes upon another, who is struggling and in obvious danger of drowning. The bystander is faced with a choice—whether to risk self-injury or death to save the victim or to leave the struggling swimmer to drown. On the basis of the assumptions that (a) the victim and rescuer are unrelated, (b) the victim will drown without help but with help will survive, (c) the energetic costs of rescue are small relative to the possibility of survival, and (d) the probability of the victim's surviving is much greater than the probability of the rescuer's also drowning, Trivers asserted that the rescuer should not save the drowning person in this isolated event. But if, at some later time, a reversed situation might occur, and hence the rescue could be reciprocated, then risking one's life for the other might be beneficial. If two people save each other on different occasions, both will have gained tremendously.

Trivers (1971) outlined several assumptions necessary for RA—a cost to the altruist, a benefit to the recipient, a significant time delay before repayment, the involvement of unrelated individuals, and opportunity for reiterated encounters. Of these, the time lag has been consistently recognized as the most crucial element, for it is this that distinguishes RA from simpler forms of cooperation, such as mutualism. However, as a result, individuals involved in RA must be characterized by a number of more complex skills. These include having the ability to (a) recognize individuals, (b) detect cheaters so as to deter those who give less than they receive (Taylor & McGuire, 1988; Wilkinson, 1987), and (c) mentally keep score (i.e., remember acts given and received).

In addition to developing the evolutionary theory of RA, Trivers showed attention to the proximate mechanisms involved. He proposed several factors that act to induce or inhibit behavior, including guilt, subtle cheating, trust, suspicion, friendship, and gratitude. The attention Trivers gave to these psychological devices is unusual, because many have neglected proximate mechanisms, even though this notion was a part of Trivers's thinking from the start. Here, we build on his thoughts about gratitude as a mediating mechanism that links the receipt of a favor to the giving of a return favor. Yet, to fully understand the role that Trivers believed gratitude to play, we must first address the various forms of reciprocity present in the animal world.

Evolution of Cooperation

Trivers (1971) emphasized a fairly complex memory-based form of reciprocity. Imagine this and other high-cost, multiparty interactions–in which the donor of services receives no immediate benefits and is dependent on the other for return benefits—as lying at one end of a spectrum. What, in contrast, is found at the other? Is there anything in between?

Evidence of cooperation in animals abounds (for a review, see Dugatkin, 1997), and without it, many life-forms could not possibly exist. The complete range of functional benefits (i.e., survival value) is too numerous to explore here. But among those benefits are the successful upbringing of offspring (e.g., alloparenting or providing care for another's offspring), predator detection and defense (e.g., alarm calls in prairie dogs [Hoogland, 1983] and vervet monkeys [Cheney & Seyfarth, 1990]), and food acquisition (e.g., group hunting in lions [Packer & Ruttan, 1988] and chimpanzees [Boesch, 1994]). For our purposes, we define cooperation as "the voluntary acting together of two or more individuals that brings about, or could potentially bring about, an end situation that benefits one, both, or all of them in a way that could not have been brought about individually" (Brosnan & de Waal, 2002, p. 130).

Gratitude implies memory, so here we are particularly interested in mechanisms of cooperation that are based on memories of previous events. Demonstrating the complexity of such interactions, however, is difficult. Nonhuman primates provide the best examples. Among cercopithecinae monkeys, preliminary evidence for an exchange between affiliative behavior and agonistic support has been reported. De Waal and Yoshihara (1983), for example, found increased grooming between previous alliance partners in rhesus monkeys (*Macaca mulatta*). Seyfarth and Cheney (1984) employed playback of vervet monkey (*Chlorocebus aethiops*) calls to measure the reaction of recently groomed individuals to a vocalization used both to threaten aggressors and to solicit the support of others. Previous grooming partners were reported as being the objects of increased attention. Finally, Hemelrijk (1994) reported that after experimentally manipulating grooming in long-tailed macaques (*Macaca fascicularis*), agonistic support was related to bouts of previous grooming, that is, Individual A supported Individual B more if B had groomed A, but not if A had groomed B. The last study suggests a temporal connection between one service and another and thus implies the need for a memory of past events. But what if, in fact, a mechanism of mental score keeping does not exist? Could there be a simpler explanation?

The Good-Mood Hypothesis: Food for Grooming in Chimpanzees

Few nonhuman primates share food outside the mother-offspring relationship. However, in chimpanzees, the exchange of food for grooming can be a common event. To examine whether these interactions are affected by previous encounters between the same individuals, de Waal (1997) investigated spontaneous food sharing and grooming in a captive group of chimpanzees. Large bundles of leaves and branches were tossed into the chimps' enclosure, before and after which grooming among the chimpanzees was measured. Results showed that adults were more likely to share food with individuals who had groomed them earlier in the day. This suggested two possible explanations. The good-mood hypothesis offers the suggestion that the receipt of a service—in this case, grooming—affects an individual's social attitude toward all possible partners. That is, receiving food results in a general benevolent mood, which makes the individual generously share with all others. On the other hand, the exchange hypothesis predicts that the recipient of grooming shares food only with the groomer. In this case, exchange is the best explanation. The data supported the second explanation, showing that sharing was specifically directed at the previous groomer—each chimpanzee appeared to remember the exact partner in the first exchange (grooming) and later directed a beneficial response (food sharing) toward that individual alone. In sum, this study suggests the presence of the prerequisites for RA outlined by Trivers (1971), including individual recognition and the ability to keep score.

Symmetry-Based Versus Calculated Reciprocity

The food-for-grooming economy involves a rather complex series of interactions. In the lives of these complex apes, do alternative mechanisms exist? In a study of chimpanzees, rhesus monkeys, and stump-tailed macaques (*Macaca arctiodes*), de Waal and Luttrell (1988) examined two types of reciprocity—symmetry-based and calculated. The first "involves exchanges between closely bonded individuals who help each other without stipulating equivalent returns. . . . The second type of reciprocity is calculated by feedback, that is, the continuation of helpful behavior is contingent upon the partner's reciprocation" (p. 103). Whereas in calculated reciprocity an intimate relationship between individuals is not required, symmetry-based reciprocity assumes a close relationship—such as those between kin and frequent associates. Interindividual associations, such that Individual A spends much time with Individual B and then B automatically spends much time with A, therefore lead to an exchange of behavior that might simply be accounted for by physical proximity rather than by any type of score-keeping system. In most species, such as vampire bats, for which costly reciprocity has been reported, symmetry-based reciprocity is the most likely mechanism (Brosnan & de Waal, 2002).

Attitudinal Reciprocity: Food Sharing in Capuchin Monkeys

Brown capuchin monkeys (*Cebus apella*) also share food. Sharing can be active or passive. The first is characterized by the actual handing or giving of food to another individual and is, not surprisingly, a rare behavior. Passive sharing, in contrast, occurs when an individual acquires food from another without active help (Brosnan & de Waal, 2002; de Waal, 1997). Passive sharing can take a variety of forms, including taking food directly from the possessor's hands without protest, and collecting bits of dropped food from the possessor sitting near by.

Spontaneous food-based interactions among captive capuchins were initially reported by de Waal, Luttrell, and Canfield (1993). In a later study (de Waal, 2000), food sharing between monkey dyads was more rigorously examined using a delayed exchange test. Monkeys were placed side by side in a test chamber and separated by wire mesh. A bowl of cucumber pieces was placed in front of the first monkey, well outside the reach of the second. Twenty minutes later, the bowl of cucumber pieces was removed, and the second monkey was given a bowl of apples. Later, the test was repeated; however, the order in which the monkeys received food was reversed. The level of reciprocal sharing and social tolerance was quite amazing. Furthermore, there was a significant correlation between the number of passive food transfers in the first phase with the number of transfers in the second. However, because the capuchins were strongly affiliated with and highly tolerant of one another, their behaviors were most easily explained by symmetry-based reciprocity.

To test whether capuchins are capable of the more complex calculated reciprocity, changes in the relationship over time were also examined. Each dyad was subjected to six delayed exchange tests in which both females were always in the same roles. The results of the six tests were then compared to the results in the first test phase. In each female-female dyad, sharing rates were found to covary significantly over time, as the second monkey shared significantly more than average if the first monkey had shared more than average as well (de Waal, 2000).

These results suggest that more than symmetry-based reciprocity is taking place. However, it is not clear that calculated reciprocity is the explanation either. Instead, de Waal proposed a mechanism of attitudinal reciprocity, in which the attitude of the partner is mirrored. The hypothesis was that, instead of keeping track of how much food is given and received, the monkeys merely respond in a positive manner (e.g., with proximity and tolerance) to a positive attitude in their partners. Such behavior, specifically the mirroring of social predispositions, may well explain the reciprocal distribution of food sharing across time without the requirement of scorekeeping of services (de Waal, 2000).

High- and Low-Cost Interactions

Reciprocal exchanges can be categorized according to the cost of the services involved as high- and low-cost interactions. Services such as grooming (de Waal, 1997; Seyfarth & Cheney, 1988), a failure to act (Seyfarth & Cheney, 1988), or any act that carries a cost (in terms of a loss in opportunity to do something else) constitute low-cost reciprocity. High-cost reciprocity, on the other hand, is rare. Blood sharing in vampire bats (*Desmodus rotundus*) provides perhaps the best illustration of reciprocity encompassing a great cost as well as a significant time delay.

Vampire bats feed exclusively on blood and must do so at least once every 3 days to survive. Adults, however, miss a meal approximately once every 10 days. In the bat society, there is no need for worry, because members of the social group regularly regurgitate blood to provision others (Wilkinson, 1990). The behavior is extremely costly and apparently altruistic, because regurgitation results solely in a cost to the donor and reaps no immediate benefit. The possibility that bats remember favors given and received for an extended period of time, that is, a minimum of one day, may explain the perpetuation of such behaviors. However, an alternative explanation is possible, because Wilkinson (1984) reported that the vast majority of blood sharing is between mother and offspring or between closely related individuals. Therefore, with no evidence that giving is contingent on previous receipt from the same individual, it is possible that the observed reciprocity results from the symmetrical components of the relationship (i.e., kinship and mutual friendship) rather than any scorekeeping and return expectation (Brosnan & de Waal, 2002).

Mutualism

The simplest cooperation involves a interaction among a dyad or small group of individuals in which the benefits are immediately gained. This is known as mutualism. For example, if wild dogs together bring down a wildebeest, all hunters benefit at the same time. Similarly, chimpanzees living in the Tai National Park, Ivory Coast, cooperate to hunt a number of species of colobus monkeys. Studies show an increased success for cooperative hunters compared with solitary hunters (Boesch, 1994). As a result of the instant payoff, this kind of cooperation is widespread.

Family Bonds

In theory, reciprocal interactions are assumed to take place between unrelated (or at least only distantly related) individuals. In reality, reciprocity may well exist among kin, and when one is evaluating a reciprocal interaction, this is often difficult to rule out. But, in addition to the normal benefits built into an exchange, helping a family member affords extra gains—namely, in terms of increased inclusive fitness for the helper. In aiding a family member, the helper ensures that copies of its own genes survive. As a result of this added benefit, when compared with the helper's cost in interactions between unrelated individuals, the cost incurred by the helper in familial relationships can be higher, whereas the exchange remains beneficial for both. Kinship, therefore, favors cooperation.

A MODEL OF GRATITUDE

To understand what role gratitude plays in reciprocal exchanges, it is necessary to expand our definition, given at the beginning of this chapter—as an emotional appreciation of and thankfulness for favors received—to include an urge to repay. We suggest that, whereas an appreciation of favors received is a necessary component of gratitude, the emotional response of feeling good by itself is not sufficient. Furthermore, we conceptualize the function of gratitude as promoting positive feelings toward the benefactor, which then induces the return of favors equivalent to those received. This implies that only those animals with advanced cognitive skills, (e.g., memory systems capable of storing past events and recognizing individuals) are capable of expressing gratitude to the extent that we humans can. Evidence from other species, nonhuman primates in particular, suggests that some of these prerequisites for gratitude are present in animals besides ourselves.

The model in Figure 11.1 represents the full human cycle (Path 3) of received benefits and the entire evaluation leading to gratitude, indebtedness, and repayment tendencies, that is, reciprocal altruism. An individual is the recipient of a good deed from another. The deed results in a good feeling and the association of this positive feeling with the actions of the donor. The receiver understands the costs of the donor's actions and attributes good intentions to him or her (i.e., the recipient understands the difference between intended and unintended benefits, feeling no gratitude for the latter). This results in the recipient being grateful not only for the action of the donor, but to the donor himself or herself. As a result, the receiver feels a debt to the donor, and an obligation to return the favor. Finally, the initial receiver returns a good deed to the donor, and the cycle continues because the initial donor (now the recipient) feels good about this, and so on. The cycle will continue as long as both individuals regularly meet each other and maintain the basic contingencies of mutually beneficial exchange.

Instances of gratitude encompassed in reciprocal exchanges are plentiful in the human world. Gift exchange, for example, has been described by sociologists Komter and Vollebergh (1997) as "the cement of social relationships" (p. 747; see also Komter, chap. 10, this volume). Although gift giving may involve a range of feelings and a variety of circumstances, the expression of gratitude for a favor received is a common occurrence. Furthermore, gift exchange is governed by the norm of reciprocity (Schwartz, 1967), and *do ut des* ("I give so that you give in return"; Komter & Vollebergh, 1997). "The counterbalancing of debt—now in favor of one member, now in favor of the other—insures that the relationship between the two continue, for gratitude will always constitute a part of the bond linking them" (Schwartz, 1967, p. 8). Gifts, however, need not only be thought of in terms of decoratively wrapped tokens of exchange. Rather, gifts can include other currencies, such as services or a meal. For example, imagine a situation in which you voluntarily assist a friend in moving. She then returns the favor by unexpectedly paying for a dinner at an expensive restaurant in town. Most likely, you considered your help a mere act of friendliness, perhaps not expecting anything in return. Your friend's appreciation for the help inspired her to treat you to the meal.

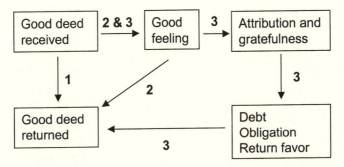

Figure 11.1. Upon receiving a good deed or service from another, the recipient can go through several cycles to return the favor. Humans often, but perhaps not always, follow the full cycle marked as 3, which includes a good feeling about the received favor, an understanding of the costs incurred by the other, attribution of intentions (e.g., feeling no gratitude for unintended benefits), and a felt obligation to repay the favor. Cycle 3 is not necessary, however, for reciprocal exchange to occur. Cycle 2 includes merely positive feelings upon the receipt of a favor, changing the attitude of the recipient such that positive behavior towards the giver, hence repayment, is likely. In an even simpler scheme, as in path 1, repayment of the favor is more or less automatic, without intermediating mechanism such as good feelings and gratitude.

Humans are not alone in this matter. As evidenced by our statistical analyses of the food-for-grooming service economy, chimpanzees remember the specific individuals who have groomed them in the past and subsequently return the favor by sharing more food with them. "Only for chimpanzees do we at present have evidence for the entire set of features expected if reciprocity were cognition-based: partner specificity, selective protest, retaliation, turn-taking, and the effect of one service on another" (de Waal, 1997, p. 384). Furthermore, although the general feel-good hypothesis could be ruled out (see previous discussion), we would replace it with one stipulating a positive feeling specifically directed at the benefactor. This seems a prerequisite for the cycle of exchange seen in the chimpanzee. If chimpanzees indeed feel good about benefactors, remember them, and have a tendency to repay favors received, it will be hard not to count the mechanism of gratitude among the possibilities. In fact, we argue that to explain their documented exchange behavior without invoking gratitude would introduce a difference in human behavior not supported by the known close relationships between the two species, humans and apes. In other words, from an evolutionary perspective, the default position ought to be that chimpanzee reciprocity relies on mechanisms similar to ours, and hence on gratitude (de Waal, 1991). The reader is welcome to treat this as a mere assumption, but it seems to us a far more reasonable one than an assumption of difference.

Alternative Pathways

Many animals, however, may be following a shorter course (Path 2) through the cycle depicted in Figure 11.1. This alternative pathway involves the psychology of feeling good about received favors but does not necessarily require the attribution of intentions and appreciation of behavioral risks and costs involved in the full cycle. Capuchin monkeys appear to follow this shorter path in the act of food sharing. As described earlier, food sharing in this species may be explained as attitudinal reciprocity, in which the reciprocation is an immediate response to the positive predisposition of the partner. Unlike the calculated reciprocity demonstrated by chimpanzees, the capuchin pathway might not involve attribution of intentions but may instead be an immediate positive response to someone's being positive, as if capuchins are simply following the rule, "If you are nice, I will be nice, too."

An even simpler scheme for exchange would be to exchange beneficial behavior simultaneously, a pattern known as barter (Path 1). This does not require individual recognition or scorekeeping of previous events; instead, it involves a direct exchange without emotional investment and likely without gratitude. Mutualistic exchanges, such as impala grooming (Hart & Hart, 1992) seem to follow this path. Impala (*Aepyceros melampus*) are large African antelope that live in either groups of females, fawns, and one territorial male or as bachelor groups of males. A grooming exchange is usually unsolicited and begins as one partner turns to groom the neck of the other. A single exchange is comprised of multiple bouts during which the groomer moves up along the neck of its partner. The recipient, in turn, reciprocates grooming for an equal period of time, and so on. The apparent function of these exchanges is to remove ticks from parts of the body unreachable by the individual itself (Hart & Hart, 1992). Among impala, no evidence exists for the recognition of previous partners or interactions.

MORALITY AND RETRIBUTION

It is clear that there is much left to be studied before we can consider that gratitude and its role within reciprocal interactions in animals are completely understood. Yet, as demonstrated by our investigations of nonhuman primates, there is every indication that the foundations of gratitude exist within our closest relatives. If we are to accept this, then can we extend the argument presented in McCullough et al. (2001), that gratitude, like empathy and guilt, can be conceptualized as a moral affect? Reciprocity, too, is arguably an essential element of moral systems. Reciprocity can exist without morality, as evident from the mutual cleaning in impala. But, as argued in *Good Natured* (de Waal, 1996), "There can be no morality without reciprocity" (p. 136). Consequently reciprocity, and therefore gratitude, may be central to theories about the origin of moral sentiments. Does the presence of gratitude, or at least of its precursors, in some primate societies suggest that morality can be found in these same animals?

The argument that reciprocity and gratitude are an integrated part of morality is by no means a novel idea. Adam Smith (1790/1976), considered gratitude to be one of the moral sentiments. Similarly, Westermarck wrote, in *The Origin and Development of the Moral Ideas* (1908), "To requite a benefit, or to be grateful to him who bestows it, is probably everywhere, at least under certain circumstances, regarded as a duty" (Vol. 2, p. 154). In later writings, Westermarck coined a unique term, "retributive kindly emotion," to describe this moral sentiment. "[Moral] approval, like gratitude, forms a subspecies of retributive kindly emotion" (1932, p. 63). Though more than a century apart, the thoughts shared by Smith (1790/1976) and Westermarck (1908) established a foundation on which modern ideas have been built.

Twentieth-century theorists have conceptualized gratitude as "the moral memory of mankind" (Simmel, 1908/1950, p. 388) and reciprocity as "a dimension to be found in all value systems and, in particular, as one among a number of 'Principal Components' universally present in moral codes" (Gouldner, 1960, p. 171). Richard Alexander (1987) expanded on these ideas, arguing that reciprocity is essential to the development of moral systems. Although he considered a somewhat different type of reciprocity—one that is dependent on a third party's providing compensation for the original act—these systems of indirect or generalized reciprocity require memory, consistency across time, and most important, a sense of social regularity or a consensual sense of right and wrong (Alexander, 1987, p. 95). De Waal (1996) and Flack and de Waal (2000) have taken these ideas one step further, arguing that a number of social behaviors suggest the possession of the first building blocks of morality in nonhuman primates.

One avenue through which social regularity is maintained in both human and nonhuman primate societies is that of obligation. In consideration of morality among chimpanzees, Harnden-Warwick (1997) wrote, "Both [calculated reciprocity and moralistic aggression] rely on cognitive processing and advanced memory, which are necessary if an individual is to express gratitude in response to positive reciprocal action or hostility in response to a negative return. . . . Thus, calculated reciprocity sets the state for the possibility of interpersonal exchanges and favors which can be mentally charted and recorded over time, thereby encouraging a sense of obligation to develop in either or both actors" (p. 35). It is no accident, then, that this obligation to return a favor is included in our model of gratitude. Chimpanzees, in their food-for-grooming economy, illustrate this idea in practice. Food sharing in chimpanzees not only demonstrates a reciprocal system, but also suggests that a sense of social regularity exists among our closest relatives.

Up to this point we have talked only of the positive role gratitude plays in eliciting obligatory feelings in reciprocal exchanges. Numerous theorists suggest that its opposite, desire for retribution, helps to maintain the cycle in an equally significant way. "The sense of obligation implied by calculated reciprocity could not be considered reciprocity at all if the possibility did not exist that an actor would fail to meet an obligation" (Harnden-Warwick, 1997, p. 35). Those who attempt to beat the system by giving less than they receive commonly elicit an unpleasant emotional response in others. Regardless of whether or not this desire for retribution is fully expressed in an act of punishment, the cheater becomes associated with a negative feeling and ultimately the positive course of the cycle is tarnished. Thus, not only are beneficial actions rewarded, but cheating becomes a costly event.

Trivers (1971) recognized that a system of favors and return favors would not last without going unchecked. He argued that, although positive emotions such as gratitude evolved to motivate altruistic behavior, negative emotions, in contrast, must exist to protect the giver from those who cheat. He labeled these negative reactions produced by perceived violations of the social code "moralistic aggression." By increasing the cost of not cooperating, and more important, associating a cost with cheating, he emphasized that this aggressive response helps to reinforce systems of reciprocity. The punitive action, then, concerns how others ought to behave.

In addition to keeping a mental record of services rendered and received, nonhuman primates appear to be capable of holding negative acts in mind as well. We now have systematic data on how chimpanzees punish negative actions with other negative actions, called a "revenge system" by de Waal and Luttrell (1988), and how a macaque attacked by a dominant member of its troop will often turn around to redirect aggression against a vulnerable younger relative of its attacker (Aureli, Cozzolino, Cordischi, & Scucchi, 1992). Building on this evidence, Clutton-Brock and Parker (1995) contrasted positive and negative reciprocity while noting that punishment can be similar to reciprocal altruism in terms of the cost endured for a deferred benefit. Of particular use to the argument at hand is that the authors cited the enforcement of cooperative behavior as one of five common social contexts in which punishment is particularly common. For example, chimpanzees often form supportive coalitions to gain access to resources. Among the chimpanzees of the Netherlands's Arnhem Zoo, whom the second author has studied intensely, such coalitions played a vital role. But when support of an ally fails or is blatantly refused, such disobedience may be punished (de Waal, 1982).

Among humans, the role of altruistic punishment may be more significant than in our nonhuman relatives. In a recent study, Fehr and Gachter (2002) showed that, in the absence of punishment, cooperation dissolves. "By showing that altruistic punishment is a key force in the establishment of human cooperation, our study indicates that there is more at work in sustaining human cooperation than is suggested by [kin selection, reciprocal altruism, indirect reciprocity and costly signaling]" (Fehr & Gachter, p. 139). With regard to proximate mechanisms of cooperation, gratitude then appears to provide support from one end, whereas punishment and retribution drive it from the other.

In our consideration of morality among nonhuman primates, we in no way suggest that human moral complexity is directly comparable to the behavior of other primates. However, it seems that, particularly among apes, at least some elements of human morality can be found in other species (Flack & de Waal, 2000). An equal conclusion can be reached about gratitude in animals—humans may be the only creatures with the full-blown reciprocity cycle of indebtedness and gratitude, but not all of its elements may be totally unique. This insight was reached long ago by Westermarck and remains valid today: "In its primitive form [retributive kindliness] is found among animals living in groups, including the small group consisting of mother, or parents, and offspring. The altruistic sentiment would never have come into existence without such a reciprocity of feeling" (Westermarck, 1932, p. 87).

CONCLUSIONS

The fact that gratitude is universal across all cultures suggests that it is part of human nature. Cultures and religions, therefore, must have acted upon an earlier psychological foundation to strengthen a mechanism that has held our societies together throughout time. We see it as having evolved for the sake of cooperation—hence as an inherently constructive switch that tries to turn us from selfish receivers into givers. But if we believe that gratitude has an evolutionary basis, we also expect to find signs of it in other animals, and our nearest relatives in particular. As demonstrated most clearly by the chimpanzee food-for-grooming economy, gratitude appears to play a vital role in the intricate reciprocal exchanges that hold these primate societies together.

The complexity of reciprocity, and reciprocal altruism in particular, demands advanced cognitive skills for recognizing partners, detecting cheaters, and mentally keeping score. More important, the cycle of give-and-take requires a feeling of appreciation associated specifically with the helpful individual. This emotional appreciation for a favor received is particularly important when the temporal delay of a returned favor is considered. Gratitude, then, acts as a mediator between give-and-take, coloring our emotions in such a way as to bring about a positive feeling of obligation to reciprocate in turn.

There is little doubt that human society could not function without reciprocity. But we are not unique in this matter—the same complex reciprocity may also be shown by some animals. We therefore assume that the mechanism driving give-and-take in humans can be found in them as well. This does not imply that animals demonstrate gratitude of the same complexity and depth that humans do. But the basic mechanism probably occurs in animals besides ourselves.

References

Alexander, R. D. (1987). *The biology of moral systems*. New York: Aldine de Gruyter.

Aureli, F., Cozzolino, R., Cordischi, C., & Scucchi, S. (1992). Kin-oriented redirection among Japanese macaques: An expression of a revenge system? *Animal Behaviour, 44*, 283–291.

Boesch, C. (1994). Cooperative hunting in wild chimpanzees. *Animal Behaviour, 48*, 653–667.

Brosnan, S. F., & de Waal, F. B. M. (2002). A proximate perspective on reciprocal altruism. *Human Nature, 13*, 129–152.

Cheney, D. L., & Seyfarth, R. M. (1990). *How monkeys see the world: Inside the mind of another species*. Chicago: University of Chicago Press.

Clutton-Brock, T. H., & Parker, G. A. (1995). Punishment in animal societies. *Nature, 373*, 209–216.

de Waal, F. B. M. (1982). *Chimpanzee politics: Power and sex among apes*. Baltimore: Johns Hopkins University Press.

de Waal, F. B. M. (1991). Complementary methods and convergent evidence in the study of primate social cognition. *Behaviour, 118*, 297–320.

de Waal, F. B. M. (1996). *Good natured: The origins of right and wrong in humans and other animals*. Cambridge, MA: Harvard University Press.

de Waal, F. B. M. (1997). The chimpanzee's service economy: Food for grooming. *Evolution and Human Behavior, 18*, 375–386.

de Waal, F. B. M. (2000). Attitudinal reciprocity in food sharing among brown capuchin monkeys. *Animal Behaviour, 60*, 253–261.

de Waal, F. B. M., & Luttrell, L. M. (1988). Mechanisms of social reciprocity in three primate species: Symmetrical relationship characteristics or cognition? *Ethology and Sociobiology, 9*, 101–118.

de Waal, F. B. M., Luttrell, L. M., & Canfield, M. E. (1993). Preliminary data on voluntary food sharing in brown capuchin monkeys. *American Journal of Primatology, 29*, 73–78.

de Waal, F. B. M., & Yoshihara, D. (1983). Reconciliation and redirected affection in rhesus monkeys. *Behaviour, 85*, 224–241.

Dugatkin, L. A. (1997). *Cooperation among animals: An evolutionary perspective*. New York: Oxford University Press.

Fehr, E. & Gachter, S. (2002). Altruistic punishment in humans. *Nature, 415*, 137–140.

Flack, J. C., & de Waal, F. B. M. (2000). "Any animal whatever": Darwinian building blocks of morality in monkeys and apes. *Journal of Consciousness Studies, 7*(1–2), 1–29.

Gouldner, A. W. (1960). The norm of reciprocity: A preliminary statement. *American Sociological Review, 25,* 161–178.

Harnden-Warwick, D. (1997). Psychological realism, morality, and chimpanzees. *Zygon, 32,* 29–40.

Hart, B. L., & Hart, L. A. (1992). Reciprocal altruism in impala, *Aepyceros melampus. Animal Behaviour, 44,* 1073–1083.

Hemelrijk, C. K. (1994). Support for being groomed in long-tailed macaques, *Macaca fascicularis. Animal Behaviour, 48,* 479–81.

Hoogland, J. L. (1983). Nepotism and alarm calls in the black-tailed prairie dog (*Cynomys ludovicianus*). *Animal Behaviour, 31,* 472–479.

Komter, A., & Vollebergh, W. (1997). Gift giving and the emotional significance of family and friends. *Journal of Marriage and the Family, 59,* 747–757.

Leuba, J. H. (1928). Morality among the animals. *Harper's Monthly, 937,* 97–103.

McCullough, M. E., Kilpatrick, S. D., Emmons, R. A., & Larson, D. B. (2001). Is gratitude a moral affect? *Psychological Bulletin, 127,* 249–266.

Packer, C., & Ruttan, L. (1988). The evolution of cooperative hunting. *American Naturalist, 132,* 159–194.

Schwartz, B. (1967). The social psychology of the gift. *American Journal of Sociology, 73,* 1–11.

Seyfarth, R. M., & Cheney, D. L. (1984). Grooming, alliances, and reciprocal altruism in vervet monkeys. *Nature, 308,* 341–343.

Seyfarth, R. M., & Cheney, D. L. (1988). Empirical tests of reciprocity theory: Problems in assessment. *Ethology and Sociobiology, 9,* 181–187.

Simmel, G. (1950). *The sociology of Georg Simmel.* Glencoe, IL: Free Press. (Original work published 1908)

Smith, A. (1976). *The theory of moral sentiments* (6th ed.). Indianapolis, IN: Liberty Classics. (Original work published 1790)

Taylor, C. E., & McGuire, M. T. (1988). Reciprocal altruism: 15 years later. *Ethology and Sociobiology, 9,* 67–72.

Trivers, R. L. (1971). The evolution of reciprocal altruism. *Quarterly Review of Biology, 46,* 35–57.

Twain, M. (1976). *Tragedy of Pudd'nhead Wilson.* Cutchogue, NY: Buccaneer Books. (Original work published 1894)

Westermarck, E. (1908). *The origin and development of the moral ideas.* London: Macmillan.

Westermarck, E. (1932). *Ethical relativity.* New York: Harcourt, Brace.

Wilkinson, G. S. (1984). Reciprocal food sharing in vampire bats. *Nature, 308,* 181–184.

Wilkinson, G. S. (1988). Reciprocal altruism in bats and other mammals. *Ethology and Sociobiology, 9,* 85–100.

Wilkinson, G. S. (1990). Food sharing in vampire bats. *Scientific American,* 76–82.

12 The Grateful Heart

The Psychophysiology of Appreciation

Rollin McCraty and Doc Childre

Throughout history and across diverse cultures, religions, and spiritual traditions, the heart has been associated with spiritual influx, wisdom, and emotional experience, particularly with regard to other-centered, positive emotions such as love, care, compassion, and gratitude. Current research provides evidence that the heart does indeed play a role in the generation of emotional experience, suggesting that these long-surviving associations may be more than merely metaphorical. In this chapter, we discuss a model of emotion that includes the heart, together with the brain, nervous, and hormonal systems, as fundamental components of a dynamic, interactive network from which emotional experience emerges. Furthermore, we review research that has identified new physiological correlates associated with the experience of heartfelt positive emotions, with a specific focus on appreciation. We discuss the use of heart-based positive-emotion-focused techniques to help people self-induce and sustain states of appreciation and other positive emotions. Finally, we summarize the outcomes of several studies in which these techniques have been introduced in organizational, educational, and clinical settings.

DEFINITION OF TERMS

Gratitude and appreciation are related, yet different, aspects of our emotional landscape. Emmons and McCullough (2003) described gratitude as "a felt sense of wonder, thankfulness and appreciation for life. It can be expressed to others, as well as to impersonal (nature) or nonhuman sources (God, animals, the cosmos)" (p. 377). In their conceptualization of gratitude as an affect that guides people's cognitions and behaviors in the moral domain (McCullough, Kilpatrick, Emmons, & Larson, 2001), they pointed out that this emotion is generally considered one that people generate in response to others who have intended to benefit them.

Although a feeling of appreciation can clearly be elicited in the context of gratitude, it is not the same emotion. Whereas appreciation may at times be generated in response to another's actions, it is not necessarily evoked in response to specific favors or benefits received from another. Consequently, generally speaking, appreciation is less likely to carry the associated feelings of indebtedness or obligation that more often overlap with gratitude. Appreciation at times may also be directed toward oneself (e.g., appreciating one's own accomplishments, one's progress or perseverance in pursuing a particular goal, or one's efforts toward positive behavioral change), whereas gratitude by definition requires an interpersonal context or external source.

Common definitions of appreciation include "the act of estimating the qualities of things according to their true worth," "grateful recognition," "sensitive awareness or enjoyment," and "an increase in value." Cooperrider and Whitney (2000) defined appreciation as "valuing—the act of recognizing the best in people or the world around us" (p. 4). In the context of this chapter, when we refer to appreciation we denote an active feeling of thankfulness, which has an energetic quality that uplifts one's energy and spirit.

POSITIVE EMOTIONS AND OPTIMAL FUNCTIONING

You feel a deep sense of peace and internal balance—you are at harmony with yourself, with others, and with your larger environment. You experience increased buoyancy and vitality. Your senses are enlivened—every aspect of your perceptual experience seems richer, more textured. Surprisingly, you feel invigorated even when you would usually feel tired and drained. Things that usually would irk you just don't get to you as much. Your body feels regenerated—your mind, clear. At least for a period of time, decisions become obvious, as priorities clarify and inner conflict dissolves. Intuitive insight suddenly provides convenient solutions to problems that have previously consumed weeks of restless thought. Your creativity flows freely. You may experience a sense of greater connectedness with others and feelings of deep fulfillment.

Most people have at some point in their lives experienced a state similar to that just described. In many cases, individuals report that such magical moments, sometimes described as periods of increased "flow" (Csikszentmihalyi, 1990), are accompanied by the experience of a heartfelt positive emotion. Perhaps it is the feeling of being in love, gratitude for another's kindness, appreciation for the majesty of nature, or a sense of fulfillment spurred by one's own accomplishments.

For centuries, religious scholars, artists, scientists, medical practitioners, and lay authors have written about the transformative power of positive emotions. However, until recently, scientific exploration of these experiences has been largely lacking. Presently, a growing body of research is beginning to provide objective evidence that positive emotions may indeed be key to optimal functioning, enhancing nearly all spheres of human experience. Positive emotions have been demonstrated to improve health and increase longevity (Blakeslee, 1997; Danner, Snowdon, & Friesen, 2001; Russek & Schwartz, 1997), increase cognitive flexibility and creativity (Isen, 1999), facilitate "broad-minded coping" and innovative problem solving (Fredrickson, 2002; Isen, Daubman, & Nowicki, 1987), and promote helpfulness, generosity, and effective cooperation (Isen, 1987).

Over the past 10 years, our research group has focused on exploring how and why positive emotions improve health and performance, and specifically on uncovering physiological correlates of positive emotional states that may help to explain these observations.

THE HEART'S ROLE IN EMOTION

Throughout the 1990s, the view that the brain and body work in concert in order for perceptions, thoughts, and emotions to emerge has become widely accepted and has challenged several long-standing assumptions about emotions. For example, psychologists once maintained that emotions were purely mental expressions generated by the brain alone. However, we now know that emotions have as much to do with the body as they do with the brain. Furthermore, of the bodily organs, the heart plays a particularly important role in the emotional system.

Recent work in the relatively new field of neurocardiology has firmly established that the heart is a sensory organ and an information encoding and processing center, with an extensive intrinsic nervous system sufficiently sophisticated to qualify as a "heart brain." Its circuitry enables it to learn, remember, and make functional decisions independent of the cranial brain (Armour, 2003; Armour & Ardell, 1994). Moreover, patterns of cardiac afferent neurological input to the brain not only affect autonomic regulatory centers, but also influence higher brain centers involved in perception and emotional processing (Frysinger & Harper, 1990; McCraty, 2003; Sandman, Walker, & Berka, 1982).

One tool that has proved valuable in examining heart-brain interactions is heart rate variability analysis. Heart rate variability, derived from the electrocardiogram, is a measure of the naturally occurring beat-to-beat changes in heart rate. The analysis of heart rate variability, or heart rhythms, provides a powerful, noninvasive measure of neurocardiac function that reflects heart-brain interactions and autonomic nervous system dynamics, which are particularly sensitive to changes in emotional states (Tiller, McCraty, & Atkinson, 1996). Our research, along with that of others, suggests that there is an important link between emotions and changes in the patterns of both efferent (descending) and afferent (ascending) autonomic activity (Collet, Vernet-Maury, Delhomme, & Dittmar, 1997; McCraty, Barrios-Choplin, Rozman, Atkinson, & Watkins, 1998; Tiller et al., 1996). These changes in autonomic activity lead to distinct changes in the pattern of the heart's rhythm, often without any change in the amount of heart rate variability. Specifically, we have found that during the experience of emotions such as anger, frustration, or anxiety, heart rhythms become more erratic and disordered, indicating less synchronization in the reciprocal action between the parasympathetic and sympathetic branches of the autonomic nervous system (ANS). In contrast, sustained positive emotions such as appreciation, love, and compassion are associated with highly ordered or coherent patterns in the heart rhythms, reflecting greater synchronization between the two branches of the ANS and a shift in autonomic balance toward increased parasympathetic activity (see Figure 12.1; McCraty, Atkinson, Tiller, Rein, & Watkins, 1995; Tiller et al., 1996).

In addition to understanding how complex ANS activity patterns correlate with differing emotions, we are beginning to understand the role played by afferent neural signals, which flow from the heart and body to the brain, in the generation and experience of feelings and emotions. A substantial body of research, dating back to the early part of the twentieth century, has explored the influence of afferent signals from the heart and cardiovascular system on brain function (see Heymans & Neil, 1958). Among the first modern psychophysiological researchers to examine the "conversations" between the heart and brain, John and Beatrice Lacey observed that afferent input from the heart could significantly affect perception and behavior (B. C. Lacey & Lacey, 1974; J. I. Lacey & Lacey, 1970). Since that time, extensive experimental data have documented the role played by cardiac afferent input in modulating such varied processes as reaction times (J. I. Lacey & Lacey, 1970), pain perception (Randich & Gebhart, 1992), hormone production (Drinkhill & Mary, 1989), electrocortical activity, and cognitive functions

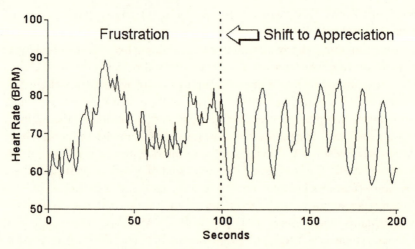

Figure 12.1. Emotions reflected in heart rhythm patterns. The real-time heart rate variability (heart rhythm) pattern, measured in beats per minute (BPM), is shown for an individual making an intentional shift from a self-induced state of frustration to a genuine feeling of appreciation by using the Freeze-Frame positive-emotion-refocusing technique. It is of note that when the recording is analyzed statistically, the amount of heart rate variability is found to remain virtually the same during the two different emotional states; however, the pattern of the heart rhythm changes distinctly. Note the immediate shift from an erratic, disordered heart rhythm pattern associated with frustration to a smooth, harmonious, sine-wave-like (coherent) pattern as the individual uses the positive-emotion-refocusing technique and self-generates a heartfelt feeling of appreciation.

(Rau, Pauli, Brody, & Elbert, 1993; Sandman et al., 1982; van der Molen, Somsen, & Orlebeke, 1985).

This research, however, did not generally consider how patterns of afferent input affect emotional processes. Our research findings have led us to support a systems-oriented model of emotion that includes the heart, brain, and the nervous and hormonal systems as fundamental components of a dynamic, interactive network that underlies the emergence of emotional experience (McCraty, 2003). The model builds on the theory of emotion first proposed by Pribram (Pribram & Melges, 1969), in which the brain functions as a complex pattern identification and matching system. In this model, past experience builds in us a set of familiar patterns, which are maintained in the neural architecture. Inputs to the brain from both the external and internal environments contribute to the maintenance of these patterns. In the body, many processes provide constant rhythmic inputs with which the brain becomes familiar. These include the heart's rhythmic activity; digestive, respiratory and hormonal rhythms; and patterns of muscular tension, particularly facial expressions. These inputs are continuously monitored by the brain and help organize perception, feelings, and behavior. Recurring input patterns form a stable backdrop, or reference pattern, against which current experiences are compared. According to this model, when an input is sufficiently different from the familiar reference, this mismatch or *departure from the familiar* underlies the generation of emotions.

The heart, as a primary and consistent generator of rhythmic patterns in the human body that possesses a far more extensive communication system with the brain than do other major organs, plays a particularly important role in this process (McCraty, 2003). With every beat, the heart transmits to the brain and throughout the body complex patterns of neurological, hormonal, pressure, and electromagnetic information, which form a major component of the physiological backdrop that ultimately determines our emotional experience.

Cardiovascular afferent signals are, therefore, a major contributor in establishing the baseline pattern or set point against which the "now" is compared. At lower brain levels, the heart's input is compared to references or set points that control blood pressure, affect respiration, and gate the flow of activity in the descending branches of the ANS (Langhorst, Schulz, & Lambertz, 1983). From there, these signals cascade up to a number of subcortical or limbic areas that are involved in the processing of emotion (Oppenheimer & Hopkins, 1994; Rau et al., 1993).

Several lines of research support the perspective that cardiac afferent input exerts an important influence on central emotional processing. For example, neural activity in the central nucleus of the amygdala, a key emotional center, is synchronized to the cardiac cycle and is modulated by cardiovascular afferent input (Frysinger & Harper, 1990). The importance of changes in the pattern of cardiac afferent signals is further illustrated by the finding that psychological aspects of panic disorder are frequently created by unrecognized paroxysmal supraventricular tachycardia (a sudden-onset cardiac arrhythmia). One study found that *DSM-IV* (American Psychiatric Association, 1994) criteria for panic disorder were fulfilled in more than two thirds of patients with these sudden-onset arrhythmias. In the majority of cases, once the arrhythmia was discovered and treated, the symptoms of panic disorder disappeared (Lessmeier et al., 1997). These arrhythmias generate a large and sudden change in the pattern of afferent signals sent to the brain, which is detected as a mismatch and consequently results in feelings of anxiety and panic.

It is interesting that when one plots the heart rhythms generated by this type of arrhythmia they appear quite similar to the incoherent heart rhythm patterns produced by strong feelings of anxiety in an otherwise healthy individual. By contrast, coherent heart rhythm patterns, which are associated with sincere positive emotions, are familiar to most brains and evoke feelings of security and well-being. If this is the case, then interventions capable of shifting the pattern of the heart's rhythmic activity should modify one's emotional state. In fact, people commonly use just such an intervention— simply altering their breathing rhythm by taking several slow, deep breaths. Most people do not realize, however, that the reason breathing techniques are effective in helping to shift one's emotional state is because changing one's breathing rhythm modulates the heart's rhythmic activity. The modulation of the heart's rhythm by respiratory activity is referred to as respiratory sinus arrhythmia (Hirsch & Bishop, 1981). Later in this chapter, we describe other, heart-focused interventions that also facilitate emotional shifts by generating changes in the heart's rhythmic patterns.

PHYSIOLOGICAL CORRELATES OF HEARTFELT POSITIVE EMOTIONS

Physiological Coherence

Our research on emotional physiology has identified distinct physiological correlates of heartfelt positive emotional states. We have introduced the term *physiological coherence* to describe a functional mode encompassing a number of related physiological phenomena that are associated with feelings of appreciation.

The term *coherence* has several related definitions applicable to the study of emotional physiology. In physics, the term describes the ordered or constructive distribution of power within a wave. The more stable the frequency and shape of the waveform, the higher the coherence. An example of a coherent wave is the sine wave. The term *autocoherence* is used to denote this kind of coherence. In physiological systems, this type of coherence describes the degree of order and stability in the rhythmic activity generated by a single oscillatory system. Methodology for computing coherence has been published elsewhere (Tiller et al., 1996).

Coherence also describes two or more waves that are phase- or frequency-locked. In physiology, coherence is used to describe a functional mode in which two or more of the body's oscillatory systems, such as respiration and heart rhythms, become entrained and oscillate at the same frequency. The term *cross-coherence* is used to specify this type of coherence.

It is of interest that both of the above definitions apply to the study of emotional physiology. We have found that sincere positive emotions such as appreciation are associated with a higher degree of coherence in the heart's rhythmic activity (autocoherence). Additionally, during such states there

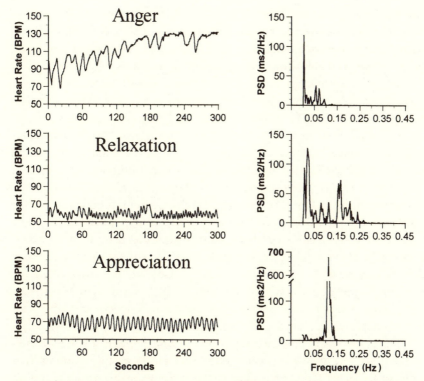

Figure 12.2. Heart rhythm patterns during different psychophysiological states. The lefthand graphs are heart rate tachograms, which show beat-to-beat changes in heart rate, measured in beats per minute (BPM). To the right are shown the heart rate variability power spectral density (PSD) plots of the tachogram at left. Anger is characterized by a lower frequency, disordered heart rhythm pattern and increasing heart rate. As can be seen in the corresponding power spectrum to the right, the rhythm during anger is primarily in the very low frequency band (0.0033–0.04 hertz), which is associated with sympathetic nervous system activity. Relaxation results in a higher frequency, lower amplitude rhythm, indicating reduced autonomic outflow. In this case, increased power in the high frequency band (0.15–0.4 hertz) of the power spectrum is observed, reflecting increased parasympathetic activity (the relaxation response). In contrast, sustained positive emotions such as appreciation are associated with a highly ordered, smooth, sine-wave-like heart rhythm pattern (coherence). As can be seen in the corresponding power spectrum, this physiological mode is associated with a large, narrow peak in the low frequency band (0.04–0.15 hertz), centered around 0.1 hertz. This indicates systemwide resonance, increased synchronization between the sympathetic and parasympathetic branches of the nervous system, and entrainment between the heart rhythm pattern, respiration, and blood pressure rhythms. The coherent mode is also associated increased parasympathetic activity, thus encompassing a key element of the relaxation response, yet it is physiologically distinct from relaxation, because the system is oscillating at its resonant frequency and

also tends to be increased coherence among different physiological oscilla-tory systems (cross-coherence/entrainment; Tiller et al., 1996). Typically, en-trainment is observed among heart rhythms, respiratory rhythms, and blood pressure oscillations; however, other biological oscillators, including very low frequency brain rhythms, craniosacral rhythms, electrical potentials meas-ured across the skin, and, most likely, rhythms in the digestive system, can also become entrained (McCraty & Atkinson, 2003).

A related phenomenon that can also occur during physiological coher-ence is resonance. In physics, resonance refers to a phenomenon whereby an abnormally large vibration is produced in a system in response to a stimulus whose frequency is the same as, or nearly the same as, the natural vibratory frequency of the system. The frequency of the vibration produced in such a state is said to be the resonant frequency of the system. Most models show that the resonant frequency of the human cardiovascular system is deter-mined by the feedback loops between the heart and brain (Baselli et al., 1994; deBoer, Karemaker, & Strackee, 1987). In humans and in many animals, the resonant frequency of the system is 0.1 hertz, which is equivalent to a 10-sec-ond rhythm. Thus, in the coherent mode, the power spectrum of the heart rhythm displays an unusually large peak around 0.1 hertz (see Figure 12.2).

The system especially vibrates at its resonant frequency when an indi-vidual is actively feeling appreciation or some other positive emotion (Mc-Craty et al., 1995), although resonance can also emerge during states of sleep and deep relaxation. In terms of physiological functioning, resonance confers a number of benefits to the system. For example, there is increased efficiency in fluid exchange, filtration, and absorption between the capillaries and tis-sues; increased ability of the cardiovascular system to adapt to circulatory re-quirements; and increased temporal synchronization of cells throughout the body. This results in increased systemwide energy efficiency and metabolic energy savings (Langhorst et al., 1984; Siegel et al., 1984). These findings provide a link between positive emotions and increased physiological effi-ciency, which may partly explain the growing number of correlations docu-mented between positive emotions, improved health, and increased longevity. Furthermore, data suggest that this more efficient functional mode also improves the cognitive processing of sensory information (McCraty, 2002b; McCraty & Atkinson, 2003).

---

there is increased harmony and synchronization in nervous system and heart-brain dynamics. In addition, the coherent mode does not necessarily involve a lowering of heart *rate* per se or a change in the *amount* of variability, but rather a change in heart rhythm *pattern*. Also note the scale difference in the amplitude of the spectral peak during the coherent mode.

Appreciation, Heart-Brain Synchronization, and Cognitive Performance

In addition to the phenomena discussed above, physiological coherence is also associated with increased synchronization between the heartbeat and alpha rhythms in the electroencephalogram (EEG). In experiments measuring heartbeat evoked potentials, we found that the brain's alpha activity (8–12 hertz frequency range) is naturally synchronized to the cardiac cycle. However, when subjects felt appreciation, their heart rhythm coherence significantly increased, as did the ratio of the alpha rhythm that was synchronized to the heart (McCraty, 2002b; McCraty & Atkinson, 2003). In another study in which subjects self-generated feelings of appreciation while listening to music designed to foster positive emotions, the percentage of alpha-electrocardiogram synchronization significantly increased in the left hemisphere, centered around the temporal lobe (see Figure 12.3). These observations may be related to findings linking increased left hemisphere activity with positive emotion (Lane et al., 1997).

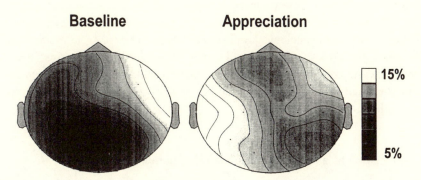

Baseline   **Appreciation**

15%

5%

Figure 12.3. Alpha activity synchronized to the cardiac cycle. Group mean topographical maps for 30 subjects show the percentage of alpha activity, in different regions of the brain, that is synchronized to the heartbeat during a resting baseline as compared with the percentage of synchronized alpha activity while the subjects were actively feeling appreciation. The plots are controlled for total amount of alpha activity (which did not change significantly) and show only the amount of synchronized activity. As can be seen in the plots, the areas with the highest degree of synchronization (the areas lightest in color) shift from the right frontal area during the baseline period to the left hemisphere, centered around the temporal area and radiating outward from there during appreciation. This change was most pronounced at EEG site T3 (left temporal area), although activity at adjacent sites was also significantly more synchronized to the heart.

In related experiments, we found that increased heart rhythm coherence correlates with significant improvements in cognitive performance in auditory discrimination tasks, which require focused attention, the ability to discriminate subtle tone differences, and the ability to react quickly and accurately. Not only did increases in heart rhythm coherence accompany increased cognitive performance, but also the degree of coherence correlated with task performance across all subjects during all tasks. The control group, which had an unstructured relaxation period in place of the positive emotion self-induction task, showed no significant increase in heart rhythm coherence or improvements in cognitive performance (McCraty, 2002b; McCraty & Atkinson, 2003). These observations directly support the concept that the pattern of cardiac afferent input reaching the brain can inhibit or facilitate cognitive processing and thus provide a potential physiological link between appreciation and improvements in faculties such as motor skills, focused attention, and discrimination.

In summary, we use the term *coherence* to describe a physiological mode that encompasses entrainment, resonance, and synchronization—distinct but related phenomena, all of which emerge from the harmonious interactions of the body's subsystems. Correlates of physiological coherence include increased synchronization between the two branches of the ANS, a shift in autonomic balance toward increased parasympathetic activity, increased heart-brain synchronization, increased vascular resonance, and entrainment between diverse physiological oscillatory systems. The coherent mode is reflected by a smooth, sine-wave-like pattern in the heart rhythms (heart rhythm coherence) and a narrow-band, high-amplitude peak in the low frequency range of the heart rate variability power spectrum, at a frequency of about 0.1 hertz.

Appreciation as a Driver of Physiological Coherence

Although physiological coherence is a natural state that can occur spontaneously, sustained episodes are generally rare. Whereas specific rhythmic breathing methods can induce coherence and entrainment for brief periods, cognitively directed, paced breathing is difficult for many people to maintain. On the other hand, our findings indicate that individuals can produce extended periods of physiological coherence by actively generating and sustaining a feeling of appreciation. Sincere feelings of appreciation appear to excite the system at its resonant frequency, allowing the coherent mode to emerge naturally. This typically makes it easier for people to sustain a positive emotion for longer periods, thus facilitating the process of establishing and reinforcing coherent patterns in the neural architecture as the familiar reference. Once a new pattern is established, the brain strives to maintain a match with the new program, thus increasing the probability of maintaining emotional stability, even during challenging situations.

EMOTIONAL MANAGEMENT: THE MISSING DIMENSION

Throughout the ages, in every culture and in countless different ways, we have been exhorted repeatedly with the same fundamental message: to love one another, to have care and compassion for our fellow human beings, and to live in appreciation of life's gifts. Yet, in our view, genuine positive emotions and attitudes are not as prevalent in most people's lives as one might presume. For the most part, such states, along with their numerous benefits, remain mental concepts, which are transient and unpredictable experiences in most people's lives. They are too often dependent on the arrangements of external events, rather than being fundamental traits. For example, people may find it relatively easy to genuinely experience feelings such as happiness, buoyancy, or appreciation during life's highs—special occasions or events that frequently involve a high degree of sensory stimulation; however, people rarely sustain such regenerative feelings as a norm in the midst of their ordinary day-to-day lives. At the other end of the spectrum, a tragedy or crisis can often elicit feelings and actions of care, compassion, and unprecedented co-operation among members of a family, community, or organization—only for people to fall back into old patterns of separation, judgment, and self-centered thought and action some time after the event has passed.

Although most people intuitively know that they feel best and operate more efficiently and effectively when experiencing positive emotions, why is it that they do not more consistently engage such states in their day-to-day lives? Why do genuine positive emotional experiences remain transient and unpredictable occurrences for most people? We propose that a main factor underlying this discrepancy is a fundamental lack of mental and emotional self-management skills. In other words, people generally do not make efforts to actively infuse their daily experiences with greater emotional quality because they sincerely do not know how.

Despite our best intentions, the human "negativity bias"—the natural tendency to focus on inputs (including thoughts and emotions) perceived as negative to a greater extent than neutral or positive stimuli—is a very real phenomenon with a sound neurophysiological basis (Ito, Larsen, Smith, & Cacioppo, 1998). Although most people definitively claim that they love, care, and appreciate, it might shock many to realize the large degree to which these feelings are merely assumed or acknowledged cognitively, far more than they are actually experienced in their feeling world. In the absence of conscious efforts to engage, build, and sustain positive perceptions and emotions, we all too automatically fall prey to feelings such as irritation, anxiety, worry, frustration, judgmentalness, self-doubt, and blame. As negative feelings are repeatedly rehashed, these patterns reinforce their familiarity in the neural architecture, thus becoming stereotyped and increasingly automatic and mechanical. Many people do not realize the extent to which these habitual response patterns dominate their internal landscape, diluting and limiting positive emotional experience and eventually becoming so familiar that they become engrained in one's sense of self-identity.

Unmanaged negative mental and (particularly) emotional processing drains vital energy from our psychological energy reserves, which we call the "emotional energy accumulators." Emotional energy or buoyancy is important for smooth mental processes. When energy accumulators are drained, this leads to unregulated nervous system activity, which decreases clarity and our ability to make accurate assessments and quick, effective decisions. This, in turn, often serves to perpetuate the cycle of stress and disturbed feelings. In essence, the inner noise generated from unmanaged mental and emotional processes consumes our energy and keeps us from functioning to our full potential.

Various stress management practices have been developed to help people manage their emotions in order to reduce these energy drains. Most of these approaches are based on a cognitive model in which all emotions follow a cognitive assessment of sensory input, which then leads to a behavioral response. Therefore, these approaches rely on strategies that engage or restructure cognitive processes. The basic theoretical framework is that if emotions always follow thought, then by changing one's thoughts, one can gain control over one's emotions. However, in the last decade, research in the neurosciences has made it quite clear that emotional processes operate at a much higher speed than thoughts and frequently bypass the mind's linear reasoning process entirely (LeDoux, 1996). Furthermore, although emotions can be induced by thoughts, they may also arise from unconscious associations triggered by external or internal events. In other words, not all emotions follow thoughts; many (in fact most, in certain contexts) occur independently of the cognitive system and can significantly bias or color the cognitive process and its output or decisions (LeDoux, 1994, 1996).

This is why strategies that encourage "positive thinking" *without also engaging positive feelings* may frequently provide only temporary, if any, relief from emotional distress. Although a conceptual shift may occur (which is important), the fundamental source of the emotional stress (a maladapted reference program) remains largely intact. This has significant implications for emotion regulation interventions and suggests that intervening at the level of the emotional system may in many cases be a more direct and efficient way to override and transform historical patterns underlying maladaptive thoughts, feelings, and behaviors, and to instill more positive emotions and prosocial behaviors.

TOOLS AND TECHNIQUES TO PROMOTE POSITIVE EMOTIONS AND PHYSIOLOGICAL COHERENCE

Positive-Emotion-Focused Techniques

The recent positive psychology movement has emphasized the importance of encouraging not only the reduction of negative emotions, but also the cultivation of positive emotions in daily life (Seligman & Csikszentmihalyi, 2000). Yet, psychology has seen a notable scarcity of interventions that focus directly and systematically on increasing positive emotional experiences. Recognizing this need many years ago, one of us (D.C.) undertook the development of practical, heart-based positive-emotion-focused tools and techniques that are designed to facilitate the self-regulation of emotions (Childre & Martin, 1999; Childre & Rozman, 2002). Collectively known as the Heart-Math[1] system, these techniques utilize the heart as a point of entry into the psychophysiological networks that underlie emotional experience. The model of emotion we briefly summarized earlier emphasizes the central role played by cardiac afferent signals in emotional perception and experience. In essence, because the heart is a primary generator of rhythmic patterns in the body—influencing brain processes that control the ANS, cognitive function, and emotion—it provides an access point from which systemwide dynamics can be quickly and profoundly affected (McCraty, 2003; McCraty & Atkinson, 2003).

In brief, HeartMath techniques combine a shift in the focus of attention to the area around the heart (where many people subjectively feel positive emotions) with the intentional self-induction of a sincere positive emotional state, such as appreciation. We have found that appreciation is one of the most concrete and easiest of the positive emotions for individuals to self-induce and sustain for longer periods.

Such a shift in focus and feeling serves to increase heart rhythm coherence, which results in a change in the pattern of afferent cardiac signals sent to the cognitive and emotional centers in the brain. This coupling of a more organized afferent pattern with an intentionally self-generated feeling of appreciation reinforces the natural conditioned response between the physiological state and the positive emotion. This subsequently strengthens the ability of a positive feeling shift to initiate a physiological shift toward increased coherence, or a physiological shift to facilitate the experience of a positive emotion.

Furthermore, our work suggests that the change in the pattern of afferent input reaching the brain also facilitates higher cognitive faculties that are normally compromised during stress or negative emotional states. This sharpens one's discernment abilities, increases resourcefulness, and often facilitates a perceptual shift, which allows problematic issues, interactions, or decisions to be assessed and dealt with from a broader, more emotionally balanced perspective.

Positive-emotion-focused techniques can thus enable individuals to effectively replace stressful thought patterns and feelings with more positive perceptions and emotions in the moment when they are needed most. However, the benefits also extend beyond reducing stress and negative emotions in the present moment. Learning to self-generate positive emotions with greater consistency can give rise to long-term improvements in emotion regulation abilities, performance, attitudes, and relationships that affect many aspects of one's life.

In keeping with our model of emotion, we suggest that these enduring benefits stem from the fact that, as people experience appreciation and its consequent physiological coherence with increasing consistency, the coherent patterns become ever more familiar to the brain. Thus, these patterns become established in the neural architecture as a new, stable baseline or norm, which serves as a set point or frame of reference that the system then strives to maintain. Therefore, when stress or emotional instability is subsequently experienced, the familiar coherent, stable state is more readily accessible, enabling a quicker and more enduring emotional shift. Even brief periods of coherence can stabilize nervous system dynamics, thereby reducing the tendency for inputs, whether internally or externally generated, to cause an emotional disturbance. Through this repatterning process, positive emotions and coherent physiological patterns progressively replace maladaptive emotional patterns and stressful responses as the habitual way of being. At the physiological level, the occurrence of this repatterning process is supported by electrophysiological evidence demonstrating a greater frequency of spontaneous (without conscious practice of the interventions) periods of coherence in the heart rate tachograms of individuals practiced in positive-emotion-focused techniques in comparison to the general population (McCraty & Atkinson, 1998).

HeartMath tools and techniques include positive-emotion-refocusing techniques such as Freeze-Frame[1] (Childre, 1998), which enables individuals to modify their responses to stress in real time, and emotional restructuring techniques such as Heart Lock-In[1] (Childre & Rozman, 2002), which builds the capacity to sustain heartfelt positive emotions and physiological coherence for longer periods. These tools are intentionally designed as simple, easy-to-use interventions that can be adapted to virtually any culture or age group. They are free of religious or cultural bias, and most people feel an enjoyable emotional shift and experience a broadened perception the first time that they use them. Although most age groups can effectively use the Freeze-Frame and Heart Lock-In techniques, tools specifically for children and young adults have also been designed (Childre, 2001). We have also created a number of tools for use in specific contexts in organizational, educational, and health care settings (Childre & Cryer, 2000; Childre & Martin, 1999).

Heart Rhythm Coherence Feedback Training

Heart rhythm feedback training is a powerful tool to assist people in using positive-emotion-focused techniques effectively and in learning to self-generate increased physiological coherence (McCraty, 2002a). Technologies have been developed that enable physiological coherence to be objectively monitored and quantified. One such device is the Freeze-Framer[1] heart rhythm monitoring and coherence-building system (Quantum Intech, Inc., Boulder Creek, CA). This interactive hardware/software system monitors and displays individuals' heart rate variability patterns in real time as they practice the positive-emotion-focused techniques taught in an included tutorial. Using a fingertip sensor to record the pulse wave, the Freeze-Framer plots changes in heart rate on a beat-to-beat basis. As people practice the techniques, they can readily see and experience the changes in their heart rhythm patterns, which generally become more ordered, smoother, and more sine-wave-like as they feel appreciation and other positive emotions. This process reinforces the natural association between the physiological coherence mode and positive feelings. The real-time physiological feedback also essentially takes the guesswork and randomness out of the process of self-inducing a positive emotional state, resulting in greater consistency, focus, and effectiveness in practicing emotional shifts.

The software also analyzes the heart rhythm patterns for coherence level, which is fed back to the user as an accumulated score or success in playing one of three on-screen games designed to reinforce the emotion-refocusing skills. Finally, the software includes a multiuser database to store results and track one's progress.

Because this technology uses a fingertip pulse sensor and involves no electrode hookup, it is extremely versatile, time efficient, and easy to use in a wide variety of settings (e.g., workplaces, homes, schools, etc.). Heart rhythm coherence feedback training has been used in diverse contexts by mental health professionals, physicians, law enforcement personnel, educators, and corporate executives to decrease stress, anxiety, depression, and fatigue; promote improved academic and work performance; lower blood pressure; and facilitate health improvements in numerous clinical disorders.

INTERVENTION STUDIES

Beneficial psychological and health outcomes associated with the use of positive-emotion-focused techniques and heart rhythm coherence feedback training have been demonstrated across diverse populations in both laboratory and field studies (McCraty, Atkinson, & Tomasino, 2001). Collectively, these results suggest that techniques that foster feelings of appreciation and increase physiological coherence are effective in producing sustained improvements in many aspects of psychological and physical health and in general well-being and performance. Furthermore, results indicate that such techniques are easily learned, have a high rate of compliance, and are highly adaptable to a wide range of demographic groups.

Health-Related Outcomes

The human body has an inherent capacity for self-healing and regeneration. However, life's hectic pace coupled with frequent inefficient mental and emotional activity can compromise the system's natural regenerative processes. The energy drains produced by unmanaged emotions burden the system, placing added stress on the entire body. The health implications are substantial, as there is now abundant evidence that the depletion of emotional energy plays a major and largely unrecognized role in both the genesis and aggravation of many health problems (Boone & Christensen, 1997; Grossarth-Maticek & Eysenck, 1995; Wickramasekera, 1998).

By fostering a state of physiological coherence, positive-emotion-focused techniques help individuals create an internal environment that is conducive to both physical and emotional regeneration. We suggest that such techniques are effective in helping to build back energy that has been depleted by persistent mental processing or negative emotional arousal, thereby enhancing health and healing. A number of research studies provide support for this hypothesis, documenting both short-term and long-term health benefits associated with the use of positive-emotion-focused techniques.

In one study, practice of the Heart Lock-In technique for 15 minutes with a focus on appreciation resulted in an immediate and significant increase in levels of secretory IgA, the predominant antibody class found in mucosal secretions, which serves as the body's first line of defense against pathogens (McCraty, Atkinson, Rein, & Watkins, 1996). Other research has documented significant favorable changes in hormonal balance with regular practice of the Heart Lock-In and Cut-Thru[1] (an emotional restructuring technique; Childre & Rozman, 2002) techniques over a period of 30 days. In a study of 30 subjects, a 23% average reduction in cortisol and a 100% increase in DHEA were measured after one month of practice. Increases in DHEA were significantly correlated to increases in the affective construct of *warmheartedness* (represented by kindness, appreciation, tolerance, and compassion), whereas decreases in cortisol were significantly correlated to decreases in stress (McCraty et al., 1998).

Improvements in clinical status, emotional well-being, and quality of life have also been demonstrated in various medical patient populations in intervention programs using positive-emotion-refocusing and emotional restructuring approaches. For example, significant blood pressure reductions in individuals with hypertension (McCraty, Atkinson, & Tomasino, 2003), improved functional capacity and reduced depression in congestive heart failure patients (Luskin, Reitz, Newell, Quinn, & Haskell, 2002), and improved psychological health and quality of life in patients with diabetes (McCraty, Atkinson, & Lipsenthal, 2000) have been demonstrated. Another study reported reductions in pathological symptoms and anxiety and significant improvements in positive affect, physical vitality, and general well-being in individuals with HIV infection and AIDS (Rozman, Whitaker, Beckman, & Jones, 1996).

Additionally, patient case history data provided by numerous health care professionals report substantial improvements in health and psychological status and frequent reductions in medication requirements in patients with such medical conditions as cardiac arrhythmias, chronic fatigue, environmental sensitivity, fibromyalgia, and chronic pain. Finally, positive-emotion-focused techniques and heart rhythm feedback have been used by mental health professionals in the treatment of emotional disorders, including anxiety, depression, panic disorder, and posttraumatic stress disorder. Many therapists find that emotional restructuring techniques are an effective means of achieving therapeutic release without retraumatization, and that such techniques frequently shorten treatment time.

Organizational Outcomes

We have examined the impact of positive-emotion-focused interventions and heart rhythm feedback training in diverse organizational settings, including high-tech companies, government agencies, global oil companies, hospitals, and law enforcement agencies. Collectively, this research shows that interventions that focus on increasing positive emotions can indeed be effectively implemented in a wide variety of workplace settings, yielding measurable improvements in both employee health and well-being and in organizational performance (Childre & Cryer, 2000). Organizationally relevant outcomes documented include increases in productivity, goal clarity, job satisfaction, communication effectiveness, and reductions in employee turnover (Barrios-Choplin, McCraty, Sundram, & Atkinson, 1999; Mc-Craty, Tomasino, Atkinson, & Sundram, 1999; Barrios-Choplin, McCraty, & Cryer, 1997; McCraty et al., 2001). Positive-emotion-focused intervention programs have also been used in helping organizations to effectively meet the demands of specific challenges, such as downsizing and restructuring initiatives.

Educational Outcomes

Programs incorporating HeartMath tools and techniques introduced at the elementary, middle school, high school, and college levels have been demonstrated to improve emotional well-being, classroom behaviors, learning, and academic performance (Arguelles, McCraty, & Rees, 2003; McCraty et al., 2001). In one study, 32 at-risk middle school students exhibited significant improvements in nearly all areas of psychosocial functioning assessed, including stress and anger management, risky behavior, work management and focus, and relationships with teachers, family, and peers. Furthermore, students were able to use the Freeze-Frame technique to quickly recover from acute emotional stress and positively modulate their autonomic response to stress in real time, thus demonstrating increased physiological stress resiliency in relation to a control group (McCraty, Atkinson, Tomasino, Goelitz, & Mayrovitz, 1999).

Another study examined the impact of tools and technology on reducing test-taking anxiety and improving test scores in high school seniors. Students who had failed their state-required exit exams and needed to retake the tests to graduate participated in a 3-week intensive program. The course included instruction in the Freeze-Frame and Heart Lock-In techniques, with an emphasis on reducing test-related anxiety and instilling greater emotional stability and self-confidence. Students also received heart rhythm feedback training to help them learn how to self-generate physiological coherence. After the program, the students demonstrated improvements in test scores and passing rates that represented 1 to 2 years' growth in academic skills and greatly exceeded those achieved through standard academic preparation alone. As compared with a control group, the trained students also demonstrated significant reductions in hostility, depression, interpersonal sensitivity, somatization, and other key indices of psychological distress (McCraty, Tomasino, Atkinson, Aasen, & Thurik, 2000).

In a study evaluating a program designed to decrease anger, improve psychosocial well-being, and engender forgiveness, Stanford University students were taught the Freeze-Frame and Heart Lock-In techniques in six weekly 1-hour sessions. Participants were assessed by psychological self-report measures and their response to a vignette at baseline, at the completion of the training, and again 10 weeks later. The students who received the training demonstrated significant reductions in both trait and reactive anger as well as interpersonal hurt, and were more willing to use forgiveness as a problem-solving strategy, compared with those in the control group. Among members of the study group, there were also significant increases in hopefulness, self-efficacy in managing emotion and interpersonal hurt, and scores on measures assessing personal growth, compassion, spiritual issues, and quality of life. These results suggest that programs that foster appreciation can be effective in modifying psychosocial traits and facilitating the release of negative emotions accumulated from past hurts in a relatively brief period of time (Luskin, 1999).

CONCLUSION AND FUTURE RESEARCH DIRECTIONS

Recent years have seen the emergence of a growing body of data linking positive emotions to the enhancement of human functioning. Collectively, these findings are beginning to substantiate what many people have long intuitively known: Positive emotions bolster one's ability to meet life's challenges with grace and ease, optimize cognitive capacities, sustain constructive and meaningful relationships with others, and foster good health. The research discussed in this chapter adds to this body of data by identifying and characterizing a distinct mode of physiological functioning, termed physiological coherence, that is associated with the feeling of appreciation. We propose that coherence may provide a physiological link between positive emotions and a range of favorable health-related, cognitive, and psychosocial outcomes.

It is our hope that the findings described here will help to lay the groundwork for future research relating the physiology of emotions to human health and performance. Our future research aims include the elucidation of additional physiological correlates of appreciation and other positive affective states. For example, a current study is examining changes in levels of atrial natriuretic peptide and oxytocin during positive as compared to negative and neutral emotional states.

Another pertinent research question is whether positive-emotion-focused coherence-building interventions can be used to improve diverse aspects of human performance. For example, preliminary evidence suggests that athletic performance and teamwork are improved by the use of such techniques.

Research discussed in this chapter has shown that positive and negative emotions can be discriminated by distinct changes in the heart's rhythmic patterns. However, we have not yet been able to clearly discriminate between specific positive or negative emotions on the basis of heart rhythm patterns alone. We anticipate that future developments in pattern analysis technologies will enable a more refined discrimination of emotions than is currently possible. This may facilitate the recognition of specific positive and negative emotions based on their heart rhythm pattern signatures.

We have argued that, for most people, the range of positive emotional experience is limited by the automaticity of historical patterns that operate at a level below conscious awareness to color perception, feelings, and behavior. It therefore requires conscious choice and commitment to recognize these maladaptive patterns and gradually replace them with ones that are more conducive to well-being. We suggest that practice of positive-emotion-focused techniques can facilitate such a repatterning process and enable people to cultivate more positive emotions, attitudes, and behaviors in daily life.

Future research studies could further substantiate the occurrence of such a repatterning process by providing additional evidence of the development of stable changes in physiological and psychosocial functioning over time. Positive-emotion-focused techniques could be readily incorporated into studies investigating the long-term effects on health and well-being of cultivating gratitude and appreciation in daily life. This research could help to answer a wide range of questions, including the following: Can interventions that foster feelings of appreciation/gratitude engender other positive emotions (e.g., love, care, joy, elevation, and contentment) and other-regarding virtues (e.g., altruism, compassion, and service)? Can such interventions enhance the quality of interpersonal relationships? Can they foster an increased sense of spiritual connectedness?

Finally, intervention studies could be designed to further determine to what degree positive-emotion-focused interventions may be effective in the treatment of people with affective disorders as well as individuals with physical pathologies. To the extent that such interventions help to facilitate the recovery process, it is of interest to determine their cost effectiveness as additions to existing treatment programs.

As increasing emphasis is placed on learning to enrich the emotional aspects of our experience, we anticipate that positive-emotion-focused techniques and intervention programs that instill feelings of appreciation and gratitude will be increasingly integrated in clinical, workplace, and academic settings for the enhancement of health, well-being, and performance. It is our hope that such interventions will help people to develop greater awareness of their emotional responses, both conscious and subconscious; to progressively learn to direct these responses in ways that benefit their health and well-being; and ultimately to take on a more proactive role in the orchestration of their own fulfillment.

Note

1. HeartMath, Freeze-Frame, Heart Lock-In, and Cut-Thru are registered trademarks of the Institute of HeartMath (http://www.heartmath.org). Freeze-Framer is a trademark of Quantum Intech, Inc. (http://www.quantumintech.com). The Heart-Math organizations—the Institute of HeartMath, HeartMath LLC (http://www.heartmath.com), and Quantum Intech—are located at 14700 West Park Avenue, Boulder Creek, CA 95006, USA.

References

American Psychiatric Association. (1994). *Diagnostic and statistical manual of mental disorders* (4th ed.). Washington, DC: Author.

Arguelles, L., McCraty, R., & Rees, R. A. (2003). The heart in holistic education. *Encounter: Education for Meaning and Social Justice, 16*(3), 13–21.

Armour, J. A. (2003). *Neurocardiology—Anatomical and functional principles.* Boulder Creek, CA: HeartMath Research Center, Institute of HeartMath, Publication No. 03–011.

Armour, J. A., & Ardell, J. L. (Eds.). (1994). *Neurocardiology.* New York: Oxford University Press.

Barrios-Choplin, B., McCraty, R., & Cryer, B. (1997). An inner quality approach to reducing stress and improving physical and emotional wellbeing at work. *Stress Medicine, 13*(3), 193–201.

Barrios-Choplin, B., McCraty, R., Sundram, J., & Atkinson, M. (1999). *The effect of employee self-management training on personal and organizational quality.* Boulder Creek, CA: HeartMath Research Center, Institute of HeartMath, Publication No. 99–083.

Baselli, G., Cerutti, S., Badilini, F., Biancardi, L., Porta, A., Pagani, M., et al. (1994). Model for the assessment of heart period variability interactions of respiration influences. *Medical and Biological Engineering and Computing, 32*(2), 143–152.

Blakeslee, T. R. (1997). *The attitude factor: Extend your life by changing the way you think.* London: Thorsons/HarperCollins.

Boone, J. L., & Christensen, J. F. (1997). Stress and disease. In M. D. Feldman & J. F. Christensen (Eds.), *Behavioral medicine in primary care: A practical guide* (pp. 265–276). Stamford, CT: Appleton & Lange.

Childre, D. (1998). *Freeze-Frame: A scientifically proven technique for clear decision making and improved health*. Boulder Creek, CA: Planetary Publications.

Childre, D. (2001). *Emotional security tool kit for children and teens*. Boulder Creek, CA: Institute of HeartMath. Retrieved May 12, 2003, from http://www.heartmath.org/estk_t/estk_home.html

Childre, D., & Cryer, B. (2000). *From chaos to coherence: The power to change performance*. Boulder Creek, CA: Planetary.

Childre, D., & Martin, H. (1999). *The HeartMath solution*. San Francisco: HarperSanFrancisco.

Childre, D., & Rozman, D. (2002). *Overcoming emotional chaos: Eliminate anxiety, lift depression and create security in your life*. San Diego: Jodere Group.

Collet, C., Vernet-Maury, E., Delhomme, G., & Dittmar, A. (1997). Autonomic nervous system response patterns specificity to basic emotions. *Journal of the Autonomic Nervous System, 62* (1–2), 45–57.

Cooperrider, D. L., & Whitney, D. (2000). A positive revolution in change: Appreciative inquiry. In D. L. Cooperrider, P. F. Sorensen, Jr., D. Whitney, & T. F. Yaeger (Eds.), *Appreciative inquiry: Rethinking human organization toward a positive theory of change* (pp. 3–28). Campaign, IL: Stipes.

Csikszentmihalyi, M. (1990). *Flow: The psychology of optimal experience*. New York: Harper & Row.

Danner, D. D., Snowdon, D. A., & Friesen, W. V. (2001). Positive emotions in early life and longevity: Findings from the nun study. *Journal of Personality and Social Psychology, 80*(5), 804–813.

deBoer, R. W., Karemaker, J. M., & Strackee, J. (1987). Hemodynamic fluctuations and baroreflex sensitivity in humans: A beat-to-beat model. *American Journal of Physiology, 253*(3, pt. 2), H680-H689.

Drinkhill, M. J., & Mary, D. A. (1989). The effect of stimulation of the atrial receptors on plasma cortisol level in the dog. *Journal of Physiology, 413*, 299–313.

Emmons, R. A., & McCullough, M. E. (2003). Counting blessings versus burdens: An experimental investigation of gratitude and subjective well-being in daily life. *Journal of Personality and Social Psychology, 84*(2), 377–389.

Fredrickson, B. L. (2002). Positive emotions. In C. R. Snyder & S. J. Lopez (Eds.), *Handbook of positive psychology* (pp. 120–134). New York: Oxford University Press.

Frysinger, R. C., & Harper, R. M. (1990). Cardiac and respiratory correlations with unit discharge in epileptic human temporal lobe. *Epilepsia, 31*(2), 162–171.

Grossarth-Maticek, R., & Eysenck, H. J. (1995). Self-regulation and mortality from cancer, coronary heart disease and other causes: A prospective study. *Personality and Individual Differences, 19*(6), 781–795.

Heymans, C., & Neil, E. (1958). *Reflexogenic areas of the cardiovascular system*. Boston: Little, Brown.

Hirsch, J. A., & Bishop, B. (1981). Respiratory sinus arrhythmia in humans: How breathing patterns modulates heart rate. *American Journal of Physiology, 241*(4), H620–H629.

Isen, A. M. (1987). Positive affect, cognitive processes, and social behavior. *Advances in Experimental Social Psychology, 20*, 203–253.

Isen, A. M. (1999). Positive affect. In T. Dalgleish & M. Power (Eds.), *Handbook of cognition and emotion* (pp. 522–539). New York: Wiley.

Isen, A. M., Daubman, K. A., & Nowicki, G. P. (1987). Positive affect facilitates creative problem solving. *Journal of Personality and Social Psychology, 52*(6), 1122–1131.

Ito, T. A., Larsen, J. T., Smith, N. K., & Cacioppo, J. T. (1998). Negative information weighs more heavily on the brain: The negativity bias in evaluative categorizations. *Journal of Personality and Social Psychology, 75*(4), 887–900.

Lacey, B. C., & Lacey, J. I. (1974). Studies of heart rate and other bodily processes in sensorimotor behavior. In P. Obrist, A. Black, J. Brener, & L. DiCara (Eds.), *Cardiovascular psychophysiology* (pp. 538–564). Chicago: Aldine.

Lacey, J. I., & Lacey, B. C. (1970). Some autonomic-central nervous system interrelationships. In P. Black (Ed.), *Physiological correlates of emotion* (pp. 205–227). New York: Academic Press.

Lane, R. D., Reiman, E. M., Bradley, M. M., Lang, P. J., Ahern, G. L., Davidson, R. J., et al. (1997). Neuroanatomical correlates of pleasant and unpleasant emotion. *Neuropsychologia, 35*(11), 1437–1444.

Langhorst, P., Schulz, G., & Lambertz, M. (1983). Integrative control mechanisms for cardiorespiratory and somatomotor functions in the reticular formation of the lower brain stem. In P. Grossman, K. H. L. Janssen, & D. Vaitl (Eds.), *Cardiorespiratory and cardiosomatic psychophysiology* (pp. 9–39). New York: Plenum.

Langhorst, P., Schulz, G., & Lambertz, M. (1984). Oscillating neuronal network of the "common brainstem system." In K. Miyakawa, H. P. Koepchen, & C. Polosa (Eds.), *Mechanisms of blood pressure waves* (pp. 257–275). Tokyo: Japan Scientific Societies Press.

LeDoux, J. E. (1994). Cognitive-emotional interactions in the brain. In P. Ekman & R. J. Davidson (Eds.), *The nature of emotion: Fundamental questions* (pp. 216–223). New York: Oxford University Press.

LeDoux, J. (1996). *The emotional brain: The mysterious underpinnings of emotional life.* New York: Simon & Schuster.

Lessmeier, T. J., Gamperling, D., Johnson-Liddon, V., Fromm, B. S., Steinman, R. T., Meissner, M. D., et al. (1997). Unrecognized paroxysmal supraventricular tachycardia: Potential for misdiagnosis as panic disorder. *Archives of Internal Medicine, 157*(5), 537–543.

Luskin, F. (1999). *The effects of forgiveness training on psychosocial factors in college-age adults.* Unpublished doctoral dissertation, Stanford University, California.

Luskin, F., Reitz, M., Newell, K., Quinn, T. G., & Haskell, W. (2002). A controlled pilot study of stress management training of elderly patients with congestive heart failure. *Preventive Cardiology, 5*(4), 168–172, 176.

McCraty, R. (2003). *Heart-brain neurodynamics: The making of emotions.* Boulder Creek, CA: HeartMath Research Center, Institute of HeartMath, Publication No. 03-015.

McCraty, R. (2002a). Heart rhythm coherence—An emerging area of biofeedback. *Biofeedback, 30*(1), 23–25.

McCraty, R. (2002b). Influence of cardiac afferent input on heart-brain synchronization and cognitive performance. *International Journal of Psychophysiology, 45*(1–2), 72–73.

McCraty, R., & Atkinson, M. (2003). *Psychophysiological coherence.* Boulder Creek, CA: HeartMath Research Center, Institute of HeartMath, Publication No. 03–016.

McCraty, R., & Atkinson, M. (1998). [Spontaneous heart rhythm coherence in individuals practiced in positive-emotion-focused techniques]. Unpublished data.

McCraty, R., Atkinson, M., & Lipsenthal, L. (2000). *Emotional self-regulation program enhances psychological health and quality of life in patients with diabetes.* Boulder Creek, CA: HeartMath Research Center, Institute of HeartMath, Publication No. 00–006.

McCraty, R., Atkinson, M., Rein, G., & Watkins, A. D. (1996). Music enhances the effect of positive emotional states on salivary IgA. *Stress Medicine, 12*(3), 167–175.

McCraty, R., Atkinson, M., Tiller, W. A., Rein, G., & Watkins, A. D. (1995). The effects of emotions on short-term heart rate variability using power spectrum analysis. *American Journal of Cardiology, 76*(14), 1089–1093.

McCraty, R., Atkinson, M., & Tomasino, D. (2003). Impact of a workplace stress reduction program on blood pressure and emotional health in hypertensive employees. *Journal of Alternative and Complementary Medicine, 9*(3), 355–369.

McCraty, R., Atkinson, M., & Tomasino, D. (2001). *Science of the heart.* Boulder Creek, CA: HeartMath Research Center, Institute of HeartMath, Publication No. 01–001.

McCraty, R., Atkinson, M., Tomasino, D., Goelitz, J., & Mayrovitz, H. N. (1999). The impact of an emotional self-management skills course on psychosocial functioning and autonomic recovery to stress in middle school children. *Integrative Physiological and Behavioral Science, 34*(4), 246–268.

McCraty, R., Barrios-Choplin, B., Rozman, D., Atkinson, M., & Watkins, A. D. (1998). The impact of a new emotional self-management program on stress, emotions, heart rate variability, DHEA and cortisol. *Integrative Physiological and Behavioral Science, 33*(2), 151–170.

McCraty, R., Tomasino, D., Atkinson, M., and Sundram, J. (1999). *Impact of the HeartMath self-management skills program on physiological and psychological stress in police officers.* Boulder Creek, CA: HeartMath Research Center, Institute of HeartMath, Publication No. 99–075.

McCraty, R., Tomasino, D., Atkinson, M., Aasen, P., & Thurik, S. J. (2000). *Improving test-taking skills and academic performance in high school students using HeartMath learning enhancement tools.* Boulder Creek, CA: HeartMath Research Center, Institute of HeartMath, Publication No. 00–010.

McCullough, M. E., Kilpatrick, S. D., Emmons, R. A., & Larson, D. B. (2001). Is gratitude a moral affect? *Psychological Bulletin, 127*(2), 249–266.

Oppenheimer, S. M., & Hopkins, D. A. (1994). Suprabulbar neuronal regulation of the heart. In J. A. Armour & J. L. Ardell (Eds.), *Neurocardiology* (pp. 309–341). New York: Oxford University Press.

Pribram, K. H., & Melges, F. T. (1969). Psychophysiological basis of emotion. In P. J. Vinken & G. W. Bruyn (Eds.), *Handbook of clinical neurology* (Vol. 3, pp. 316–341). Amsterdam: North-Holland Publishing Company.

Randich, A., & Gebhart, G. F. (1992). Vagal afferent modulation of nociception. *Brain Research Reviews, 17*(2), 77–99.

Rau, H., Pauli, P., Brody, S., & Elbert, T. (1993). Baroreceptor stimulation alters cortical activity. *Psychophysiology, 30*(3), 322–325.

Rozman, D., Whitaker, R., Beckman, T., & Jones, D. (1996). A pilot intervention program which reduces psychological symptomatology in individuals with human immunodeficiency virus. *Complementary Therapies in Medicine, 4*(4), 226–232.

Russek, L. G., & Schwartz, G. E. (1997). Feelings of parental caring predict health status in midlife: A 35-year follow-up of the Harvard Mastery of Stress Study. *Journal of Behavioral Medicine, 20*(1), 1–13.

Sandman, C. A., Walker, B. B., & Berka, C. (1982). Influence of afferent cardiovascular feedback on behavior and the cortical evoked potential. In J. T. Cacioppo & R. E. Petty (Eds.), *Perspectives in cardiovascular psychophysiology* (pp. 189–222). New York: Guilford.

Seligman, M. E. P., & Csikszentmihalyi, M. (2000). Positive psychology: An introduction. *American Psychologist, 55*(1), 5–14.

Siegel, G., Ebeling, B. J., Hofer, H. W., Nolte, J., Roedel, H., & Klubendorf, D. (1984). Vascular smooth muscle rhythmicity. In K. Miyakawa, H. Koepchen, & C. Polosa (Eds.), *Mechanisms of blood pressure waves* (pp. 319–338). Tokyo: Japan Scientific Societies Press.

Tiller, W. A., McCraty, R., & Atkinson, M. (1996). Cardiac coherence: A new, noninvasive measure of autonomic nervous system order. *Alternative Therapies in Health and Medicine, 2*(1), 52–65.

van der Molen, M. W., Somsen, R. J. M., & Orlebeke, J. F. (1985). The rhythm of the heart beat in information processing. In P. Ackles, J. R. Jennings, & M. G. H. Coles (Eds.), *Advances in Psychophysiology* (Vol. 1, pp. 89–165). London: JAI Press.

Wickramasekera, I. (1998). Secrets kept from the mind but not the body or behavior: The unsolved problems of identifying and treating somatization and psychophysiological disease. *Advances in Mind-Body Medicine, 14*(2), 81–132.

PART V

Discussion and Conclusions

13 Gratitude

Considerations from a Moral Perspective

Charles M. Shelton

> My fiftieth year had come and gone,
> I sat, a solitary man,
> In a crowded London shop,
> An open book and empty cup
> On the marble table-top.
> While on the shop and street I gazed
> My body of a sudden blazed;
> And twenty minutes more or less
> It seemed, so great my happiness,
> That I was blessed and could bless.
> —William Butler Yeats ("Vacillation," IV)

It is not an overstatement to maintain that few emotions hold gratitude's magnetic appeal. This emotion's attraction arises from several sources: its linkage to other positive emotions (Emmons & Shelton, 2002); its power to evoke a focus by the recipient on the benevolence of others, thereby ensuring a perception that kindness has been offered (Roberts, chap. 4, this volume); and its beneficial consequences, which frequently are the motive to respond favorably toward another (McCullough, Kilpatrick, Emmons, & Larson, 2001; McCullough & Tsang, chap. 7, this volume). In most situations, a grateful state requires a relationship. Accordingly, if we accept the premise that discourse and actions between human beings are legitimate moral concerns (e.g., how one speaks and relates to others), and that morality itself is indispensable for the functioning of relationships whether they be at an interpersonal or societal level, then it is incumbent on academics and scholars to explore critically the relationship between morality and gratitude. Of equal importance, as this volume points out, gratitude merits an interdisciplinary inquiry.

Noting both the attractiveness and interdisciplinary nature of gratitude, the need for two cautions looms. The first caution is best expressed in the form of three biases: empirical, idealizing, and Pollyannish. The first bias, the empirical, is psychologists' frequent penchant for viewing ideas as significant solely if they are subject to some type of measurement or quantifiable formulation. Although such thinking rightly offers the benefit of rooting psychology in the everyday world, it leads to a narrowing of perspective that, when reflected in its extreme form, obscures human beings' complexity and their search for meaning.

Second, philosophers and theologians are susceptible to committing the idealizing bias. More than those in the social sciences, philosophers and theologians are often prone to emphasize the noetic, thereby moving away from concrete and everyday occurrences. Additionally, this bias is sometimes displayed by centering on the exemplary while skipping over daily struggles and conflicts. And last, the Pollyannish bias comes into play when one naively assumes that the nature of a specific entity is always positive. This final bias, as shown later in this chapter, complicates the study of gratitude as it relates in general to the nature of morality and, more specifically, when it is joined to an analysis of moral behavior.

In sum, all three of these biases come into play at one time or another when one examines the relationship between academic inquiry and morality's domain. Fortunately, the first two biases have receded dramatically, because interdisciplinary study encourages the interaction between psychology and the humanities, thereby tempering each discipline's tendency for distortion. The most fruitful example of this trend is the growing hospitable relationship between religion and psychology (Jones, 1994). The final bias, however, remains a looming concern and requires monitoring. When formulating a definition for gratitude, only critical scrutiny precludes one-dimensional gullibility.

The second caution concerns the very meaning of morality. As pointed out later in the chapter, psychological researchers speak with anything but a clear voice when setting forth morality's nature (Lapsley, 1996). Of equal if not greater importance, this fractured state of affairs is underscored by the general populace's lack of consensus in regard both to the meaning of morality and to its application (Wolfe, 2001). As an example, Walker and Pitts (1998) concluded that there exists no clear consensus among the general population as to what constitutes a truly moral person. Rather, participants judged moral exemplars from a variety of perspectives, each of which usually clustered around a wide assortment of principles, personal qualities, and behaviors. These findings led Walker and Pitts to consider that "a questionable implication that might be drawn from the present research, and one that should prompt further research, is whether there is a single prototype for moral maturity" (p. 415).

PSYCHOLOGY AND MORALITY

Over decades, commentators and social scientists have linked psychology and the moral life (e.g., Berkowitz & Oser, 1985; Kurtines & Gewirtz, 1984; Lapsley, 1996; Wilson, 1995). Initially, a psychoanalytic approach controlled psychology's contribution and placed emphasis on an intrapunitive superego. Over time, this view came to dominate both popular and clinical discussion; indeed, the superego became a substitute for conscience. Over the past several decades, however, research efforts have exploded, providing, in turn, both original and rich conceptual understandings of morality. Though several decades old, the most elaborately constructed model remains Kohlberg's (1981, 1984) rationally based moral reasoning perspective. Illustrative though not exhaustive with regard to moral psychology, other models of morality include the empathic focus of Hoffman (1975, 1981, 2000); Haan's (1982; Haan, Aerts, & Cooper, 1985) interactional viewpoint; the feminist critique, most notably as advocated by Gilligan (1982); and the confluence of developmental and social psychology to spawn fruitful elaborations of prosociality (e.g., Bridgeman, 1983; Eisenberg, 1982). Except for Kohlberg's, none of these viewpoints succumbs to the biases noted previously. To be fair, Kohlberg's (1984) major theme—the centrality of justice as the meaning of morality—was continually applied to everyday situations to achieve some practical bent. In spite of these attempts, Kohlberg nonetheless continually enshrined the justice principle as fundamental, indeed isomorphic, to the notion of morality. In effect, a principled justice theme subsumed his model of morality and, in the process, made the notion of morality a totally rational process. Because the imperative of justice was so rationally based, it was only a matter of time before critics pointed out that an affective element was integral to conceptualizing morality's meaning (e.g., Hinman, 1985; Hogan, 1995; Shelton, 1990). A number of educators and psychologists have remarked to me that only an Ivy League academic was capable of constructing an idealized world wherein a principle (such as justice) solely guided—from a moral perspective—the discussion, the perception, and the evaluation of human behavior.

Of late, several theories of moral psychology have presented a striking contrast to Kohlberg's primarily cognitive viewpoint. When examined, each of these competing theories incorporates or at least is compatible with the integration of an affective element into the moral discussion. For example, Hoffman (1975, 1981, 2000) has focused on empathy's role in eliciting the moral emotion of guilt and explores empathy's dynamics, including, for example, sympathetic distress, empathic anger, prosocial behavior, and empathic overarousal. Though some more obviously than others, all of these experiences contain some affectively tinged element. More tellingly, Hoffman elegantly weaves together and makes a compelling case for empathy's complexity, arguing persuasively for the need to integrate both cognitive and affective components to formulate a definition of empathy.

Haan et al. (1985) likewise have presented emotion as absolutely integral for any adequate theory of moral psychology. They forcefully and unstintingly maintained that "emotions accompany and enrich understandings, and they convey far more authentic information about a person's position in a dispute than any well-articulated thoughts. In ordinary circumstances, emotions instruct and energize action" (p. 147). Not surprisingly, Haan and colleagues have underscored emotion's role when negotiating life's practical realities and the integral part emotion plays in individuals' lives as they construct defenses for defining themselves, in the context of frequent stress and daily struggles, as moral beings. Gilligan (1982) more pointedly challenged the fundamental core of the Kohlbergian paradigm not only by suggesting another framework for morality (i.e., care as opposed to justice), but, at the same time, by escalating considerably the moral debate when positing possible differences in how men and women view morality (hence the position that some women speak, from Gilligan's perspective, through a possibly "different voice"). Though this last point need not concern us here, it must be pointed out that the notion that men and women have different moral experiences has met with challenging if not compelling criticism (Lapsley, 1996; Walker, 1984). Finally, a flourishing theme found today in psychological perspectives on morality is social and developmental psychology's emphasis on prosocial behavior. A focus on prosocial behavior sets up a framework for fruitful research in comprehending how people actually live their moral lives.

MORALITY AND EMOTION

As might be expected, philosophy's heavily weighted cognitive dimension (e.g., Rawls, 1971), tilts toward an idealizing bias that frequently eclipses the ability to conceive of people's daily lives; moreover, at times it sets up a nearly affectless world, one far removed from the moral struggles individuals encounter in their everyday lives. Though one can only surmise the reasoning behind this discipline's stance, one likely candidate, according to Lazarus and Lazarus (1994), points to Western culture's bias toward rationality. This triumph of cognition over affect in comprehending a source and motive for morality has met with strong dissent among some psychologists (Kagan, 1984; Shelton, 1990, 2000). Indeed, Kagan (1984) went so far as to say, "Construction of a persuasive rational basis for behaving morally has been the problem on which most moral philosophers have stubbed their toes. I believe they will continue to do so until they recognize what Chinese philosophers have appreciated for a long time: namely, feeling, not logic, sustains the superego" (p. xiv).

Frequently, theology, too, succumbs to the idealizing bias. Yet, unlike philosophy, whose bias is rooted in cognition, theology's idealizing bias has roots in an overly enthusiastic and far too uncritical stance in regard to the relationship of everyday human functioning and people's transcendent ideals. For example, the emotion of gratitude receives nearly unabashed endorsement in theological writings. Many seem to believe erroneously that extolling gratitude, a common theme in Christian tradition, has been unequivocally successful in helping people heed St. Paul's admonition, "In every thing give thanks; for this is the will of God in Christ Jesus concerning you" (1 Thessalonians 5:18 AV). To illustrate, the ethicist Edward Vacek (2000), in one of the more judicious and realistic commentaries on gratitude, pointed out with thoughtful skepticism the prevailing viewpoint held by Christian scholars, that "gratitude is not only important, not only essential, but the center of the Christian life" (p. 81). Moreover, he bolstered his position by quoting a sampling of several contemporary Christian moralists: "It is no exaggeration to claim that this wondrous spiral of grace descending and thanks ascending forms the very axis of Christian faith." Or take the statement that gratitude is "the basic motive and perspective for all true worship and faithful living" (p. 81). Finally, he referred to another moralist's belief that gratitude reflects "the pivotal virtue of the moral life" (p. 81). In particular, a subdiscipline of theology, spiritual (or ascetical) theology, is egregiously prone to overplay gratitude's significance. To illustrate, foundational to Jesuit spirituality is the gratuitous nature of God's grace, of which the believer is most apt to be aware (and frequently acutely sensitive to) when he or she participates in an 8- or 30-day retreat based on a rigorous set of prayerful practices (spiritual exercises). Such conscious experiences lead to deeply felt experiences of gratitude (for an overall summary of Jesuit spirituality, see Fagin, 1995). However, the critical point is not the focus on gratitude per se. Rather, the significant issue is the propensity to slide loosely into a conceptualization of gratitude that is uncritical and naively construed. For example, I have witnessed retreatants concluding their retreats with a fresh perspective on the world, in which everything is viewed as a gift for which the person feels immense gratitude. However, such optimistic exuberance sometimes covers up or gives an overly optimistic interpretation of issues needing to be addressed, such as personal pathologies that are often crippling, relationships that are unhealthy, or naive perceptions of a complex world that need reappraisal. Under the guise of gratitude, these critical issues are unwittingly swept aside. Personally speaking, as a Jesuit priest who has both made and directed others in retreats, I have often thought that a series of questions, best termed a reality check, would be of immense help to the retreatant as he or she concludes the experience.

Although the idealizing bias is alive and well, moralists and spiritual theologians more and more have advocated the idea that emotion is a vital aspect for integrating everyday human, moral, and spiritual growth (Shelton, 1982, 1990; Spohn, 1983, 2000; Vacek, 2001). This progress has come about not only because of the growing rapport between the disciplines of psychology and theology, but also, equally important, because of the resurgent interest in virtue ethics. Its content and focus reflect a natural receptivity to emotion. Moreover, virtue ethics accommodates nicely academic psychology's growing interest in positive psychology, which stands behind the belief that the discipline must shift its focus, in part, to include human strengths, character, and virtues as suitable areas for study and research (Emmons & Shelton, 2002; McCullough & Snyder, 2000; Seligman & Csikszentmihalyi, 2000). In brief, virtue ethics concerns itself with good habits that bring about right or exemplary living. Virtuous behavior reflects a character well formed. Roberts (chap. 4, this volume) is correct to point out that virtues must be cultivated through the community; in other words, they require some form of moral socialization. Besides academic psychology's increasing openness to discussions of virtue, professional practitioners have shown growing interest in the role virtues might play in professional ethics. For example, Meara, Schmidt, and Day (1996) have pointed out the importance of virtues for coming to well-thought-out moral decisions in clinical situations. All in all, to speak of habitual behaviors, character, moral socialization, and ethical decision making opens the door for discussing the role of emotion, because these topics encroach on a vast range of responses and subsequent commitments that are emotionally laden.

GRATITUDE AND MORALITY

The study of moral development and emotion has signaled an emerging focus on the role of moral emotions (Hoffman, 1982; Tangney, 1991). To date, the most compelling case for defining gratitude as a moral emotion comes from McCullough and colleagues (McCullough, Emmons, & Tsang, 2002; McCullough & Tsang, chap. 7, this volume; McCullough et al., 2001). McCullough and his colleagues posit three essential prerequisites for gratitude to qualify as a moral emotion. Briefly stated, gratitude functions as (1) a moral barometer that tells a person he or she has personally benefited from another's kindness; (2) a moral motivation that fosters the inclination to behave prosocially; and (3) a moral reinforcer that, when expressed by the beneficiary, increases moral behavior on the part of the benefactor. Gathering together a wealth of available literature, these researchers show how gratitude meets all three requirements, thereby qualifying as a moral emotion.

Though a finer weaving together of research findings to develop a coherent theory of moral emotion might be beneficial, it seems obvious that gratitude is prominently involved, indeed vital, for living a good life. For centuries, learned individuals and scholars have extolled gratitude's merits and viewed its lack as a human deficiency. A small sampling of various thoughts on gratitude includes the following statements:

> "Gratitude, as it were, is the moral memory of mankind." (Georg Simmel, as quoted in Harpham, chap. 2, this volume)
>
> "Blow, blow, thou winter wind! / Thou art not so unkind / As man's ingratitude." (William Shakespeare, as quoted in Harpham, chap. 2, this volume)
>
> "Ingratitude . . . is the essence of vileness." (Immanuel Kant, as quoted in Emmons & Shelton, 2002, p. 463)
>
> "Men detest one forgetful of a benefit." (Cicero, as quoted in Emmons & Shelton, 2002, p. 463)
>
> "I had not noticed how the humblest, and at the same time most balanced and capacious minds, praised most, while cranks, misfits, and malcontents praised least." (Lewis, 1958, p. 95)
>
> "The modern cynic says 'Blessed is he who expects nothing for he shall be satisfied.' Francis of Assisi says 'Blessed is he who expects nothing, for he shall appreciate everything.'" (G. K. Chesterton, as quoted in Watkins et al., 1997)

Even today, popular personalities such as Oprah Winfrey acclaim gratitude's positive and worthwhile effects, implicitly imbuing it with a moral stance (Breathnach, 2000). Though not all commentators are sanguine about this trend (e.g., Duplantier, 1998), most writers (Brokaw, 1998; Buckley, 2000) hail gratitude's merits, particularly in regard to its role in historical remembrance. In the hope of bringing further clarity to this issue, though my research was admittedly neither methodologically sound nor scientifically rigorous, I have probed gratitude's meaning by collecting surveys and conducting interviews over the past 3 years with approximately 150 young and middle-aged adults, garnering their thoughts on gratitude's meaning and purpose. To date, no individual in any way whatsoever has offered a position casting gratitude in a negative light. On the contrary, the thread that weaves consistently through these individuals' comments is their unambiguously positive view of gratitude.

Yet herein lies the problem. More specifically, a point raised at the beginning of this chapter looms enormously pertinent. In light of the above-mentioned Pollyannish bias, a fairly unequivocal conclusion is gratitude's overwhelming popularity, casting it as a prime example of the Pollyannish bias. Naturally, this observation in no way obviates gratitude's key role when conceptualizing the meaning of a moral or good life. However, at the same time, caution is warranted, for such a naive view obscures gratitude's moral limitations.

Perhaps posing the question in the extreme makes this point best: How does evil relate to gratitude? To explain by way of example: Heretofore, scholars studying the Third Reich have been fascinated by the question, To what degree did the German populace accede to, collude in, or enthusiastically endorse the horror of the Nazi state and its carrying out of the ensuing pogrom? Building on Goldhagen's (1996) highly publicized yet provocative theory of Germany's historical anti-Semitism, utilizing the latest research to date, Gellately (2001) wove a fascinating account of the German people's tolerance of executions and state terrorism; in addition, such activities more often than not received the citizenry's tacit and, quite frequently, its active support. Furthermore, he goes on to show that many Germans were well aware of sizable portions of the regime's horrific undertakings. Though the Nazi regime and Hitler come immediately to mind when one is addressing the question of evil, the Nazi state and its demented dictator are hardly alone. To further focus this issue, Becker (1998) cited credible sources in positing the thesis that the greatest mass murderer of the twentieth century (if not all time), was Mao Tse-tung, whose engineering of the Great Leap Forward cost the lives of 40 to 60 million human beings. Expanding the list of horrors still further, Stalin's unmerciful orders sent millions of Ukrainians to their deaths by mass starvation while the purge trials and gulags took the lives of countless others. Less known perhaps but equally revolting and almost incomprehensible is Pol Pot's fanaticism that, in the name of ideological purity, led to the death of 15% of the Cambodian population. Were any of these leaders capable of gratitude? The frightening implications of these questions are, *a fortiori*, further brought to bear when we include the ideologues, cronies, government bureaucrats, and sympathetic citizenry who supported in one way or another or contributed to such butchery.

Yet we need not confine ourselves to tyrants. Were the terrorists who forever changed the lives of U.S. citizens on September 11, 2001, capable of gratitude? Perhaps equally unsettling are individual examples such as the Richard Specks, Ted Bundys, and other serial killers or, clinically speaking, those diagnosed as having antisocial personality disorder. Are these individuals capable of gratitude?

To focus our discussion, let's now reiterate the point made earlier in light of the preceding discussion: In the broadest sense, the question must be faced as to how gratitude relates to evil. In a more specific sense, to force the issue, the question can be asked, Was Hitler capable of gratitude? The question is hardly a rhetorical one. For most people, Hitler represents the personification of the twentieth century's yielding to evil (Rosenbaum, 1998). Even so, Hitler was, obviously, a human being. Human beings possess the faculty, barring some severe neurological impairment, for experiencing a wide scope of emotions, of which gratitude must be considered a rightful candidate. Hence the question is begged, Was Hitler a grateful person? The frightening implications of answering yes to this question makes many readers ill at ease, I'm sure. (The reader might take a moment and try to be aware of what he or she is currently feeling.) Even more unnerving, can any of us truthfully say that, given the pre–World War years in Nazi Germany and the Party's relentless mass indoctrination, we ourselves would have abstained from being sympathetic to at least some Nazi programs and, in effect, becoming grateful for the opportunity to offer such support? On one hand, the common conception of gratitude calls, viscerally, for an outright rejection of the notion that people who hold or perhaps even flirt with such ideas could be grateful. I suspect that most readers would wish to embrace this stance.

On the other hand, the experience of gratitude is so pervasive in the human life cycle that to deny some level of grateful response with one or another person or because of some event at some time, though albeit meager, is unrealistic if not fanciful. And when considering the supportive stance of the countless millions who in one way or another colluded with such horror (and hence experienced gratitude at the actions or consequences of such evil), to deny the affirmative to such a question becomes ludicrous. Even the prototypic example of evil, Adolf Hitler, used the highly personal and intimate *du* form with some individuals (D. Clayton, personal communication, October 26, 2000), thereby adding some plausibility to the belief that a form of appreciative sense existed at least at some specific points with some people. This view is bolstered by the foremost Hitler scholar of our time, Ian Kershaw (1999), who recently pointed out that Hitler was filled with almost unbearable grief on the death of his mother. Certainly such evidence is suggestive of some type of gratefulness. To extend this line of thinking, from all accounts he most certainly was thankful for being born into an Aryan lineage. He was, perhaps, appreciative (or had some measure of consideration) for the adulators who surrounded him.

After all that has just been noted, gratitude can be shown to be associated with either ideologies that are motivating or blinding or with individual criminals who commit illegal acts containing various degrees of illegality. Either way, I suspect, the vast majority of human beings would, if asked, balk at linking such behaviors with gratitude. For clarity's sake, let's term the former phenomenon an ideology of gratitude, whereas the latter (the cases of individual criminals—those whose actions are not motivated by deeply held ideological goals) as *deviant gratitude*. Nonetheless, even though we might distinguish between them, it is clear by the very fact of being human that those motivated and capable of using power to evil ends or those best characterized as individuals who deviate from societal norms are both capable of some type of gratitude given the range of possibilities—from having underlings carry out their maniacal orders to criminals' gratitude for the good-hearted individual who is manipulated to aid unknowingly, even in a small way, the carrying out of some illegal act.

THREE MAJOR POINTS

Three essential points are born of the previous discussion. First, there exists no one definition for gratitude. The attributes and descriptors making up the domain of gratitude are both varied and numerous. Whether this view is described as common sense psychology, folk psychology, or an implicitly held theory of emotion, individuals view gratitude as possessing a number of (for lack of a better term) degrees of gratitude. I suspect that the vast majority of readers grapple with the questions posed here and employ some mental gymnastics to accommodate their personal unease. In other words, the aforementioned questions regarding evil and gratitude force the issue of confronting gratitude's complexity and range. In regard to my discussion of Hitler, devising varieties of an appreciative sense allows for a reality-based description of Hitler while preserving gratitude's integrity as a moral emotion.

Besides the degrees of gratitude that one might conceive, a second consideration flowing from this discussion is the need for gratitude to be rooted in a moral standard. To state that it is otherwise precludes the notion of gratitude as a moral emotion. In other words, despite the optimistic renderings of gratitude, there exists no unyieldingly compelling reason to view gratitude as necessarily wedded to a moral framework. Though research grounds gratitude in some commonly accepted moral system, there is no reason that *every*

experience of gratitude should be so rooted. Likewise, though everyday definitions of gratitude convey its moral flavor, it does not follow that *every* definition must be framed as such. Moreover, without a compelling moral standard to ground gratitude, wayward behaviors not typically associated with
gratitude grow abundant. Let's take just one of many examples, using the
previously mentioned example of Hitler to demonstrate gratitude's potentially perverted state. Let's take the political participants in 1930s Germany
(a typical non–National Socialist voter). Even by the most minimal elements
of a gratitude definition, such an individual could be rightfully assigned the
definition of *grateful*. He or she could perceive the benefit of a gift (the Nazi
crackdown on hooligans and lawbreakers and the emphasis on economic bet-
terment, even if achieved by drastic, brutal, or barbaric means) that afforded
safety and economic security. Such a gift was perceived by the individual as
emanating from the desire of government officials to help Germany. German
citizens responded by being dutiful, being law-abiding, and tolerating
heretofore unimaginable methods to sustain the gift received. Is it reasonable
to contest this label of *grateful*? I think not. Therefore, unless we identify
some specific moral underpinning, the possibility remains that one or another type of gratitude might actually be associated with or reinforce wrong-
ful or truly wicked behaviors.

But doesn't the seeking of some standard open up the temptation to
commit the idealizing bias? When we examine the third consideration that
emerges from the earlier discussion, the answer is, not necessarily. Struggling to deal with the Hitler question or, more broadly, the question that, in
one way or another, the possibility exists for the collusion of gratitude and
evil, offers an opportunity to look for ways that the idealizing and empirical
traditions shed their biases and are transformed to perspectives that are informative to rather than adversarial toward one another. One standard that
allows for this blending of traditions is the notion of the good, or the living
of a good life. At first glance, this position hardly appears a viable option.
Few moral perspectives are more elusive than conceptualizing the meaning
of *the good*. Yet, when probed more carefully, the notion of the good is compatible both with aspirations that flow from ideals and with everyday
human experience established through an empirical tradition. In this context, philosophical viewpoints merge with psychology's empiricism to bring
about an enriching notion of the good that situates gratitude within a moral
framework.

Blending the perspectives of the humanities and psychological science
generates, I believe, five substantive criteria that, taken together, convey a viable notion of the good, or, more concretely, a standard for living a good life.
When employed as a foundation for this emotion, gratitude, no matter how
defined, firmly becomes a morally anchored emotion.

TOWARD A DEFINITION OF THE GOOD

Five criteria establish a notion of the good, thereby allowing for a moral framework for gratitude. The first is the existence of some standard that is acknowledged as worthwhile and intrinsically contains some quality people aspire to attain. According to Kagan (1984), at a very young age a child develops an idea of competence. Successful completion of tasks and mastery of situations provide the child with a sense of goodness because the pursuit is successfully completed. A not unrelated example to which parents can relate is taking a 3-year-old shopping. The child sees an adult whose facial features or body deviates from the child's standard of what an adult should be (e.g., a person with a noticeably red face caused by a rash, or an amputee who has lost a leg), which often leads the child to point to the perceived "deviated" human and immediately and loudly announce to all who can hear (and to the embarrassment of parents) the distinguishing characteristic that violates the child's notion of the way something should be (standard). Over time, obviously, standards grow more sophisticated as socialization, the development of empathy and guilt, and cognitive maturation evolve into complex evaluations of self and others, thereby leading to judgments of good and bad. As Kagan (1984) noted, "Humans are the only species that applies a symbolic evaluation of good or bad to actions, thoughts, feelings, and personal characteristics and tries continually to choose acts that make it easier to regard the self as good" (p. 155). Indeed, humans go to great lengths to believe in their own goodness, as seen in the vast array of defense mechanisms they employ to subvert guilt or render themselves oblivious to their morally questionable behaviors. Ironically, the striving to be good is seen starkly in everyday gang behavior, in which gang members are expected to adhere to a code (standard) and any violation of the code leads to harmful if not deadly consequences.

Though the earlier discussion argues forcefully for a moral motivation in human behavior, the characteristics that make up such goodness are of equal relevance. People frequently and, at times, violently disagree about the nature of goodness. Cultural, ethnic, and religious wars attest all too well to the extremes to which humans will go to assert what they believe is the good's essence. At this point, four observations are required. First, humans must continually strive to be conscious of and sensitive to their standards of goodness. Second, the goodness they endorse is intentional. That is, it is felt as something out there, that for the sake of which they behave. Thus, goodness has a decidedly teleological dimension. We aspire, in other words, to live out more completely this goodness. Tying these thoughts to gratitude, a grateful person is grateful first and foremost because he or she evaluates the gift received as in accordance with a standard of goodness. Even if this is only tacitly perceived, the grateful person has some sense that the gratitude experienced is moral precisely because it measures up to and is inextricably interweaved with some moral standard the individual has come to accept and aspires to uphold.

Even so, a culture's standards can be closed-minded (the Nazi culture being a fitting case in point). A third observation is that a feature of the standard must also be a continuing effort to transcend specific cultural contexts. This lack of universality explains why racism, sexism, and prejudice are so commonly culturally endorsed and, more germane to the position being developed here, why we can be grateful for believing in and adhering to beliefs and practices that are racist, sexist, and prejudicial. In such instances, individuals erroneously believe that they are good persons whose gratitude is morally felt. Thus, in the segregated South of the early twentieth century, a white person more likely than not used a culturally accepted standard to define himself or herself as moral *and* grateful. Discrimination was a "good" that many Southern whites practiced (living the standard), and they felt grateful not only for the cultural tradition in which they were raised, but also for the opportunity to act with prejudice, leading in some cases to extreme cruelty. Thus, when commonly acknowledging his or her moral standard, the individual must make the conscious effort to examine it in light of differing cultural standards. And last, when addressing the specific psychological ramifications for the individual, internalizing and living up to a standard invites a sense of self-appreciation for the goodness that is inside the self. This inner appreciative sense is commonly viewed as self-esteem. (For an overview of self-esteem from a psychological perspective, see Bednar, Wells, & Peterson, 1989.)

Second, obviously, people embrace various standards. Characteristics making up such standards can of course lead to serious disagreement. But psychology can contribute to allaying conflict and by containing the possibility that a standard can justify immoral actions. Such interventions help at least to provide some boundaries for a standard's characteristics, thereby, minimally at least, offering some more or less permeable domains in which reasonable people will explore and talk out their differences and that help to mitigate the most extreme acts motivated by salient and highly emotionally charged standards (e.g., terrorist activity, dogmatic fundamentalism). Psychology's contribution resides in two intrinsic features in human development. First, in line with Hoffman's theory of empathy, the standard of the good must encompass what is a naturally occurring perspective of the other. This in turn leads to understanding, which, at the same time, encourages compassionate responding through prosocial actions. These two dimensions of empathy cannot help but facilitate dialogue and relationship, essential elements for interpersonal and societal functioning. Second, in accord with and extending Kohlberg's model, the standard articulates a clear message of fairness (the moral principle of justice). Through the course of their development, children quite naturally increasingly come to attribute meanings to justice. The first moral statement of a young child, for example, is most likely the emotion-filled utterance, "That's not fair." Moreover, these naturally developing inclinations in which people are conscious of and sensitive to empathic stirrings and ways of responding fairly provide some helpful though certainly by no means foolproof check on the standard itself, thereby limiting its ability to create inflexible, self-righteous, and unreflective responses in the moral agent that lead inevitably to knee-jerk reactions and foreclosed dialogue.

Third, the development of empathic and equitable qualities, as features of the good, propels the standard, like gratitude itself, to be a form of gift giving, because empathy and justice are overwhelmingly motivations for initiating and maintaining human connection, an essential starting point for gift giving. (Perhaps this is one reason we so naturally assign a moral quality to gratitude.) Moreover, the essential ingredients for the good as discussed thus far, (a) a standard and the twin features it contains all foster sensitivity to otherness for the reasons that (b) a standard dictates overall behaviors toward another, (c) empathy evokes compassion for another, and (d) justice pinpoints some form of exchange with another. With a specific focus on gratitude in mind, acknowledging this awareness of otherness sets the stage for recognizing and taking seriously another's offer of kindness, thus strengthening a person's inclination to be receptive (to a gift), which, arguably, fosters the case for gratitude's moral thrust.

It most certainly is not lost on the many authors in this volume, as well as other notable scholars, that a defining feature of gratitude is giving and receiving a gift. Nonetheless, the giving and receiving of a gift is fraught with a widely diverging assortment of perceptions, psychological states, and conflicting emotions. Scheibe (2000) remarked, concerning the exalting and humiliating properties of gifts, "Gifts bring pride, and also envy, hatred, greed, jealousy. People are literally the creative products of the gifts they receive. But people can also be destroyed by their gifts, or by the perverse effects of the gift-giving process gone awry" (pp. 209–210). Whenever done improperly, gift giving can engender insult, anger, hurt, disgrace, remorse, or even rage. Some examples of gratitude "gone awry" include giving a gift to flaunt one's wealth (thereby humiliating the beneficiary or to making him or her envious) or giving a gift to exert one's power over another (thereby evoking feelings of anger-triggering sadness). Pulling together these examples, use of a gift to bring about a beneficiary's gratitude (which in reality masks negative feelings such as hurt or anger) is termed *fabricated gratitude*. In conclusion, from a *moral* perspective, in addition to the ideology of gratitude and deviant gratitude spoken of previously, there exists fabricated gratitude. These three classes of gratitude, though distinct, are joined by some moral deficiency in the gift-giving process.

Thus the question becomes, How do we avoid such gratitudes? The answer, put simply, is that only continual articulation of and commitment by the benefactor and the beneficiary to a standard, as described previously, offers an adequate solution. But one problem remains. Recall the problem of how to configure a credible definition of gratitude that can account for the commonly occurring everyday gratitude of a Hitler (or some other evil character) while preserving a moral flavor for gratitude ranging from the simple "thanks" to profoundly felt gratitude. The only possible resolution to this quandary is to allow for a gratitude by degrees, or what I depict as a *depth model* of gratitude. It should be noted that Komter (chap. 10, this volume) speaks of layers of gratitude. However, these distinctions describe various dimensions or functions of gratitude rather than qualitative differentiations as expressed through a gratitude gradient. There is ample evidence from the vocabulary of gratitude that a viewpoint encompassing depths of gratitude mirrors people's everyday experience. A short list of qualitative differentiations of gratitude includes an attitude, an emotion, a habit, a disposition, a trait, and a way of being. Enlisting such refinements helps to advance a folk theory of gratitude. More important, consideration of qualitative distinctions helps to capture philosophic and theological conceptualizations of gratitude that move beyond psychology's empirical findings. To state this another way, psychology's contribution is necessary but not sufficient to explain the moral quality of gratitude or its effects on human behavior, especially when the behavioral patterns described contain a broad spectrum of patterned, consistent, and time-tested behaviors. To illustrate, to describe a person by saying that he or she always seems to have a deeply grateful heart, no matter what the circumstance, is far more compellingly robust than to comment merely that he or she is appreciative of, grateful for, or thankful that some occurrence or experience has taken place. These statements point not only to a theory of moral mindfulness, they also depict, qualitatively speaking, distinct gradients of gratitude.

At the risk of flirting with if not succumbing to the idealizing bias, I propose that the deepest form of gratitude is viewed as a way of life that is best defined as *an interior depth we experience, which orients us to an acknowledged dependence, out of which flows a profound sense of being gifted. This way of being, in turn, elicits a humility, just as it nourishes our goodness. As a consequence, when truly grateful, we are led to experience and interpret life situations in ways that call forth from us an openness to and engagement with the world through purposeful actions, to share and increase the very good we have received.* The discerning reader might note the similarity of this definition to Fredrickson's (chap. 8, this volume) broaden-and-build theory of emotion. To summarize,

Fredrickson notes that positive emotions broaden the capacity to be creative and expands one's viewpoint and understanding of life situations. Such cognitive expansion serves to increase flexible and maneuverable responses to life events. The *build* part of the theory comes into play when such emotions cultivate skills associated with furthering attainment of goals such as increasing optimism and fostering subjective well-being. Thus, the deepest form of gratitude fits nicely with a comprehensive theory of positive emotions.

Finally, from a psychological perspective, this fullest sense of gratitude represents a substantial altering of a person's outlook. To elaborate, experiencing this degree of gratitude brings about a expansive enlargement of a perceptual hermeneutic. In short, this degree of gratitude nourishes a more or less all-encompassing hermeneutic of appreciation. This appreciative lens fosters in individuals a radical openness to and receptivity of the world. This openness and receptivity allows for an altruistic acuity that enhances the *giving away of goodness*. Stated succinctly, as one experiences life, gratitude's intrinsic function allows one to approach the world by *embracing it, nourishing it, and transforming it*. A corollary to this definition involves the language of gratitude. If this portrayal of gratitude is accurate—a range stretching from the commonplace "thanks" to a profound way of being—it might prove more precise when discussing gratitude to incorporate periodically specific phrases such as *true gratitude, authentic gratitude*, or *genuine gratitude*, to convey that inherent in the experience of gratitude is the capacity for it to root more deeply in a person and with an end point (gratitude as defined earlier) that one can strive for but never *totally* attain. The aforementioned definition reflects gratitude as a way of life. Is such gratitude something that one experiences all the time and in every situation? Hardly. But it does suggest that if there are gradients of gratitude as I have argued here, then one could have on a daily basis a rather deep form of gratitude (e.g., a disposition), and perhaps periodically, in specific situations, one could plumb to a depth that reaches gratitude as a way of life. The more one has experiences of gratitude at this most deep level, it is reasonable to conclude that one moves closer to experiencing gratitude as a way of life. To illustrate from the survey I conducted, take the following story written by a young resident physician:

> Doctor, please come look at Baby M.; he's not breathing! The baby in question had been born ten days earlier after 26 weeks gestation (normal is 40 weeks), weighed 600 grams (1.5 lbs.), and had had a disastrous brain hemorrhage; the doctor was struggling through her fifth day as an intern, second night on call in the neonatal ICU, exhausted at 2 a.m. and anxious. Indeed, the infant only breathed

when someone gently tapped the soles of his feet: absent simulation, absent breath. The young intern doubted her ability to successfully intubate the baby and place him on the ventilator (breathing machine), but even as she considered this, a nurse stated that she thought the baby was a "DNR," and therefore should be allowed to die without intervention. A thorough review of the baby's chart, however, failed to reveal any note or order pertaining to a DNR. Reluctantly, the doctor realized that she would have to call the attending neonatologist, whom she did not yet know, for guidance. She felt inadequate, insecure and embarrassed as she dialed, fearing a negative response. It was by now 3 a.m. and she was incompetent. Her attending's sleepy voice startled her and she apologetically outlined the situation. Dr. L. listened, and then said quietly, "This baby has been so very sick since birth. We've had many talks with his mother and about the seriousness of his condition and I think she knows he will probably die. We have done all that we can for this child. So, I recommend that you just stop stimulating." The intern gasped and without thinking blurted, "Then he'll die." Dr. L. apparently heard the desperation in her voice and immediately replied, "Just keep doing what you're doing and I'll be there in thirty minutes." He was. He found his intern still keeping vigilance at the tiny crib. Dr. L. stood closely beside her and smiled with so much gentleness and understanding the young doctor was overwhelmed with relief and gratitude. Together they told the nurse to stop tapping the tiny feet, and waited. To everyone's amazement, Baby M. chose that moment to start breathing again; he lived six days longer and died peacefully.

The young doctor eventually became a faculty member herself. Always she kept the memory of that night, of the generosity, support, and kindness her mentor had shown, and she has tried to emulate his example in her own life as teacher-physician.

I don't think anyone could deny the good lived out by the two physicians in this story. One could easily infer that both lived by standards, felt empathy, and thought justly. Truly, it is a story of goodness given away (the resident to the intern, the intern to Baby M). Furthermore, the gift giving was not only inspiring but continues via the intern-turned-faculty-member's ability to harbor the memory of her mentoring attendant and in her continuing to share this gift with her own students. By the experience she described, I argue that this resident had pierced what it means to have gratitude as a way of life. Given her story, she most likely lives a life of deep gratitude, yet because of the experience she described and most likely other similar experiences, her gratitude draws her closer to living gratitude as a way of life.

Returning to the five criteria that establish a notion of the good, a fourth quality needed for the good as a standard for gratitude is a stance of respect toward others. The most concrete form of this respect is the advancement of human rights, which has become a moral end that more and more countries have adopted as national policy (Ignatieff, 1999), even though in practice these principles are only adhered to in various degrees. Charles Taylor (1989) noted the significance of respect when he wrote, "The moral world of moderns is significantly different from that of previous civilizations. This becomes clear, among other places, when we look at the sense that human beings command our respect. In one form or another, this seems to be a human universal; that is, in every society, there seems to be some such sense. The boundary around those beings worthy of respect may be drawn parochially in earlier cultures, but there always is such a class. And among what we recognize as higher civilizations, this always includes the whole human species" (p. 11).

Though this issue is not treated in the emotion literature, it is inconceivable how individuals could not help but feel a diminution in terms of their positive emotional responses (e.g., joy, gratitude) toward others if a warranted level of consideration for them is lacking. Without respect, a dismissive or false perception of the other is apt to occur, thereby undercutting an adequate gratitude response.

The final quality requisite for the good as a standard for ensuring gratitude's integrity, and closely linked to the aforementioned respect owed others, is an attribute of openness. Without openness, an individual is unable or only partially able to trigger an adequate gratitude response. Without sufficient openness, defensive reactions breed unencumbered, and imagination shrivels. When human beings are defensive and unimaginative, their understandings of others falter and their aspirations are compromised. Philosopher Jonathan Lear (1998) accurately portrayed this all-too-human yet existentially pitiable state: "One of the most important truths about us is that we have the capacity to be *open minded*: the capacity to live nondefensively with the question of *how to live* [emphasis added]. Human life in general is a study of why this capacity is not exercised: why open-mindedness is, for the most part, evaded, diminished, and attacked" (p. 8).

To summarize: Ideally, gratitude roots itself in a standard pointing more fully toward compassion and fairness and acted on with an eye toward a universal respect for and openness to others. It goes without saying that such gratitude is an ideal standard humans can only achieve to various degrees. Nonetheless, we can conclude that when humans actively strive toward this ideal, then the Hitler question is resolved sufficiently, and gratitude's integrity as a moral emotion is secure.

FUTURE RESEARCH

From the previous discussion, some potentially fruitful areas for research on the relationship between gratitude and morality become apparent. A critical task requiring psychologists' attention is the development of self-report measures of gratitude. Fortunately, work in this area looks highly promising (McCullough et al., 2002; Watkins, chap. 9, this volume). In addition, a prime research area worthy of serious consideration is the question as to how grati-tude relates to empathy. Davis's (1980) Interpersonal Reactivity Index, which measures multiple components of empathy, offers fertile possibilities for understanding the intricacies of the empathy-gratitude link. Moreover, Shelton and McAdams (1990) explored empathy's multidimensional fea-tures with various notions of morality, and extending such inquiry to the area of moral emotions such as gratitude seems a fitting next step. Likewise, the connections between prosocial behavior and measured states of gratitude offer the same encouraging research prospects. Another area worth probing is how gratitude manifests itself during young, middle, and late adulthood. More specifically, life-span researchers could pinpoint the saliency of grati-tude in various phases of adult development. For this to happen requires finely sharpened delineations between gratitude and somewhat related con-structs such as generativity. McAdams and Bauer (chap. 5, this volume) pro-vide a useful springboard by establishing both the presence and interweaving of generativity and gratitude during the adult years.

More speculative in nature, though equally intriguing, is the question as to how the gratitude experience aids the functioning of conscience when the latter is understood in more multidimensional and complex conceptualiza-tions (Callahan, 1991; Shelton, 2000). Finally, though there is a need to tread cautiously to avoid the idealizing bias, psychology's perhaps most adventur-ous task is to construct measures, to the extent possible, that attempt to cap-ture depth-related types of gratitude. To illustrate where such a venture might lead, Oliner and Oliner (1988) posited the existence of an altruistic personality. From a personological standpoint, is it unrealistic to consider a trait of gratitude or even a grateful personality? If the latter construct could be sustained through coherent theoretical underpinnings and rooted in rig-orous empirical testing, how would such a personality and its complex dy-namics and functioning be described?

CONCLUSION

Ironically, the various types of biases with which this chapter began can be recast as positive elements for gratitude's moral conceptualization. Whereas the original perspective was to construe the potential pitfalls of an empirical, idealizing, or Pollyannish bias, it remains even more likely that substituting *theme* for *bias* proves a fitting way to unearth and bring clarity to gratitude's moral basis. Most certainly, empirical studies thus far look promising for advancing the theme that gratitude engenders behaviors typically endorsed as moral (e.g., some caring attitude or prosocial inclination). Likewise, gratitude frequently possesses an aspirational quality, particularly when linked to spiritual and religious themes; in other words, gratitude offers ideals to strive for. Finally, shedding the Pollyannish bias's negative nuance, gratitude is acknowledged as a highly desirable emotion both prized and cherished. The appeal of gratitude arises to a considerable degree from its perceived moral quality. No inquiry, no matter how massive in scope or sophisticated in its conceptualization, can deny the necessity of cementing a link between gratitude and a (moral) standard, thereby ensuring gratitude's allegiance to and position within some commonly accepted moral framework.

The mention of one of the acknowledged saints of the twentieth century, Mother Teresa, aptly proves a fitting end to this discussion. Mother Teresa was, unconditionally, a gift giver. But this fact pales in comparison with a more dominant theme pervasive throughout her adult life. Above all, she was acutely aware that the poor to whom she devoted her life returned to her gifts far more abundant than she could ever repay. It was this standard of humility, a lens that allowed her to view the power of the powerless and to be a receptacle for this power, that served to both elicit and nourish the gratitude she felt.

> Mother Teresa's friendship with humanity was perfect. Let no one say that she was secretly self-serving and inauthentic, lest these words be stripped of their meaning. If grace is the bestowing of unmerited favor, then giving to unrelated or unknown parties without thought of return is a graceful act. Mother Teresa's life is testimony to this possibility. This poor Albanian missionary had the gift of giving. She did not reject worldly plenty, but set about to redistribute it as best she could, without being absorbed or spoiled by her contact with riches. She was a net giver to humanity. It is possible. (Scheibe, 2000, pp. 217–218)

Few if any of us are called to or even capable of such profound gift giving. Nonetheless, each of us, like her, is capable of aspiring to—even if necessarily heroically—a standard that calls for the gifts that we possess or that are bestowed on us to be given away. When viewed from this perspective, gratitude's essence can be construed not only from behaviors that are measurable, but also from ways of living that are both pathways for aspiring to the good and passages for attaining it.

References

Becker, J. (1998). *Hungry ghosts: Mao's secret famine.* New York: Henry Holt.

Bednar, L. G., Wells, M. G., & Peterson, S. R. (1989). *Self-esteem: Paradoxes and innovations in clinical theory and practice.* Washington, DC: American Psychological Association.

Berkowitz, M. W., & Oser, F. (Eds.). (1985). *Moral education: Theory and application.* Hillsdale, NJ: Erlbaum.

Breathnach, S. B. (2000, November). November calendar: The path to gratitude. *O, The Oprah Magazine,* 51–53.

Bridgeman, D. L. (Ed.). (1983). *The nature of prosocial development: Interdisciplinary theories and strategies.* New York: Academic Press.

Brokaw, T. (1998). *The greatest generation.* New York: Random House.

Buckley, W. F. (2000). *Let us talk of many things.* Roseville, CA: Prima.

Callahan, S. (1991). *In good conscience: Reason and emotion in moral decision making.* San Francisco: HarperCollins.

Davis, M. H. (1980). A multidimensional approach to individual differences in empathy. *JSAS Catalog of Selected Documents in Psychology, 10,* 85.

Duplantier, F. R. (1998, November). An epidemic of gratitude is sweeping the nation. *New Oxford Review, 65,* 23–27.

Eisenberg, N. (Ed.). (1982). *The development of prosocial behavior.* New York: Academic Press.

Emmons, R. A., & Shelton, C. M. (2002). Gratitude and the science of positive psychology. In C. R. Snyder & S. J. Lopez (Eds.), *Handbook of positive psychology* (pp. 459–471). New York: Oxford University Press.

Fagin, G. M. (1995). Stirred to profound gratitude. *Review for Religious, 54,* 237–252.

Gellately, R. (2001). *Backing Hitler.* New York: Oxford University Press.

Gilligan, C. (1982). *In a different voice: Psychological theory and women's development.* Cambridge, MA: Harvard University Press.

Goldhagen. D. J. (1996). *Hitler's willing executioners: Ordinary Germans and the Holocaust.* New York: Knopf.

Haan, N. (1982). Can research on morality be "scientific"? *American Psychologist, 37,* 1096–1104.

Haan, N., Aerts, E., & Cooper, B. A. (1985). *On moral grounds: The search for practical morality.* New York: New York University Press.

Hinman, L. (1985). Emotion, morality, and understanding. In C. G. Harding (Ed.), *Moral dilemmas: Philosophical and psychological issues in the development of moral reasoning* (pp. 57–70). Chicago: Precedent.

Hoffman, M. L. (1975). Developmental synthesis of affect and cognition and its implications for altruistic motivation. *Developmental Psychology, 11,* 607–622.

Hoffman, M. L. (1981). Is altruism part of human nature? *Journal of Personality and Social Psychology, 40,* 121–137.

Hoffman, M. L. (1982). Development of prosocial motivation: empathy and guilt. In N. Eisenberg (Ed.), *The development of prosocial behavior.* New York: Academic Press.

Hoffman, M. L. (2000). *Empathy and moral development: Implications for caring and justice.* New York: Cambridge University Press.

Hogan, R. (1995). Personality and moral development. In W. M. Kurtines & J. L. Gewirtz (Eds.), *Moral development: An introduction* (pp. 209–228). Needham Heights, MA: Allyn & Bacon.

Ignatieff, M. (1999, May 20). Human rights: The midlife crisis. *New York Review of Books*, 58–62.

Jones, S. (1994). A constructive relationship for religion with the science and profession of psychology: Perhaps the boldest model yet. *American Psychologist, 49,* 184–199.

Kagan, J. (1984). *The nature of the child.* New York: Basic Books.

Kershaw, I. (1999). *Hitler: 1889–1936: Hubris.* New York: Norton.

Kohlberg, L. (1981). *The philosophy of moral development: Essays on moral development* (Vol. 1). San Francisco: Harper & Row.

Kohlberg, L. (1984). *The psychology of moral development: Essays on moral development* (Vol. 2). San Francisco: Harper & Row.

Kurtines, W. M., & Gewirtz, J. L. (Eds.). (1984). *Morality, moral behavior, and moral development.* New York: Wiley.

Lapsley, D. K. (1996). *Moral psychology.* Boulder, CO: Westview Press.

Lazarus, R. S., & Lazarus, B. N. (1994). *Passion and reason: Making sense of our emotions.* New York: Oxford University Press.

Lear, J. (1998). *Open minded: Working out the logic of the soul.* Cambridge, MA: Harvard University Press.

Lewis, C. S. (1958). *Reflections on the Psalms.* New York: Harcourt Brace.

Meara, N., Schmidt, L., & Day, J. (1996). Principles and virtues: A foundation for ethical decisions, policies, and character. *Counseling Psychologist, 24,* 4–77.

McCullough, M. E., Emmons, R. A., & Tsang, J. (2002). The grateful disposition: A conceptual and empirical topography. *Journal of Personality and Social Psychology, 82,* 112–127.

McCullough, M. E., Kilpatrick, S. D., Emmons, R. A., & Larson, D. B. (2001). Is gratitude a moral affect? *Psychological Bulletin, 127,* 249–266.

McCullough, M. E., & Snyder, C. R. (2000). Classical sources of human strength: Revisiting an old home and building a new one. *Journal of Social and Clinical Psychology, 19,* 1–10.

Oliner, S. P., & Oliner, P. M. (1988). *The altruistic personality: rescuers of Jews in Nazi Europe.* New York: Free Press.

Rawls, J. (1971). *A theory of justice.* Cambridge, MA: Harvard University Press.

Rosenbaum, R. (1998). *Explaining Hitler.* New York: Random House.

Scheibe, K. E. (2000). *The drama of everyday life.* Cambridge, MA: Harvard University Press.

Seligman, M. E. P., & Csikszentmihalyi, M. (Eds.). (2000). Positive psychology [Special issue]. *American Psychologist, 55*(1).

Shelton, C. M. (1982). Discernment in everyday life: Spiritual and psychological considerations. *Spirituality Today, 34,* 326–334.

Shelton, C. M. (1990). *Morality of the heart: A psychology for the Christian moral life.* New York: Crossroad.

Shelton, C. M. (2000). *Achieving moral health.* New York: Crossroad.

Shelton, C. M., & McAdams, D. P. (1990). In search of an everyday morality: The development of a measure. *Adolescence, 25,* 923–943.

Spohn, W. C. (1983). The reasoning heart: An American approach to Christian discernment. *Theological Studies, 48,* 30–52.

Spohn, W. C. (2000). Conscience and moral development. *Theological Studies, 61,* 122–138.

Tangney, J. P. (1991). Moral affect: The good, the bad, and the ugly. *Journal of Personality and Social Psychology, 61,* 598–607.

Taylor, C. (1989). *Sources of the self: The making of modern identity.* Cambridge, MA: Harvard University Press.

Vacek, E. C. (2000). Gifts, God, generosity, and gratitude. In J. Keating (Ed.), *Spirituality and moral theology: Essays from a pastoral perspective* (pp. 81–125). Mahwah, NJ: Paulist Press.

Vacek, E. C. (2001). The emotions of care in health care. In F. Cates & P. Lauritzen (Eds.), *Medicine and the ethics of care* (pp. 105–140). Washington, DC: Georgetown University Press.

Walker, L. J. (1984). *Sex differences in the development of moral reasoning: A critical review, 55,* 677–691.

Walker, L. J., & Pitts, R. C. (1998). Naturalistic conceptions of moral maturity. *Developmental Psychology, 34,* 403–417.

Wilson, J. Q. (1995). *The moral sense.* New York: Free Press.

Wolfe, A. (2001). *Moral freedom: The search for virtue in a world of choice.* New York: Norton.

14 Gratitude as Thankfulness and as Gratefulness

David Steindl-Rast

At this early stage of concerted scientific research concerning gratitude, it is essential to fine-tune our terminology. Precise terminology is a necessary instrument for clear thinking. Scientific terminology differs from conversational usage by its precision. Emmons and Shelton (2002) noted, "Given that gratitude is a commonly occurring affect, it is remarkable that psychologists specializing in the study of emotions have, by and large, failed to explore its contours" (p. 461). Because we have failed to explore even the contours, we lack the terminology necessary for more detailed exploration. My effort at precision is twofold: linguistic and psychological. In this chapter, I examine idiomatic usage and etymological derivation of the terms I suggest, and also I base my choice of terms on a rigorous analysis of the ways we experience gratitude. For the sake of clarity and succinctness, I propose a series of theses and attempt to substantiate each of them briefly. In conclusion, I point out why the terminological distinction I propose has weighty consequences for the scientific study of gratitude.

THESIS 1: GRATITUDE IS ESSENTIALLY A CELEBRATION

By focusing on the way we experience gratitude, we become aware that it is more than a feeling. Besides its emotional component, we find in gratitude an element of recognition, in both its cognitive and its volitional senses. Gratitude not only presupposes that I recognize the gift as gift, but this recognition increases in proportion to my gratitude: The more I allow my gratitude to take hold of me, the more I come to understand the gift. The more I understand the gift, the more also the volitional aspect grows: I want to acknowledge my appreciation by giving recognition for the gratuitousness of the gift. All three components of gratitude resonate together in the French expression *Je suis reconnaissant* (I am grateful)—I recognize (intellectually), I acknowledge (willingly), I appreciate (emotionally). Only when all three come together is gratitude complete.

All three of these aspects are integral also to the phenomenon of celebration, a phenomenon that deserves careful psychological analysis. By *celebration* I mean an act of heightened and focused intellectual and emotional appreciation. In this working definition, *act* means an operation of the mind; *appreciation* stands for estimation, sympathetic recognition, perception, understanding, gratitude (Brown, 1993). *Heightened* may refer to an overwhelming increase of intensity, as in peak experiences; in any case, appreciation has to be raised above its normal level before we can speak of celebration. Our working definition applies to any form of celebration and distinguishes celebration from all other activities.

The object of celebration may be a thing (e.g., a celebrated piece of art singled out by a whole culture for heightened appreciation), a person (e.g., one's hero), an activity (e.g., the solemn signing of a document), an event—past or present (e.g., the saving event celebrated in religious ritual), a situation (e.g., time spent with a friend), or a state (e.g., euphoric intoxication with beauty or alcohol). Our working definition will apply also if the object is present only in one's imagination or memory. This points to an often overlooked fact: Celebration need not be externally expressed, although it often is. Your birthday is a day that you celebrate, even if no one else remembers it and you yourself do not mark the day, externally, as different from any other.

My claim that gratitude is essentially a celebration is based on the fact that its essential characteristics are heightened and focused intellectual and emotional appreciation. Our intellectual focus is sharpened and our emotional response intensified in the act of (spontaneous or deliberate, but in either case willing) appreciation that we call gratitude. This conformity with the definition of celebration justifies us in speaking of gratitude as essentially a celebration. It differs from all other celebrations by its object, that is, undeserved kindness.

The references to celebration in Komter's "Gratitude and Gift Exchange" (chap. 10, this volume) are of interest in this context. Referring to Bonnie and de Waal's chapter (chap. 11, this volume) on "Primate Social Reciprocity and the Origin of Gratitude," Komter remarks, "In his experiments, [de Waal] has observed chimpanzees watching a caretaker arrive with bundles of blackberry, sweet gum, beech, and tulip branches. Characteristically, a general pandemonium ensues: wild excitement, hooting, embracing, kissing, and friendly body contact, which he has called a 'celebration.' De Waal has noted that he considers this a sign indicating the transition to a mode of interaction characterized by friendliness and reciprocity. . . . De Waal's results clearly demonstrate that celebration is followed by a pattern of reciprocal giving and receiving" (Komter, this volume, p. 204). Reciprocity plays a decisive role in Komter's understanding of gratefulness. Thus, from an altogether different perspective, she also focuses on a deep connection between gratitude and celebration.

THESIS 2: GRATITUDE IS A CELEBRATION OF UNDESERVED KINDNESS

At first glance, it would appear that gratitude can celebrate a great variety of objects. One may experience gratitude for any item on our list of potential objects of celebration: for a thing (e.g., a Christmas present), a person (e.g., one's child), an event (e.g., the first snowfall), an activity (e.g., ice skating), a situation (e.g., one's vacation time), or a state (e.g., one's good health). Note, however, that in all these cases it is the sense of receiving something undeservedly that triggers gratitude. If what we receive is ours by right, our appreciation will not pick up that special flavor of something *undeserved*, something gratis. But this is essential, as even the stem (*grati*) of the word *gratitude* indicates.

Invariably something undeserved is the formal, constituent object on which gratitude focuses. But why do I speak of this undeserved something as "kindness"? Admittedly, I could also call it "undeserved admittance into a state of mutual belonging," but this sounds more than clumsy, and the term that comes closest to conveying the same idea is *kindness*. Kindness implies solidarity. We tend to like those who are like us and to be kind to those of our own kind. Kindness is a display of mutual belonging. Even a trivial kindness shown to a stranger, or even to an animal, expresses some sense of solidarity. The prototype of kindness is the relationship between mother and child. (The German word for child is *Kind*.) Hence Shakespeare's metaphor, "the milk of human kindness" (*Macbeth*, Act 1, Scene 5). Until the late seventeenth century, *kindness* meant kinship, close relationship. To show kindness meant therefore to display the mutual belonging implied by kinship. The idiom has changed, but the experiential connection between belonging together and being kind is still strong enough to revive some of the original meaning of the term.

If we look again at our list of potential objects for the celebrative act of gratitude, we notice that it seems more natural to speak of kindness when we receive a tangible gift, than, say, in a peak experience, when we are looking up at the starry sky in grateful wonder. Yet the sense of belonging is strong in both cases. We would not be stretching the term too far, it seems, if we called a peak experience an experience of cosmic kindness. All of the other objects of gratitude could be lined up to form a spectrum of which the two extremes are personal kindness, on one end, and cosmic kindness on the other. A sense of belonging characterizes every sector of that spectrum; careful analysis shows, however, that its two poles can be distinguished by several different characteristics.

THESIS 3: GRATITUDE CAN BE EXPERIENCED IN TWO CHARACTERISTIC MODES, SUFFICIENTLY DISTINCT TO DESERVE TWO DIFFERENT DESIGNATIONS

The distinction is clearest when we compare the extreme poles of the spectrum of gratitude. Typical examples would be, for one pole, receiving a gift package from another person; for the opposite pole, a peak experience in the solitude of a mountain top. In both cases, we have an instance of genuine gratitude: an act of heightened intellectual and emotional appreciation for gratuitous belonging. In the first case, we experience gratuitous belonging as undeserved kindness, in the other as an overwhelming cosmic oneness, typically associated with a sense of "I don't deserve this." Though both cases fit our working definition, gratitude in the first case is *personal*, and in the other, *transpersonal*. Gratitude for a personal kindness focuses on one specific instance of undeserved belonging; the gratitude integral to the peak experience is universal.

Transpersonal, universal gratitude, although unreflective, is no less genuinely cognitive than its typically reflective personal and specific counterpart. It ought not to be called *precognitive*, for cognition of gratuitousness is not an afterthought but an integral aspect of the oceanic feeling of universal belonging. Both modes of gratitude are cognitive; both are also volitional. Although transpersonal gratitude arises spontaneously, whereas personal gratitude cultivates spontaneity deliberately, we can detect a strong volitional element also in transpersonal gratitude—a willingness to open oneself to given reality, to make oneself vulnerable to say an unconditional yes to all that is. This unconditional response of universal gratitude is an other distinguishing characteristic. A specific act of gratitude is always conditional, depending, for example, on whether or not the giver acted out of unselfish motives.

It seems appropriate, then, to find a special term for spontaneous, unreflective, unconditional, and universal transpersonal gratitude to distinguish it from deliberate, reflective, conditional, specific personal gratitude, which deserves its own special designation.

THESIS 4: GRATEFULNESS AND THANKFULNESS SUGGEST THEMSELVES AS PSYCHOLOGICALLY AND LINGUISTICALLY FITTING DESIGNATIONS FOR TWO DISTINCT MODALITIES OF GRATITUDE

The terms *grateful* and *thankful* are interchangeable in most situations of everyday parlance. There remains, however, a subtle distinction. To say that one is thankful *to* someone and grateful *for* something seems to be the more commonly preferred usage. More significant is the fact that *thanking* and *thinking* are cognates. To thank meant originally to think of a gift and has come to mean the feeling aroused by these thoughts and their expression in a thankful attitude (*Duden Etymologie*, 1989, s.v. "*Dank*"; see also Barnhart, 1994, p. 806). When we thank, we think—namely, in terms of giver, gift, and receiver. This is necessary for personal gratitude, but transpersonal grati-tude—though cognitive—lies deeper than thinking and precedes it. When it is an integral element of the experience of universal wholeness, gratitude does not yet distinguish between giver, gift, and receiver.

Transpersonal gratitude belongs to our inner realm and we often find no words for it; personal gratitude belongs to the social realm and we most often express it. Hence, the verb that goes with gratitude is *thanking*. There is no action word for gratefulness; its dynamism is self-contained. Being grateful is a state; thanking is an action.

These considerations seem to me to justify the terminology I propose. Personal gratitude deserves to be called *thankfulness*, because it typically ex-presses itself in thanks given to the giver by the receiver of the gift. Transper-sonal gratitude deserves to be called *gratefulness*, because it is typically the full response of a person to gratuitous belonging.

I find a parallel to this distinction between gratefulness and thankfulness in Komter's chapter 10 (this volume) when she speaks of two layers of grati-tude: "The first layer of gratitude is a spiritual, religious, or magical one. . . . The moral and psychological aspects of gratitude constitute its second layer" (p. 209). McAdams and Bauer (chap. 5, this volume) wrestle with the tension between gratitude aimed at someone—a person or persons, and gratitude for simply being here. Only thankfulness fits into their conviction that gratitude typically has as its object an intentional agent beyond the self. They realize, however, that some people are grateful for receiving the precious gift of life, even if they do not identify a personified target for their gratitude. They admit that further research is needed, agreeing with McCullough and Tsang (chap. 7, this volume) who warn, "In this early stage of empirical work on gratitude, it might be useful to remain mindful of these obvious and seem-ingly trivial distinctions between the various perspectives from which grati-tude might be conceptualized and measured" (p. 135). My own distinction between thankfulness and gratefulness results from two such different perspectives from which gratitude might be conceptualized.

THESIS 5: FOR SCIENTISTS WHO EXPLORE THE RELIGIOUS AND SPIRITUAL SIGNIFICANCE OF GRATITUDE, IT IS OF PRIME IMPORTANCE TO FOCUS ON GRATEFULNESS

The spiritual core of every religion is mysticism. By *mysticism*, I mean experiential communion with transcendental reality. This belongs to the transpersonal realm of gratefulness, in contrast to the social realm of thankfulness. Admittedly, thanksgiving occupies a wide space in religious thought and practice; it deserves to be studied. But, like all thanking, it is based on thinking; it uses concepts—such as the basic distinction of giver, gift, and receiver—and it interprets experience. The religious experience itself—mystic intuition—is preconceptual cognition. Gratefulness is the mystical element of religious gratitude, thankfulness is its theological one. As scientists we will do well to study the mystic experience of religious gratitude before turning to its theological interpretations.

Two fine examples of theological interpretation of gratitude in this book are "Gratitude in Judaism" by Solomon Schimmel (chap. 3) and "The Blessings of Gratitude: A Conceptual Analysis" by Robert C. Roberts (chap. 4). "I mean *conceptual* as contrasted with *empirical*," Roberts warns the reader (p. 59). But what happens when empirical reality does not fit our concepts? It is always difficult to readjust an accustomed conceptual framework to empirical reality, particularly a theological one. But it helps to remember that all theology is merely an attempt to conceptualize mystic experience. The mystical experience—though cognitive—is preconceptual. Roberts's construal of gratitude in terms of beneficiary, benefice, and benefactor is closely tied up with theistic theology. It produces many valuable insights regarding thankfulness but is ill-equipped to deal with gratefulness. To our surprise, we might discover that gratitude as gratefulness is more deeply and universally religious than its theological restriction to thankfulness ever allowed us to see.

William James (1842–1910) and Abraham Maslow (1908–1970), as pioneers in the psychology of mystic experience, amassed a wealth of research data still awaiting analysis and evaluation. Maslow's study of the hierarchy of human needs eclipsed his explorations of the peak experience, a term he coined. The peak experience is at one and the same time a key moment of spiritual awareness and a moment of overwhelming gratefulness. Maslow wrote, "People during and after Peak-experiences characteristically feel lucky, fortunate, graced. A common reaction is 'I don't deserve this.' A common consequence is a feeling of gratitude, in the religious persons, to their God, in others, to fate or to nature or to just good fortune. . . . This can go over into worship, giving thanks, adoring, giving praise, oblation, and other reactions which fit very easily into orthodox religious frameworks" (1964, p. 68).

Maslow's own account shows how clearly he recognized and tackled, 40 years ago, the task that Sir John Templeton's *Humble Approach* (1998) has taken up in our time:

> When I started to explore the psychology of health, I picked out the finest, healthiest people, the best specimens of mankind I could find, and studied them to see what they were like. . . . I learned many lessons from these people. But one in particular is our concern now. I found that these individuals tended to report having had something like mystic experiences. . . . I gave up the name 'mystic' experience and started calling them peak-experiences. They can be studied scientifically. . . . They are within reach of human knowledge. . . . Peak-experiences can be considered to be *truly* religious experiences in the best and most profound, most universal, and most humanistic sense of that word. . . . Peak-experiences are far more common than I had expected. . . . I now suspect they occur in practically everybody although without being recognized or accepted for what they are. (Maslow, 1962, p. 9)

To recognize our mystical moments and to accept them for what they are—there lies the challenge. A mystic is not a special kind of human being; rather, every human being is a special kind of mystic—potentially, at least. What is in question is not whether all of us do have those "*truly* religious experiences," but rather what we make of them. We can realize our mystical potential through grateful living. If we want to live deliberately, the study of gratefulness can become an integral part of our lives. This exploration is open to all of us. Once we distinguish gratefulness from thankfulness (Step 1), and recognize gratefulness as the mystic dimension of gratitude (Step 2), we are challenged to explore gratefulness—with reverent, yet resolute scrutiny—as the ground zero of religious experience. This is what Sir John Templeton called "wide-ranging, open-minded research into the laws of the spirit"(p. 118). Christopher Fry (1951/1953) called it "exploration into God."

References

Barnhart, R. K. (Ed.). (1994). *The Barnhart concise dictionary of etymology.* New York: HarperCollins.

Brown, L. (Ed.). (1993). *The new shorter Oxford English dictionary on historical principles*. Oxford, UK: Clarendon.

Emmons, R. A., & Shelton, C. S. (2002). Gratitude and the science of positive psychology. In C. R. Snyder & S. J. Lopez (Eds.), *Handbook of positive psychology* (pp. 459–471). New York: Oxford University Press.

Fry, C. A. (1951/1953). "A Sleep of Prisoners" [play]. New York: Acting Edition. (Original work published 1951)

Maslow, A. H. (1962). Lessons from the peak-experiences. *Journal of Humanistic Psychology, 2,* 9–18.

Maslow, A. H. (1964). *Religions, values, and Peak-experiences*. New York: Penguin Press.

Templeton, J. M. (1998). *The humble approach*. Radnor, PA: Templeton Foundation Press.

Appendix

Annotated Bibliography of Psychological Research on Gratitude

Jo-Ann Tsang and Michael E. McCullough

With the recent resurgence of positive psychology, many researchers have a renewed interest in the concept of gratitude. Though the current empirical work on gratitude is exciting and promising, such studies are few in number. It is our hope that this annotated bibliography will aid psychologists in their investigation of the nature and effects of gratitude, spurring further advances in theory and research in gratitude.

The studies summarized in this bibliography are both descriptive and experimental. Choosing from research that best illustrated the nature and effects of gratitude, we included experiments that employed vignettes, narratives, and behavioral measures, as well as correlational studies of personality and even telephone surveys. Although there is not complete consensus among these studies, they do come together to paint a rather coherent picture of the nature of gratitude: People experience gratitude in response to a valued positive outcome that another individual intentionally caused. This grateful emotion leads people to desire to act prosocially themselves, at least in the short run. Feelings of gratitude are reported to be pleasant and are experienced often in the course of everyday life.

There is much room for further research in this area of psychology. Future studies can move beyond the reliance on vignette manipulations and self-report measures evident in much previous work on gratitude. Instead, we can look at the effects of actual gratitude experienced by research participants, both in their everyday lives and in situations experimentally manipulated to produce gratitude. Given that we have at least a rudimentary understanding of what gratitude is, we can also develop additional studies to answer questions about the effects of gratitude. For example, if gratitude does increase prosocial behavior, is this behavior directed only at the benefactor, or will those experiencing gratitude act more prosocially toward anyone? What are the effects of gratitude on health? In addition, we can look more deeply at the dispositional side of gratitude. Is there such a thing as a grateful personality? What is the relationship between the disposition toward gratitude and variables such as religiousness or the Big Five model of personality? Using the present studies as a foundation, psychologists can continue to explore the complex emotion of gratitude.

Baron, R. A. (1984). Reducing organizational conflict: An incompatible response approach. *Journal of Applied Psychology, 69,* 272–279.

Objective: To apply the technique of incompatible response strategy to the reduction of destructive organizational conflict.

Design: Between-subjects experiment.

Setting: This study was conducted in a laboratory setting.

Participants: Participants were 85 male and 71 female undergraduate students.

Manipulated variables: The accomplice's behavior and the incompatible response induction served as the manipulated variables. The participant and a male accomplice of the experimenter were asked to imagine that they were executives who were employed at a large company. Their task was to discuss solutions to a particular problem in their company. The accomplice disagreed with the participant's statements in one of two ways: In the *disagreement* condition, the accomplice disagreed with the participant calmly and rationally. In the *condescension* condition, the accomplice disagreed in a condescending and conceited manner. After the accomplice's behavior, the experimenter asked the participant and accomplice to wait while she searched for some questionnaires. During this time, the incompatible response variable was manipulated. The accomplice either waited quietly (*control* condition), offered the participant a piece of candy (*gift* condition), apologized for his rude behavior and explained that he was stressed out by exams (*sympathy* condition), or asked the participant to read some cartoons in his notebook (*humor* condition).

Assessment of outcome variables: After the incompatible response induction, the experimenter returned with the questionnaires containing the dependent variables. These included self-report measures of current mood, personal impressions of the accomplice (liking, reasonableness, and pleasantness), and job-related impressions of the accomplice. Participants were also asked to predict how they would behave in future conflicts with the accomplice, rating the likelihood of engaging in the conflict be-haviors of accommodation, competition, compromise, and collaboration.

Main results: Looking at the effects relevant to gratitude (the gift condition), partic-ipants had a marginally more positive mood in the gift condition than in the control condition. Participants in the gift incompatible response condition reported liking the accomplice more, and rated him as more pleasant in comparison to participants in the control condition. In addition, none of the incompatible response conditions had a significant effect on participant's job-related ratings of the accomplice. Regarding fu-ture conflict behaviors, participants in the gift condition were significantly more likely to engage in the strategy of collaboration, in comparison to participants in the control condition. Effects of the gift condition were similar to effects of the other in-compatible response conditions, with a few small differences.

Conclusions: The author concluded that responses incompatible with the anger can be successfully used to reduce negative affect and increase constructive responses to conflict. The author noted that the incompatible response inductions used in this study were minimal, and that stronger levels of incompatible responses may lead to even more constructive responses to conflict.

Commentary: One limitation of this experiment, from the standpoint of gratitude research, is that the specific emotion of gratitude was not measured in the gift condi-tion. However, since the gift condition produced similar effects to the other incom-patible response conditions, it is likely at least a small amount of gratitude, which is theorized to be positively valenced, was experienced by participants. This experi-ment underscores the prosocial nature of grateful feelings, which caused these par-ticipants to rate the accomplice more positively as well as to endorse a more con-structive conflict strategy in the future, in comparison to participants who did not experience positive emotions. More research is needed to differentiate between any specific effects of gratitude on impressions and behaviors, independent of other pos-itive emotions.

Correspondence: Author was at Purdue University when this study was published.

Baumgarten-Tramer, F. (1938). "Gratefulness" in children and young people. *Journal of Genetic Psychology, 53,* 53–66.

Objective: In the context of a theoretical analysis of gratitude, to categorize different types of gratitude and to examine whether children and adolescents recognize that certain situations are relevant to gratitude.

Design: Qualitative.

Setting: Elementary and secondary schools in the city of Bern, Switzerland.

Participants: In the first study mentioned, participants included 1,059 school chil-dren between the ages of 7 and 15. The second study mentioned included 530 chil-dren between the ages of 10 and 15 years.

Assessment of outcome variables: Participants in the first study responded to questionnaires that asked, "What is your greatest wish?" and "What would you do for the person who granted you this wish?" Participants in the second study were presented with a scenario in which an individual saved a rich person's life, but the rich person was injured in the process and took the other individual to court. Participants were asked what they thought the court's decision should be in the case.

Main results: The author found that participants' responses in the first study could be grouped into four categories: verbal gratefulness, concrete gratefulness, connective gratitude, and finalistic gratefulness. These different forms of gratitude differed in frequency depending on the age of the participant. In the second study, 14.71% of participants directly mentioned the concept of ungratefulness in reaction to the scenario, whereas the remainder of the participants described the scenario in terms of unfairness.

Conclusions: There are individual differences between children in their expressions of gratitude. Some of these differences are related to age. Whereas results from the second study revealed that children are not always aware of the relevance of gratitude to certain situations, the first study demonstrated that children express gratitude when a situation clearly calls for gratefulness.

Commentary: Although not methodologically or statistically rigorous, this article presents good theoretical material that will be of interest to gratitude researchers.

Correspondence: The author was at the University of Bern, Switzerland, when these studies were published.

Bar-Tal, D., Bar-Zohar, Y., Greenberg, M. S., & Hermon, M. (1977). Reciprocity behavior in the relationship between donor and recipient and between harm-doer and victim. *Sociometry, 40,* 293–298.

Objective: To investigate the effect of relationship closeness on the reciprocation of favors and harm.

Design: Between-subjects experiment.

Setting: The setting of the experiment is not explicitly stated, but it was most likely conducted in a laboratory or classroom setting.

Participants: Participants were 50 male and 50 female undergraduate students from a course in introductory social psychology.

Manipulated variables: The two manipulated variables were the nature of the relationship between the potential helper and the person in need, and the sex of the participant. Each participant read two similar scenarios about a protagonist who missed a bus to an important event and did not have a car. He/she then called someone to ask for a ride. The scenarios varied in outcome: In one scenario, the person gave the protagonist a ride (*help-giving*), and in the other scenario, the person refused to give the protagonist a ride (*harm-doing*). The nature of the relationship was varied by manipulating the identity of the potential helper: parent, sibling, friend at dormitory, acquaintance at dormitory, or stranger at dormitory (parent = closest relationship, stranger = least close).

Assessment of outcome variables: Items at the end of each scenario asked participants to rate the extent to which the called person was under an obligation to help. For the help-giving scenarios, participants also rated how grateful they felt toward the person who helped them, and for the harm-doing scenarios, they rated how resentful they felt toward the person who refused to help. Participants were also asked open-ended questions about why they thought the person they called did/did not help them, and how they felt toward the person who helped/didn't help them.

Main results: The authors first examined participant ratings of the help-giving scenarios. Male participants thought close friends and acquaintances were the most obligated to help, whereas female participants felt that parents had the most obligation to help. Across both sexes, closer relationships were related to increased obligation to help. Conversely, less close relationships were related to increased gratitude. In other words, parents were seen as the most obligated to help, but participants said they would feel most grateful when receiving help from a stranger. Responses to the open-ended questions were content-analyzed and coded. Using the author's coding system, participants were more likely to state that strangers and acquaintances helped for social responsibility reasons, whereas participants who read about calling a parent, sibling, or close friend were more likely to mention role obligation as the main reason for help. Participants who read about being helped by a stranger or acquaintance were more likely to mention they felt indebtedness and attraction for the helper, and participants reading about the three closer relationships were also most likely to report feeling indebted.

With the harm-doing scenarios, participants also rated that parents and siblings were under the most obligation to help, with close friends under an intermediate obligation, and acquaintances and strangers under the least obligation. Participants felt the most resentment toward parents and siblings who had refused to help and the least resentment toward nonhelping strangers. Regarding open-ended questions, participants who read about acquaintances and strangers were most likely to mention fear as an explanation for their refusal to help.

Conclusions: The nature of the relationship between the potential benefactor and recipient affects individuals' reactions when they are helped or refused helped. Closer relationships, such as those with parents and siblings, bring with them increased obligation to help, decreased gratitude in response to help, and increased resentment in response to the refusal to help.

Commentary: This experiment demonstrates that role obligation is an important component of gratitude. Individuals feel most grateful for help when they do not feel entitled to that help out of relationship obligations. Researchers would be wise to take into account the relationship between benefactor and recipient when investigating grateful responses to help.

Correspondence: Daniel Bar-Tal was at Tel-Aviv University when this study was published.

Baumeister, R. F., & Ilko, S. A. (1995). Shallow gratitude: Public and private acknowledgement of external help in accounts of success. *Basic and Applied Social Psychology, 16,* 191–209.

Objective: To test the hypothesis of "shallow gratitude," that people privately take credit for their successes, but publicly express gratitude by sharing the credit with others.

Design: Between-subjects experiment.

Setting: Laboratory.

Participants: Participants were 67 undergraduate students.

Manipulated variables: Participants were asked to write two stories, one concerning an important success experience that occurred in the past 2 years, and the other concerning a major failure experience. Participants in the *private* condition were asked not to put any identifying information in the stories. Participants in the *public* condition were asked to write their names on every sheet of paper they filled out, and were told that they would discuss their stories with a small group after completing the two stories.

Assessment of outcome variables: Stories were coded for mentions of direct help, emotional support, direct hindrance, and emotional hindrance from others. They were also coded for fairness and contradictory material (self-enhancing statements in failure stories or self-deprecating statements in success stories).

Main results: Mentions of help from others occurred mainly in success stories, whereas mentions of hindrance from others occurred mainly in failure stories. For success stories, mentions of direct help were significantly more frequent in the public condition, compared to the private condition. A marginal effect occurred for emotional support in the same direction. In other words, participants seemed more likely to express gratitude to others for their successes when their accounts were to be made public, rather than kept private. Regarding failure stories, participants were equally likely to mention direct hindrance and emotional hindrance from others in both the public and private stories. The authors also present supplementary findings regarding their fairness and contradictory statements variables.

Conclusions: These results support the "shallow gratitude" hypothesis, that individuals exhibit less self-serving bias when their success stories are public versus private. Because failure accounts did not show a public-private difference in the mention of the actions of other people, these results cannot be explained by the nonmotivational cue of the presence of others in the public condition. This implies that public expressions of gratitude are not always genuine, but part of a motivated self-presentation strategy.

Commentary: Although this study does not directly assess grateful emotions, it has important ramifications for gratitude research. Expressions of gratitude may vary depending on the self-presentational motivations of the participants, especially in retrospective accounts.

Correspondence: Roy M. Baumeister, Department of Psychology, Case Western Reserve University, Cleveland, OH 44106.

Becker, J. A., & Smenner, P. C. (1986). The spontaneous use of *thank you* by preschoolers as a function of sex, socioeconomic status, and listener status. *Language in Society, 15,* 537–546.

Objective: Researchers investigated whether preschoolers would spontaneously say "thank you" in a familiar social setting when their parents were not present, and whether certain demographic variables were related to spontaneously saying "thank you."

Design: Between-subjects experiment.

Setting: Day care centers in a southeastern metropolitan area.

Participants: Participants were 250 children (129 girls, 121 boys) between the ages of 3.5 and 4.5 years. Of the participants, 146 children were from low-income families, whereas 104 children were from middle-income families.

Assessment of predictor variables: Children from low-income families were drawn from day care centers that did not charge a fee for services. Children from middle-income families were drawn from day care centers that charged the highest rates in the area, and these children had parents employed in professional occupations. Experimenters also noted the sex and ethnicity of children. Children played a color-naming game with teachers, and after correctly guessing the color on a card, each child went to another room, where he or she was given a sticker by a child model or an adult model.

Assessment of outcome variable: Responses to the receipt of the sticker were recorded on audiotape and noted by the adult model. Researchers noted whether participants said "thank you" or related phrases.

Main results: Thirty-seven percent of children said "thank you" in response to receiving a sticker. Girls were more likely to respond with "thank you" than boys. Children from lower income families said "thank you" more often than children from middle-income families, but no effects were found for ethnicity. Children were more likely to say "thank you" to the adult model than to the child model.

Conclusions: Previous studies cited by the authors revealed a lower frequency of children responding "thank you" in the presence of parents. The authors argued that young children may see parental prompting to say "thank you" as part of the politeness routine, and that they then wait for the parent to prompt them before they say "thank you." However, in the absence of parents, the authors posited, children can recognize when a situation calls for saying "thank you." Demographic variables such as sex, socioeconomic status, and benefactor status all affected children's use of "thank you." The authors suggested that these differences may be caused by differences in socialization.

Commentary: Although these researchers did not measure children's perceptions or experiences of gratitude, it is possible that saying "thank you" in response to a gift is indicative of some amount of gratitude, even in children. The authors mentioned this when they discussed the relationship between socioeconomic status and frequency of saying "thank you." Although it is possible that children from lower income families are socialized to say "thank you" more frequently, the authors noted that these children also seemed to be more excited about receiving the stickers than did children from middle-income levels. Therefore, the fact that children from lower income families said "thank you" more often may indicate that they also felt more gratitude. At the least, these studies show that some children as young as 3.5 years old recognize that expressions of gratitude are relevant in certain situations, without being prompted by their parents.

Correspondence: Both authors were affiliated with the Department of Psychology at the University of South Florida at the time of their research.

Biner, P. M., & Kidd, H. J. (1994). The interactive effects of monetary incentive justification and questionnaire length on mail survey response rates. *Psychology and Marketing, 11*, 483–492.

Objective: To test equity theory in the context of responding to a mail survey. These researchers believed that feelings of obligation would lead to an increase in the number of surveys sent back by respondents. Specifically, they wished to explore the effects of under- and overcompensation on response rates.

Design: Between-subjects experiment.

Setting: A midwestern city with a population of 120,500.

Participants: Participants were 200 people whose names were selected from a telephone directory using a systematic random sampling technique. Approximately 90% of the residents of the city were listed in the directory.

Manipulated variables: Participants were assigned to one of four conditions in a 2 x 2 design using a randomized blocks procedure. Participants in all conditions were sent a questionnaire ostensibly designed to assess community needs, along with a cover letter and a $1 bill. The first manipulation was presented in the cover letter. Half of the participants read that the $1 was included to make individuals obligated to return the questionnaires (equity-salient condition). The other half of the participants read that the $1 was a token of appreciation in advance for filling out the questionnaire (standard condition). The other manipulation consisted of the length of the questionnaire. Half of the participants received a one-page questionnaire with 10 questions (short questionnaire condition), and the other half received a five-page questionnaire with

50 questions (long questionnaire condition). Researchers hypothesized that participants who received $1 with the short questionnaire would feel overcompensated, and that participants who received $1 for the long questionnaire would feel undercompensated.

Assessment of outcome variables: Questionnaires were coded to determine participants' treatment conditions. The dependent measure consisted of the number of completed questionnaires returned within a 3-week period.

Main results: The equity-salient letter produced a significantly higher response rate than the standard letter, but only with the short questionnaire. With the long questionnaire, the effect was reversed but nonsignificant.

Conclusions: These results support an equity interpretation of monetary compensation's effects on response rates. Overcompensation—in this case, receiving payment for a short questionnaire—along with a statement of obligation caused participants to increase their rates of response.

Commentary: On the surface, these results seem to contradict other research reviewed in this bibliography. Other studies suggest that expression of gratitude, as in the standard condition of the present study, should increase response rates. However, there are a number of differences between the present study and other research. One difference is that the present study did not have a control condition in which neither equity nor gratitude was made salient. It may be that the standard cover letter expressing gratitude led to a higher response rate than a letter that had no gratitude or equity at all. Additionally, this study can be seen as consistent with Carey, Clicque, Leighton, and Milton's (1976) results. (See the next entry in this bibliography.) Carey et al. compared the effects of saying "thank you" to customers with the effects of thanking customers and telling them about a new sale. The "thank you" plus information about a sale did not increase sales as much as the simple "thank you" did. This may have occurred because the information about the sale made customers think that the person calling them had ulterior motives. In the same way, the inclusion of $1 with all questionnaires in the present study could have been perceived by participants as coercive, nullifying any effects the expression of gratitude might have had on response rates. More directly, this present study also demonstrates that the expression of gratitude is different from (or at least weaker than) a direct statement of obligation or equity.

Correspondence: Paul M. Biner, Department of Psychological Science, Ball State University, Muncie, Indiana 47306

Carey, J. R., Clicque, S. H., Leighton, B. A., & Milton, F. (1976). A test of positive reinforcement of customers. *Journal of Marketing, 40,* 98–100.

Objective: To explore whether thanking customers for their business would serve as positive reinforcement, thereby increasing sales.

Design: Controlled field experiment.

Setting: A central Texas city of 22,000.

Participants: Participants were 440 customers of M&M Jewelers.

Manipulated variables: Customers were randomly assigned to one of three conditions. For the first condition, customers were called and thanked for their business. In the second condition, customers were thanked for their business and told of a special sale. In the control group, no call was made.

Assessment of outcome variables: Overall sales for the retail establishment were measured. Additionally, individual sales from customers from the different conditions were also recorded.

Main results: The store experienced a 27% increase in sales during the test month as compared with the previous month. This increase in sales was due to participants in the two experimental groups. The largest increase in sales came from customers who were simply thanked (70%), whereas there was a small increase for those who were thanked and told about the sale (30%), and no increase for customers in the control group. The increase in sales seemed due to the renewed interest of dormant rather than regular customers. In addition to increased sales, there was also an increase in payment of delinquent accounts by customers.

Conclusions: Thanking customers can serve as a form of positive reinforcement, stimulating increased spending, especially among customers who make purchases less regularly.

Commentary: It is interesting to note that the thank-you condition had a much bigger effect than the condition in which customers were also told about a sale. It may be that news about a sale cheapened the expressed gratitude in the second condition, making it seem as though store employees were calling customers expressly to increase sales. The differences between conditions suggest that the increase in sales was caused, not so much by general positive reinforcement, but by the reinforcing nature of gratitude.

Correspondence: No designated mailing address, but the first author listed his affiliation at the University of Texas at San Antonio at the time of the study.

Clark, H. B., Northrop, J. T., & Barkshire, C. T. (1988). The effects of contingent thank you notes on case managers' visiting residential clients. *Education and Treatment of Children, 11,* 45–51.

Objective: To explore whether thank-you letters would increase the frequency with which case managers visited their adolescent clients in a residential program.

Design: Controlled field experiment.

Setting: Adolescent residential unit at a community mental health center.

Participants: Case managers from the welfare department or juvenile court who were assigned to youth in the residential unit.

Intervention: After a baseline period of 20 weeks during which no special interactions occurred between staff and case managers, staff implemented the intervention phase. During the intervention phase, thank-you letters were sent to case managers and their supervisors, contingent upon each case manager's visiting the residential unit. Letters thanked the case manager for his or her visits, underscored the importance of the visits, and indicated that the supervisor was sent a copy of the letter. The intervention phase lasted 20 weeks. After this intervention, there was a third period of 10 weeks in which no letters were sent, approximating the previous baseline phase.

Assessment of outcome variables: Throughout the three phases of the study, case manager visits were recorded in two ways. First, case managers were required to sign a log book during each visit and to list the client or staff members they were visiting. Second, case managers were required to meet with one of the staff before or after meeting with their clients. At the end of each week, each staff member checked off which case managers they had seen that week, and each staff member indicated whether he or she had met with his or her client. Reports by staff members produced over 98% agreement with the log book.

Main results: Results were reported separately for two different social service agencies by which the case managers were employed. Case managers from the different agencies showed a similar pattern: Case managers' visits to their clients increased during the intervention period (74%, 81%) when compared with the baseline (45%, 40%) and postintervention (44%, 55%) periods.

Conclusions: Thank-you letters served as effective reinforcers for case managers' visiting their clients. There were certain qualifications to the data: Some case managers and clients changed during the 50 weeks of the study, and the increase in visits began to drop off during the end of the intervention phase. This graded reduction in the potency of the intervention may reveal the existence of habituation effects. Suggestions by the authors for further research include investigation of the specific content of thank-you letters and the effect of increased visits on clients.

Commentary: This study provides strong support for the reinforcing nature of gratitude. The advantages of this study include its location in the field, as well as its use of behavioral measures. A small weakness of this study is that perceptions of gratitude were not actually measured, but this would have been difficult, given the naturalistic nature of the study.

Correspondence: Hewitt B. Clark, Associate Chairperson, Department of Child and Family Studies, University of South Florida, Tampa, Florida, 33612

Emmons, R. A., & McCullough, M. E. (2003). Counting blessings versus burdens: An experimental investigation of gratitude and subjective well-being in daily life. *Journal of Personality and Social Psychology, 84,* 377–389.

Objective: To test the causal effect of gratitude on physical and psychological well-being.

Design: Between-subjects experiment.

Setting: Participants completed questionnaires in their homes and returned questionnaires either directly to the experimenter in a classroom setting (Studies 1 and 2) or by mail (Study 3).

Participants: Participants for Studies 1 and 2 consisted of college students. Study 1 included 146 female and 54 male undergraduate students. Study 2 participants consisted of 125 female and 41 male undergraduate students. Participants in Study 3 were 44 female and 21 male adults with congenital and adult-onset neuromuscular disorders.

Manipulated variables: In Study 1, participants were asked to complete 10 weekly reports of either gratitude, hassles, or meaningful events. In Study 2, participants were asked to complete 14 daily reports of either gratitude, hassles, or downward social comparisons. In Study 3, half of the participants completed 21 daily reports of gratitude, and the other half of the participants were assigned to a control condition and only completed the dependent measures for 21 days.

Assessment of predictor variables: In Study 1, dependent variables included self-reports of the following: mood (including grateful mood, as well as positive and negative affect), physical symptoms, reactions to aid received, time spent exercising, and global life appraisal.

In Study 2, dependent variables included self-reports of the following: mood, physical symptoms, health behaviors (including amount of strenuous and moderate exercise, number of caffeinated and alcoholic beverages consumed, number of pain relievers taken, and amount and quality of sleep), and prosocial behaviors.

In Study 3, dependent variables included self-reports of the following: mood, global life appraisals and feelings of connection with others, health behaviors (including amount and quality of sleep, ratings of physical pain, and amount of exercise), and difficulties with daily activities. In addition, the participants' significant others completed observer reports of the participants' positive and negative affect and life satisfaction.

Main results: In Study 1, participants who completed weekly gratitude reports rated their lives more favorably than those participants who wrote about hassles or meaningful events. Gratitude participants also reported fewer symptoms of physical illness than participants in the other two groups and spent more time exercising than participants in the hassles group. Across all three groups, feelings of gratitude in response to aid received was positively related to feelings of joy and happiness, favorable life appraisals, and optimism about the coming week.

In Study 2, participants who completed daily gratitude forms experienced an increase in positive affect over the 13 days of the study, when compared with participants who completed daily hassles forms. The effect that the daily gratitude versus daily hassles interventions had on positive affect was mediated by self-reported feelings of daily grateful mood. Writing daily about gratitude did not have an effect on physical symptoms or health behaviors, in contrast to Study 1. Participants in the daily gratitude condition reported offering more emotional support, in comparison with participants in the hassles and downward comparison groups, and gratitude participants also showed a marginal effect of self-reported helping of others, in comparison with the hassles participants.

In Study 3, writing about daily gratitude increased daily positive affect and decreased daily negative affect in participants, and these effects were mediated by daily felt gratitude. Participants in the gratitude condition also felt more satisfied with their lives, felt more optimism about the coming week, and felt more connected with others, relative to participants in the control condition. Gratitude participants also reported getting more sleep at night than control participants. Observer reports also rated participants in the gratitude condition as having higher positive affect and higher life satisfaction, in comparison with observer reports of participants in the control condition.

Conclusions: Focusing on gratitude rather than hassles, life events, downward social comparison, or a control group increases components of both psychological and physical well-being. These positive effects of writing about gratitude are mediated by the experience of gratitude and are not simply a general increase in positive affect.

Commentary: These studies provide good support for the positive potential of a grateful outlook on life. Researchers provided a number of different comparison conditions and dependent measures, and results generalized beyond college students to adults coping with neuromuscular disorders. These studies made good use of experimental design to test the causal relationship between a grateful outlook and well-being.

Correspondence: Robert A. Emmons, Department of Psychology, University of California, One Shields Avenue, Davis, California 95616, e-mail: raemmons@ucdavis.edu

Farwell, L., & Wohlwend-Lloyd, R. (1998). Narcissistic processes: Optimistic expectations, favorable self-evaluations, and self-enhancing attributions. *Journal of Personality, 66,* 65–83.

Objective: The study described here is the third in a series of three. Studies 1 and 2 demonstrated that individuals high in narcissism tended to have more optimistic expectations for the future and to possess enhanced self-evaluations. Study 3 investigated the effect of narcissism on perceptions of a collaborator in the context of a collective group project.

Design: Correlational.

Setting: This study was conducted in a laboratory setting.

Participants: Participants were 37 female and 30 male undergraduate students enrolled in an introductory psychology class.

Assessment of predictor variables: Participants' narcissism scores were collected using the Narcissistic Personality Inventory (Raskin & Hall, 1979).

Assessment of outcome variables: Individuals were paired with partners. Participants were asked to predict how successful they and their partners would be on a joint creativity test. Each participant was asked to predict his or her own performance on the test and his or her partner's individual performance, as well as their joint performance. After being given bogus positive feedback about the outcome of the task, participants were asked to rate the extent to which they thought their own performance was due to luck, task ease, own ability, own effort, as well as partner ability and effort. Participants also rated items measuring personal affect (e.g., pride) and interpersonal affect (e.g., gratitude).

Main results: Narcissism was positively related to prediction of a participant's own performance on the upcoming test and negatively related to predictions of a partner's performance. Narcissism was not related to predictions of joint performance. Narcissism was related positively to individuals attributing test success to their own ability and efforts, but it was unrelated to ascribing the success to external factors such as luck, task ease, or a partner's ability and effort. Interpersonal affect (gratitude) was negatively related to narcissism.

Conclusions: The trait of narcissism is comprised of optimistic expectations about the future, as well as positive overassessments of one's current outcomes. Narcissism is related to attributing success to one's own efforts, but is not related to a disinclination to attribute success to a collaborator's effort or ability. This suggests a self-aggrandizement component to narcissism, rather than other-derogation. Narcissism was also related to less liking and gratitude toward one's collaborator. These results raise the possibility that narcissism can be disruptive in interpersonal contexts.

Commentary: Although not direct measures of gratitude, increased attributions to one's own ability and effort can be related to the inhibition of gratitude, in that the experience of gratitude requires that one recognize the contributions of others. If one is too caught up in self-aggrandizement (as narcissists appear to be), this may take one's attentional focus off other-oriented attributions necessary for gratitude.

Correspondence: Lisa Farwell, Department of Behavioral Studies, Santa Monica College, 1900 Pico Boulevard, Santa Monica, California 90405

Fredrickson, B. L., Tugade, M. M., Waugh, C. E., & Larkin, G. R. (2003). What good are positive emotions in crises? A prospective study of resilience and emotions following the terrorist attacks on the United States on September 11th, 2001. *Journal of Personality and Social Psychology, 83,* 365–376.

Objective: To examine the occurrence and function of positive emotions following a crisis. Specifically, researchers tested the hypotheses that positive emotions such as gratitude, interest, and love would have calming physiological effects, broaden people's ways of thinking, and build resources for future coping.

Design: One-group pretest-posttest.

Setting: Laboratory.

Participants: Participants were 18 male and 29 female undergraduates and recent graduates of the University of Michigan.

Assessment of predictor variables: Participants completed a number of questionnaires before the September 11, 2001 crisis, including measures of ego-resiliency (Block & Kremen, 1996), a selection of three of the Big Five personality measures (Neuroticism, Extraversion, and Openness; Costa & McCrae, 1992), the Satisfaction with Life Scale (SWLS; Diener, Emmons, Larsen, & Griffin, 1985), the Life Orientation Test (LOT; Scheier & Carver, 1985), and a measure of tranquility constructed from two tranquility-related filler items from the LOT.

Assessment of outcome variables: Participants returned to the lab for the post-crisis measures from September 23, to November 6, 2001, during which a number of world events related to the September 11th crisis continued to unfold. Participants rated their current mood, and wrote about the most important problem or stressor they had experienced since September 11, 2001. They completed a questionnaire about finding positive meaning in their current problems, and rated the extent to which they had experienced numerous positive and negative emotions since the September 11th attacks. Participants also noted their depressive symptoms on the Center for Epidemiological Studies-Depression Measure (CES-D; Radloff, 1977). Finally, participants completed post-crisis questionnaires of the SWLS, the LOT, and tranquility, using the same questionnaires that were used precrisis.

Main results: None of the participants reported losing a loved one in the September 11th attacks. The most frequently experienced emotions after the attacks were sympathy/compassion, gratitude, interest, love, and anger. Higher levels of trait resiliency were related to lower levels of sadness, and higher levels of interest, joy, hope, sexual desire, pride, and contentment. Individuals with high trait resiliency also reported less depression and increased psychological resources, and these effects were mediated by the experience of positive emotions (including gratitude).

Conclusions: After the September 11th crisis, gratitude was one of the positive emotions experienced by individuals with both high and low trait resiliency. Participants felt grateful for their own safety and the safety of those close to them. Although all participants experienced negative emotions in the aftermath of this crisis, the experience of positive emotions such as gratitude, love and interest helped to buffer resilient individuals from the negative emotions and psychological symptoms that a crisis normally brings. The authors concluded that the experience of positive emotions is one of the key components of trait resilience.

Commentary: Although not centered specifically on gratitude, this study demonstrates some adaptive functions that grateful feelings might share with other positive emotions in the context of a crisis. It also suggests that gratitude can occur not only in response to positive outcomes, but also in the midst of negative world events. Teigen (1997), reviewed below, discusses the role of counterfactual thinking in the experience of gratitude, and counterfactual thinking ("It could have been worse") may be an important factor in the experience of gratitude in response to negative outcomes such as the September 11th attacks.

Correspondence: Barbara L. Fredrickson, Department of Psychology, University of Michigan, 525 East University Avenue, Ann Arbor, MI, 48109–1109. E-mail: blf@umich.edu.

Gallup, G. H., Jr. (1998, May). *Thankfulness: America's saving grace.* Paper presented at the National Day of Prayer Breakfast, Thanks-Giving Square, Dallas.

Objective: To explore the nature of gratitude in adults and teenagers in the United States.

Design: Two telephone interview polls.

Setting: The adults were surveyed from U.S. homes in mid-April, 1998. Teenagers were surveyed during the period between January and March, 1998.

Participants: There were 482 adults, aged 18 and older, and 500 teenagers between the ages of 13 and 17.

Assessment of predictor variables: Participants were from one of two samples: an adult sample or a sample of teenagers.

Assessment of outcome variables: Participants answered self-report rating measures on the following topics: frequency of expressing gratitude to others, frequency of expressing gratitude toward God, different ways they might express gratitude, whether expressing gratitude makes them happy, and how many people they know who seem to be grateful all the time for no reason.

Main results: Most adults in the United States say that they express gratitude to God (54%) and to others (67%) "all the time." The rank order of endorsed ways of expressing gratitude were as follows: telling family and friends that one is grateful to them (96%), worshipping and praying (85%), giving money to charity (81%), community service (70%), and saying grace at meals (64%). The majority of adults said that expressing gratitude made them "extremely happy" (60%). Only 25% of adults said that they know a lot of people who are dispositionally grateful, whereas 68% said that they know a few people who are grateful all the time. Results for teenagers paralleled those for adults, although teens tended to express less gratitude.

Conclusions: The author contrasts gratitude with the negative view that many have of society. The fact that so many people report gratitude, and endorse so many different forms of gratitude, paints a more optimistic picture of humanity.

Commentary: This study is useful in showing the importance of gratitude in the everyday lives of individuals. People seem to perceive an abundance of gratitude in society, and to see gratitude as a positive emotion, the expression of which brings happiness into their lives.

Correspondence: No information listed.

Gillani, N. B., & Smith, J. C. (2001). Zen meditation and ABC relaxation theory: An exploration of relaxed states, beliefs, dispositions, and motivations. *Journal of Clinical Psychology, 57,* 839–846.

Objective: To investigate the psychological effects of Zen meditation on experienced practitioners.

Design: Between-subjects quasi-experiment.

Setting: All participants were tested in the Chicago area. Participants in the Zen meditation group were tested during regularly scheduled weekly group meditation in their Buddhist temples. Participants in the control group were tested in a general psychology class at a junior college.

Participants: Participants included 59 Zen meditators from local Japanese Zen temples, and 24 students from a local junior college.

Assessment of predictor variables: Participants in the meditation group engaged in Zen meditation for about an hour during a regularly scheduled group meditation session. Participants in the control group engaged in a silent 60-minute relaxation activity that consisted of reading leisure material during class. Participants were not randomly assigned to experimental conditions.

Assessment of outcome variables: Outcome variables consisted of self-report responses to items from the Smith Relaxation Inventory Series (Smith, 2001), which assesses variables associated with successful relaxation. In constructing the Smith Relaxation Inventory Series, Smith and his colleagues used a lexicographical technique to identify words that people used to describe experiences that they had while engaging in methods of relaxation, such as yoga and meditation. Through factor analysis, Smith and his colleagues constructed 15 relaxation state factors (R-States), including the relaxation state most relevant to gratitude: *Love and Thankfulness.* Participants filled out reports about their experiences of relaxation states before and after the experimental intervention. In addition, they filled out questionnaires about their relaxation beliefs (R-Beliefs), their propensities to experience a particular relaxation state over a 2-week period of time (R-Dispositions), their motivations to experience more of a given relaxation state (R-Motivations), and attitudes they might have that are not conducive to relaxation (R-Attitudes). The factor *Love and Thankfulness* took the form of an R-State, an R-Belief, and R-Disposition, and an R-Motivation. All scales were given before the intervention, and the R-State items were given again after the intervention.

Main results: Meditators scored higher than control participants on the pretest of the R-Motivation of *Love and Thankfulness.* In other words, experienced meditators were more motivated to experience the relaxation state of *Love and Thankfulness* than were control participants. There were no group differences on pre-session measures of the R-State *Love and Thankfulness,* but after the intervention, participants who had meditated reported higher levels of love and thankfulness, whereas control participants did not report change in this variable.

Conclusions: Because of the quasi-experimental nature of this experiment, it was not possible to know whether differences between mediators and controls were due to meditation or to other demographic variables. It is also possible that individuals who are more prone to focus on love and thankfulness are also more likely to engage in Zen meditation. However, the fact that meditators experienced a change in presession to postsession love and thankfulness suggests that thankfulness is an important component of Zen meditation.

Commentary: The results of this research suggest that gratitude is an important outcome of Zen meditation. In light of the possible positive effects of gratitude on psychological and physical well-being (see Emmons & McCullough, 2003, listed previously), the exploration of different techniques of inducing gratitude is important for practitioners and researchers alike.

Correspondence: Jonathan C. Smith, Director, Roosevelt University Stress Institute, Roosevelt University, 430 South Michigan Avenue, Chicago, Illinois 60605

Graham, S. (1988). Children's developing understanding of the motivational role of affect: An attributional analysis. *Cognitive Development, 3,* 71–88.

Objective: These researchers used two studies to explore the development of the understanding of attributional processes behind complex emotions.

Design: Laboratory experiment.

Setting: Research rooms at a university-affiliated elementary school.

Participants: Study 1 participants consisted of 125 children from three age groups: 5- to 6-year-olds ($n = 34$), 7- to 8-year-olds ($n = 46$), and 10- to 11-year-olds ($n = 39$), divided approximately evenly by sex within each age group. Only children who had some knowledge about pride, gratitude, and guilt were included in the study. The experimenter asked children to tell her what would make them proud/grateful/guilty. Children were retained as participants if they mentioned an accomplishment as a source of pride, another's actions as a source of gratitude, and a wrongdoing as a source of guilt.

Study 2 participants were recruited from the same elementary school as those from Study 1, and consisted of 105 children from three different age groups: 5- to 6-year-olds ($n = 38$), 7- to 8-year-olds ($n = 32$), and 10- to 11-year-olds ($n = 35$).

Manipulated variables: In Study 1, children were presented three stories, each involving a different emotion: pride, gratitude, or guilt. In the pride scenarios, the situation was either caused by the protagonist of the story, or by other people/outside forces (locus). In the gratitude and guilt scenarios, the protagonist either did or did not have control over his or her actions (controllability). In Study 2, the same three scenarios were presented, with similar variations. In addition, researchers manipulated how much of the emotion the protagonist in each scenario might feel. Target children in the scenario were either said to have felt a lot or none of the emotion in question (pride, gratitude, and guilt).

Assessment of outcome variables: In Study 1, after being told each scenario, children were asked to rate the causes of the outcome of each scenario in terms of locus for the pride scenario and controllability in the gratitude and guilt scenarios. Next, they were asked to rate the affective responses of the target child—how proud, grateful, and guilty the target child would be for the respective scenarios. They were also asked to rate the intensity of an irrelevant affect for each scenario: *angry* (pride scenario), *scared* (gratitude scenario) and *glad* (guilt scenario). Last, children rated a series of behavioral intentions. In the pride scenario, they rated how many gold stars the child would give himself or herself for getting an *A* on a test; in the gratitude scenario, they rated how likely the target child would be to give a gift to the team captain who picked him or her for a team; and in the guilt scenario, they indicated how much money the target child should give to another child whose bike he or she had damaged.

In Study 2, children were asked to rate the same behavioral intentions of the target children presented in Study 1. In this way, the researchers investigated in Study 2 whether attributions and affect were direct causes of behavioral intentions.

Main results: In Study 1, irrelevant affect was not rated highly by children in any age group. Looking specifically at gratitude, all age groups perceived that controllable causes elicited more gratitude, but this was perceived significantly more distinctly by the 8- and 10-year-olds. Additionally, all children were more likely to say that the target child would reciprocate with a gift when the cause was controllable, but again this effect was significantly more prominent for the 8- and 10-year-olds. Correlational analyses showed that, as children get older, their evaluations of characters' likely attributions, affects, and behavioral intentions become more highly interrelated.

In Study 2, a significant main effect was present for affect: The amount of pride, gratitude, or guilt that the target child was said to have felt influenced participants' judgments of behavioral intentions. In relation to gratitude, feelings of gratitude in the target child caused participants to rate that the child was more likely to reciprocate a positive outcome with a gift. There was also a main effect for controllability, with participants inferring gift giving when the cause was controllable, but this accounted for much less variance than felt gratitude. Although there were age by affect interactions with pride and guilt, there was no significant interaction with gratitude.

Conclusions: As children age, their understanding of complex emotions, including gratitude, increases. Children as young as 5 understand that a controllable positive event elicits more gratitude than one that was uncontrollable, and that gratitude leads to a greater probability of reciprocating a favor. As children grow older, these associations between controllability, gratitude, and reciprocation become more developed and interrelated.

Commentary: This set of studies shows that even young children have some knowledge about the events that elicit gratitude, as well as the behavioral intentions paired with this emotion. Future developmental studies could move beyond the sole use of scenarios, to behavioral measures of gratitude.

Correspondence: Sandra Graham, Graduate School of Education, University of California, Los Angeles, California 90024

Graham, S., & Barker, G. P. (1990). The down side of help: An attributional-developmental analysis of helping behavior as a low-ability cue. *Journal of Educational Psychology, 82,* 7–14.

Objective: To investigate whether the receipt of help can serve as a cue for low ability, and whether this effect differs for children of various age groups.

Design: Between-subjects experiment.

Setting: An elementary school room outside of participants' classrooms.

Participants: Participants were 90 elementary school children. Children were selected to vary by age, with 15 female and 15 male participants from each of the following age categories: ages 4–5, ages 7–8, and ages 11–12.

Assessment of predictor variables: Experiment 2 contained the gratitude-relevant measures; therefore only information from Experiment 2 will be reported. The predictor variable (help/not help) was manipulated by having children watch a video where a teacher is supervising a math test. She glances at the paper of one student and walks by, then glances at the paper of another student and gives him unsolicited help. Both students are then seen turning in their papers, and are told that they did well on the test (scored 8 out of 10 problems).

Assessment of outcome variables: After watching the video, participants filled out questionnaires about the effort and ability of each of the two students in the video. Additionally, they rated the extent to which each of the students would feel happiness, pride, gratitude, sadness, and worry. Participants were also asked which of the two students they would choose to work with in a group math task.

Main results: Children age 7 and older rated the helped students as lower in ability than the nonhelped student. Children of all age groups rated the nonhelped student higher on effort. Ratings of happiness differed by age, with the oldest children rating the helped and nonhelped students as equally happy. Older children rated the nonhelped student as higher in pride, whereas younger children did not make a distinction between students in ratings of pride. All children rated the helped child as feeling more gratitude than the nonhelped child, demonstrating a link between attributing success to an external source, and feelings of gratitude. Though this effect was significant, it is interesting to note that children still rated grateful feelings of nonhelped children between 2 and 3 on a 1–7 scale. Children did not rate the students as overly sad or worried. Lastly, older children were more likely than younger children to pick the nonhelped student as a future group member.

Conclusions: Receiving unsolicited help in an achievement context serves as a low-ability cue, especially after ages 5–6.

Commentary: The gratitude-relevant dependent measure provides further support for the hypothesis that gratitude is elicited by positive outcomes due to external agents. The low but nonzero ratings of gratitude of the nonhelped student also point to the possibility that people may perceive a least a small amount of gratitude for positive outcomes, regardless of agent. This study is limited by its scenario methodology (the children were not actually experiencing gratitude themselves, but inferring it in others), but also contains a strong point in its developmental perspective.

Correspondence: Sandra Graham, Graduate School of Education, University of California, Los Angeles, CA 90024.

Graham, S., Hudley, C. & Williams, E. (1992). Attributional and emotional determinants of aggression among African-American and Latino young adolescents. *Developmental Psychology, 28,* 731–740.

Objective: To determine whether aggressive children differed in the intentionality attributions they made for others' ambiguous behavior with negative outcomes, and whether this increase in intentionality attribution led to increases in anger and aggressive action tendencies.

Design: Mixed-model experiment.

Setting: Classrooms and resource rooms in a junior high school that primarily served students from families with low socioeconomic status.

Participants: Participants were 88 students (74 males and 14 females) from the 7th and 8th grades.

Assessment of predictor variables: An aggressive group of 44 students was created through peer and teacher nominations. A control group was created of 44 nonaggressive students that matched the aggressive group by gender and ethnicity. Children were presented with 8 stories in which they were to imagine themselves as the protagonist. In the stories, the protagonist experiences a negative outcome, caused by a hypothetical peer. Each story had 4 different versions which differed by intention: prosocial, accidental, ambiguous, and hostile. Children read one story paired with a prosocial intent, one with a hostile intent, two with accidental intent, and four with ambiguous intent. The authors presented an example of one of the 8 stories, which asks children to imagine that one of their homework papers blows away, and another child steps on the paper and leaves a muddy footprint on it. In the prosocial intent condition (which is the condition most relevant to feelings of gratitude), the story continues, "The other kid turns to you and says, 'I could see that your paper was going to blow in the gutter. I'll help you copy it over'" (p. 734). In comparison, the hostile version of the story reads "The other kid laughs at you, says, 'That was your tough luck,' and then turns and runs into the school."

Assessment of outcome variables: Children responded to dependent measures on questionnaires. They were asked about the intentionality in each of the stories, as well as how mad, angry, and thankful they would feel for each story. Lastly, children were asked to rate their behavioral intentions for each story, with behavioral intentions ranging from prosocial to indirectly and directly aggressive.

Main results: Ratings of intentionality were lowest for the accidental and prosocial versions of the stories, and highest for the hostility versions of the stories, with ambiguous stories rated as intermediate in intentionality. Aggressive children rated ambiguous stories as more intentional than did nonaggressive children. Participants also reported lower levels of anger for the prosocial stories, and higher levels of anger for hostile stories. There was also a main effect for aggression, with aggressive children feeling more anger than nonaggressive children. All children reported feeling more gratitude for the prosocial story, compared to all the other story versions. Regarding action tendencies, aggressive children were more likely to endorse the behavioral options of "get even" and "have it out right then and there," compared to nonagressive children. The authors then used EQS to test an attributional explanation of aggression, which states that attributions cause emotions, which in turn cause action tendencies. The attributional model was the best fit to the data.

Conclusions: The attributional model provides a good explanation for childhood aggression. Aggressive children were more likely to perceive intention in ambiguous negative situations, and reported more feelings of anger in reaction to negative situations.

Commentary: Both aggressive and nonaggressive children inferred gratitude when the story stated that the other child was trying to help the protagonist. This provides further support that gratitude serves as an indicator that one has received a benefit from an external agent.

Correspondence: Sandra Graham, Graduate School of Education, University of California, Los Angeles, CA 90024.

Harris, M. B. (1972). The effects of performing one altruistic act on the likelihood of performing another. *Journal of Social Psychology, 88,* 65–73.

Objective: To determine whether engaging in a prosocial action in the absence of reinforcement will make one more likely to act prosocially in the future, and to compare the effects of reward, punishment, and no reinforcement on later prosocial behavior.

Design: Study 1 was a controlled field experiment. Study 2 was a laboratory experiment.

Setting: Study 1 was conducted on a street in the Albuquerque, New Mexico, area. Study 2 was conducted in classrooms from 12 classes at the University of New Mexico. These classes ranged from freshman to graduate level and were in four different departments.

Participants: Participants in Study 1 were 54 people walking down the street. Locations varied from campus to different shopping centers to busy streets. Participants in Study 2 were 276 students from the University of New Mexico.

Manipulated variables: In Study 1, participants were randomly assigned to one of three conditions. The experimenter stopped participants on the street. In the time condition, the experimenter asked the participant what time it was. In the directions condition, the experimenter asked participants for directions to another street. When the time or directions were given, the experimenter repeated the information in a neutral tone and then asked participants for a dime. In the dime-only control condition, the experimenter said only, "Excuse me" and asked participants for a dime.

In Study 2, participants were asked to volunteer to write a letter to a high school student and offer to answer any questions the student might have about the university. After writing the letters, participants were randomly assigned to one of three response conditions. Participants in the no-response control condition did not receive responses to their letters. Participants in the positive-response condition and the negative-response condition received letters, ostensibly from the high school students to whom they had written. Letters in the positive-response condition expressed gratitude at participants' offer to help them out. Letters in the negative-response condition contained negative comments in response to the participants' offer of help.

Assessment of outcome variables: In Study 1, after the experimenter made his or her first request (if any), he or she then asked participants for a dime. The dependent measure was whether the participant gave the experimenter a dime.

In Study 2, participants received a second, unrelated request for help 2 weeks after the first request and 10 days after receiving a response, if any. A student made an announcement to all 12 classes asking for volunteers to help with a publicity campaign to inform people about the work the university does with the community. The dependent measure was whether participants signed up to help with this project.

Main results: In Study 1, more participants in the Time condition (44.4%) and the Directions condition (38.9%) gave the experimenter a dime, as compared with those in the control condition (11.11%). In Study 2, more students who had heard the original request to write letters (17.6%) signed up to help with the publicity campaign, as compared with students who were absent or in a control class and did not hear the first request (8.9%). However, there were no significant differences in subsequent helping between the positive-, negative-, and no-response conditions.

Conclusions: These studies suggest that helping someone makes a person more likely agree to subsequent requests for help, at least if the subsequent request occurs relatively close in time to the first request. This effect is independent of the type of feedback received, as participants who were both positively and negatively reinforced showed increased rates of subsequent helping. Nor is actual helping necessary to increase later helping: Participants in Study 2 who heard the first request but did not help (16.7%) still showed increased subsequent helping when compared with the students who were absent when the request was made (9.5%) or enrolled in another section (8.8%). The author explains these results using a social norm interpretation: Being asked for help makes a norm of social responsibility salient, causing an increase in later help.

Commentary: The results of this experiment contrast with other studies summarized in this bibliography that showed increased helping following a positive reinforcement (Clark et al., 1988; Moss & Page, 1972; Rind & Bordia, 1995). However, Harris found that this effect does not necessarily occur if the second request occurs a relatively long time after the initial helping behavior. One aspect of the present study that is different from the others is the time lag between the positive and negative reinforcement and the second request (10 days). In contrast, the time lags for the Clark et al. and the Moss and Page studies were only a few minutes, whereas the time lag in the Rind and Bordia study was undetermined, but potentially only a day or two. These differences suggest that, if there is a reinforcing effect of gratitude, it may last only a short while. Further studies need to explore the effects over time that factors such as gratitude and the salience of social norms have on future prosocial behavior. Alternatively, it may be that the positive reinforcement of gratitude may only increase prosocial behavior toward the person who originally expressed the gratitude. Of the previously cited studies, the two that found effects for gratitude (Clark et al., Rind & Bordia) showed that participants were more likely to help the same person who expressed gratitude to them. Study 2 of the present set of experiments, which compared the effects of positive, negative, and no reinforcement, presented participants with opportunities to help two different sets of individuals. If, instead, participants were given a second opportunity to help the same individuals who gave them reinforcement, the effects of gratitude might be seen more clearly.

Correspondence: Mary B. Harris, Department of Educational Foundations, University of New Mexico, Albuquerque, New Mexico 87106

Harris, P. L., Olthof, T., Meerum Terwogt, M., & Hardman, C. E. (1987). Children's knowledge of the situations that provoke emotion. *International Journal of Behavioral Development, 10,* 319–343.

Objective: To investigate children's understanding of the situational determinants of complex emotions.

Design: Mixed model experiment. Researchers presented two studies; however, only Study 1 contained measures relevant to gratitude.

Setting: The setting is not explicitly stated; however it is assumed that children were tested at their respective schools.

Participants: Participants were 80 children from Oxford or Amsterdam. Although not directly noted, it is assumed that researchers recruited equal numbers of English and Dutch children.

Assessment of predictor variables: Twenty children each were recruited from each age group: 5 years, 7 years, 10 years, and 14 years. Children were presented with 20 emotion terms, including *grateful.* English-speaking children were presented stimuli in English, and Dutch children in Dutch.

Assessment of outcome variables: For each emotion term, children were asked to describe a situation that would evoke that particular emotion. Children ages 5 and 7 years were interviewed individually, whereas children ages 10 and 14 completed questionnaires. Two judges read children's responses and rated the emotion that was most likely to have been the stimulus. Responses were given 1 accuracy point if one judge picked the actual stimulus emotion, and 2 points if both judges picked the correct term.

Main results: Older children were more accurate than younger children in describing situations that elicited particular emotions. For English children, very few 5 year olds gave accurate descriptions of gratitude situations, whereas children 7 years and older were more accurate in their gratitude descriptions. Effects for gratitude in Dutch children were seen at age 10 and older. Cluster analyses revealed an "all-or-nothing" process of understanding emotion, with complex emotions (including gratitude) being acquired by children abruptly at later ages.

Conclusions: Results demonstrated that children were able to describe situations for more complex emotions that did not have distinctive facial expressions.

Commentary: These data speak to the complexity of gratitude. Unlike simple emotions such as *happy* or *angry*, gratitude takes longer for children to acquire. This study suggests that children understand the situations that elicit gratitude at around age 7 or older.

Correspondence: First author was at the University of Oxford at the time of this study.

Hegtvedt, K. A. (1990). The effects of relationship structure on emotional responses to inequity. *Social Psychology Quarterly, 53,* 214–228.

Objective: To examine the determinants of emotional responses to inequity. Specific to gratitude, this researcher predicts that overreward will be related to feelings of deservingness and gratitude, in addition to guilt. High status should be associated with feelings of deservingness, whereas low status should be associated with gratitude.

Design: Between–subjects experiment.

Setting: Classroom.

Participants: Participants were 118 female and 97 male undergraduate sociology students.

Manipulated variables: Participants were each given a vignette which described a student who needed a paper typed by a student typist. Participants imagined themselves in the role of the typist. Half of the vignettes portrayed the student seeking typing services as male, and the other half portrayed the student as female. Gender of the student was varied in order to manipulated status: Male participants typing for a female student were inferred to have higher status, whereas female participants typing for a male student were inferred to have lower status. Participants typing for same-sexed students were assumed to be equal in status. Vignettes were also written to vary in power: in the low power condition, the typist needed the job but few people needed typing services, and the student casually sought services among the many typists available. In the high power condition, the typist did not need the job and many students needed typing services, and the student desperately sought services from the few available typists. Finally, equity was manipulated by stating that the going rate for the job that the student needed was $30, and that the student either paid the typist $30 (equity), $20 (underreward), or $40 (overreward).

Assessment of outcome variables: Emotional responses were measured via questionnaire, and included ratings of satisfaction, deservingness, gratefulness, anger, resentfulness, helplessness, and guilt.

Main results: Underrewarded participants reported more distress than equitably rewarded participants, and overrewarded participants showed the least amount of distress. Higher power participants who had been equitably or overrewarded rated themselves as more deserving than did low power participants who were similarly rewarded. In contrast, low power participants who were equitably or overrewarded rated themselves as more grateful than high power participants receiving the same pay. There were no effects of status on deservingness or gratitude.

Conclusions: Rather than a simple relationship between inequity and emotional responses, this researcher found that reactions to inequity depended not only on the outcome/input ratio, but on the individual's power in the relationship.

Commentary: These results underscore the importance of expectations and deservingness in the experience of gratitude. Individuals who feel that they deserve beneficial treatment will be less likely to feel grateful for a benefit, whereas individuals who do not feel that they deserve a benefit will be grateful for it. One factor that determines feelings of deservingness and gratitude is relationship power, which in this study incorporated the need of the recipient and the value of the benefit.

Correspondence: Karen A. Hegtvedt, Department of Sociology, Tarbutton Hall at Emory University, 1555 Pierce Dr., Atlanta, GA, 30322.

Jackson, L. A., Lewandowski, D. A., Fleury, R. E., & Chin, P. P. (2001). Effects of affect, stereotype consistency, and valence of behavior on causal attributions. *Journal of Social Psychology, 141,* 31–48.

Objective: To compare the effects of anger and gratitude with sadness and happiness on causal attributions when target behavior varied in stereotype consistency and valence.

Design: Randomized experiment.

Setting: Laboratory.

Participants: Participants were 229 Anglo-American undergraduate psychology students (133 women, 96 men).

Manipulated variables: Participants were induced to experience an angry, sad, grateful, happy, or neutral mood. Participants in the four affect conditions were asked to think of an event that evoked the target affect in vivid detail and write about the event on a blank piece of paper. Participants in the neutral condition were asked to recall places they had been the previous day and write about those places and routes on a blank sheet of paper. Participants were then presented with a scenario about an African American man. This scenario manipulated stereotype consistency and valence. The stereotype-consistent positively valenced behavior presented the target as receiving a full athletic scholarship to play basketball at Duke University. Stereotype-consistent negatively valenced behavior presented the target as having been convicted of armed robbery. Stereotype-inconsistent positively valenced behavior presented the target as having received a full academic scholarship to Harvard University to study business administration. Stereotype-inconsistent negatively valenced behavior presented the target as having been convicted of computer theft and the diversion of corporate assets into a personal account.

Assessment of outcome variables: Causal attributions for the target's behavior were measured using the revised Causal Dimension Scale (CDSII) (McAuley, Duncan, & Russell, 1992), which assesses locus of causality, stability, personal control, and external control.

Main results: Positive affect, including gratitude, caused participants to attribute causality more strongly to the target than to the situation, to make more stable attributions, and to view the behavior as more controllable by the target and slightly less controllable by others. When compared with happy participants, participants induced to feel gratitude viewed the cause of positive behavior as more stable and slightly more controllable by the target. In contrast, happiness was related to more stereotypic thinking when the behavior was negative.

Conclusions: Cognitive appraisal dimension is an important factor to consider when looking at the effects of affect on social judgments. Additionally, it is important to consider both positively and negatively valenced behaviors when looking at attributions of behavior.

Commentary: Although gratitude is an affect or emotion, it has important cognitive components that may have consequences for other cognitions. The differential effects that gratitude and happiness had on attributions of behavior also underscores the idea that gratitude is not reducible to general positive affect.

Correspondence: Linda A. Jackson, Department of Psychology, Michigan State University, East Lansing, Michigan 48824, e-mail: jackso67@msu.edu

Lane, J., & Anderson, N. H. (1976). Integration of intention and outcome in moral judgment. *Memory and Cognition, 4,* 1–5.

Objective: To explore whether moral judgments follow the same cognitive algebra as nonmoral decision making. Specifically, these researchers were interested in whether a benefactor's *intention* in providing a benefit and the *value* of the benefit affect gratitude in a multiplicative manner.

Design: Randomized experiment.

Setting: Participants were tested individually in the laboratory. Sessions lasted about 30 minutes.

Participants: Participants were 20 students at the University of California, San Diego.

Manipulated variables: Participants were given paragraph vignettes as well as simple assertions that varied in intentionality and value. Each story contained a description of either a high, medium, or low intention, as well as a high, medium, or low benefit value. In addition, paragraph vignettes contained an additional condition in which value was not specified. Thus, the paragraph variables were arranged in a 3 x 4 design, and simple assertions were arranged in a 3 x 3 design. Participants read 12 randomly ordered paragraph vignettes, followed by 15 randomly ordered simple assertions.

Assessment of outcome variables: Participants were asked to rate how grateful the average person would be for each description.

Main results: Results for both paragraph and simple statement stimuli showed evidence for an averaging rule rather than a multiplicative one. Information about intentionality and value were averaged to determine level of gratitude, with higher levels of intentionality and value leading to greater anticipated experiences of gratitude.

Conclusions: The authors concluded that individuals weigh information about intentionality and value similarly. The averaging rule found in these studies is not intuitive, because the two pieces of information were not superficially similar. The authors cited other studies in which an additive-type rule was found when a multiplicative rule was instead expected. They speculated that deservingness might mediate the effect that intentionality and value have on gratitude—that when a well-meaning person tries hard to help us but fails, we still feel that the person deserves our gratitude.

Commentary: This experiment shows that, although intentionality and value are sufficient to elicit gratitude, both may not be necessary. Specifically, high value without intention may still bring forth some feelings of gratitude, and vice versa. This study has the advantage of an experimental design; however, this advantage is somewhat offset by the fact that hypothetical vignettes were used rather than actual gratitude situations that participants experienced. A good next step would be to look at participants' reactions to gratitude-eliciting stimuli in the laboratory.

Correspondence: Jeneva Lane, University of Oklahoma, Norman, Oklahoma 73069

McCullough, M. E., Emmons, R. A., & Tsang, J. (2002). The grateful disposition: A conceptual and empirical topography. *Journal of Personality and Social Psychology, 82,* 112–127.

Objective: To develop a measure of the disposition to experience gratitude, and to examine the correlates of gratitude as a personality trait.

Design: Correlational, using both self-reports and peer reports.

Setting: Studies 1 and 3 were conducted in undergraduate classrooms. Study 2 was based on a survey conducted on the Internet. Study 4 examined the extent to which the relationships found in Studies 1, 2, and 3 remained when extraversion/positive affect, neuroticism/negative affect, agreeableness, and social desirability were controlled.

Participants: Participants in Study 1 were 238 undergraduate psychology students (174 women, 57 men, 6 unrecorded). Study 1 also included 639 informants who were peers or family of 168 of the original participants. Participants in Study 2 consisted of 1,228 visitors (80% women, 15% men, 5% unrecorded; mean age = 44.6, *SD* = 12.0, *range* = 18–75) to the Web site for the magazine *Spirituality and Health* (http://www.spiritualityhealth.com) or other Web sites linked to the *Spirituality and Health* Web site. Participants in Study 3 were 156 undergraduate psychology students. Study 4 was based on a reanalysis of the data collected for Studies 1, 2, and 3.

Assessment of predictor variables: The grateful disposition was measured using the newly developed Gratitude Questionnaire-6 (GQ-6). In Study 1, this six-item questionnaire was created from a pool of 39 self-report items. The resultant GQ-6 was again administered in Studies 2 and 3. Study 2 also included an additional three-item adjective measure of the disposition to experience gratitude (using the adjectives *grateful, thankful,* and *appreciative*).

Assessment of outcome variables: Outcome variables in Study 1 included self-report questionnaire assessments of the following variables: life satisfaction (SWLS; Diener, Emmons, Larson, & Griffin, 1985), vitality (Ryan & Frederick, 1997), subjective happiness (Lyubomirsky & Lepper, 1999), optimism (LOT; Scheier, Carver, & Bridges, 1994), hope (Adult Hope Trait Scale; Snyder et al., 1991), positive and negative affect (PANAS; Watson, Clark, & Tellegen, 1988), anxiety and depressive symptoms (BFI; Derogatis & Spencer, 1982), dispositional empathy (empathic concern and perspective taking subscales of the Interpersonal Reactivity Index; Davis & Oathout, 1987), social desirability (BIDR; Paulhus, 1998), spiritual transcendence (STS; Piedmont, 1999), self-transcendence (Kirk, Eaves, & Martin, 1999) several single-item measures of religiousness, and the Big Five Inventory (John, Donahue, & Kentle, 1991). Study 1 also included peer reports of participants' gratitude (using a 12-item gratitude scale drawn from the same item-pool as the GQ-6), frequency of participants' prosocial action, participants' general prosocial tendencies, and participants' Big Five traits.

Study 2 also included identical self-report measures of positive and negative affect, life satisfaction, and spiritual transcendence. In addition, scores on the Big Five were assessed using Saucier's (1994) Big Five Mini-Markers scale, and the disposition to forgive was measured using 10 items based on McCullough, Worthington, and Rachal's (1997) theory of forgiveness.

Study 3 included identical measures of the Big Five Inventory (John, Donahue, & Kentle, 1991), anxiety and depressive symptoms, dispositional empathy, optimism, spiritual transcendence, and other religious variables. In addition, Study 3 also assessed materialism (Values-Oriented Materialism Scale—Richins & Dawson, 1992; and Belk Materialism Scale—Ger & Belk, 1990) and envy (Dispositional Envy Scale; Smith, Parrott, Diener, Hoyle, & Kim, 1999).

Main results: In Study 1, factor analyses revealed that the 39-item pool of gratitude items loaded strongly on a single factor. From this item-pool, six items were chosen that loaded strongly on the first factor and assessed unique aspects of the grateful disposition. This GQ-6 scale demonstrated good internal consistency reliability (α = .82). Discriminant validity was established by distinguishing the GQ-6 from measures of happiness, vitality, satisfaction with life, optimism, and hope. Self-reports and observer reports of grateful disposition were moderately positively correlated. Grateful disposition was moderately positively related to self- and peer reports of positive affect and well-being, prosociality, religiousness and spirituality, social desirability, extraversion, and agreeableness, and moderately negatively related to negative affect and neuroticism. When the GQ-6 was regressed on the Big Five, agreeableness predicted unique variance in GQ-6 scores.

Study 2 involved a cross-validation of the single-factor measurement model of the GQ-6. Both the GQ-6 and the adjective measure of grateful disposition were positively and moderately related to positive affect, life satisfaction, spiritual transcendence, forgiveness, agreeableness, conscientiousness, extraversion, and openness. Both gratitude measures were also moderately negatively related to negative affect and neuroticism. Agreeableness and neuroticism uniquely predicted scores on the GQ-6, whereas agreeableness and openness predicted unique variance in the adjective measure of the grateful disposition.

Study 3 provided additional support for the single-factor measurement model of the GQ-6. Dispositional gratitude was again positively associated with measures of positive affect and well-being, prosociality, spirituality/religiousness, and social desirability. Additionally, dispositional gratitude was negatively related to materialism and envy. Gratitude was positively correlated with agreeableness, extraversion, and conscientiousness, and negatively correlated with neuroticism. Agreeableness, neuroticism, and extraversion predicted unique variance in grateful disposition.

Results of Study 4 showed that relationships between the grateful disposition and other variables remained significant, though substantially reduced, when extraversion and positive affect were statistically controlled. The only exception was self-transcendence, whose correlation was not significant after controlling for extraversion and positive affect. Likewise, the relationships between grateful disposition and most other variables were reduced but still significant after controlling for neuroticism and negative affect. The only correlations that did not maintain their valence and statistical significance were correlations with anxiety and the possessiveness subscale of the Belk Materialism Scale. Similarly, correlations between grateful disposition and other variables, though reduced, maintained their valence and statistical significance after controlling for agreeableness, with the exception of the possessiveness and nongenerativity subscales of the Belk Materialism Scale. Last, correlations between the grateful disposition and other variables were reduced but still statistically significant after controlling for social desirability, with the exception of the success subscale of the Richins Materialism Scale.

Conclusions: Measures of the grateful disposition are related to other variables such as positive and negative affect, well-being, spirituality/religiousness, prosociality, materialism and envy. Though gratitude is related to different factors of the Big Five, the Big Five do not account for all of the variance in the grateful disposition. The relationship between the grateful disposition and other variables remains even after controlling for extraversion, agreeableness, positive and negative affect, and social desirability.

Commentary: This set of studies provides a gratitude questionnaire with good internal consistency reliability and discriminant validity. The grateful disposition was related in theoretically expected ways to other variables of interest. These studies provide a tool for examining the grateful disposition and its relationship to outcomes such as health and well-being.

Correspondence: Michael E. McCullough, Department of Psychology, University of Miami, 248185 Coral Gables, Florida, 33124-2070; e-mail: mikem@miami.edu

Robert A. Emmons, Department of Psychology, University of California, 1 Shields Avenue, Davis, California 95616; e-mail: raemmons@ucdavis.edu

Moore, D. W. (1996). Americans most thankful for family and health: Youth also thankful for career/job. Lincoln, NB: *The Gallup Poll Monthly.*

Objective: To explore what U.S. citizens list as the things they are most thankful for as the Thanksgiving season approaches.

Design: Telephone interview polls.

Setting: Polls were taken from U.S. homes from November 21 to November 24, 1996.

Participants: A randomly selected national sample of 1,003 adults, aged 18 years and older.

Assessment of predictor variables: Demographic information collected included participant age, ethnicity (black or white), and income.

Assessment of outcome variables: Interviewers asked participants, "As the Thanksgiving holiday approaches, we'd like to know what two or three things are you most thankful for in your life right now?" Participants were asked to provide up to three responses to this open-ended question.

Main results: The most common response was to mention family (61%), followed by own health (50%), job/career (21%), child/children (20%), spouse (12%), my life/just being alive (12%), freedom/living in the U.S. (10%), friends (8%), income/financial security (7%), home (7%), and God (5%). Older people were more likely to mention being thankful for their health, whereas younger people were more likely to mention their jobs or careers. More blacks mentioned being thankful for being alive (22%) than did whites (9%). This effect was also related to income, with lower income families more likely to be thankful for being alive.

Conclusions: U.S. citizens are most thankful for their families and their health, with certain demographic differences.

Commentary: This survey helped to flesh out the objects of many people's gratitude. It included individuals of many different ages, and compared ethnicities. A good first step in the study of gratitude is to find out what people are grateful for.

Moss, M. K., & Page, R. A. (1972). Reinforcement and helping behavior. *Journal of Applied Social Psychology, 2,* 360–371.

Objective: To determine the effects of positive versus negative reinforcement, as well as attractiveness of the reinforcer, on subsequent helping behavior.

Design: Controlled field experiment.

Setting: A main street in Dayton, Ohio, similar to many other metropolitan shopping areas.

Participants: Participants were 140 white individuals between the ages of 18 and 60, walking individually along the street. There were equal numbers of men and women.

Manipulated variables: Two female confederates administered the manipulation and dependent measures. The first confederate walked up to a participant and asked for directions to a popular local department store. After the participant gave directions, the confederate gave either a positive, neutral, or negative statement in response to the help. The positive response consisted of saying "thank you" and smiling. In the negative condition, the confederate cut the participant off just before he or she finished giving directions and said "I can't understand what you're saying, never mind, I'll ask someone else" (Moss & Page, 1972, p. 363). In the neutral condition, the confederate said "Okay" after receiving directions. There was also a control condition in which participants did not interact with the first confederate before encountering the second confederate. Attractiveness of the first confederate was also varied, so that she appeared attractive for half of the participants and unattractive for the other half.

Assessment of outcome variables: A second confederate was stationed about 75 feet from the first confederate. The second confederate began to walk toward the participant, and when she was within 6 feet of the participant, she dropped a small bag and continued walking down the street. The dependent measure consisted of whether the participant helped the second confederate by either picking up the bag or calling out to her.

Main results: Participants who received a negative response from the first confederate were less likely to offer subsequent help (43% helped) than participants in other conditions. There were no significant differences in helping between participants in the positive (93%), neutral (88%), and control (90%) conditions. There was an effect for attractiveness of the first confederate, in that participants were more likely to give physical help to the second confederate after interacting with an attractive first confederate, and they were more likely to give verbal help after interacting with an unattractive first confederate.

Conclusions: Individuals who are negatively reinforced for helping are less likely to give help in the future. The authors explained the lack of results for positive reinforcement by pointing to a possible ceiling effect in helping.

Commentary: We concur with the authors' explanation for the lack of effects of positive reinforcement. The prosocial behavior in this experiment involved little cost to participants, and therefore many participants in the control condition ended up helping. The effects of gratitude might be more clearly seen with helping behaviors that occur with less naturalistic frequency. Additionally, it may be that gratitude may only be effective as a positive reinforcer for prosocial actions toward the same reinforcing agent. In other words, expressed gratitude might have increased helping toward the first confederate but left behaviors toward the second confederate unchanged.

Correspondence: Martin K. Moss, Department of Psychology, Wright State University, Dayton, Ohio 45431

Okamoto, S., & Robinson, W. P. (1997). Determinants of gratitude expressions in England. *Journal of Language and Social Psychology, 16,* 411–433.

Objective: To explore factors affecting expressions of gratitude in England. These researchers hypothesized that expressions of gratitude would increase in politeness as the benefactor experienced more imposition when helping the receiver.

Design: Study 1 was a between-subjects field design. Study 2 was a questionnaire study.

Setting: Study 1 took place at the doors of the main library of the University of Bristol. Study 2 was administered during an introductory psychology class at the University of Bristol.

Participants: In Study 1, participants were 228 people (108 males, 120 females), mostly students, passing through doors of the main library of the University of Bristol. In Study 2, participants consisted of 120 undergraduates (39 males, 81 females) from the same university.

Manipulated variables: In Study 1, the experimenter opened doors for people passing singly through the doors. The experimenter held the door open in one of four ways, each way increasing in imposition to himself: 1) Experimenter going in same direction as participant, without looking back after opening the door (least imposition), 2) Experimenter going in same direction as the participant and making eye contact after opening the door; 3) Experimenter going in the opposite direction as participant, with the experimenter going through the door first, then holding open the door and making eye contact with the participant; and 4) Experimenter going in the opposite direction from the participant, letting the participant in first and making eye contact (most imposition).

For Study 2, participants were presented with one of two questionnaires that contained different versions of six randomly ordered vignettes. In the vignettes, a giver does a favor for the receiver. The vignettes were written to correspond to three responsibility conditions (neither person responsible for giver's behavior, receiver responsible, and giver responsible) along with two imposition conditions (large and small). For example, the neither/large vignette consisted of a giver lending valuable photos for the receiver's exhibition; for the receiver/small condition, the vignette described the giver's picking up a pen that the receiver had just dropped; for the giver/large condition, the vignette described the giver's returning money that was borrowed from the receiver, long after he or she had agreed to repay it. Participants were asked to imagine that they were the receiver in these scenarios under both of two status conditions (equal-status giver and high-status giver).

Assessment of outcome variables: In Study 1, the experimenter wrote down what participants said after the door was held open. In the condition in which the experimenter did not make eye contact with the participant, an observer noted what the participant said. These verbal expressions were coded for politeness.

In Study 2, participants wrote down what they would say in response to each vignette, depending on the status of the giver. Responses were coded for politeness. Participants also rated the imposition present in each vignette if a friend were the giver.

Main results: In Study 1, gratitude was expressed least frequently in the minimal imposition condition, where eye contact not made and the experimenter was the least imposed on. Accordingly, gratitude was expressed most frequently in the condition that posed the greatest imposition on the experimenter. When comparing the three conditions with the greater imposition, the condition with the most imposition elicited the most polite expressions of gratitude, and the condition that contained the least imposition of the three elicited more colloquial forms of gratitude.

Greater imposition led to greater politeness in Study 2 as well. For both equal-status and higher status givers, the greater the imposition, the longer the gratitude expressions and the more modifiers they contained. However, politeness was lower in response to giver-responsible vignettes. Along with gratitude expressions, researchers also looked for apology expressions in response to the vignettes. Expressions of apology were used most often in receiver-responsible vignettes but least often in the neither-responsible vignettes.

Conclusions: These studies reveal that more polite forms of gratitude expressions are used for favors of greater imposition. This effect occurred across different measurement designs and manipulations, with both equal-status and high-status benefactors. However, this effect was not present when the receiver was responsible for the imposition.

Commentary: Benefits that cause larger imposition to the benefactor call for more politeness and more expressed gratitude than smaller impositions. Future research can explore whether individuals who do not express the requisite level of gratitude in a situation with large imposition are seen as ungrateful, or whether there is a corresponding increase of actual experienced gratitude with increased imposition.

Correspondence: Shinichiro Okamoto, Department of Psychology, Faculty of Letters, Aichi Gakuin University, Nisshin-shi, Aichi 470–01, Japan, e-mail: okamoto@dpc.aichi-gakuin.ac.jp

Pyke, K., & Coltrane, S. (1996). Entitlement, obligation, and gratitude in family work. *Journal of Family Issues, 17*, 60–82.

Objective: To investigate how experience in a previous marriage affects feelings of gratitude and obligation in response to the division of household labor in second marriages.

Design: Correlational.

Setting: Questionnaires were filled out by participants at home and mailed back to the researchers. Interview setting was not specified.

Participants: Participants consisted of 97 husbands and 96 wives who had remarried. Spouses of participants were not allowed to participate in the study. Further qualifications included having at least one child in the home half the time, having a first marriage that had lasted one year or longer, and a second marriage that occurred at least one year ago. These 193 participants represented the survey sample. From this sample, 70 participants were selected for a follow-up interview.

Assessment of predictor variables: Predictor variables were assessed via questionnaire and interview questions. Predictor variables from the interviews included extramarital affairs during the first marriage, and the use of social comparison to previous marriages by participants. Predictor variables assessed in the questionnaires included family/gender ideology, employment hours, total household income, extramarital affairs during the first marriage, wife's earnings, wife's age, and presence of preschool children in the household.

Assessment of outcome variables: Dependent variables in the interview section included assessment of the proportion of household labor the husband contributed in a relationship (as rated by husbands or wives), and feelings of entitlement, obligation, and gratitude experienced by participants in their marriages. The dependent variable in the survey data was also the proportion of household labor contributed by the husband.

Main results: Interview data revealed that women tended to compare their second marriage with their first marriage, and this mitigated feelings of entitlement and bolstered feelings of gratitude. The authors also provided examples of men who compared their second marriage to their first. In some instances, men engaged in social comparison in order to justify a more traditional division of labor in their second marriage, and other times as an explanation for the high importance they now placed on egalitarianism. Interview data also revealed an effect for first marriage extramarital affairs by men. Women whose first husbands had engaged in extramarital affairs tended to experience gratitude at their current husband's fidelity. Similarly, men who had cheated in their first marriage felt entitled to gratitude from their wives for their current fidelity.

Questionnaire data revealed that remarried wives spent twice as much time on household labor as husbands. Husbands with more egalitarian family ideologies, and husbands who worked fewer hours contributed more to household labor. Wife's earnings and husband's family ideology were positively related to husband's household labor, whereas wife's family ideology and husband's first-marriage extramarital affair were negatively related to husband's proportion of household labor.

Conclusions: Experiences from prior marriages, such as experiences of husband's extramarital infidelity, affected division of household labor in second marriages, and feelings of entitlement and gratitude for the spouses' efforts in the home.

Commentary: Although this study did not contain an actual quantitative measure of gratitude, it still made some important theoretical and empirical points about the determinants of gratitude. Whereas results from Teigen (1997) and Fredrickson et al. (2003) focus on the role of "what could have been" in eliciting gratitude, this study shows that social comparison to "what was before" can also affect gratitude and related emotions. The results suggest that social comparison to past relationships might be an important determinant of gratitude in current relationships. Additionally, this study highlights the importance of individual construal in gratitude: the cost and value of various benefits are not static and objective—different benefits are worth more to some people than others, and some people feel entitled to more benefits than others. These differences in construals can be affected by factors such as previous relationship experience or sex role ideology, and they determine whether someone responds with gratitude to the action of a benefactor.

Correspondence: Contact information not provided. The first author was associated with the University of Southern California at the time of this study.

Rind, B., & Bordia, P. (1995). Effect of server's "thank you" and personalization on restaurant tipping. *Journal of Applied Social Psychology, 25,* 745–751.

Objective: To determine whether a server's expression of gratitude through writing "thank you" on the back of the check would increase the server's tip amount. Researchers also tested if adding a personal signature after writing "thank you" increased tips.

Design: Controlled field experiment.

Setting: Lunch hours (11:00 a.m. to 3:00 p.m.) at an upscale restaurant in Philadelphia, located on the University of Pennsylvania campus. The experiment was conducted in late spring over a 5-day period, from Monday through Friday.

Participants: Participants were 51 dining parties having lunch. Many of the participants were faculty and other university staff. Total participants were 137 customers, with a mean of 2.69 customers per party.

Manipulated variables: Dining parties were randomly assigned to one of three conditions. In the control condition, the server delivered the check without writing anything on the back of it. In the thank-you condition, the server wrote "thank you" on the back of the check. In the thank-you-plus-name condition, the server wrote "thank you" on the back of the check and signed her name directly under it. After writing the message, if any, on the check, the server placed the check on the party's table, face down, and had no further interactions with the party.

Assessment of outcome variables: The server recorded the tip amount, bill before taxes, size of the dining party, and method of payment for each party.

Main results: Tip amounts were larger for the thank-you condition (18.10%) and the thank-you-plus-name condition (18.01%) when compared with tip amounts in the control condition (16.28%). The two experimental conditions did not differ significantly. Tip amounts did not differ by party size or method of payment.

Conclusions: The authors framed the results in terms of impression-management theory, positing that expressing gratitude increased the server's perceived likability and friendliness, leading to increased influence and greater tip percentages. They listed several alternative explanations, such as increased perception of servers' expectations for tips; self-perception; or reciprocity

Commentary: This study supports the theory of gratitude as a moral reinforcer (McCullough, Kilpatrick, Emmons, & Larson, 2001). Benefactors—dining parties—who became the targets of gratitude from the server later increased their prosocial behavior by leaving higher tips. The strong point of this study is that it looks at behavioral outcomes of gratitude in a field setting. However, because perceived gratitude was not actually measured, the exact mechanisms driving the results of this study are not clear-cut. This shortcoming is small, because this study speaks to expressed rather than perceived gratitude.

Correspondence: Bruce Rind, Department of Psychology, Temple University, Philadelphia, Pennsylvania 19122, e-mail: rind@templevm

Russell, J. A., & Paris, F. A. (1994). Do children acquire the concepts for complex emotions abruptly? *International Journal of Behavioral Development, 17,* 349–365.

Objective: This set of two studies looked at the course of development of more complex emotions, such as gratitude or pride. Study 1 sought to determine whether children acquire concepts for complex emotions abruptly or in a gradual manner. Study 2 investigated the hypothesis that children initially understand complex emotions in terms of the bipolar dimensions of pleasure and arousal.

Design: Study 1 was a laboratory experiment employing a within-subjects, cross-sectional design. Study 2 was also a laboratory experiment, using a mixed-model, cross-sectional design with participants randomly assigned to rate a number of different emotions on one of two bipolar scales.

Setting: In Study 1, children were tested individually by an experimenter. Although the location was not explicitly stated, this study most likely was conducted in a laboratory. In Study 2, children were tested in a laboratory setting, whereas adults were presented the rating scales individually in public places such as shopping malls.

Participants: Study 1 participants were 96 children—12 girls and 12 boys at each of four ages: 4, 5, 6, and 7 years. Study 2 participants were 20 boys and 20 girls at each of two ages (4 and 5 years), as well as 20 women and 20 men older than 16 years.

Assessment of predictor variables: The predictor variables in Study 1 were the child's age and the specific emotion the child was asked to describe. The complex emotions examined were *proud, grateful, jealous, ashamed,* and *worried. Happy* was also included as a noncomplex control emotion. In Study 2, the predictor variables were the participants' age, the scale on which participants were rating emotions (pleasure or arousal), and the specific emotion participants were rating: complex emotions—*grateful, proud, ashamed, jealous,* and *worried;* and simple emotions—*happy, calm,* and *sad.*

Assessment of outcome variables: In Study 1, the experimenter asked children to tell a story about a fictional child who was feeling one of the tested emotions. The child was instructed to explain why the target child was feeling that emotion, and whether the target child was feeling good or bad. Children were asked to tell a separate story regarding each emotion. Their responses were coded first on the good/bad dimension (good = *happy, proud, grateful;* bad = *ashamed, jealous, worried).* Judges then rated whether the story the child gave for each emotion was appropriate to the given emotion, and a content analysis was done for each emotion. A correct response for *grateful* appeared when a story included "a positive event (statement, action, affection) from someone" to the target child (p. 353, Table 1). A modified version of the Harris, Olthof, Meerum Terwogt, and Hardman (1987) *best guess* procedure was also employed to differentiate emotion stories.

In Study 2, children were told that a stick figure was feeling a particular emotion and were asked to place this figure into one of five boxes corresponding to different ratings of either pleasure or arousal. Adults filled out a comparable rating questionnaire of either pleasure or arousal. Participants rated all eight emotions on the particular scale they were given.

Main results: In Study 1, results did not support either a strong or weak abruptness hypothesis; rather, they supported a gradual acquisition hypothesis. Children in the youngest age groups told better stories for some complex emotions than for others, with *jealous* producing the worst stories at the youngest ages, and *gratitude* producing slightly better stories. Additionally, the oldest children (7-year-olds), though they exhibited greater knowledge of the complex emotions, did not show complete knowledge when their stories about complex emotions were compared with their stories about the noncomplex emotion, *happy.* Many children showed a partial knowledge of complex emotions, their stories demonstrating knowledge of the emotion's positive or negative valence.

In Study 2, patterns of pleasure and arousal ratings given by children were similar to those given by adults, though the average pleasure and arousal scores did differ by age. For all age groups, the emotion *grateful* was rated above the mean on both pleasure and arousal.

Conclusions: The authors concluded that complex emotions are learned gradually, rather than abruptly. Younger children have some knowledge about the nature of complex emotions, such as their dimensions of arousal or pleasure. Older children, such as 7-year-olds, have a greater knowledge of complex emotions but do not have complete knowledge.

Commentary: These studies are an important step in determining the acquisition patterns of more complex emotions such as gratitude. They provide evidence that knowledge about gratitude is not acquired abruptly; rather, there is at least one inter-mediate stage in which children know general information about gratitude, such as its arousal and pleasure level. They demonstrate that children as young as 4 can have at least a rudimentary idea of what gratitude is like as an emotion.

Correspondence: James A. Russell, Department of Psychology, University of British Columbia, Vancouver, British Columbia, Canada V6T 1Y7, fax (604) 822 6923, email: jrussell@cortex.psych.ubc.ca

Saucier, G., & Goldberg, L. R. (1998). What is beyond the Big Five? *Journal of Person-ality, 66,* 495–523.

Objective: To find clusters of adjectives for describing people that are independent of the Big Five personality factors.

Design: Factor-analysis.

Setting: Not explicitly stated, but it is assumed that participants completed ratings in a classroom or related setting.

Participants: Participants were distributed among four original samples and one cross-validation sample. Of the original samples, Sample 1 consisted of 320 partici-pants and 316 of their peers. Sample 2 included 187 participants. Sample 3 consisted of 360 participants and 329 of their peers. Sample 4 consisted of 201 peer ratings. The cross-validation sample consisted of 694 participants, about 57% of whom were women, with an average age of approximately 50.

Derivation of clusters: The authors used a combination of factor analysis and intuitive methods to derive 53 clusters to identify sources of variance peripheral to the Big Five.

Cross-validation: These 53 clusters of adjectives were rated by the cross-validation sample in two iterations using a 7-point scale.

Main results: A "minimax" criterion was used to determine whether a given cluster was peripheral to the Big Five: minimum multiple correlation with the Big Five fac-tors, and maximum reliability. Using this criterion, the six clusters that stood out as being independent were *short-tall, busy-overworked, employed-unemployed, religious-nonreligious, young-youthful,* and *slim-slender.*

In contrast, the cluster *grateful-thankful* was not independent of the Big Five. Its multiple correlation with the Big Five was .40, and it was especially positively correlated with *agreeableness* ($r = .31$) and negatively correlated with *openness* ($r = -.24$).

Conclusions: "Gratefulness" (gratitude) does not seem to be an independent personality trait. Instead, the tendency to feel grateful is related to other personality characteristics, such as agreeableness and openness.

Commentary: Though not an independent personality dimension in its own right, gratitude might be thought of as the emotional and behavioral outcome of a combination of Big Five traits.

Correspondence: Gerard Saucier, Department of Psychology, 127 University of Oregon, Eugene, Oregon 97403, email: gsaucier@oregon.uoregon.edu

Teigen, K. H. (1997). Luck, envy, and gratitude: It could have been different. *Scandinavian Journal of Psychology, 38*, 313–323.

Objective: To investigate the relationship between good or bad luck, feelings of envy and gratitude, and the role of counterfactual thinking. Study 1 explored the meanings behind people's statements of luck in comparison to statements of goodness. Study 2 investigated the extent to which luck implied comparison with others, envy, gratitude, sympathy, and positive or negative impressions of the speaker. Study 3 tested whether the experience of gratitude makes people feel lucky, and whether the experience of envy causes people to feel unlucky and that someone else has been lucky.

Design: All three studies were within-subjects laboratory experiments.

Setting: Though not explicitly stated, it is assumed that all studies took place in a classroom or laboratory setting.

Participants: Study 1 participants consisted of 60 first-year psychology students at the University of Bergen, Norway. Study 2 participants were 262 first-year psychology students at the same university. Study 3 participants were 60 students from the same university.

Manipulated variables: Participants in Study 1 were presented with two pairs of statements. For each pair, one statement included the term *lucky*, and the other statement included the word *good*. For example, one pair of statements was as follows: "It is lucky that you have a job" and "It is good that you have a job." One pair of statements was phrased in first person: "I am lucky that . . ." whereas the second pair was phrased in second person "You are lucky that. . ."

Participants in Study 2 were presented with two out of 16 statement pairs. There were four sets of phrases, with each set having permutations: lucky/good second person—"It is lucky that you have a job" and "It is good that you have a job," and lucky/good first person—"It is lucky that I have a job" and "It is good that I have a job," and so on (unlucky/bad second person and unlucky/bad first person).

Participants evaluated one second-person and one first-person pair, with one statement in each pair being negative and the other positive.

Participants in Study 3 were asked to write two brief descriptions of situations in which they felt grateful for something. One description was to be of a situation in which participants had felt grateful to a specific person, and the other description was to be of a situation in which they felt a more abstract gratitude, perhaps toward life, or fate. After writing these descriptions of gratitude, participants were asked to write about a situation in which they felt envious of someone.

Assessment of outcome variables: Study 1 participants were asked to give a brief explanation of the meaning of both statements in each of the two pairs presented.

Study 2 participants rated each statement (using a 3-point scale) on whether it expressed *sympathy, envy, comparison with others*, and *expressing/requesting gratitude*. They also rated their impressions of the person issuing the statement, on a 3-point scale.

After completing the descriptions of gratitude and envy, participants in Study 3 completed questionnaires about each description. For the gratitude descriptions, participants rated the extent to which they felt *unlucky* and *lucky*, the extent to which the situation was *pleasant* or *unpleasant*, and whether *something else* could have easily happened. Participants also answered an open-ended question regarding other possible outcomes of the situation and rated this possibility in terms of pleasantness and unpleasantness. For the envy description, participants answered the same question, except that they rated the extent to which they felt someone else was lucky, rather than themselves.

Main results: In Study 1, several respondents perceived second-person luck statements to be more judgmental and demanding that the lucky person feel grateful, whereas similar goodness statements were perceived to be more neutral. First-person luck statements were also more likely than first-person goodness statements to elicit comments implying gratitude. In Study 2, positive first-person luck statements were seen as more expressive of gratitude than positive first-person goodness statements.

In Study 3, when asked to write descriptions of gratitude, most participants wrote about being grateful to specific people (personal gratitude) but seemed to have no problem generating descriptions of being grateful to abstract entities (impersonal gratitude). Of the 60 personal gratitude stories, 27 were about close friends, 12 were about parents or other relatives, and 21 were about strangers or more distant acquaintances. For strangers, the main elicitor of gratitude was lack of expectation, as when a stranger helps beyond the call of duty. Other objects of gratitude were concrete assistance, services, pleasant surprises, or emotional support. Of the impersonal gratitude stories, 27 cases were about particular episodes, such as dramatic situations that turned out better than expected, and 32 were more permanent descriptions of affairs, such as having healthy children or being alive in general. Both types of gratitude situations were described as lucky, and luck was independent of perceived pleasantness of the situation. Gratitude situations also elicited high ratings of "it could easily have been otherwise," and counterfactual alternatives were always rated as worse than what actually happened. In contrast, when people rated envy situations, they rated themselves as unlucky, whereas the objects of their envy were thought of as very lucky. Envy situations also elicited high counterfactual ratings, but these alternatives were always thought to be more positive than reality.

Conclusions: This study demonstrated the importance of counterfactual thinking in the relationship between attributions of luck, and envy and gratitude. Envy is felt if "things could have been better," whereas gratitude is often felt if "things could have been worse." In instances of envy, the self is seen as unlucky, whereas the self is seen as lucky in cases of gratitude. Although attributions of positive outcomes to external agents are an important source of feelings of gratitude, gratitude may be elicited by counterfactual thinking and feelings of luck.

Commentary: This set of studies is important for a number of reasons. First, Study 3 gives a sketch of the content of grateful descriptions. More important, it shows how different factors—attributions, counterfactual thinking, comparisons—play complex roles in the arousal of gratitude. Although external, intentional attributions for success are sufficient to elicit gratitude, they may not be the only possible antecedents of grateful emotion.

Correspondence: Karl Halvor Teigen, Department of Psychology, University of Tromsø, N-9037 Tromsø, Norway, email: karlht@psyk.uit.no

Tesser, A., Gatewood, R., & Driver, M. (1968). Some determinants of gratitude. *Journal of Personality and Social Psychology, 9,* 233–236.

Objective: To examine the effects of intention of benefactor, cost to benefactor, and value of benefit on receiver's feelings of gratitude.

Design: Randomized experiment.

Setting: Classroom of undergraduates at Purdue University.

Participants: Participants were 126 undergraduate men.

Manipulated variables: Three scenarios were written, with each scenario reflecting every possible combination of intention, cost, and value at three intensity levels. This led to 27 different vignettes. Each participant was asked to read one randomly assigned vignette from each of the three scenarios, imagining himself or herself as the receiver of the benefit in the scenario.

Assessment of outcome variables: Following each scenario were a number of questions. Participants were instructed to answer the questions from the point of view of the receiver. Manipulation checks asked about intentionality, cost, and value. Two 6-point scales were used to assess gratitude: Participants rated how grateful they felt toward the benefactor, and how indebted they felt.

Main results: The two items asking about felt gratitude and indebtedness were highly correlated, and the authors combined these items as a measure of gratitude. There was a significant main effect on felt gratitude for intention, cost, and value, and there were no interactions. Further analysis revealed that felt gratitude was a linear function of each of the independent variables. Regressions run separately on each scenario showed that intentionality and value significantly predicted gratitude with all three scenarios, but that cost was significant for only two scenarios.

Conclusions: These data support the hypothesis that intentionality, cost, and value are significant in determining feelings of gratitude.

Commentary: This study's strong point is the use of a randomized experiment to directly test hypotheses about gratitude. Its results show the importance of the factors of intentionality, cost, and value. However, a weakness in this study is its use of scenarios instead of actual gratitude situations. Regardless, this experiment is an excellent starting point in the study of gratitude.

Correspondence: No mailing address listed. The first author was affiliated with the University of Georgia at the time of this publication.

Van Overwalle, F., Mervielde, I., & De Schuyter, J. (1995). Structural modelling of the relationships between attributional dimensions, emotions, and performance of college freshman. *Cognition and Emotion, 9,* 59–85.

Objective: To use structural equation modeling to test Weiner's (1986) attribution model of emotions.

Design: Correlational.

Setting: Classroom.

Participants: Study 1 participants were 585 undergraduate students at two universities in Belgium. Study 2 participants were 621 undergraduate students from the same universities.

Assessment of predictor variables: In Study 1, participants were given questionnaires during class a few days after receiving scores on their midterm exams. Participants were asked for their midterm score, and rated their expectations about final exams, emotional responses to their midterm exams, and causal attributions about their midterms. The emotional dimension of *gratitude* was assessed using the items "gratefulness," "trust," and "appreciation" (p. 71). The causal attribution assessed that was relevant to gratitude was an external attribution of success to others.

   Study 2 measures were similar to those in Study 1, with the exception of the following: Participants were asked the extent to which they experienced gratitude and anger "toward the teachers who examined" (p. 76), and participants were asked attributional questions about external control that referred to "teachers who examined" rather than "other people" (i.e., "The cause of something is something I/teachers who examined can(not) do something about") (p. 76)

Assessment of outcome variables: In Study 1, academic performance was assessed through participants' scores on final exams. Study 2 outcome variables were identical to those in Study 1.

Main results: In Study 1, gratitude was significantly positively correlated with happiness, pride, hope, and expectation. It was not significantly correlated with other, negative emotions such as shame and anger. Structural equation models showed that gratitude was significantly related to a positive outcome on the midterm, but counter to predictions it was not significantly correlated with external attributions to others. (Another hypothesized effect between external attributions to others and anger also failed to materialize.)

In Study 2 the relationship between gratitude and midterm grade failed to reach significance. Like Study 1, there was no relationship between external control and gratitude and anger. However, when participants were divided into groups based on positive or negative outcome on their midterm exams, effects for gratitude and anger emerged: For participants who did well on their midterms, the path from gratitude to external control was significant and positive.

Conclusions: The authors explained the lack of significant effect between external control and gratitude and anger in Study 1 by suggesting that external attribution questions asking about "other persons" was too general. This led to the use of "the teacher" as a referent in Study 2. The results of Study 2 emphasized the importance of taking outcome into account when investigating social emotions such as anger and gratitude. In general, the authors found support for the relationship between attributions and emotion and for Weiner's (1986) idea of outcome-related and attribution-related emotions.

Commentary: These studies provide support for the proposal that gratitude is elicited by positive outcomes that are attributed to others, and underscore the positive emotional valence of gratitude.

Correspondence: Frank Van Overwalle, Pleinlaan 2, B-1050 Brussels, Belgium.

Ventimiglia, J. C. (1982). Sex roles and chivalry: Some conditions of gratitude to altruism. *Sex Roles, 8,* 1107–1122.

Objective: To investigate the effects of sex role on grateful responses of recipients of chivalrous action.

Design: Between-subjects experiment.

Setting: This study is a field experiment conducted in the entrances of a city library and a university library.

Participants: Participants were 479 individuals, 52% men and 48% women.

Assessment of predictor variables: The experimenter approached library doors shortly before the participant arrived, and held open the door for the participant. An observer recorded relevant predictor variables, including the participant's physical attractiveness, age, race, and need state. Setting was manipulated by gathering half of the data outside of a city library, and half of the data outside a university library. Sex of the benefactor was manipulated by using one male experimenter and one female experimenter.

Assessment of outcome variables: The observers coded participants' responses to the favor.

Main results: The two most frequent positive responses to door opening were thanking the benefactor, and smiling, whereas the two most frequent negative responses were obliviousness to the favor and hesitation. Examining these four responses, female participants were more likely to have higher percentages of positive responses and lower percentages of negative responses, when compared to male participants. Male experimenters were more likely to elicit negative responses from participants than were female experimenters. Setting (city vs. university library) had no interpretable effect on these positive or negative responses, aside from an effect of increased disapproval in city versus university libraries.

Coders used four categories to further classify participant responses: gratitude, *confusion, disapproval,* and *avoidance.* Gratitude responses included participant expressions of thanks, reciprocation, and smiles and nods directed at the experimenter; confusion responses consisted of puzzled looks, disagreements, and blushing; disapproving responses included frowns, laughter, and obliviousness toward the benefactor; and avoidance responses consisted of avoidance of eye contact with the experimenter, and hesitation. Participants demonstrated more gratitude in response to the favor when they had a higher need state, were older, more attractive, and female. More disapproval was elicited when the participant was entering the university library, when the person holding open the door was male, and when the participant was more attractive. Confusion occurred most often when the participant was male, or when the experimenter was female. Avoidance was more likely when the participant was physically attractive or male. Whereas female participants showed more gratitude, male participants tended to emit more confusion and avoidance.

Regarding the effect of sex roles on responses to a favor, male participants helped by a woman showed more confusion than did female participants helped by a man. Women helped by another woman exhibited more gratitude, less disapproval, and less avoidance than did men helped by another man.

Looking at the impact of physical attraction on the sex role effect on responses, unattractive female recipients helped by male benefactors showed the most gratitude, whereas unattractive male recipients helped by a female benefactor exhibited the least gratitude. With confusion, attractive female recipients helped by a male benefactor were least confused, whereas attractive male recipients helped by a female benefactor were most confused. Looking at same-sex recipient-benefactor pairs, attractive male and female recipients both showed more disapproval at a benefactor of the same sex, when compared with less-attractive participants.

Conclusions: The most frequent response to having a door held open was the expression of gratitude, either by saying "Thanks" or smiling or nodding. The effect of sex roles on gratitude—the most gratitude occurred when a man held open a door for a women—demonstrates that traditional norms regarding sex roles still affect individual's responses.

Commentary: Although these results are to a certain extent tied to the context of the "door-opening ceremony" (p. 1122), they underscore the importance of normative context in the study of gratitude. A benefit or favor that has negative ramifications for one's self-image, whether it be in the realm of sex roles, self-efficacy, or some other domain, may not be interpreted as a benefit, effectively tempering any gratitude effects.

Correspondence: The author was affiliated with Memphis State University at the time of this study.

Weiner, B., Russell, D., & Lerman, D. (1978). Affective consequences of causal ascriptions. In J. H. Harvey, W. J. Ickes, & R. F. Kidd (Eds.), *New directions in attribution research* (Vol. 2). Hillsdale, N. J.: Erlbaum.

Objective: To investigate the emotions elicited in an achievement context, and to examine the effects of internal and external attributions on these emotional responses.

Design: Between–subjects experiment.

Setting: Laboratory.

Participants: 90 undergraduate students.

Manipulated variables: Participants were given two achievement scenarios: one with a positive outcome, and one with a negative outcome. The scenario relevant to gratitude was the positive outcome scenario. Scenarios varied by the attributions presented for the outcome. Positive outcome scenarios contained one of following attributions: ability, personality, unstable effort, stable effort, other's effort, other's motivation and personality, task difficulty, luck, mood, and intrinsic motivation.

Assessment of outcome variables: After each scenario, participants rated 85 emotions that the researchers predicted would be related to success or failure. Participants only rated success-relevant emotions for the positive outcome scenario, and failure-relevant emotions for the negative outcome scenario.

Main results: Researchers listed the 10 most frequent emotions experienced for each attribution. Looking at the positive outcome scenario, the emotion *appreciative* was tied for second place for the attribution "other's effort" and tied for 6th for the attribution "other's motivation and personality." The emotion *thankful* was tied for first place for the attribution of "luck." Next, researchers determined "discriminating affects," or emotions that did not appear across all attributions. An emotion was considered discriminating if it's mean for one attribution was higher than the mean across the other attributions. The emotions *appreciative* and *grateful* appeared as discriminating affects for attributions to "other's effort." The emotions *grateful* and *appreciative* appeared for attributions to "other's motivation and personality." The emotion of *thankful* appeared for attributions to "luck." Other discriminating emotions that were associated with attributions to others effort and other's motivations were *composed, relaxed, proud, modest, thoughtful,* and *charmed.*

Conclusions: Gratitude is listed as a "dominant discriminating affect" for successes attributed to "other's effort and personality" (p. 76). The authors conclude that different attributions for success lead to specific emotional responses.

Commentary: These results support the prediction that feelings of gratitude are related to external attributions of positive outcomes to help from other people or from abstract external agents such as luck.

Correspondence: No contact information is listed; however the authors were affiliated with the University of California at Los Angeles at the time of this research.

Weiner, B., Russell, D., & Lerman, D. (1979). The cognition-emotion process in achievement related contexts. *Journal of Personality and Social Psychology, 37,* 1211–1220.

Objective: To investigate the effect of attributions on emotions in an achievement context. Researchers were elaborating and improving upon their previous work in Weiner, Russel, & Lerman (1978).

Design:

Setting: Laboratory.

Participants: In Study 1, participants were 79 undergraduate students enrolled in general psychology. In Study 2, participants were 48 undergraduate students.

Assessment of predictor variables: In Study 1, participants were asked to remember 12 instances where they found out the outcome of a test. For six of these times, participants were asked to remember a time when they did well; for the other six instances, participants were asked to remember a time when they did poorly. Each scenario asked participants to think of a time when they made a different attribution for their failure or success: ability, unstable effort, stable effort, personality, others, and luck.

   In Study 2, participants were presented with 12 scenarios that randomly varied by outcome (positive or negative) and six possible emotion descriptions (the descriptions relevant to gratitude included the emotion terms *appreciative, grateful,* and *modest,* and *surprised, astonished,* and *thankful*). A sample scenario described a student who just received a *high score* on an important example and felt *surprised, astonished,* and *thankful.*

Assessment of outcome variables: In Study 1, after writing about the details of an outcome, participants were asked to list three emotions that they felt in that situation, and then to rate the intensity of different emotions listed on the questionnaire.

In Study 2, after each scenario, participants were asked to rate the attribution the person in the scenario would have made for his/her success or failure. Attributions rated for the success stories (which are the stories relevant to gratitude) included ability, unstable effort, stable effort, task ease, luck, and others.

Main results: In Study 1, gratitude and thankfulness were among the emotions that participants listed in the free-response portion of the questionnaire. Gratitude was most often mentioned for successful outcomes that were attributed to others, as was thankfulness. Both emotions were also mentioned a number of times when attributing success to luck. Gratitude arose as a discriminating emotion for attributions to others. Discriminating emotions were emotions that were mentioned significantly more for one attribution than for all others. Gratitude and thankfulness were not mentioned by participants in relation to failure outcomes.

In Study 2, the emotion cluster of appreciative, grateful, and modest had the highest rating for the attribution of success to others, and the emotion cluster of surprised, astonished, and thankful had the highest rating for the attribution of success to luck. The differences between the attribution ratings for these two clusters of emotion were significantly different from each other.

Conclusions: Attributions of success to an external agent lead to the emotions of gratitude and thankfulness. The authors found support for a three-step cognitive process of emotions, where the individual first evaluates performance based on success or failure (leading to outcome-dependent emotions such as happiness), then makes an attribution for that outcome (leading to attribution-dependent emotions such as gratitude), and finally the individual makes causal judgments relevant to the self-concept (leading to low or high self-esteem). The authors generalized past research using hypothetical achievement scenarios, to methodologies employing recollections of achievement, and explored the use of emotions as cues for attributions.

Commentary: These experiments provide further support for the hypothesis that gratitude and associated emotions such as appreciation and thankfulness stem from attributions of success to external agents, whether those external agents be other people, or abstract agents such as luck.

Correspondence: Bernard Weiner, Department of Psychology, University of California, Los Angeles, Los Angeles, California, 90095.

Zaleski, Z. (1988). Attributions and emotions related to future goal attainment. *Journal of Educational Psychology, 80*, 563–568.

Objective: To investigate attributions for the attainment of anticipated goals, and their concomitant emotional reactions.

Design: Study 1 was a between-subjects experiment, whereas Study 2 was a correlational study.

Setting: Although not explicitly stated, it is assumed that Study 1 took place in a laboratory setting. Study 2 was conducted in students' classrooms.

Participants: In Study 1, participants were 166 male and 165 female graduate and undergraduate students. In Study 2, participants were 392 undergraduate students from a university in the United States, and from a university in Canada.

Assessment of predictor variables: In Study 1, participants were asked to write down goals that they had set for one of five time-periods: 1 week, 1 month, 1 year, 10 years, or a life goal. In Study 2, participants noted their year in college (freshman, sophomore, etc.) on a questionnaire.

Assessment of outcome variables: In Study 1, after participants wrote about their goal, they filled out a questionnaire with the dependent measures, which included value of the goal, expectancies, effort and persistence, and attributions about attainment of the goal. Attributions that were relevant to the study of gratitude involved attributions of success to luck, and to "external conditions."

In Study 2, dependent measures were collected on a questionnaire, and included ratings of internal and external attributions for current academic performance as well as future graduation. Participants were also asked to rate the emotional reactions they would have upon graduation, which included *proud, surprised,* and *grateful.* Participants answered similar questions regarding their attributions and emotions if they were to fail to graduate.

Main results: In Study 1, the most frequently cited attribution for success was effort and ability, followed by attributions to external circumstances. Participants were more likely to attribute successes to internal factors, and less to external factors. The longer the time range of the goal, the less participants attributed external factors to success, and the more they attributed external factors for failure. This effect was particularly driven by external attributions to task difficulty.

Like Study 1, in Study 2, successes were attributed more to internal factors than external factors. When asked about emotional reactions to successful graduation, participants rated that they would feel a high amount of pride, and intermediate amount of gratitude, and only a small amount of surprise. Emotions of surprise and gratitude were positively correlated with external attributions of success. There was no effect of year in school on these variables.

Conclusions: Attributions of anticipated outcomes coincided with research on attributions for past outcomes. The author found mixed results for the time variable between the two studies.

Commentary: These studies provide further research for gratitude's link with attributions of success to others. Although participants probably were not experiencing the emotions in question during the studies, these studies have the advantage of examining participants' own goals and anticipated outcomes, rather than presenting participants with hypothetical scenarios.

Correspondence: Zbigniew Zaleski, Department of Psychology, Catholic University of Lublin, Al. Ralawickie 14, Poland, 20–950.

References

Block, J., & Kremen, A. M. (1996). IQ and ego-resiliency: Conceptual and empirical connections and separateness. *Journal of Personality and Social Psychology, 70,* 349–361.

Costa, P. T., & McCrae, R. R. (1992). *Revised NEO Personality Inventory (NEO-PI-R) and NEO Five-Factor Inventory (NEO-FFI) professional manual.* Odessa, FL: Psychological Assessment Resources.

Davis, M. H., & Oathout, H. A. (1987). Maintenance of satisfaction in romantic relationships: Empathy and relational competence. *Journal of Personality and Social Psychology, 53,* 397–410.

Diener, E., Emmons, R. A., Larsen, R. J., & Griffin, S. (1985). The Satisfaction with Life Scale. *Journal of Personality Assessment, 49,* 71–75.

Derogatis, L. R., & Spencer, P. M. (1982). *The brief symptom inventory: Administration, scoring, and procedures manual.* Baltimore, MD: Clinical Psychometric Research.

Harris, P. L., Olthof, T., Meerum Terwogt, M., & Hardman, C. E. (1987). Children's knowledge of the situations that provoke emotion. *International Journal of Behavioral Development, 10,* 319–343.

John, O. P., Donahue, E. M., & Kentle, R. L. (1991). *The Big Five Inventory—Versions 4a and 54.* Berkeley, CA: University of California, Berkeley, Institute of Personality and Social Research.

Ger, G., & Belk, R. W. (1990). Measuring and comparing materialism cross-culturally. *Advances in Consumer Research, 17,* 186–192.

Kirk, K. M., Eaves, L. J., & Martin, N. G. (1999). Self-transcendence as a measure of spirituality in a sample of older Australian twins. *Twin Research, 2,* 61–87.

Lyubomirsky, S., & Lepper, H.S. (1999). A measure of subjective happiness: Preliminary reliability and construct validation. *Social Indicators Research, 46,* 137–155.

McCullough, M. E. Kilpatrick, S. D., Emmons, R. A., & Larson, D. B. (2001). Is gratitude a moral affect? *Psychological Bulletin, 127,* 249–266.

McCullough, M. E., Worthington, E. L., Jr., & Rachal, K. C. (1997). Interpersonal forgiving in close relationships. *Journal of Personality and Social Psychology, 73,* 321–336.

Paulhus, D. L. (1998). Interpersonal and intrapsychic adaptiveness of trait self-enhancement: A mixed blessing? *Journal of Personality and Social Psychology , 74,* 1197–1208.

Piedmont, R. L. (1999). Does spirituality represent the sixth factor of personality? Spiritual transcendence and the five-factor model. *Journal of Personality, 67,* 985–1013.

Radloff, L. S. (1977). The CES-D Scale: A self-report depression scale for research in the general population. *Applied Psychological Measurement, 1,* 385–401.

Richins, M. L., & Dawson, S. (1992). A consumer values orientation for materialism and its measurement: Scale development and validation. *Journal of Consumer Research, 19,* 303–315.

Ryan, R. M., & Frederick, C. (1997). On energy, personality, and health: Subjective vitality as a dynamic reflection of well-being. *Journal of Personality, 65,* 529–565.

Saucier, G. (1994). Mini-markers: A brief version of Goldberg's unipolar big-five markers. *Journal of Personality Assessment, 63,* 506–516.

Scheier, M. F., & Carver, C. S. (1985). Optimism, coping, and health: Assessment and implications of generalized outcome expectancies. *Health Psychology, 4,* 219–247.

Scheier, M. F., Carver, C. S., & Bridges, M. W. (1994). Distinguishing optimism from neuroticism (and trait anxiety, self-mastery, and self-esteem): A reevaluation of the Life Orientation Test. *Journal of Personality and Social Psychology, 67,* 1063–1078.

Smith, R. H., Parrott, W. G., Diener, E., Hoyle, R. H., & Kim, S. H. (1999). Dispositional envy. *Personality and Social Psychology Bulletin, 25,* 1007–1020.

Watson, D., Clark, L. A., & Tellegen, A. (1988). Development and validation of brief measures of positive and negative affect: The PANAS scales. *Journal of Personality and Social Psychology, 54,* 1063–1070.

Weiner, B. (1986). *An attributional theory of motivation and emotion.* New York: Springer. ublin, Al. Ralawickie 14, Lublin, Poland, 20–950.

Index